THE PROFANE BOOK
OF IRISH COMEDY

THE
PROFANE BOOK
OF
IRISH
COMEDY

DAVID KRAUSE

Ithaca · CORNELL UNIVERSITY PRESS · *London*

First published 1982 by Cornell University Press.
Published in the United Kingdom by Cornell University Press Ltd.
Ely House, 37 Dover Street, London W1X 4HQ.

Extracts from *John Bull's Other Island* by George Bernard Shaw appear by permission of The Society of Authors on behalf of the Bernard Shaw Estate. Extracts from Brendan Behan's *The Quare Fellow* and *The Hostage* are reprinted by permission of Grove Press, Inc. *The Quare Fellow* copyright © 1956 by Brendan Behan and Theatre Workshop; *The Hostage* copyright © 1958 by Theatre Workshop; Extracts from *Cartney and Kevney* by George Shiels are reprinted from *Two Irish Plays* by permission of Macmillan, London and Basingstoke.

International Standard Book Number 0-8014-1469-5
Library of Congress Catalog Card Number 81-17454
Printed in the United States of America

Librarians: Library of Congress cataloging information
appears on the last page of the book.

The paper in this book is acid-free, and meets the guidelines
for permanence and durability of the Committee on Production
Guidelines for Book Longevity of the Council on Library Resources.

To My Father,
who, throughout the first
ninety-four years of his great good
life, always assured us after
we had encountered some misfortune,
"Now you can laugh."

CONTENTS

8   CONTENTS

PREFACE

Perhaps the first suggestion of a laugh accompanies the title of this book, for some readers may feel that I have written a profane book on Irish comedy, which bright temptation was not part of my plan, though I recognize that it might be taken that way. Actually, I have tried to illustrate the overwhelming extent to which the Irish dramatists themselves have, instinctively or mythically, through the dynamism of their plays, written what amounts to a profane book of Irish comedy, a body of theatrical literature that comically desecrates whatever is too sacred in Ireland. Somewhat like the Messenger in Greek drama, who was often the inadvertent occasion of laughter, I bring the tidings about comic profanation—I didn't create them. I am surprised that it has taken so long for this critical message to come to light; and, in what may be a conscious attempt to improve on the effort of that innocent Messenger, I have come fully prepared to interpret as well as deliver this crucial information about the comic and the profane in Irish drama.

I must acknowledge an indirect debt to Herbert Howarth, whose book originally provoked me to investigate the subject; in it he claimed that the modern Irish writers were trying to write a sacred book about Ireland. They were all, he insisted, driven by "the Irish passion for a sacred book."[1] Howarth made no attempt, however, to examine Irish comedy, particularly comic drama, and he limited himself to a consideration of six writers in relation to the force of Irish nationalism: George Moore, Lady Gregory, Yeats, AE, Synge, and Joyce. Except for the minor mysticism of AE, and Yeats's conscious attempt to write *A Vision* as a sacred book, in contrast to many of his magnificently profane poems and plays, all of these writers, and many more, notably the significantly omitted O'Casey, were in their various ways really driven by what I would call the Irish passion for a profane book of comedy, as well as by a sardonic disillusionment with the mythical queen of Irish nationalism, Cathleen Ni Houlihan, the old sow who, according to Joyce's tragicomic jest, tries to devour her farrow.

Everyone interested in nondramatic Irish comedy owes a direct debt to the wise Vivian Mercier, who in his pioneering and important book *The Irish Comic Tradition* (1962) analyzed and traced the major works of Irish poetry and prose back to the rich Gaelic tradition of comedy and satire. Nevertheless, Mercier properly felt he had to apologize in his Preface for having largely ignored the study of comic drama, partly because he believed it was a genre that had no direct link to the Gaelic tradition: "Also, in the absence of a chapter on stage comedy, I have said less than I should have liked to about Synge and O'Casey. Both studied Gaelic, and the work of both shows a general affinity with the Gaelic tradition, but their very originality has made it difficult to link them with any one specific branch of that highly conservative heritage."[2]

It is therefore one of my main concerns to illustrate how not only Synge and O'Casey but most of the major comic dramatists in Ireland are emotionally and thematically linked to one specific branch of Gaelic literature, the tragicomic tradition of the mythic Oisín or Usheen, the last great playboy of the pagan world, who in the medieval and later Ossianic ballad-dialogues with Patrick, the first great saint of Ireland in the Christian world, emerges as an archetype for the various "playboys" and "paycocks" of dark and wild Irish comedy. In its comic darkness and wildness, qualities Synge in a related context called a "barbarous" or daimonic impulse, this Celtic tradition presided over by the rebellious Oisín stands out as a radical and comically profane departure from what Mercier described as an otherwise "highly conservative heritage."

Perhaps it was the moral and aesthetic rigidity of that conservative heritage which prompted the writers who followed in the mainstream of this folk-inspired comic tradition to mock oppressive authority, now represented by the austere St. Patrick, with its condemnation of emotional pleasure and its threat of eternal damnation. With the function of this comic catharsis in mind, I have suggested a structural affinity between the comic and the mythmaking energies, the need to use laughter as a creative means of fulfilling unconscious or hidden wishes by achieving a temporary release from repression. It will be obvious that I owe a deep debt to the illuminating work of Freud in the area of catharsis—the psychically more than the sexually oriented Freud; the comically irreverent Freud of *Jokes and Their Relation to the Unconscious* (1905); the symbolically prophetic Freud of *Civilization and Its Discontents* (1930). In a series of connected motifs on comedy and guilt, comic liberation, the high power of low comedy, comic Satanism, denied expectation, the principle of disintegration, the ironic victory of comic defeat, and many interrelated themes, it will be clear that I have been strongly influenced by the comic theories of Charles Baudelaire, Samuel Beckett, Eric Bentley, Northrop Frye, Susanne Langer, and Wylie Sypher.

Many other debts will emerge from my comments on comedy and the Pelagian heresy, some Polish and Irish correspondences in the game of role playing, comic antiheroism and Irish nationalism, stage-Irish stereotypes and archetypes, contentious comedy and the weapon of the flyting, the technique of comic discrediting, the desecration of Ireland's household gods, the structural inversion of the double plot, the comfort of comic failure. In many instances I have felt compelled to allow the discussion of some of these topics to overflow into the Notes and Comments, where I have tried to qualify some fine points, suggest alternative sources of investigation, and sometimes amuse myself, as well as, I hope, some readers.

On the basis of five chapters with twenty subheadings, which are arranged according to thematic connections rather than any chronological order, I have examined the major comedies of fourteen Irish dramatists: Dion Boucicault, Bernard Shaw, J. M. Synge, Lady Gregory, W. B. Yeats, William Boyle, Lennox

Robinson, George Fitzmaurice, Sean O'Casey, George Shiels, Paul Vincent Carroll, Denis Johnston, Brendan Behan, and Samuel Beckett. If Synge and O'Casey have occupied much of my attention, it is because I feel they are the seminal figures who have most effectively dramatized what I have called the barbarous sympathies of antic Irish comedy.

Since it is likely that those barbarous sympathies strike a universal impulse, a common cause for men and women to mock repressive conformity and authority, what I have said about Irish comedy can probably be extended to include the comic literature of many nations. To the degree that most of us regularly need the catharsis of a comically inspired *non serviam*, a declaration of individual independence, whether we find it in the comic mythology of the creative arts or in compensatory dreams, we are all potentially Irish. To that metaphoric degree, then, we are all tentatively if only emotionally free.

To those readers who might take offense—especially the Irish themselves, who in view of their long and tragic history as a subject nation might feel that I am libeling their national character by associating them with the *barbarous* and sustaining element of comedy—I would reply that I am using this strong term in its most positive if paradoxical meaning, as a source of the instinctive and unfettered power of the creative imagination, untainted and unintimidated by the mechanical pressures of what passes for "civilized" society. Camus probably had the poetic victory of this barbarous impulse in mind when he said somewhere that "the opposite of a civilized people is a creative one." I believe that the Irish people, Irish audiences as well as their dramatists, are comically creative in this special barbarous sense.

I am grateful to the Musée de Trondheim for kind permission to reproduce the six ornamental designs of crosses taken from Celtic bronze and stone carvings and the illuminated Book of Kells. The anonymous artists who carved and drew these delightfully enigmatic religious emblems displayed that comic treatment of a sacred subject which often characterized medieval Irish art, and which has for many centuries consistently appeared in Irish literature, particularly modern Irish drama.

Finally, I should say that earlier versions of some of the material in this book have appeared in *Modern Drama, Studia Hibernica, The Dolmen Boucicault, Malahat Review, Theatre and Nationalism in 20th Century Ireland, James Joyce Quarterly,* and *Sean O'Casey Review.* My students at Brown University have also been exposed to much of this material over the years, and I am grateful to them for the challenging way they have responded to my views, questioning some of my judgments and forcing me to clarify them. I owe a special debt of gratitude to Bernhard Kendler for his reassuring faith in the book, and to Barbara H. Salazar for her palpably indispensable copy editing of the manuscript. In conclusion, I could not have finished this book without the valuable help of a fellowship from the National Endowment for the Humanities; nor could I have survived the antic effort without the comic patience of my Irish wife and children, who never stopped grinning and bearing it.

DAVID KRAUSE

Killybegs,
Inch, Gorey,
Co. Wexford

THE PROFANE BOOK
OF IRISH COMEDY

Chapter 1

THE BARBAROUS SYMPATHIES

OF ANTIC IRISH COMEDY

THE man who feels most exquisitely joy in what is perfect in art and nature is the man who from the width and power of his mind hides the greatest number of Satanic or barbarous sympathies.

—J. M. Synge

THE ban on laughter stretches back to the day when man wore skins and defended himself with the stone hammer. Many enemies have always surrounded laughter, have tried to banish it from life; and many have perished on the high gallows tree because they laughed at those who had been given power over them. Hell-fire tried to burn it, and the weeping for sins committed did all that was possible to drown it; but laughter came safely through the ordeals of fire and water; came smiling through.

—Sean O'Casey

DREAMS, then, are often most profound when they seem most crazy. In every epoch of history those who have had something to say but could not say it without peril have eagerly assumed a fool's cap.

—Sigmund Freud

Comedy and Myth

The comic impulse shares with the mythic impulse the fictive power of reconstructing and releasing our unconscious aspirations, our private desires that are frustrated in the conscious or public world. These submerged or repressed emotions find a liberating outlet in the legends of laughter that grow out of a nation's folk imagination. Needless to say, not all myths are comic, not all comedy is mythic; however, when these two creative impulses are felicitously united, as they are in some early Celtic poetry and modern Irish drama—for example, in the medieval flytings of Oisín and Patrick, or in the plays of a Synge and an O'Casey—then the comic mythmaking process finds its archetypal sources of inspiration hidden in the rich folk memory of the Irish people. Perhaps Claude Lévi-Strauss can shed some light on this hidden ritual of creation. He says of the mythmaking impulse: "Is it not the character of myths, which have such an important place in our research, to evoke a suppressed past and apply it, like a grid, upon the present in the hope of discovering a sense in which the two aspects of his own reality man is confronted with—the historic and the structural—coincide?"[1] This concept of myth as an evocation of a suppressed past that emerges creatively, structurally, in the present time clearly has a profound Freudian resonance; and, indeed, Lévi-Strauss borrowed his basic premise from Freud's dream psychology, from the view that "myths express unconscious wishes which are somehow inconsistent with conscious experience."[2]

Comedy and myth coincide at precisely this point, the pivotal point at which the frustrations of conscious experience are creatively circumvented by unconscious wishes, instinctive wishes that assume an artistic response in the form that Northrop Frye calls the pastoral mythos of comedy, although in the antic Irish experience it is more often a mock-pastoral mythos. The legendary laughter imitates the cathartic function of dreams, and its structural artifact can be applied, like a grid, upon the present state of mythic comedy in Ireland, or in any country where a subject people, unified by repression or humiliation, must resort to comic strategies rather than physical violence to compensate for their personal and national frustrations. According to Freud's safety-valve theory of dreams, "all kinds of harmful things are made harmless by being presented in dreams."[3] And by the parallel association of empathetic values, the following corollaries are inescapable: all kinds of harmful things are made harmless by being presented in myths; all kinds of harmful things are made harmless by being presented in comedy. The nature of the comic circumvention in the second corollary is explained by Freud in *Jokes and Their Relation to the Unconscious* when he tells us that jokes "represent a rebellion against authority, a liberation from its pressure"; that the psychological purpose of jokes is that "they make possible the satisfaction of an instinct (whether lustful or hostile) in the face of an obstacle that stands in its way. They circumvent this obstacle and in that way draw pleasure from a source which the obstacle had made inaccessible."[4] In the context of the traditionally comic confrontation between a flexible *eiron* and a rigid *alazon,* the source of the obstacle is usually some form of impersonal authority, or the restraining superego characterized as an *alazon;* and the source of the circumventing satisfaction is usually some form of private desire, or the primordial id characterized as an *eiron.* Freud goes on to examine this classic confrontation in an inevitable situation that is at once psychological and literary, mythic and comic: "The repressive activity of civilization brings it about that primary possibilities of enjoyment, which have now, however, been repudiated by the censorship in us, are lost to us. But to the human psyche all renunciation is exceedingly difficult, and so we find that tendentious jokes provide a means of undoing the renunciation and retrieving what was lost."[5] Commenting on this Freudian function of low comedy, Eric Bentley has wisely observed: "Like dreams, farces show the disguised fulfillment of repressed wishes. That is a Freudian formula, but not, surely, one that only Freudians can accept."[6] The mythic game of comic circumvention may therefore be a universal impulse.

It is perhaps the main joke or comic purpose of modern Irish drama, and probably of all compensatory laughter, to undo the burden of Apollonian renunciation and retrieve the mythic sense of a denied or lost Dionysian freedom and joy. Wylie Sypher suggests such a comic purpose when, by linking the views of Freud and Nietzsche, he describes this wild and liberating spirit of comedy as "a mechanism for releasing powerful archaic impulses always there below the level of reason. . . . This un-civilized but knowing self Nietzsche once called Dionysian, the self that feels archaic pleasure and archaic pain. The substratum of the world of art, Nietzsche says, is 'the terrible wisdom of Silenus,' and Silenus is the satyr-god of comedy leading the ec-static 'chorus of natural beings who as it were live ineradicably behind every civilization.' The confused statements of the dream and the joke are intolerable to the daylight, sane, Apollonian self."[7] At the continual rebirth of comedy in the theater, the ecstatic impulses of Dionysian laughter cathartically overwhelm the sane, Apollonian self, for it is the natural and perpetual function of the wild comic spirit to recreate mythically that in-tense and transient ritual of archaic joy.

In an insular and parochial country such as Ireland, where, as Joyce and O'Casey have consistently illustrated, the Apollonian nets of religion, nationality, and family are tightly strung and calculated to frustrate the ecstatic impulses of the satyr-god, the Dionysian ritual of comic renewal has often been greeted with suspicion, violence, or censorship. No less aware of those tight nets than Joyce and O'Casey, Yeats made an attempt to break them when he unsuccessfully opposed the government's Cen-sorship of Publications Bill of 1928. As a member of the Irish Senate, Yeats protested against the repressive measures in the bill, at one point in a speech referring to the pro-censorship vigilante campaign of an Irish cleric as a symptom of the times: "A Christian Brother publicly burnt an English magazine because it contained the Cherry Tree Carol, the lovely celebration of Mary's sanctity and her Child's divinity, a glory of the mediaeval church as popular in Gaelic as in English, because, scandalised by its naiveté, he believed it the work of some irreligious modern poet."[8] Then Yeats went on to draw the following analogy between this song-burning incident and the riots at the Abbey Theatre against the plays of Synge and O'Casey in 1907 and 1926: "Synge's 'Playboy' and O'Casey's 'Plough and the Stars' were attacked because, like 'The Cherry Tree Carol,' they contain what a belief, tamed down to a formula, shudders at, something wild and ancient."[9]

Behind that symbolic shudder of fear Yeats had identified the ignorant enemy of the artistic imagination, the religious puritanism of Joyce's boorish rabblement; but he had also defined one of the central conflicts in Irish life, the recurring confrontation between a wild myth and a tamed formula, between barbarous impulses and benign dogma. It is therefore axiomatic in Irish literature, and most particularly in modern Irish drama, that the tigers of comic wrath must collide with and mock the horses of dogmatic instruction. That inevitable collision between pagan and pious values provides one of the predominant dramatic and comic tensions in Irish life and art, as is so tragicomically highlighted in the plays of Synge and O'Casey, in the Crazy Jane poems of Yeats, in the Christmas dinner episode in Joyce's *Portrait of the Artist as a Young Man,* in the later poetry of Austin Clarke. One must look to modern fiction and poetry as well as drama, since there was no native Irish drama before the literary renaissance of the twentieth century. Douglas Hyde's *Casadh an tSugain* (The Twisting of the Rope, 1901) was the first Irish play written in Irish; Yeats's *Land of Heart's Desire* (1894) was the first Irish play written in English, with the exception of Boucicault's mid-nineteenth-century comic melodramas. The Anglo-Irish-born or -educated dramatists who achieved their success on the London stage—Congreve, Farquhar, Goldsmith, Sheridan, Wilde, and Shaw—and who wrote what is euphemistically called English comedy between the seventeenth and twentieth cen-

turies cannot properly be considered part of the tradition of
Irish comedy, that is, that body of work written by the Irish in
Ireland for Irish audiences. It is therefore necessary to examine
the roots of that uniquely wild and ancient laughter in early
Celtic poetry, as well as in modern Irish drama, in order to
retrieve and celebrate that comic ritual of archaic joy.

In a mock-heroic legend that goes back to the Gaelic folk
poetry of twelfth-century Ireland, with earlier roots in the ninth
century, and which remained popular among the peasants into
the nineteenth and twentieth centuries in many oral and written
versions, two archetypal Irish figures confront each other in a
heroic and comic collision between irreconcilable ways of life:
Oisín, the last of the pagan poet-heroes, and St. Patrick, the first
of the new proseletyzing Christian priests. This symbolic poem,
the *Agallamh Oisín agus Padraig*, the "Dialogue between Oisín
and Patrick," composed in over a hundred ballad stanzas and in
the form of a dramatic flyting for two epic voices, rehearses the
perennial Irish debate between the representatives of wild myth
and tamed dogma; and though, with historical accuracy, Patrick
and his dogma must be victorious, it is the defeated Oisín, the
sympathetic victim who comically and rebelliously attempts to
retrieve his lost pagan freedom, that dominates the work. It is
the humorously profane and naive manner in which the aged
Oisín dreams of his past Dionysian glories and refuses to be
converted by the ascetic Patrick that allows him to circumvent if
not overcome the Apollonian rigors of the new dispensation.

The old pagan way of life is doomed in fifth-century Ireland,
when pagan and priest are brought together in the dramatic
setting of the poem, yet the fact that Oisín is a defeated comic
hero only serves to emphasize the prevailing motif of failure in
Irish comedy, which thrives on adversity as invention relies on
necessity. Adversity is a spur to the comic imagination; it is an
occasion when the fool's cap of antic laughter offers a grotesque
way of mitigating disaster, of learning to mock at despair, not
only for the unrepentant Oisín, whose barbarous affinities hover
like a giddy spirit of defiance over the tradition of Irish comedy,
but for all the kindred characters of comic imagination, for a
Mak or a Falstaff, a Tony Lumpkin or a Huck Finn, a Chaplin
tramp or the Marx Brothers; for a Christy Mahon or a Fluther

Good, a Crazy Jane or a Borstal Boy, a Leopold Bloom or a Gogo and Didi. These comic characters must be failures or outcasts before they can be mythically liberated, for low comedy is the last and perhaps only refuge of the defeated. They are defeated or dispossessed from the start; they enter defeated; and it is precisely their ability to live cheerfully and resourcefully with defeat that distinguishes them from tragic characters, who are broken and destroyed by defeat. The absurdity and anarchy of the comic fall has saved the comic characters from the terrible burden of responsibility and guilt that accompanies the tragic fall. Unlike tragic hubris, which destroys individual freedom through the chastising terror of outrageous deeds, comic hubris affirms individual freedom through merry indulgence in outrageous deeds. In order to sustain their compensatory laughter, therefore, the mythic and comic Irish characters, like their antic counterparts in all countries who are able to survive the ordeals of fire and water, must not only reject St. Patrick's hard life of renunciation, they must also circumvent his threat of guilt and eternal damnation.

Comedy and Guilt

The comic act of liberation is so primitive in its origins that it creates a temporary suspension of inhibiting guilt, a psychic suspension that can last only as long as the joke, or, theoretically, as long as the mythic structure that contains and forever celebrates the laughter. Barbarous comedy is the repressed person's vicarious holiday from original sin. There is no room for the "aginbite" of conscience in the atavistic energy released by rebellious laughter. This form of profane humor functions as an act of emotional release, a comic impulse of insurrection that achieves its impermanent yet palpable victory in the nervous system and therefore cannot be suppressed by force or law. It is the instinctive person's creative act of faith in his ability to survive by laughing, by committing the comic crime without punishment. In the protective sanctity of a darkened theater, then, where dramatic art makes life plausible and bearable, knockabout comedy enacts a ritualistic escape from sin for a random audience of empathetic revelers. Civilization itself, with all its restraining force, is the archenemy that must be mocked; it is the comic villain of the piece in which there is desecrating laughter without damnation, antic comedy without guilt. For the audience as well as the characters, such laughter releases such liberty.

In the final chapter of *Civilization and Its Discontents,* Freud, in concluding his profound investigation into the mortal unhappiness of the civilized, observes that it has been his intention "to represent the sense of guilt as the most important problem in the evolution of culture, and to convey that the price of progress in civilization is paid in forfeiting happiness through the heightening of the sense of guilt."[10] In this manner civilized society has frustrated us by making us the prisoner of our sickly consciences; and therefore any comic conjurer who can tentatively diminish or paralyze the sense of guilt possesses the source of our brief but life-sustaining happiness. The system of guilt is based on self-denial and mortification, and Freud may have been preparing the justification for a comic rebellion against the system when he stated that, "most important of all, it is impossible to ignore the extent to which civilization is built upon renunciation of instinctual gratifications, the degree to which the existence of civilization presupposes the non-gratification (suppression, repression or something else?) of powerful instinctual urgencies."[11] In one of his more sanguine moods, Freud realized that the comic impulse, like the sexual impulse, was one of those "powerful instinctual urgencies" that might help to release one from the guilt trap of renunciation and repression. He found what he called "a liberating element" in rebellious humor, something he described as "fine and elevating":

> Obviously what is fine about it is the triumph of narcissism, the ego's victorious assertion of its own invulnerability. It refuses to be hurt by the arrows of reality or to be compelled to suffer. It insists that it is impervious to wounds dealt by the outside world, in fact, that these are merely occasions for affording it pleasure. This last trait is a fundamental characteristic of humour.... Humour is not resigned; it is rebellious. It signifies the triumph not only of the ego, but also of the pleasure principle, which is strong enough to assert itself here in the face of the adverse real circumstances.[12]

With this fine comic stance of narcissistic liberation we have entered the anarchic realm of the antic comedian—antic because he can be crazy or grotesque, fantastic or irresponsible, a law unto his resilient self in his daimonic struggle against repressive civilization. The antic comedian is beyond retribution because he has no quarrel with the omnipotent and inscrutable gods; his defiant laughter is aimed at the household gods, those fallible and worldly hierarchies of power, the state and the church, which more for worse than for better organize and control society, and are therefore destined to frustrate us. These solemn guardians of the guilt system must consistently be mocked, desecrated by rough and impious laughter, if the pleasure principle is to gain a psychic triumph for the antic comedian and his merry knockabouts.

The antic mood and the knockabout method of comedy might be illustrated by these two working definitions:

> *antic:* an instance of grotesquely ludicrous or other unusual or unpredictable behavior ... one who performs a grotesque or ludicrous part (as in a play); buffoon, merry-andrew ... characterized by ludicrous or clownish extravagance or absurdity ⟨the first specific instance of Hamlet's assumed antic disposition ... ⟩; fantastic in a light gay fashion: frolicsome. ...
> *knockabout:* marked by, given to, or skilled at boisterously funny antics and farce and often extravagant burlesque or slapstick ... ⟨knockabout comedians in baggy pants ...⟩... a performance or instance of knockabout comedy ⟨a grave ceremony that gradually turned into hilarious knockabout ... ⟩; boisterous farcical humor of the kind found in knockabout comedy. ...
> [*Webster's Third New International Dictionary*, 1971]

Not only do these terms clearly overlap and complement each other, they both carry a functional as well as a gratuitous comic meaning. The parenthetical reference to Hamlet's "antic disposition" suggests that the grotesque or ludicrous behavior could be a disguise or a stratagem to be used against one's tormentors or oppressors. And the parenthetical reference to the "grave ceremony that gradually turned into hilarious knockabout" suggests that a once sacred ritual has been mocked and transformed into a profane farce. In both instances, along with the sheer fun and frolic, a psychological weapon for triumph might be hidden in the wild comic experience.

In his earlier studies Freud traced this psychological triumph back to the unconscious yet functional strategy of dreams, and significantly he related this process to the compensatory mythos of comedy, even linking it to the sometimes conscious and deliberate game of Hamlet's "antic disposition":

> Dreams, then, are often most profound when they seem most crazy. In every epoch of history those who have had something to say but could not say it without peril have eagerly assumed a fool's cap. The audience at whom their forbidden speech was aimed tolerated it more easily if they could at the same time laugh and flatter themselves with the reflection that the unwelcome words were clearly nonsensical. The Prince in the play, who had to disguise himself as a madman, was behaving just as dreams do in reality; so that we can say of dreams what Hamlet said of himself, concealing the true circumstances under a cloak of wit and unintelligibility: "I am but mad north-north-west: when the wind is southerly, I know a hawk from a hand-saw."[13]

Hamlet contrives "to put an antic disposition on" in order to expose a tyrannical king, and the comic fool contrives to hide behind his antic disposition in order to expose a repressive society. Except for the fact that the exposure leads to a tragic resolution in one instance and a comic resolution in the other, the antic contrivance on both occasions involves a mask of seeming nonsense calculated to catch one's enemies off guard.

By the method of this madness, then, the antic comedian temporarily blunts the sharp arrows of reality by paralyzing the superego long enough for the comic id to release its jokes and spread hilarious disorder. The antic comedian's laughter is cathartic and functions somewhat like the libido: intense and brief, these giddy bursts of apocalyptic joy can momentarily set men and women free in their source of vital energy, bring them back to their primitive origins in a state of barbarous grace, and thereafter enable them to endure their daily repressions with uncivilized equanimity while they wait hopefully for their next climactic laugh.

"A laugh," O'Casey wrote, "is a great natural stimulator, a pushful entry into life; and once we can laugh, we can live."[14] The desecrating laughter we find in O'Casey's plays is a natural celebration as well as a provocation; it is a defiant assertion of our ability to survive the repressive ordeals of fire and water: the intimidation of hell-fire and the mortification of guilty tears. This is the implicit yes behind the antic comedian's *non serviam*. And Synge—for whom the wild and brutal impulses were at the heart of comic celebrations—might have been playing with the barbarous gift of profane laughter when he described some of the comic tramps of the west of Ireland as men of "extraordinary ugliness and wit" who revealed a "half-sensual ecstasy of laughter" while they poured out "a medley of rude puns and jokes that meant more than they said."[15] Contemplating the coarse and ecstatic laughter of these grotesque vagabonds, who were the originals for the characters in his plays, Synge concluded, with a profound understanding of gallows humor, that such a man "must have a sense of intimate misery before he can set himself to jeer and mock at the world."[16]

Ironically and necessarily, therefore, the awareness of one's misery, one's original sin, precedes and provokes the most antic comedy. Excessive guilt is the goad for excessive laughter, and the rigid pieties of the world must be profaned in the name of freedom. This antic signal for a comic *non serviam* quickly brings to mind the compensatory blasphemies of Joyce; and from his extravagant word hoard of impious prayers in *Finnegans Wake*, here is a supplication and a remonstrance to the Loud/Lord that human misery cannot be tolerated without barbarous laughter:

Loud, heap miseries upon us yet entwine our arts with laughters low!
Ha he hi ho hu
Mummum.[17]

The artistic presentation of this act of comic faith and rebellion is lowly humanity's affirmation of life as an alternative to inevitable despair. Bred out of the misery of our uneasy burden of guilt, profane laughter without remorse is the wild and joyous revenge of the antic comedian. It is also partially Satanic in its narcissistic triumph in defeat, as Freud explained psychologically, as Synge felt intuitively, and as Baudelaire argued logically with respect to the comic act of disobedience. In his essay "On the Essence of Laughter," Baudelaire claims that "the comic is a damnable element, and one of diabolic origin,"[18] beginning with the proud and superior laughter of Satan. "Holy books never laugh," he tells us, "to whatever nations they may belong."[19] Then, as a contrast to the laughing Satan, Baudelaire posits a trembling Sage—a Christian representative of orthodox and ordered society, who does not dare to laugh except in the fear and trembling of guilt:

> The Sage, that is to say he who is quickened with the spirit of Our Lord, he who has the divine formulary at his finger tips, does not abandon himself to laughter save in fear and trembling. The Sage trembles at the thought of having laughed; the Sage fears laughter, just as he fears the lustful shows of this world. He stops short on the brink of laughter, as on the brink of temptation. There is, then, according to the Sage, a certain secret contradiction between his special nature as Sage and the primordial nature of laughter. . . .
>
> If you are prepared, then, to take the point of view of the orthodox mind, it is certain that human laughter is intimately linked with the accident of an ancient Fall, or a debasement both physical and moral.[20]

Perhaps an enormous paradox is emerging: for if our ancient Fall was provoked by a comic rebellion, our psychic survival may depend on our ability to conquer fear and trembling through disobedient and debasing laughter. Confronted by the choice of salvation through fear or damnation through laughter, empirical men and women may have had no option but to lose their immortal souls in order to find their vital selves. So there is a connection as well as a contradiction between the formalized sense of guilt and the primordial sense of laughter. In order to rise, comic humankind must fall, again and again. The archetypal pratfall is part of the ritualistic comic Fall. Unlike the orthodox mind, the comic imagination does not stop at the brink, it risks temptation and accepts the metaphor of hell as a fortunate fall.

The unfortunate fall of tragedy is also beyond the reach of the orthodox mind, beyond divine intervention, as I. A. Richards pointed out in his classic statement on the Manichean assumptions inherent in the tragic condition. What Richards and his critics overlooked, however, is the parallel process that similarly locates the comic condition beyond divine intervention. If the Manichean heresy denies the certainty of salvation in tragedy and makes us responsible for our irrevocable damnation, the Pelagian heresy denies the concept of original sin in comedy and makes us responsible for our inevitable salvation. The comic figure, like the tragic figure, stands alone, in control of his own destiny, confronted by a personal, not a divine, imperative: he can and must save himself, just as the tragic figure can and must damn himself, without seeking the guarantee of redemption from the Son of God. In comedy as in tragedy—in the genres of art, that is, in contrast to the orthodoxies of religion—there must always be a suspension of absolute faith, what Richards called a temporary agnosticism, for the central characters in the piece: for them, mythology replaces theology; humanistic heresy replaces scriptural doctrine. In those aesthetic moments of suspended faith, the dramatic mythos cannot accommodate preordained resolutions of human fate; with due respect, it cannot allow the noble Jesus to transform tragic and comic tigers into shriven lambs.

Here are two statements on the tragic and comic conditions of drama. The first is by Richards on the Manichean assumptions for tragedy; the second is a slight but significant modification of the same statement to show how it can also support the Pelagian assumptions for comedy:

> It is essential to recognize that in the full tragic experience there is no suppression. The mind does not shy away from anything, it does not protect itself with any illusion, it stands uncomforted, unintimidated, alone and self-reliant. The test of its success is whether it can face what is before it and respond to it without any of the innumerable subterfuges by which it ordinarily dodges the full development of experience. Suppressions and sublimations alike are devices by which we endeavour to avoid issues which might bewilder us. The essence of Tragedy is that it forces us to live for a moment without them. When we succeed we find, as usual, that there is no difficulty; the difficulty came from the suppressions and sublimations. The joy which is so strangely the heart of the experience is not an indication that "all's right with the world" or that "somewhere, somehow, there is Justice"; it is an indication that all is right here and now in the nervous system. Because Tragedy is the experience which most invites these subterfuges, it is the greatest and rarest thing in literature, for the vast majority of works which pass by that name are of a different order. Tragedy is only possible to a mind which is for

the moment agnostic or Manichean. The least touch of any theology which has a compensating Heaven to offer the tragic hero is fatal.[21]

It is essential to recognize that in the full comic experience there is subtle suppression. The mind must shy away from everything, it must protect itself with illusions, it stands comforted, unintimidated, alone and self-reliant. The test of its success is whether it can avoid what is before it with the innumerable subterfuges by which it regularly dodges the full development of experience. Suppressions and sublimations alike are comic devices by which we endeavour to avoid issues which might bewilder us. The essence of Comedy is that it forces us to live for a moment with them. When we succeed we find, as usual, that there is no difficulty; the difficulty came from the lack of suppressions and sublimations. The joy which is so strangely the heart of the experience is not an indication that "all's right with the world" or that "somewhere, somehow, there is Justice"; it is an indication that all is right here and now in the nervous system. Because Comedy is the experience which most depends upon these subterfuges, it is the greatest and rarest thing in literature, for the vast majority of works which pass by that name are of a different order. Comedy is only possible to a mind which is for the moment agnostic or Pelagian. The least touch of any theology which has a compensating Heaven to offer the comic hero is fatal.[22]

These contrasting statements illustrate the common ground of self-reliance that is essential to tragedy and comedy, but above all they indicate the sharp differences between the two genres. The tragic figure in his Manichean isolation must face the truth without any subterfuges or sublimations; the comic figure in his Pelagian independence must use subterfuges and sublimations to bend the truth to his own purposes. The tragic figure must come to terms with the distressed world and affirm sacred values; the comic figure must escape from the oppressive world and mock sacred values. It is quite appropriate that Pelagius, the fifth-century heretic, was in all probability a disobedient Irishman. One cannot be certain, but it is generally believed that he was born in Britain of Irish stock, and that his name is very likely a hellenized form of the Irish Muirchu, son of the sea. His heresy grew out of his rejection of the doctrine of original sin and his belief that human beings, with their unaided will power, are capable of achieving spiritual good. With such attractively irreverent credentials, with his stubborn faith in individual grace, Pelagius might well be qualified to serve as the mock patron saint of Irish comedy.

Unlike the form of most works that pass by the name of comedy, the mainstream of Irish comedy is noncorrective and nonromantic. Irish comedy does not reform its outrageous clowns or allow them to live happily ever after. There are no enduring love matches or moralistic happy endings in the comedy of Synge, Lady Gregory, Fitzmaurice, O'Casey, Beckett, and Behan. All's not right with their world, a world without truth or justice, a world of "chassis" that encourages subterfuges and sublimations, anarchic games and disguises of comic survival. There are, of course, other forms of comedy that do invoke sacred concepts of truth and justice in order to reform the wayward characters and restore a golden mean of ideal behavior. Albert Cook, for example, in his book on the golden mean of comedy, has described this conventional view of comedy in predictably corrective terms: "The function of comedy is to adjust the manners of people to the healthy norms of nature, to avoid excesses presented on the stage."[23] This approach to comedy suggests a utilitarian exercise in emotional restraint for the audience, rather than an uninhibited indulgence in laughter as an emotional release from the oppressive norms of society. It is a moralistic view with Bergsonian implications which ignores the clever *eirons* and can be applied only to the mechanical *alazons* or "humour" characters, though it is inherently too homiletic to account for some of the richly comic villains in Jonson and Molière, or Dickens and Twain, who in their fraudulent excesses are too full of vitality and irreverent mischief to be passed off as mere agents of moral instruction.

A similarly therapeutic but less homiletic view of comedy as a romantic reformation is posited by Northrop Frye when he tells us that the comic plot

> normally presents an erotic intrigue between a young man and a young woman which is blocked by some kind of opposition, usually paternal, and resolved by a twist in the plot which is the comic form of Aristotle's "discovery," and is more manipulated than its tragic counterpart. At the beginning of the play the forces thwarting the hero are in control of the play's society, but after the discovery in which the hero becomes wealthy or the heroine re-

spectable, a new society crystallizes on the stage around the hero and his bride. The action of the comedy thus moves towards the incorporation of the hero into the society that he normally fits.[24]

This stock and sentimental plot in which temporarily disobedient young lovers are finally restored to respectable society can be found in much eighteenth- and nineteenth-century drama and fiction, as well as in the romantic comedies of Shakespeare; but it cannot be applied to the wild and barbarous clowns in Shakespearean and Irish comedy. It is a transparent formula that may work its cure for all the misunderstood swains and nymphs who can easily be reconciled to society, but not for the unreconstructed Falstaffs and Sir Tobys, not for the shrewd and rude Celtic mechanicals, who in demanding their freedom and their excess of cakes and ale feel no pangs of guilt and refuse to fit naturally into normal society.

It is partly a difference between high comedy and low comedy, between the corrective comedy of manners and the noncorrective comedy of farce. Antic comedians cannot be reformed. They are unsalvageable heretics or Pelagians when it comes to sin and atonement. The "playboys" and "paycocks" of Synge and O'Casey recognize no culpability in their redeeming excesses, in the instinctive follies that save them from the orthodoxies of the respectable world. To become incorporated into that normal world would mean the sacrifice of their laughter and liberty. Traditionally located in the comic subplot, these irreverent clowns become the central figures of the main plot in Irish comedy.

Lead me into comic temptation; lead me into the lustful shows of this world; lead me into comic disobedience!—this barbarous and Satanic prayer could well be the profane credo of the antic comedian.

Comedy and Profanation

Whenever the sacred rituals become too sacred, too rigid, the profane and flexible spirit of knockabout comedy is close at hand. The sacred must then be mocked not because it is false but because its original truths have become too hard and brittle.

This is the ironic compliment that the profane pays to the sacred: it is a catalytic impulse that knocks in order to save. This paradoxical view of comic disobedience as a profane act of liberation is undoubtedly a universal as well as a uniquely Irish characteristic. The knockabout spirit of desecration had its origins in the clowns of the Greek satyr plays and Roman comedy, the "vice" or "devil" of the medieval miracle plays, and the buffoon or Punchinello that the English folk theater borrowed from the Italian marionette theater. Susanne Langer identifies this farcical character with the archetypal clown or Punch, the Harlequin, the Pierrot, the Persian Karaguez, the Elizabethan jester, the Vidusaka of Sanscrit drama, the pantomime clown:

These anciently popular personages show what the buffoon really is: the indomitable living creature fending for itself, tumbling and stumbling (as the clown physically illustrates) from one situation into another, getting into scrape after scrape and getting out again, with or without a thrashing. He is the personified *élan vital;* his chance adventures and misadventures, without much plot, though often with bizarre complications, his absurd expectations and disappointments, in fact his whole improvised existence has the rhythm of primitive, savage, if not animalian life, coping with a world that is forever taking new uncalculated turns, frustrating but exciting. He is neither a good man nor a bad one, but is genuinely amoral,—now triumphant, now worsted and rueful, but in his ruefulness and dismay he is funny, because his energy is really unimpaired and each failure prepares the situation for a new fantastic move.[25]

Langer also draws our attention to the significant fact that the pagan Punch made his earliest recorded appearance in religious drama in England, in puppet plays of the Creation of the World and the Deluge. Confronted by this curious combination of profane and sacred impulses, Langer calls to mind Baudelaire's "trembling Sage" when she comments on the reaction of the "solemn religious mind" to the appearance of the Punch or comic devil in medieval drama: "To the modern, solemn religious mind, scriptural stories may seem a strange context for such a secular character, and perhaps this apparent incongruity has led to the widespread belief that the clown in modern comedy derives from the devil of mediaeval miracle plays."[26] This strange yet psychologically understandable connection between

the archetypal fool and the antic devil then led Langer to the
following conclusion about the diabolical origins of laughter:

> The devil is, of course, quite at home in sacred realms. It is not
> impossible that this relation between devil and fool (in his various
> forms as clown, jester, freak) really holds; yet if it does, that iden-
> tifies the devil with the flesh, and sin with lust. Such a conception
> brings the spirit of life and the father of all evil, which are usually
> poles apart, very close together. For there is no denying that the
> Fool is a red-blooded fellow; he is, in fact, close to the animal
> world; in French tradition he wears a cockscomb on his cap, and
> Punchinello's nose is probably the residue of a beak. He is all
> motion, whim, and impulse—the "libido" itself.[27]

The impulse is universal, yet no one knew better than the antic
Irish comedians that profane or devilish laughter is our emotional protection against deadly solemnity and the cruel arrows
of reality. In the oral and written Irish tradition, language itself,
the power of words, is a great offensive weapon, a potent and
public act of comic aggression that fortifies one against one's
enemies. In his important study "Satirists and Enchanters in
Early Irish Literature," F. N. Robinson provides many striking
illustrations of the magical and maledictive word power of the
medieval Irish bards. These wandering poets used their satiric
verses and songs to punish their opponents, or anyone who mistreated them, with a comic assault of invective, ridicule, curses,
spells, and coarse knockabout associated with the tradition of the
flyting. Understandably these sharp-tongued poets were more
feared than respected, and they were more often condemned
than rewarded for their literary and supposedly supernatural
talent. They were sly and dangerous vagabonds who lived outside society and its restricting laws. Robinson stresses the precarious nature of the poet's life as literary outlaw by examining
the massive evidence in the Brehon laws, those invaluable tracts
that tell us so much about the conditions of ancient Irish life, and
he reveals countless instances of legal actions against satiric slan-
der, as well as a pervasive disparagement of poets:

> In decidedly the greater number of passages in the [Brehon] laws
> satire is treated as a kind of misdemeanor and the satirist con-

demned. Thus satirists are classed among the men for whom no one may go surety; and the woman-satirists, along with thieves, liars, and bush-strumpets, are said to have no claim to an honor-price. Similarly, the son of a woman-satirist, like the son of a bondmaid, is declared to be ineligible to chieftaincy. And the same disparagement of the class appears in the definition of a demon-banquet as "a banquet given to the sons of death and bad men, *i.e.* to lewd persons and satirists, and jesters, and buffoons, and mountebanks, and outlaws, and heathens, and harlots, and bad people in general; which is not given for earthly obligation or for heavenly reward—such a feast is forfeited to the demon."[28]

One might safely conclude that there would be more freedom and fun at such a "demon-banquet" than in heaven; a lively Satanic festival of antic Irish comedians—poets, jesters, buffoons, woman-satirists, thieves, liars, mountebanks, outlaws, heathens, harlots, and bush-strumpets! It would not be difficult to draw up a guest list of medieval and modern Irish writers who would be cordially welcome at such a barbarous banquet. And if one had to arrange a program of entertainment to be presented before such a profane company of merry rogues, one might begin by suggesting some spirited readings from the following works: the twelfth-century *Vision of MacConglinne,* and the *Buile Suibne* (Mad Sweeney); the later medieval *Agallamh Oisín agus Padraig;* the eighteenth-century Brian Merriman's *Midnight Court;* Synge's *Playboy of the Western World* and *Tinker's Wedding;* Joyce's "Holy Office" and "Gas from a Burner," as well as the Christmas dinner scene from *A Portrait of the Artist as a Young Man,* and some choice passages from Molly Bloom's immortal sentences and Earwicker's fabulous dream; selections from the autobiographies of George Moore and O'Casey, as well as O'Casey's *Plough and the Stars* and *Cock-a-Doodle Dandy;* selections from the later poems of Yeats, Austin Clarke, and Patrick Kavanagh; Brendan Behan's *Borstal Boy* and *Hostage.* So much for a sample of curtain raisers.

There can be little doubt that Synge and Joyce and O'Casey would have been fortunate enough to be condemned to appear at that demon-banquet. Besides the profane nature of his plays, Synge was following directly in the maledictive tradition of the medieval Irish poets when he resorted to the comic savagery of

his "The Curse" ("To a sister of an enemy of the author's who
disapproved of 'The Playboy'"):

> Lord, confound this surly sister,
> Blight her brow with blotch and blister,
> Cramp her larynx, lung, and liver,
> In her guts a galling give her.
> Let her live to earn her dinners
> In Mountjoy with seedy sinners:
> Lord, this judgment quickly bring,
> And I'm your servant, J. M. Synge.[29]

In a similar spirit of comic malediction, Joyce also uttered a
magical curse in the form of a prayer that probably should have
been addressed to Satan, and perhaps it was:

> O, Vague Something behind everything . . . Give me for Christ's
> sake a pen and an ink-bottle and some peace of mind, and then,
> by the crucified Jaysus, if I don't sharpen that little pen and dip it
> into fermented ink and write tiny little sentences about the people
> who betrayed me, send me to hell.[30]

O'Casey's contribution to this Celtic game of rhetorical malediction was provoked when Charlotte Shaw urged him to avoid
vindictive fights, and in his withering reply he ironically called
upon God to judge and damn him if he ever put aside his aveng-
ing sword:

> God is my judge that I hate fighting. If I be damned for anything,
> I shall be damned for keeping the two-edged sword of thought
> tight in its scabbard when it should be searching the bowels of
> knaves and fools.[31]

God and/or Satan must have been confused or amused by all
these intemperate outbursts of profane Irish prayer. All three
writers were beyond orthodox salvation, along with many of
their creative countrymen and -women, and a universal company of artists, for they have in most of their works expressed
varying aspects of this theme of malediction and profanation.
Creative artists have often been looked upon with suspicion by
the guardians of society, since Plato ruled them out of his ideal
state, since the early church fathers warned the faithful to beware of the evils of secular literature, since the Faustian myth
associated creativity with the transgressions of black magic and

blasphemy. Commenting on this conflict between the artist and society, Robert C. Elliott refers to Seanchan in Yeats's *King's Threshold,* the Celtic poet who sacrificed his life for the freedom of poets. Elliott then points out that the poet's association with magical powers has always been considered a profane encroachment upon sacred ground:

> In early European culture the association led directly into the realms of the forbidden; the artist was regarded as the heritor of the mythical beings whose "creativity" was rebellion and who were punished for their awful audacity: Daedalus, who was imprisoned; Wieland and Hephaestus, both crippled; Prometheus, the great prototype, chained to his rock. For man to create—a statue, a building, a painting, a poem—has always been in some sense to encroach on divine prerogative.[32]

Censorship of the arts has therefore been one of the most common weapons of political and religious orthodoxy, invoked in the name of the divine prerogative. What passes for morality in society is antithetical to laughter as well as art. As Brecht's anarchic poet Baal reminds us, "The righteous one has no sense of humor."[33]

In a righteous country such as Ireland, then, the artist often resorts to the rebellion of profane laughter. Early in his life Synge began to rebel against the repression of organized religion. In his fragments of autobiography Synge gives an account of his terrifying religious experiences as a child, when he was confronted by the Christian scourge of sin and damnation—the guilt and hell-fire of the Church of Ireland, a Protestant nightmare that he shared and rejected with O'Casey, and whose Roman Catholic counterpart afflicted the young Joyce. These Irishmen shared the Satanic sympathies of Prometheus' and Dedalus' *non serviam.* And O'Casey, who abandoned his Protestant faith in his twenties to become a communist worshiper of comic joy, who felt that the Christians had used the terrible threat of damnation to undermine the vital human spirit, later cried out in profane protest: "Original sin has got us all by the short hairs!"[34]

The skeptical Synge, who lost his faith at the age of sixteen, wondered if organized religion "might not all be a fraud got together to aid the bringing-up of children.... Still the well-meant but extraordinary cruelty of introducing the idea of Hell into the imagination of a nervous child has probably caused more misery than many customs that the same people send missionaries to eradicate."[35] How appropriately ironic it was, then, and how predictable from a compensatory Freudian view, that the young Synge should have been attracted to precisely those wild pagan attitudes that he had been conditioned by his religion to fear. Consider the startling revelations in these two crucial paragraphs from his autobiography, in which he explains his fascination for the primitive and the profane, his affinity for "the wildness of evil," and his confession of "satanic or barbarous sympathies":

> What is elemental and untamed seems always to have drawn me, and as a boy I studied the arabs of the streets. They provide one of the clearest examples of the links that are thought to exist between primitive man and the child. I remember coming out of St. Patrick's Sunday after Sunday and as the lamps were lit walking through the slums of Harold's Cross where hordes of wild children were playing. There was something appalling—a proximity of emotions as conflicting as the Black Mass—in emerging from the white harmonies of the St. Matthew Passion among this blasphemy of childhood. The boys and girls were always in separate groups, for the utterly wild boy seems to regard a woman with the instinct of barbarians. I have often stood for hours in a shadow to watch their manoeuvres and extra-ordinarily passionate quarrels.
>
> If we find in Bach an agreeable vibration of some portion of the brain and in the study of these children the vibration of another portion a little inferior—the attitude of science—we give release in the music to a transcendent admiration, and in the slums to an ecstasy of pity coupled with the thin relish of delightful sympathy with the wildness of evil which all feel but few acknowledge even to themselves. The man who feels most exquisitely joy in what is perfect in art and nature is the man who from the width and power of his mind hides the greatest number of Satanic or barbarous sympathies. His opposite is the narrow churchman or reformer who knows no ecstasy and is shocked chiefly by the material discomforts of earth or Hell.[36]

It is a profound and paradoxical experience to observe how Synge, an accomplished musician, was instinctively impelled to suspend his transcendent admiration of Bach and "the white harmonies of the St. Matthew Passion" in order to participate vicariously in a psychic celebration of the dark harmonies that suggested a Black Mass to him, as it was reflected in the blasphemous rituals of those magnificently barbarous slum children. Instead of trailing clouds of glory, these savage little street vagabonds, the little blood brothers of the tramp poets and poetic tinkers in Synge's plays, possessed ecstatic intimations of wild and profane glory—the elemental id impulse "which all feel but few acknowledge even to themselves." This untamed impulse is "hidden," as we know from Freud's theory of repression, and the thesis of his *Civilization and Its Discontents,* because we have been conditioned by civilized society and its "narrow churchman," a carbon copy of Baudelaire's "trembling Sage," to fear and reject it or suffer the pain of eternal damnation.

Synge had apparently read Baudelaire's essay on Satanic laughter, for he alluded to it in his Preface to *The Tinker's Wedding* in 1907:

> Of the things which nourish the imagination humour is one of the most needful, and it is dangerous to limit or destroy it. Baudelaire calls laughter the greatest sign of the Satanic element in man; and where a country loses its humour, as some towns in Ireland are doing, there will be morbidity of mind, as Baudelaire's mind was morbid.
>
> In the greater part of Ireland, however, the whole people, from the tinkers to the clergy, have still a life, and a view of life, that are rich and genial and humourous. I do not think that these country people, who have so much humour themselves, will mind being laughed at without malice, as the people in every country have been laughed at in their own comedies.[37]

It is strange that Synge should have associated morbidity with Baudelaire's enlightened view of Satanic laughter, for as it turned out Synge had miscalculated the temper of the Irish people as well as the insight of Baudelaire, since many Irish certainly did mind being laughed at in his plays, with what they felt was malice, morbidity, and worse, profanation. The hypersensitive nationalists and Catholics who rejected the dark laughter in all of his comedies and rioted at *The Playboy* were in sympathy with Synge's "narrow churchman" and Baudelaire's "trembling Sage," for if they had had their hard way they would have censored or destroyed the antic comedy of Synge; and Joyce and Yeats and O'Casey. In one of his early notebooks

Synge wrote: "When the body dies the soul goes to Heaven or Hell. So our modern art is—must be—either divine or satanic."[38] Modern Irish comedy is never divine.

Divinity cannot shape the ends of antic comedy. George Santayana must have been aware of this profane attitude when he described "the enemies of comedy" as antipagan, excessively melancholy, rational, and moralistic, in contrast to the "spontaneous passions" and "wild voices" of the Dionysian revelers. Synge would surely have agreed with the substance of these relevant passages from Santayana's "The Comic Mask":

> Paganism was full of scruples and superstitions in matters of behaviour or of *cultus*, since *cultus* too was regarded as a business or a magic craft; but in expression, in reflection, paganism was frank and even shameless; it felt itself inspired, and revered this inspiration. It saw nothing impious in inventing or recasting a myth about no matter how sacred a subject.
>
> Objections to the comic mask—to the irresponsible, complete, extreme expression of each moment—cut at the roots of all expression. Pursue this path, and at once you do away with gesture: we must not point, we must not pout, we must not cry, we must not laugh aloud. . . .
>
> Where the spirit of comedy has departed, company becomes constraint, reserve eats up spirit, and the people fall into a penurious melancholy in their scruple to be always exact, sane, and reasonable, never to mourn, never to glow, never to betray a passion or a weakness, nor venture to utter a thought they might not wish to harbour for ever.[39]

In view of Santayana's unconstrained and primordial associations, the "barbarous sympathies" of Synge and the Irish comedians take on a universal quality. Observed through an impious comic mask, those wild sympathies have an affinity with Nietzsche's concept of a fierce Dionysian energy, with the power of Ibsen's daimonic trolls, and perhaps most of all with Lorca's atavistic metaphor of the *duende,* that folk myth of an earth force whose "dark sounds" can inspire and liberate men and women. "These 'dark sounds,'" Lorca wrote, "are the mystery, the roots that probe through the mire that we all know of, and do not understand, but which furnishes us with whatever is sustaining in art."[40] It is also probable that Lorca had something like Satanic sympathies in mind, for he contrasted his dark duende with its opposite, a white angel muse, a sterile influence that must be rejected if art is to be fully powerful and free. In Ireland the equivalent of the duende is primarily if not exclusively a comic Dionysian force, an irreverent Celtic daimon.

The works of Synge, then, are inspired and sustained by his Irish duende. He seemed to realize that his art depended on those mysterious "dark sounds" or "barbarous sympathies," for in the Preface to his *Poems* he insisted that poetry "is not made by feeble blood," that it must have "strong roots among the clay and worms," and that "before verse can be human again it must learn to be brutal."[41] The ultimate achievement of his dramatic art depends on the unique manner in which, in the sense of Dr. Johnson's famous conceit, he yoked together the brutal and the comic impulses, most notably through the profane theme of mock patricide in *The Playboy of the Western World*. In the startling pattern of comic ironies in this work, savage deeds and dreams are rewarded, romantic and religious ideals are ridiculed. For a brief interlude of barbarous freedom the repressed Mayo peasants transform the miserable Christy Mahon into a strutting playboy and share the glory of his mock-heroic triumph; but they lose their romantic courage at the moment of tragicomic crisis when, in fear and trembling, they reject their potential liberator; they fall back into the mortifying guilt system of Father Reilly and the law, which once again deprives them of their "powerful instinctual urgencies." Most poignantly and tragically, Pegeen Mike is aware of that loss of love and joy. Only the comically messianic Christy escapes to conquer adverse reality, as do the alienated and barbarous vagrants in Synge's other dark comedies. All his mock-heroic characters pursue their liberating sins with unrepentant high spirit and low comic rebellion. The Tramp and Nora in *In the Shadow of the Glen;* Mary Byrne in *The Tinker's Wedding;* Martin Doul in *The Well of the Saints*—they are all repressed by a rigid world that conspires against their aspirations and gratifications, forcing them to celebrate their precarious existence outside the borders of civilized society.

A somewhat similar pattern of antic and rebellious laughter is exploited by O'Casey's profane "paycocks," the braggart "Captain" Jack Boyle and his clever parasite, Joxer Daly, those outrageously mendacious clowns who opt out of a world of "chassis" and barely survive in a tragicomic no-man's-land at the end of *Juno and the Paycock,* a desolate condition not unlike the Godot-less world of Beckett's tramps, Gogo and Didi. In parallel worlds of comic disorder in the midst of war we find the mordant and hilariously skeptical pedlar Seumas Shields in *The Shadow of a Gunman;* the Falstaffian Fluther Good and his merry company of inept rogues and sharp-tongued women in *The Plough and the Stars.* And in his neglected later plays O'Casey creates comic variations of this dark and antic condition: in the sardonic mock-heroics of Harry Heegan and his defenders and de-tractors in *The Silver Tassie;* in the gallery of cockney jesters in *Within the Gates;* in the subversive and sly rustic clowns in *Purple Dust, Cock-a-Doodle Dandy, The Bishop's Bonfire,* and *The Drums of Father Ned;* and in the knockabout disintegration let loose by the buffoons and wise fools in his one-act farces, and in his au-tobiography. O'Casey's antic comedians are all outsiders, dispos-sessed laborers and peasants who must resort to shrewd or sav-age jests for survival, even when their profane salvation is in doubt or denied. Some of them, like Harry Heegan, become tragicomic martyrs; but most of them fight back with comic fury, even when they are reduced to their barbarous skins and have only their stone hammers to beat against the laughter-negating system. They fight back with comic stratagems and exuberant invective, the gaudy and self-sustaining rush of words that are their major defense and delight; or, to paraphrase Fluther, they fight back even when they have to come out in their skins and throw words as well as stones.

Less aggressive but equally barbarous and damned by respect-able society are the tragicomic dreamers of George Fitzmaurice. In the too long neglected plays of Fitzmaurice, which have at last been made available in the Dolmen Press editions, the typical comic antihero is often a Faustian jester, a strangely obsessed peasant with a daimonic and absurd vision of private salvation that mocks and confounds the orthodox world. In *The Pie-Dish* (1908), after having dedicated fifty years of his eccentric life to the making of a mysterious pie-dish, the dying Leum Donoghue rejects his unsympathetic family, who refer to the pie-dish as a "pagan" object, and refuses to be anointed by the priest. When he suspects that God may have forsaken him and prevented him from finishing his miraculous emblem—"My wonderful pie-dish! It's my heart's blood is in you, my pie-dish!"—Leum profanely calls on the devil to help him, offering his body and soul to Satan. At that moment the pie-dish symbolically falls and breaks, and Leum screams, collapses, and dies. "Dead and damned," his daughter laments.[42] The family and the priest are bewildered by this seemingly terrible punishment, but we are led to believe that it is a comic damnation because the Faustian Donoghue has at last escaped from their narrow and pious world, which could not tolerate or understand the burning desire to create a mundane and magical pie-dish. Fitzmaurice's Kerry peasants who ostracized Leum, as Synge's Mayo peasants rejected Christy, are damned to go on living without dreams, a greater punishment than the fate of Leum, who has taken his daimonic dream with him to the liberating grave.

Fitzmaurice often stressed the scapegoat motif of tragicomic damnation in his plays, for his Jaymony Shanahan in *The Magic Glasses* (1913) and Roger Carmody in *The Dandy Dolls* (1914) are similarly sacrificial outcasts with fantastically profane dreams, failed poets who in their farcical lives and absurd deaths win a victory of spirit that is infinitely preferable to an ignoble existence in the insensitive and repressed world. And like Synge and O'Casey, Fitzmaurice also compensated for the indignities and miseries of so-called civilized life by creating a uniquely rich and mock-heroic lingo that revitalizes his characters, a folk idiom that gives them a lyrical power of imagination in hard times. Again we see that the very language of the darkly comic characters in Irish drama is quintessential to survival; for even in the face of death it can be an instrument of graveyard humor that mocks that final indignity. When Roger Carmody fears for the safety of his life and his dandy doll—the miraculous doll that is his symbolic equivalent of a pie-dish or the magic glasses, a private talisman of mysterious folk art—he tries to whip up his courage in the following speech to his shrewish wife:

> What way is it for you, woman, to be tormenting me now? Sure, if I was talking brave about my doll itself, what was it but to keep the heart in bloom, while all the time there was a little doubt, and, like 'twould be in the air, for weeks past something was foreshowing

me the calamity of the woful hour. For it's as queer in myself I felt as ever I did after a topping feed of goose, the brain dull, a ton weight in every limb, and I walking the ground, and I couldn't lep the height of a sod of turf; the strangest things coming into my head; it's a fit of crying I got itself seeing the youngsters playing in Barton's field—it brought back to me so piercing the time I was likewise gay and hearty, tasby in me and high glee.[43]

Concern for the fate of his dandy doll forces Roger to keep his "heart in bloom," and memories of his wild youth bring back the "high glee" and the "tasby"—from the Gaelic *teasbhach,* excessive animal spirit, or spontaneously wanton energy, the "tasby" as the primitive life force that sustains the Roger Carmodys of Ireland. It was probably this same wild force that Synge recognized in the savage slum children of Harold's Cross, and Fitzmaurice's Roger recalled in the children in Barton's field, the mysterious and liberating "tasby," which could be an Irish version of the Spanish *duende.* In its comic thrust this life force defines one of the main sources of inspiration in Irish literature, the comic profanation that develops from the medieval to the modern period, and is especially fulfilled in the modern dramatists. It is not only at work in the plays of Synge, O'Casey, and Fitzmaurice, for we also see it in the mock-heroic fiction of Maria Edgeworth, William Carleton, James Joyce, and Flann O'Brien; in Patrick Kavanagh's autobiographical *Green Fool* (1939) and *Tarry Flynn* (1948); in Brendan Behan's plays and his autobiographical *Borstal Boy* (1958); in Austin Clarke's *Flight to Africa* (1963); in the Crazy Jane poems of Yeats, and in a more sustained effort in his two atypical and dark allegorical comedies, *The Player Queen* (1922) and *The Cat and the Moon* (1926).

In *The Cat and the Moon* Yeats moved in a new direction and wrote what might be called a comic variation of *At the Hawk's Well,* this time allowing an antiheroic couple, the Lame Beggar and the Blind Beggar, to achieve their miracle at the holy well. First, however, the beggars must engage in their farcical fights, which suggest an uncanny anticipation of Beckett's knockabout tramps in these Yeatsian clowns who scold and need each other. Nevertheless, although the mode is farcical now, Yeats is still writing one of his characteristic miracle plays with mythic implications. He gives his Lame Beggar affinities with the passionate young Cuchulain, and the Blind Beggar is linked to the intellectually sterile Old Man in *At the Hawk's Well.* The symbolic guardians of the wells in the two plays are different: the sacred and mysterious hawk is replaced by a sacred but mundane cat, the wise Minnaloushe, who is in harmony with the subjective moon and presides over the Lame Beggar's blessed dance of victory. If *The Cat and the Moon* is a comic salvation play, *The Player Queen* is a comic damnation play.

Yeats struggled unsuccessfully for many years to write *The Player Queen* as an illustration of his theory of masks, a play in which each character finds or fails to find his secret daimon, his liberating antithetical self. Only after he finally decided to turn the play into a comedy and mock his allegory of heroic idealism was Yeats able to resolve the difficulty and finish the play: "I could not write the play I had planned, for all became allegorical, and though I tore up hundreds of pages in my endeavour to escape from allegory, my imagination became sterile for nearly five years and I only escaped at last when I had mocked in a comedy my own thought."[44] But instead of escaping from allegory, Yeats was forced to transform a tragic allegory into a comic one. The noble pursuit of the passionate daimon was no longer possible in the disordered and cynical world of the play—"this vile age," as Yeats later called the modern world in *The Death of Cuchulain*—and so he felt he had to show this collapse of tradition and heroism through malicious farce. Where once he had presented the noble figure of the poet as the prophetic and martyred Seanchan in *The King's Threshold,* he now saw his poet as the drunken and abused Septimus, a mock-heroic figure of ridicule whose prophecies are ignored. In the play-within-a-play structure of *The Player Queen,* Septimus is rehearsing to play the redemptive role of Noah in *The Tragical History of Noah's Deluge,* an allusion to the Chester cycle miracle play, a work that depends on low comedy for its symbolic theme of damnation and salvation. Yeats, however, deflates all possibilities of salvation and stresses the comic damnation of a world that has lost its vital center of faith and poetry. His confused and rootless players struggle unsuccessfully and absurdly in their attempts to discover their identities and perform their Noah play. Yeats's Noah, like Beckett's Godot, is not capable of appearing and assuming his role as potential savior.

Septimus, the mock Noah and failed poet, is beaten, abused, and finally ostracized; and he remains drunk throughout the play as if to anaesthetize himself from disaster. Only when he is sober, he claims, is he unfaithful to his bad wife, Decima, the player queen who is the comic-ironic antagonist of the play. In a cabal with the forbidding Prime Minister, the scheming Decima replaces the impotent and silly queen of this mythical country— it is one of Yeats's few plays set outside of Ireland—and when she becomes the despotic Player Queen, she banishes her husband, Septimus, and all the players involved in the Noah play. Earlier as a discredited oracle, with blood on his face from his beatings, Septimus had proclaimed that a New Dispensation of the Unicorn would replace the fading old order and mark the end of the Christian Era. At the conclusion of the play, however, when Decima assumes her terrible reign and condemns the poet and the players, all creativity, to exile, there is no sign of a redemptive unicorn. Antiheroic puppets, in the guise of an unholy couple, Decima and the Prime Minister, now represent a travesty of a "second coming."

It is as if Yeats had decided to dramatize a farcical version of his poem "The Second Coming" (1921) in *The Player Queen* (1922), for in this play mere *comic* anarchy is loosed upon a world in which "the ceremony of innocence is drowned." The banished Septimus is one of the best who "lack all conviction" now, while the devious Decima and her Prime Minister are the worst who are "full of passionate intensity." There may be no direct sign of a rough beast slouching toward Bethlehem, but, symbolically, Decima at the end picks up and wears the mask of Noah's unbelieving sister, she of the "wicked mouth" who was drowned because she thought her player brother, Noah-Septimus, "was telling lies." Septimus at the end is the antic martyr as mock savior, the wise fool who is sacrificed for his hidden wisdom. He is the comic scapegoat, the subversive poet who has played the game of his sublime folly in order to expose the sinister folly of the terrible new dispensation.

In his treatment of the theme of farcical damnation in this

tragicomedy, Yeats comes close to echoing Synge and anticipating O'Casey and Beckett; nevertheless, his comic imagination is not quite as low and wild—as outrageously barbarous—as theirs. Perhaps there is more of the failed poet than the uninhibited clown in Septimus. As Yeats often confessed, he was not comfortable with low comedy in his own writing. In any case, by presenting the traditional Irish theme of the exiled poet through the allegorical action of comic disobedience, he associated himself once more with the artist's rebellion against the repressive enemy.

Yeats was aware of the choices open to the artist in Ireland when he wrote, in the final entry of *Per Amica Silentia Lunae* (1917), about the alternatives of "barbarous words" and "simple piety":

> As I go up and down my stair and pass the gilded Moorish wedding-chest where I keep my "barbarous words," I wonder will I take to them once more, for I am baffled by those voices that still speak as if to Odysseus but as the bats; or now that I shall in a little be growing old, to some kind of simple piety like that of an old woman.[45]

Like so many of his creative countrymen, Yeats had to choose the pagan rage of his "barbarous words" to comfort his rebellious old age in pious Ireland. And there must have been many echoes of profane laughter in those batlike and mythical voices that reverberated in his Celtic tower.

Comedy and Ketman

Whether they are sacrificed or damned, all failed poets, tramps, playboys, paycocks, and pagan dreamers of antic Irish comedy are wise fools who keep their squint-eyed watch over the hardening orthodoxies of society. The main strategy of their comic resistance is to fight against institutional folly with mad folly; to create their disguises and grotesque diversions without fear and trembling. They are the comic gargoyles who profane the household gods and protect us from our grim fellows. They are the daimonic liberators whose comic crimes against society are committed as irreverent metaphors and mimes that carry no burden of guilt. The majority of people are understandably frightened by the threat of civil or religious condemnation, but the wise fool is most rebellious and laughs most profoundly when he is damned or exiled. And it seldom hurts when he laughs.

Nevertheless, though G. Wilson Knight has assured us that "it is an error of aesthetic judgement to regard humour as essentially trivial,"[46] some critics who write about comedy are suspicious of laughter in drama and treat it as a trifling or innocuous affair. Andrew E. Malone, one of the first critical historians of modern Irish drama, takes a patronizing view of the comic genre as a cheap concession to the masses when he tells us that "comedy is the path of popularity, if it be not always the path to great art."[47] L. J. Potts, a critic who specializes in comedy, solemnly distinguishes between the elevation of pure comedy and the emptiness of impure farce when he states: "More simply, and perhaps more accurately, [farce] might be described as comedy with the meaning left out; which is as much as to say, with the comedy left out."[48] Enid Welsford, the highly regarded critical historian of the Fool, recognizes that the meaning is not left out in comedy, but even she tends to reduce it to a rather insipid meaning when she describes the wise fool as little more than a harmless entertainer: "The Fool does not lead a revolt against the Law," she insists, "he lures us into a region of the spirit where, as Lamb would put it, the writ does not run. . . . There is nothing essentially immoral or blasphemous or rebellious about clownage."[49] It might equally be argued that there is nothing essentially moral or pious or respectable about clownage. Housebroken or amenable clowns might be found in Ruritania but not in Ireland; not in the Athens or Rome of the braggart warrior and the parasite slave; not in the England of Falstaff and Tony Lumpkin; not in the Germany of Zarathustra and Azdak; not in the America of Huck Finn and Buster Keaton. So Welsford's whimsical sentiments, with their quaint appeal to Charles Lamb's airy-fairyland of benign comedy, cannot help us in our pursuit of the sharp meanings that emerge from the antics of the wise fool.

Nor can Meredith help us with his genteel concept of the "silvery laughter" of the mind, which might set off some delicate ripples of delight in the nervous system, but which would exclude the intoxicating belly laughter of a barbarous Falstaff or Fluther. Meredith is distressed by what he calls the perverse and brutal aspects of low comedy. Unhappily he concedes that "laughter is open to perversion, like other good things; the scornful and the brutal sorts are not unknown to us"; but he hastens to assure us that "the laughter directed by the Comic Spirit is a harmless wine, conducing to sobriety in the degree that it enlivens."[50] There can be little doubt that such conducive sobriety is alien to the anarchic spirit of antic comedy.

Even Bergson cannot help us here, since his classic essay on laughter is limited to a brilliant study of the *alazons* or "humour" characters, those rigid impostors whose automatism exposes their comic villainy. Bergson concentrates on the solemn or one-track fools, the Malvolios and Misers who are laughed at, not the merry and malicious fools, the Sir Tobys and rude mechanicals who do the laughing. He therefore ignores the clever *eirons* who, while they may for extra measure also serve as the butt of the jest, are wise buffoons or clowns primarily endowed with a flexibility of instinctive wit that deflates the inflexible *alazons*. Bergson is therefore an enlightened moralist who analyzes the sources of comic sin, not the resources of comic salvation.

In antic comedy the rigidly ordered world itself is the ridiculous *alazon*, the inflexible enemy that cannot be defeated and must therefore be circumvented by comic stratagems. These subversive games of survival are among the main resources available to the lowly in what Susanne Langer calls their comic "contest with the world," their pragmatic reliance on "brainy opportunism in the face of an essentially dreadful universe."[51] Along with a capricious destiny presided over by an array of indifferent gods, what usually makes the universe so dreadful is that the army of mortal *alazons* who rule and regiment, all levels of secular and religious officialdom, cannot resist adopting a noble or even sublime infallibility, which automatically becomes the target of the antic comedian's mockery. It is highly significant, then, that Freud should have pointed out that the techniques of comedy are often directed at "the degradation of the sublime": "Caricature, parody and travesty (as well as their practical counterpart, unmasking) are directed against people and objects which lay claim to authority and respect, which are in some sense 'sublime.'"[52]

In his seminal investigation into the origins of comedy, Francis Cornford followed a similar path by defining one essential aspect of the comic strategy as a mock-heroic gesture, a profane impulse that instinctively deflates the sublime or heroic image of authority:

> When Comedy touched the figures of heroic legend, it was to shatter their sublimity and degrade them below the level of decent human beings—to make Ajax as vulgar as Thersites, and much more stupid. The Gods in Aristophanes, again, are always inferior to the human protagonist. These figures that might threaten to trail some clouds of glory from above and beyond the mortal scene, must be not merely brought down to the same footing with human characters, but thrust still lower.[53]

Cornford also stressed the fact that the wise fool as *eiron* had to make an indirect attack on the entrenched *alazons* by assuming a shrewd disguise of self-deprecation: "The *eiron* who victimises the Impostors masks his cleverness under a show of clownish dullness. He is a fox in the sheep's clothing of a buffoon."[54]

Further confirmation of this foxy game of antic disguises can be found in some significant affinities between Irish comedy and Polish theory. There is something refreshingly conspiratorial about the wise folly of Irish clowns, and a convincing rationale for this comic insurgence might be located in the conspiratorial ideas of three Polish writers: in Czeslaw Milosz's concept of Ketman as a psychological weapon; in Leszek Kolakowski's concept of the archetypal confrontation between a priest and a jester; in Jerzy Grotowski's concept of theater as a performing art of "sacral parody."

Having been forced into the repressed role of subject nations for many centuries, agrarian Ireland and Poland shared an inbred suspicion of foreign authority, with the added implication that all authority might be an alien influence, and they suffered from an inferiority complex that demanded, along with the movement for national freedom, the tentative yet potent compensations of comedy, a psychological need for devious profanations of the tyrannous invaders. The rise of the Irish insurrectionary spirit was of course the result of over 700 years of British misrule and suppression, and, besides the ranks of the rebel patriots, any rebel clown who could mock or unnerve the tyrant was to be encouraged and admired. Wise fools are therefore plentiful in Ireland, for they are the lifeblood of the comic resistance, and Irish dramatists, and also poets and novelists, have made the most of this historical condition that creates the need for psychic survival. And it is perhaps no accident that similarly subjugated and agrarian Poland, for many centuries exposed to invasions and repressions by Russia and Germany, should sometimes be called the restless Ireland of Central Europe. It is not a general rule, since there are notable exceptions, but superior nations often excel in the secure affirmations of tragedy, while inferior nations often excel in the insecure profanations of comedy. People subjected to the nightmare of famine and concentration camps, ghettos and Harlems, instinctively develop their underground weaponry of profane jokes and gallows humor.

The Poles therefore had to create their own foxy stratagems for survival, and Milosz in *The Captive Mind* devotes a chapter to the subversive art of Ketman, a psychological game of deception that supposedly had it origins in Islam—one is tempted to suggest that it began in the Garden of Eden—and, according to Milosz, became a necessary way of life in the Iron Curtain countries of Europe. Milosz has the credentials to write an ironic book on the diseases and defenses of mental as well as physical captivity. A poet and translator of the plays of Shakespeare into Polish, he fought in the Polish underground during World War II, served in the postwar Polish government, and subsequently rejected the terrorizing tactics of Polish communism and went into self-exile in Paris. His description of the technique of Ketman is influenced by the Comte de Gobineau's highly controversial nineteenth-century work *Religions and Philosophies of Central Asia;* and while Milosz warns us about the unfounded conclusions of this racist author, he also assures us that the concept of Ketman is a universal strategy that must have had its primordial origins in people's initial attempts to construct a gratifying defense against repression:

> Ketman fills the man who practices it with pride. Thanks to it, a
> believer raises himself to a permanent state of superiority over the
> man he deceives, be he a minister of state or a powerful king; to

him who uses Ketman, the other is a miserable blind man whom
one shuts off from the true path whose existence he does not
suspect; while you, tattered and dying of hunger, trembling ex-
ternally at the feet of duped force, your eyes are filled with light,
you walk in brightness before your enemies. It is an unintelligent
thing that you make sport of; it is a dangerous beast that you
disarm. What a wealth of pleasure![55]

It should be apparent, then, that the ancient art of Ketman
offers a psychological justification for the comic art of the traditional *eiron* or flexible clown. The mask of Ketman provides
the double-edged instrument of comic revenge for the supposedly inferior person who uses this self-deprecating disguise
in order to become the rightfully superior being, no matter how
lowly or oppressed he may be. The strategy of Ketman involves a
theatrical game played for very high stakes that could hold in the
balance a person's will to live, his determination to keep his mind
and imagination free, even though he may literally be an abject
slave. It is a virtuoso performance of deceptions played before a
double audience of one's enemies and friends; it is an ironic
performance calculated to lull the inflated beholder or *alazon*
into a state of false security by convincing him that he is superior
to the antic fool who daily makes a comic spectacle of himself in
the marketplace, where the friends of the fool are similarly or
emotionally disguised as an audience and overhear everything.
Everyone who might be distressed or confused by the barbarous
fool in broad daylight empathizes with his antics in a darkened
theater. From the perspective of an audience now, the vicarious
thrill of the theatrical performance reenacts the wish fulfillment
of dreams. In a dramatic context, the wise fool may be alienated
but he is never alone and seldom afraid; he provokes his laughter for his fellows as well as himself; and he twists the tail of the
unsuspecting dragon. The antic Hamlet plays Ketman with Den-
mark; the antic Falstaff plays Ketman with England; the antic
Irish clown, Christy Mahon or Fluther Good or Leopold Bloom,
plays Ketman with Ireland. As characters in works of literature
or as underground citizens, the players of Ketman are the necessary survivors in every country.

There are as many varieties of Ketman as there are players of
the game, disguised fools who are motivated by a wide range of

personal, economic, or political urgencies; but what we are mainly concerned with here might be called aesthetic or comic Ketman. Milosz could have been describing the emotional climate that calls for the barbarous and rebellious defenses of antic Irish comedy when he wrote the following passage:

> In short, Ketman means self-realization *against* something. He who practices Ketman suffers because of the obstacles he meets; but if these obstacles were suddenly removed, he would find himself in a void which might perhaps prove much more painful. Internal revolt is sometimes essential to spiritual health, and can create a particular form of happiness. What can be said openly is much less interesting than the emotional magic of defending one's private sanctuary.[56]

The antic clown thrives on adversity and he would paradoxically find himself disarmed in a void of easy and excessively liberal tolerance. The challenge of a world that provokes comic Ketman is good for the soul, and a country without sufficient *alazons* to goad the comic *eirons* into action would be an impossible and unlikely utopia. There would be no need for humor in such a dull heaven. A socially and religiously conservative country such as Ireland, therefore, creates a favorable climate for the dangerous risks and rewards of comic rebellion. The comic characters in Irish drama are able to act against the grain of orthodox behavior and play Ketman in order to guard the private sanctuaries of the alienated.

Comic Ketman takes on an extra dimension in the contribution of Milosz's philosophic countryman Leszek Kolakowski. In his remarkable essay "The Priest and the Jester," Kolakowski suggests that the ultimate function of the wise fool or rebellious jester is part of an ever-recurring and universal dialectic, an inevitable collision between sacred and profane values. Again the Polish and Irish connection is strikingly significant because Kolakowski might have been describing one of the archetypal motifs of Irish literature, particularly Irish comedy, the dialectic between a sacred priest and a profane jester. This modern motif goes back to the mock-heroic dialogues of twelfth-century Celtic literature, the comic confrontations between Oisín, the poet-jester and playboy of the pagan world, and St. Patrick, the austere Christian priest of fifth-century Ireland. Collisions between representatives of these contending voices can be heard throughout Irish literature, in drama, poetry, and fiction, and Kolakowski invested them with universal implications when he wrote:

> The antagonism between a philosophy consolidating the absolute and a philosophy questioning the accepted absolutes appears to be incurable, as incurable as the existence of conservatism and radicalism in all areas of human life. It is the antagonism of a priest and a jester; and in almost every historical epoch, the philosophy of the priest and the philosophy of the jester have been the two most general forms of intellectual culture. The priest is the guardian of the absolute who upholds the cult of the final and the obvious contained in the tradition. The jester is he who, although a habitué of good society, does not belong to it and makes it the object of his inquisitive impertinence—he who questions what appears to be self-evident.[57]

An independent Marxist philosopher who, like Milosz, turned his back on Polish communism and went into self-exile, Kolakowski is skeptical about political as well as religious absolutes; he realizes that commissars think and act as secular priests, not as jesters. But although his sympathies lie with the inquisitive and impertinent jesters, Kolakowski is aware of the danger inherent in the profane as well as the sacred: "Both the priest and the jester violate the mind: the former by strangling it with catechism, the latter by harassing it with mockery. At a royal palace there are more priests than jesters—just as in a king's realm there are more policemen than artists. It does not seem possible to change this."[58] If this is the inevitable nature of things, that jesters and artists must be outnumbered or outcast, that priests and police must be part of the power structure of any realm, then it should be understandable that harassment by mockery is a more essential and less deadly alternative than strangulation by catechism, religious or political. As every jester knows, it is wiser to laugh restlessly with skepticism than to rest solemnly with absolutes.

This dichotomy, however, does not take into account the Irish phenomenon of impertinent priests who sometimes feel compelled to become jesters in the church, such rebel priests as Father Michael O'Flanagan and Dr. Walter McDonald, who bravely mocked the religious and political hierarchies of Ireland for their strangling tactics. Shaw created a memorable jester-priest in *John Bull's Other Island*, the defrocked Father Keegan, who had the improbable vision of a communion of sacred *and* profane ideals in the Ireland of his mad dreams. O'Casey made a special point of celebrating the memory of Ireland's jester-priests in his autobiography, particularly Father O'Flanagan and Dr. McDonald; and he created his own mythical jester-priest in his last major play, *The Drums of Father Ned*, the mysterious title character who never appears on stage, a visionary drum-beating and apocalyptic figure in the improbable disguise of a cheerful Godot and a Celtic Dionysus in a Roman collar.

Perhaps this phenomenon is not limited to Ireland, since we have in our time witnessed the anomaly of one of the truly great jester-priests, Pope John XXIII, the inspired papal jester who revolutionized his church by exposing and reforming many of its sacred anachronisms and follies with his wise humor and inquisitive impertinence. And more recently in America we witnessed the imprisonment of those two militant jester-priests, Fathers Daniel and Philip Berrigan, who, along with a number of kindred rebel priests and nuns, committed their outrageous deeds of antic protest by desecrating the sacred records of the Vietnam War with chicken blood and fire. If Jerzy Grotowski, the brilliant theater revolutionary, founder-director of the Polish Laboratory Theatre, were to dramatize the sacred and profane aspects of the Berrigan saga, the result would reflect what has appropriately been called by Grotowski the "dialectics of mockery and apotheosis," or "religion expressed through blasphemy; love speaking out through hate."[59]

These resonant paradoxes bring us back to the barbarous aspects of Irish comedy, even though the intense Grotowski, to invoke yet another paradox, lacks a sense of humor, particularly low humor; he has the gift of dramatic Ketman without the comedy. Nevertheless, his concept of a theatrical experience that profanes sacred myths in order to transcend them goes to the heart of the theatrical experience in Ireland, if we add the catalytic agent, the grotesque art of antic comedy. The Irish dramatists have for a long time been challenging their audiences in Grotowski's terms, "by violating accepted stereotypes of vision, feeling, and judgment"; by creating "transgressions" that defy taboos and "shocks" that enable us to give ourselves "to something which is impossible to define but which contains Eros and Caritas."[60] The Irish dramatists have known instinctively that this mysterious expression of Eros and Caritas can be achieved through a daimonic release of laughter that suspends our debilitating sense of guilt so that we can attain a Pelagian acceptance of life without fear and trembling. The artistic transgression, the shock of barbarous laughter is necessary because the political and religious systems of society have conditioned men and women to resist anything less outrageous, to reject anything less rebellious. This is part of what Synge meant when he insisted that poetry "is not made by feeble blood . . . it must learn to be brutal."

Grotowski seeks to create this elemental force in the theater by establishing connections with the "sacral parody" of medieval drama, the tradition of religious profanation through antic comedy in the mock rituals of the Feast of Fools and the Lord of Misrule, and in that classic example of "religion expressed through blasphemy," the comic *Second Shepherds' Play.* He looks back to the ritualistic sources of power and parody in that early theater with this observation: "The theatre, when it was still part of religion, was already theatre: it liberated the spiritual energy of the congregation or tribe by incorporating myth and profaning or rather transcending it. The spectator thus had a renewed awareness of his personal truth in the truth of the myth, and through fright and a sense of the sacred he came to catharsis. It was not by chance that the Middle Ages produced the idea of 'sacral parody.'"[61]

In the modern secularized theater the sacred values of the congregation, religious or ethical, are still profaned and transcended, and Grotowski borrows the form of "sacral parody" for his concept of theater in order to achieve a heightened awareness of personal truth or myth, a cathartic release of unconscious aspirations. That mythic quality, which Yeats called "something ancient and wild," becomes the center of Grotowski's ritualistic theater, a theater structured on violent actions of parody that provide the function of profanation and liberation through the "dialectics of mockery and apotheosis." In this theater, and most particularly in the Irish theater, nothing is so sacred that it cannot be purified by comic profanation.

Antic Irish comedy is based on a theater of "sacral parody." It was not by chance that Ireland, one of the most profoundly religious and genuinely medieval of modern nations, produced a theatrical feast of wise fools that has its roots in the early Celtic literature and medieval drama of comic desecration. All that is sacred is purged by profanation in the antic comedy of Synge, Yeats, Shaw, Lady Gregory, Fitzmaurice, O'Casey, Shiels, Beckett, and Behan. It is a drama of "mockery and apotheosis" in which the profane redeems the sacred by violating it with comic and barbarous sympathies.

Chapter 2

THE HIDDEN OISÍN

O, dear me now! Another grand discobely! After Make-
fearsome's Ocean. You've actuary entducked one! Quok!

... make the Rageous Ossean kneel and quaff a lyre!
— James Joyce, *Finnegans Wake*

AND Saint Patrick told him about Adam and Eve and how
they were turned out and lost for eating the forbidden fruit,
an apple he called it. And Usheen said, "Although God has
all my friends shut up in hell, if I knew fruit was so scarce
with him, and he to think so much of it, I'd have sent him
seven carloads of it." It was very decent of Usheen to say
that; he always had a very decent name for those sort of
things. And Usheen said another thing to Patrick. He said,
"Don't the blackbird and the thrush whistle very well, and
don't they make their nests very nice, and they never got
any instruction or teaching from God?" And what Patrick
answered to that I don't know.
— Lady Gregory, *The Kiltartan History Book*

Oisín vs. Patrick

The mythic Oisín or Usheen is a mock-heroic figure in medieval and later Celtic literature who releases the repressed wishes of the Irish folk imagination that created him. Once the great poet-warrior of the Fenian cycle, he now appears as a lamentable and seemingly foolish old man, almost Lear-like in his barbarous rage and comic hubris, when he is confronted by St. Patrick in fifth-century Ireland. In his final days of antiheroic victory in defeat he is determined to retrieve and celebrate the lost heritage of the pagan world through his comic rebellion and profanation. "The Rageous Ossean" will not bend his knee to the saint, but he does "quaff his lyre" to the vanishing Fenians and the pleasure principle of their joyous way of life. Beyond fear and trembling, beyond guilt and mortification, the sly old pagan plays the game of Ketman with the new Christian order of solemn clerics. The flyting between Oisín and Patrick is a "sacral parody" of conversion, an early Irish dramatization of the "dialectics of mockery and apotheosis."

Traditionally it was assumed that Oisín himself, famous as a poet as well as a warrior, was the author of the Ossianic ballads and stories about the Fenians and St. Patrick. Actually these works must have originated as part of an oral folk tradition and were then written down and preserved by anonymous Irish bards and the Irish people, who apparently felt the need to project their unfulfilled dreams through the *persona* of a once heroic but now comically absurd figure of fallen glory. It is of course a common strategy of Ketman to hide one's frustrations in the guise of a fool or comic scapegoat such as Oisín. One might say that the power of a myth helped to overcome the burden of reality in this mock-heroic legend. When the mythological Oisín collided with the historical Patrick, the world of imagination scored a vicarious triumph over the world of fact; the pagan victim circumvented the obstacle of adverse circumstances by mocking the Christian victor. This expression of mockery did not mean that the faith or the clergy in medieval Ireland were in any danger; on the contrary, it only served to stress the implacable position of Patrick and his church, which was strong enough to be laughed at. It is probably an inevitable consequence that entrenched orthodoxies as well as dispossessed clowns gain strength from adversity. Kolakowski's priests and jesters feed on each other's follies.

Some of the earliest texts of the Ossianic literature, in verse and prose, are preserved in Gaelic manuscripts of the eleventh and twelfth centuries, dating back originally at least 250 years, when presumably the oral tradition began; some are to be found in manuscripts of the fourteenth and fifteenth centuries, going back about 200 years. The largest group of works, however, mostly dramatic in structure, among which the "Dialogues" between Oisín and Patrick appear, were composed in the sixteenth century, though the oral tradition for these comic debates probably existed as early as the twelfth century. Thus the Gaelic-speaking peasants of Ireland and Scotland (Irish and Scottish Gaelic were one language and one literature in medieval times) orally created and passed on to the bards the ballads and sagas about the legendary Finn MacCool (Fionn MacCumhail), chief of the Fianna, one of the most famous warrior tribes of the ancient Celts, his son Oisín, Oisín's son Oscar, and Finn's nephew Cailte MacRonan.

In some of the dialogues it is Cailte (Cweelt-ya) who shares with Oisín a supernaturally prolonged life, and both heroes— represented as old men living on several hundred years after the passing of the Fenians, until the fifth century, when Patrick set out to convert them—lament the passing of a golden age. In his book of translations from Gaelic poetry, *Kings, Lords, & Commons,* Frank O'Connor reproduces the tone of nostalgic and comic protest in his fine rendering of several Oisín and Cailte ballads. O'Connor remarks that what emerges from this poetry is a picture of "an Ireland where, because of St. Patrick, everything seems to have become cheapened and diminished";[1] and he also says that this irreverent tone of dissatisfaction can be found not only in the Fenian or Ossianic poems but in some of the later Christian poetry:

> ... Irish poetry is haunted by the revenant, the figure who has escaped death only to return and find that Ireland, under the Christians, has gone to Hell. But this note characterizes not only the Pagans, but also the Christians themselves. The hermit-poems, too, show the archaelogizing tendency, because, like the poems dealing with the Fenians, they look back to a golden age. The Irish are like Orpheus, forever looking back to the Eurydice they are attempting to bring home from the Shades.[2]

And like Orpheus they failed, sometimes comically as well as elegiacally. Nevertheless, there is an unmistakable ring of naive integrity and honor in Oisín's mock-heroic failure. Unable to rescue the dead Fenian heroes from hell, where, according to St. Patrick, the Christian God had placed them for refusing to submit to his will, Oisín remained true to his pagan code. Defiantly he chose to be in hell with his comrades rather than accept the strictures of the new religion.

In some treatment of the legends the pagan values are assimilated and diminished by the Christian way of life, for example, in the tales that deal with Cailte, who is willingly converted by Patrick. But the proud Oisín invokes his rebellious *non serviam;* however, in some later versions, where a religious hand apparently modified the myth, Oisín is also converted, though in a characteristically farcical manner. While Patrick, in conducting the ritual of baptism, inadvertently drives his crozier through Oisín's foot, the courageous old pagan does not cry out, for he stoically assumes that foot piercing must be a part of the quaint Christian ceremony.

The account of Cailte's conversion occurs in the *Agallamh na Senorach,* "Colloquy of the Elders," a loosely constructed long work in prose and verse, probably written in the twelfth century, in which Cailte and Patrick are the principal characters, and Oisín makes only a brief appearance. Here there is no conflict between the pagan and Christian worlds. At first the saint has some misgivings about listening to Cailte's stories and songs of the Fenian heroes, which he honestly but not without some guilt enjoys, for he fears they may undermine his life of devotion and prayer. His two guardian angels, however, come to assure him that it is quite safe and proper for him to listen. The angels also tell Patrick that his scribes must record the ancient tales for posterity so that future generations may learn of the noble past. Meanwhile Cailte looks forward as well as back, for though he regrets the loss of his pagan pleasures, he accepts the blessings of Patrick, who emerges as an attractive figure in this work.

In a dramatic reversal, Patrick's character changes sharply in his tragicomic confrontation with Oisín, which is recorded in the *Agallamh Oisín agus Padraig*, "The Dialogue between Oisín and Patrick," a long poem of more than one hundred ballad stanzas, probably written in the sixteenth century, though the original oral form goes back several hundred years, to medieval Ireland. In this new anticlerical context Patrick has been forced to reveal the rough side of his proselytizing nature, for his adversary is now an intransigent and colorful old pagan who cannot be won over by a mystical promise of heaven, and even less by the threat of hell and eternal damnation. In fact, Patrick becomes so hard and vindictive in his authoritarian treatment of the blind and childlike Oisín, who is virtually his prisoner, that the great Christian saint emerges as the choleric and comic villain of the piece. All the sympathy belongs to the pagan scapegoat, the helpless and raging Oisín.

Oisín appears as a comic desecrator of patriarchal authority in one of the earliest surviving Gaelic poems, "The Quarrel between Finn and Oisin," again a flyting or contest of comic invective in which a son mocks a father. This Old Irish poem, which Kuno Meyer has edited and translated from a late-eighth-century manuscript, rehearses the comic tone and form of the later Ossianic ballad dialogues. Although Oisín never fights with his generous and freedom-loving father in the Fenian cycle, the anonymous early poet decided to invent a comic quarrel be-

tween father and son, and coincidentally he happened to anticipate the comic spirit of rebellion in the later Oisín. Meyer
associates this quarrel with the traditional theme of a combat between father and son which appears in the epic and ballad literature of many nations, often, as in the Irish versions, in the form
of a lampoon. As a result of the quarrel, Finn and Oisín have
been separated for a whole year, and the father searches for his
rebellious son in a furious mood that is obviously more mock-
heroic than tragic. Meyer tells us the poet probably realized that
the Ossianic legend was not adaptable to tragedy, and "so a
humorous and burlesque treatment is substituted, such as we
find occasionally in the literature of other nations who have
introduced the motive. Here the combat is merely a bit of rough
horse-play or wrangle of words."[3]

The wandering Oisín is cooking a pig when Finn appears in
this eighth-century poem, and the father gives his errant son a
clout on the head. A mock fight follows in which they brag and
roar at each other, both hot with threats and comic insults, and
Oisín desecrates his father, rejecting him and calling him a senile
maniac. This particular father-son motif is not developed in the
later Ossianic poems, yet the tone of burlesque humor provides
a striking hint of what we can expect from the later Oisín. When
he returns to Ireland from his wandering in Tir na nOg, the
Land of Youth, this time having been absent for three hundred
years, he meets his surrogate father in the person of St. Patrick
in the ballad dialogues, and we get comic variations of the
father-son combat in Patrick's patriarchal prohibitions and
Oisín's willful disobedience. They mock each other and present
counterarguments, Patrick calling for the graces of the next
world, Oisín for the glories of this world; and in this context of a
fundamental disagreement the horseplay becomes more than a
mere wrangle of words. Now father and son represent the Oedipal clash between two irreconcilable minds, two opposing ways
of life.

This verbal combat reflects the tragicomic conflict between
father and son that is so dominant in Irish literature, in the
works of Synge and Joyce and O'Casey, for example; in Christy
Mahon's triple attempt at comic patricide; in Joyce and

O'Casey's comic rebellion against the patriarchal clergy and the matriarchal Cathleen ni Houlihan. Oisín may well be the guiding spirit behind this mock-heroic impulse of Oedipal profanation in Ireland.

Oisín vs. Ossian

The guiding spirit of Oisín has been the subject of much disagreement among Celtic scholars for many years. They disagree about whether the comic irreverence in the Ossianic poems is anti-Christian or anticlerical. They disagree about whether the comic profanation should be taken seriously, that is, viewed comically in all its rebellious implications. They disagree about who Patrick was historically, and argue over whether he was a Catholic or a Protestant saint; or whether there were not in actuality two Patricks, both Catholic, the first, the Roman missionary Palladius Patricius, who arrived in Ireland in A.D. 432, and the second, who followed Palladius by some thirty years, the Romanized Patrick the Briton, author of the *Confessio*. The controversy over the two Patricks has become so massive that the subject is now referred to as Patriciology. While one is disinclined to launch a parallel endeavour to be known as Oisínology, it is apparent that there are also two Oisíns: the genuine mythic hero, who remains largely hidden or ignored today, and the spurious Ossian, on whom most of the debate has been concentrated.

It is evident now that the Ossianic poems supposedly "translated" by James Macpherson more than two hundred years ago, between 1760 and 1763,[4] reveal more about the sentimental impulses of the late eighteenth century than they tell us about early Celtic literature. Working with a minimum of original material, which he distorted, and a maximum of rhetorical extravagance, which was his own fiction, Macpherson provided a convenient hero to suit the mood of his time. His Ossian was a noble savage from the mysterious Celtic past who wandered lonely in the misty hills, enjoying his sweet melancholy as he played his harp and sang of epic battles against insuperable odds, of the ghosts of the dead heroes that hovered in the magic Celtic moonshine, finding his only comfort in the sorrows of defeat and the pantheistic mysteries of nature. Lo, the poor Ossian! But he wasn't Irish, not even stage Irish.

In an age that yearned for the primitive virtues of the noble savage, lingered over the lamentations of the Graveyard poets, indulged its fancy for Gothic mysteries, wept pleasurable tears over Richardson's pathetic heroines, and generally exulted in a kind of genteel emotionalism, this romanticized Ossian was destined to become a popular success. To illustrate some of his sentimental and stereotyped attraction, as well as his non-Celtic temperament, here is a sample of Ossian in *Fingal*, setting the scene for a battle between the invading king of Lochlin and Cuthullin (Cuchulain: the heavy-handed Macpherson anachronistically brings this hero of the early Ulster cycle into the later Ossianic cycle), and one can observe a typical instance of Macpherson's embellishments of melancholia and mystery, his inflated diction which sounds like artificial blank verse rendered in prose:

> As the dark shades of autumn fly over the hills of grass: so gloomy, dark, successive came the chiefs of Lochlin's echoing woods. Tall as the stag of Morven, moved stately before them the king. His shining shield is on his side, like a flame on the heath at night; when the world is silent and dark, and the traveller sees some ghost sporting in the beams! Dimly gleam the hills around, and shew indistinctly their oaks! A blast from the troubled ocean removed the settled mist. The sons of Erin appear, like a ridge of rocks on the coast; when mariners, on shores unknown, are trembling at veering winds![5]

Almost immediately this melodramatic flourish of pseudo-primitivism inspired a cult of worship and imitation that spread the fame of Ossian round the world, and was well over a century in running its bathetic course. Macpherson's prose poems were translated into German, French, Italian, Spanish, Dutch, Danish, Polish, and Russian. Napoleon carried his copy of Ossian with him like a Bible and read it before going into battle. Goethe's sorrowing Werther read a characteristically lugubrious passage from it to his beloved before committing suicide. And so on through the works and theories of German, English, and American Romantics, in Schiller and Herder, Byron and Blake,

Poe and Whitman, the charismatic Ossian prefigured some of the brooding heroism of the nineteenth century, in spite of a continuing controversy over the authenticity of the poems.

Apparently it mattered little that the poems were fabrications, as the shrewd and blunt Dr. Johnson had insisted from the start. "I look upon Macpherson's *Fingal* to be as gross an imposition as ever the world was troubled with," Johnson wrote. "Had it been really an ancient work, a true specimen how men thought at that time, it would have been a curiosity of the first rate. As a modern production, it is nothing."[6] Nevertheless, something came of nothing, for few people bothered or knew enough Gaelic to go back to the "true specimen."

Eventually such scholars as Alfred Nutt and J. S. Smart doubted the authenticity of the poems and pointed out that the so-called Ossianic mood of melancholy and defeat could be attributed to the prior outbreak of a similar reaction in Macpherson's native Scottish Highlands in the middle of the eighteenth century.[7] Furthermore, Macpherson must have decided to eliminate St. Patrick from his version of the poems, for in his "Dissertation Concerning the Poems," an essay that appeared in the two-volume edition of 1765, he indicated that he was aware of the saint's presence in the original work. But he must have had a rather cracked conception of Patrick, since he tells us that this holy celibate was married to Oisín's daughter, and that "on account of this family connection" Patrick sat in the house drinking merrily as he listened to his father-in-law's great tales of the good old pagan days![8] On second thought, perhaps it was a fortunate folly that prompted Macpherson to omit this incredible fabrication of a domesticated Patrick from his Ossianic poems.

It is indeed ironic that the revival of interest in Irish literature should have begun with Macpherson's spurious Ossian. When interest in the Irish gained further impetus in the mid-nineteenth century from the Celtophilic essays of Ernest Renan and Matthew Arnold, the irony continued, for while both men served the important function of calling attention to Celtic literature, they were variously limited in their enthusiasm: they could not avoid the misleading influence of Macpherson; they had not read much of the original poetry; and they were bent on constructing psychological race theories to explain the secret of the Celts. Renan, in his *Poetry of the Celtic Races*, assumed that the Celts had no aptitude for political life, since they had suffered bitter defeats throughout their long history, and therefore their poetry, like their history, had to be "only one long lament." It is apparent that he must have based this psychic sadness on his reading of the fabricated Ossian, if one is to judge from the following typical comment on the Irish temperament:

> If at times it seems to be cheerful, a tear is not slow to glisten behind its smile; it does not know that strange forgetfulness of human conditions and destinies which is called gaiety. Its songs of joy end as elegies; there is nothing equal to the delicious sadness of its national melodies. One might call them emanations from on high which, falling drop by drop upon the soul, pass through it like memories of another world. Never have men feasted so long upon the solitary delights of the spirit, these poetic memories which simultaneously intercross all the sensations of life, so vague, so deep, so penetrative, that one might die for them, without being able to say whether it was from bitterness or sweetness.[9]

Renan was simply carried away by his urbane Macphersonism. And finally he accounted for all that bittersweet melancholia with a French touch: the Celts, he assured us, are "an essentially feminine race"; presumably, if one attempts to follow his male chauvinist logic, because women are supposedly addicted to "delicious sadness," and because "one might die for them" quite nobly, as for the sorrowing Celts.

Partially influenced by Renan and Macpherson, but working with what must be called a masculine theory, Matthew Arnold also stressed the melancholy and mysterious spirit of the Celts, but he attributed it to a psychic quality that he identified as Titanism: "There is the Titanism of the Celt, his passionate, turbulent, indomitable reaction against the despotism of fact."[10] But then most people, as Freud reminds us in *Civilization and Its Discontents*, not only the so-called titanic Celts, are enraged or repressed by "the despotism of fact." And if Arnold had encountered the genuine Oisín, he might have modified his concept to something that could be called "comic Titanism." While Arnold is generally more enlightened than Renan—though similarly misdirected toward a race theory with all its racial clichés—he almost predictably made the error of illustrating what he meant by Titanism by quoting a characteristically gloomy passage from none other than Macpherson. Arnold was ready to concede that a considerable "part" of Macpherson's Ossian was a forgery, yet he went on to insist that "there will still be left in the book a residue with the very soul of the Celtic genius in it."[11] It seems that after a hundred years Macpherson, like Ossian, was still dying hard, even to the last spurious residue. What really made Arnold's theories suspect, then, as John V. Kelleher pointed out in his definitive essay "Arnold and the Celtic Revival,"[12] is the evidence that he had read Macpherson and some books *about* Celtic literature but very little of the authentic literature itself.

Clearly, after so much Macphersonism and distortion, what was sorely needed was a legitimate translation of the Ossianic poems. Some fragmentary but faithful versions had already appeared, notably one by Charlotte Brooke in *Reliques of Irish Poetry* (1789); however, it was the Ossianic Society, founded in Dublin in 1853, that finally took the first important step. Over a period of seven years, 1854–61, the society published its six-volume edition, *Transactions of the Ossianic Society,* a bilingual collection of poems and tales taken from authentic Irish manuscripts, with the Gaelic and English texts placed side by side. The poems were set down in their original ballad stanzas and dialogue form, with Oisín and St. Patrick as the principal speakers, and although the translations were rendered in a somewhat stilted Victorian diction and prosody that fell far short of the poetic quality of the originals, they at least achieved the initial goal of textual accuracy and availability. At the same time, in 1862, Thomas McLauchlan brought out a Scotch-Gaelic version, in Gaelic and English, containing twenty-eight Ossianic poems, in an edition of *The Dean of Lismore's Book,* a collection of sixteenth-century texts.

By the turn of the twentieth century a considerable number of other translations had appeared, including J. F. Campbell's *Leabhar na Feinne* (1871), Standish Hayes O'Grady's *Silva Gadelica* (1892), Eoin MacNeill's Part I of the *Duanaire Finn* (1904), and Kuno Meyer's *Fianaigecht* (1910). Meanwhile, the Celtic revival of the 1890s had inspired many important studies in Celtic mythology, folklore, manners, history, and philology, which contributed valuable information about the composition

and background of the Ossianic poems, as well as more translations in the works of Douglas Hyde, Lady Gregory, P. W. Joyce,
Eleanor Hull, T. W. Rolleston, and Alfred Nutt.

At last one might be led to believe that there was enough
translation and information in hand to discover what Dr.
Johnson had called "the true specimen," the genuine Oisín.
What actually happened, however, has remained one of the mysteries of Celtic scholarship. With a few well-directed yet incon-
clusive exceptions, no attempt has been made, up to the present
day, to launch a comprehensive critical analysis of the Ossianic
poetry, with the aim of examining its dramatic tensions and the
mock-heroic mode of the Oisín and Patrick dialogues.

As one of the notable exceptions, Alfred Nutt raised the whole
problem initially as early as 1899 in his still excellent little book,
Ossian and the Ossianic Literature. He surveyed and commented on
all the extant manuscripts and translations, and identified the
two major works as the *Agallamh na Senorach,* "The Colloquy of
the Elders," and the *Agallamh Oisín agus Padraig,* "The Dialogue
between Oisín and Patrick." Both pieces are partly written in the
tradition of the *Dinnshenchas,* the topographical naming of ancient places. A loosely constructed mixture of verse and prose,
with the Christianized Cailte as narrator and with some amiable
dialogue between Cailte and St. Patrick, the "Colloquy" is mainly
a romantic and didactic work that celebrates the world of nature
and reflects the assimilation of paganism by Christianity. Nutt
drew some mixed conclusions about it when he wrote: "There is
no unity in the *Colloquy,* no connecting link save the personality
of the narrator. Close upon a hundred legends are given in full
or in brief, the latter as a rule. The allusions are often so curt
and remote as to be unintelligible to us nowadays.... Whereas
the fighting pieces strike the reader as perfunctory and conventional, all that relates to woodcraft and woodland life is treated
with a deep-felt joyousness."[13]

It is the more complex "Dialogue between Oisín and Patrick,"
however, that contains the heart of the Ossianic challenge, for
here we find a tragicomic and scapegoat Oisín who is so unlike
any of his pagan counterparts in Macpherson or the "Colloquy"
that a completely new frame of emotive and literary references
must be brought into play. On one level Oisín and Patrick wan-

der through Ireland in the general pattern of the discursive
Dinnshenchas, with Oisín singing about the legendary places and
battles, much to the delight of Patrick; but on another and deeper level of dramatic irony the two men keep interrupting the
elegiac songs in order to assail and mock each other and their
respective pagan and Christian values in a grotesque display of
antiromantic comedy. In these set pieces of contrasting moods
the two men almost remind one of the alternately friendly and
belligerent couples or paired clowns in an O'Casey or Beckett
play.

More than anyone else, perhaps, Nutt was fully aware of the
significance of the dramatic tension in the Ossianic poetry. In his
illuminating comment on the pagan and Christian conflicts he
indicated that the greater humanity, as well as sympathy, was on
the side of Oisín and the folk imagination:

> Ossian, in the ballads, is a pagan, defiant and reckless, full of
> contempt and scorn for the howling clerics and their churlish
> low-bred deity. The Patrick with whom he has to do well deserves
> this scorn. The benignant and gracious gentleman of the *Colloquy,*
> keenly appreciative of the great-hearted generosity of the Fenian
> chiefs, is replaced by a sour and stupid fanatic, harping with
> wearisome monotony on the damnation of Finn and all his com-
> rades; a hard taskmaster to the poor old blind giant, to whom he
> grudges food, and upon whom he plays shabby tricks in order to
> terrify him into acceptance of Christianity. . . . [Oisín] is old and
> feeble and blind, the delights of the chase and of love are denied
> him; these things are hard to bear, but the causes of his resent-
> ment lie deeper. He cannot away with the new world of which the
> Christian cleric is the symbol and the embodiment; he loathes the
> ascetic, churlish ideal unworthy of a warrior and a gentleman,
> and he contrasts it with the delights that were once his, with the
> joy of life wholly simple and unsophisticated, finding perfect
> satisfaction in battle, woodcraft and dalliance. He never wavers in
> his loyalty to the past; if his comrades are in hell, he is content to
> be there likewise.[14]

Nutt was also aware that this deeper level of comic and ironic
tension had not been picked up and explored by Celtic scholars,
and he protested: "The literary problem disclosed by these facts
has scarce been noted, still less has any serious attempt at its
solution been essayed."[15] Therefore, he went on to pose a series
of historical and textual questions about the possible origins of

the new motifs in the "Dialogue," but unfortunately he did not go beyond this speculation, or himself try to cope with the immediate literary problem, that of beginning a critical assessment of the motifs themselves, an investigation that has been mentioned in passing by some scholars and critics but never carried out. Some brief and superficial comment on the profane and farcical elements in the Ossianic poetry appear in Standish James O'Grady's *History of Ireland* (1878) and in Douglas Hyde's *Literary History of Ireland* (1899); and more important, Lady Gregory recorded some of the comic episodes from the oral folk versions of the poetry and sagas in her *Gods and Fighting Men* (1904) and *The Kiltartan History Book* (1926). But beyond these efforts, as well as some general and often belittling commentaries, it is difficult to find any analytical treatment of the poetry, and as a result the mock-heroic strategy of the work has been ignored and the essential Oisín has remained hidden. In the mythic terms of Lévi-Strauss, then, the hidden or suppressed structure of this Celtic legend has not yet been evoked and made accessible.

One can only guess at the reason for this failure of omission, though it obviously has something to do with the comic and irreverent nature of the poetry. In his Introduction to the *Duanaire Finn*, Part I, Eoin MacNeill seems to be embarrassed by the motif of low humor in the poetry, though he gives the impression that he considers all comedy to be "low" and alien to the epic form. He insists that the Ossianic poetry was epic and tragic in its origins and was later corrupted by the intrusion of mock-heroic or "facetious" comedy: "The early epic is a tragedy, not admitting laughter even into its peaceful interludes. The sole humorous element is late and external to the story—Oisín's difficulty in embracing Christian ideals of life. This feature already appears in the Duanaire, but is treated with great reserve. In later poems, it becomes a subject of free facetiousness."[16] This solemn pronouncement is at some variance with the view expressed by Kuno Meyer in his edition of the earliest surviving Ossianic poem, the eighth-century "Quarrel between Finn and Oisín," where Meyer, in accounting for the "humorous and burlesque" elements, tells us that from the start "the tragic issue was not adaptable to the Ossianic saga."[17] Far from being external to the story, then, the comic conflict between Oisín and Patrick, arising out of "Oisín's difficulty in embracing Christian ideals of life," is an organic part of the "Dialogue," since the theme and structure of the poem clearly involve a double story: one concerning the collapse of the pagan past, and the other its collision with the Christian present. There is no evidence that there might have been an early "tragic" version of the "Dialogue" which related the single story of the end of the pagan world with an epic idealization of Oisín and Patrick that is untainted by comic conflict. One soon gets the impression that many Celtic scholars devoutly wish there had been such a decorous version. But though the comic tone of the poem grew broader in later versions between the fourteenth and sixteenth centuries, the irreverent mockery of Oisín and the churlish fanaticism of Patrick are clearly indigenous to the poem. To dismiss the antic comedy as a mere game of "free facetiousness" is to dismiss the work itself, which is really what MacNeill does.

Gerard Murphy at least recognized that the Ossianic poetry is more comic than tragic, but he was not amused by this revelation. Murphy's Introduction and Notes to the *Duanaire Finn*, Part III, make up a monumental work of outstanding scholarship; nevertheless, throughout this volume he is uneasy about the element of comedy in the Ossianic cycle, and he calls it a "decay of the heroic tradition" and a "degeneration" of the heroic ideals.[18] He is even reluctant to concede that Kuno Meyer had accurately described "The Quarrel between Finn and Oisín" as "humorous and burlesque," though it is impossible to read the poem in any other way. And when he comes to a comparison of the two main works, the "Colloquy" and the "Dialogue," he has an unreserved preference for the former work, in which the characters are "idealized" and "there is no conflict between the heroes and the saint, their relations being those of mutual understanding and goodwill."[19] But he is full of reservations about the "Dialogue," in which he finds too much comic discord: Oisín "is often depicted in an amusing light. He is ridiculously blind to the true meaning of Christianity. Patrick has also degenerated: appreciation of natural goodness is entirely lacking in him: his interpretation of Christian dogma is narrow and often perverted: harsh words come to his lips more frequently than blessings."[20]

Now, for idealistic and didactic purposes it is no doubt more efficacious to have harmony and goodwill; but for poetic and dramatic purposes it is probably more effective to have conflict and comedy. Apparently the bards who wrote the "Dialogue" held the latter view. Murphy once tried to account for this bardic propensity for low comedy by making a class distinction between aristocratic and folk tastes in medieval Ireland; between the aristocratically oriented Ulster cycle dominated by the heroic Cuchulain and the folk-orientated Fenian cycle dominated by the mock-heroic Oisín: "When those aristocratically-conditioned tales [of the Ulster cycle] were being told in kings' palaces and at royal *oenaige* [fairs] in ninth and tenth-century Ireland, simple folk, seated by their firesides or in their fishing-boats, probably preferred to tell magically-controlled tales about Fionn Mac-Cumhaill and his Fianna, such as their descendants have continued to tell down to the present day."[21] Fair enough. But Murphy does not hide his belief that the uninhibited folk imagination gradually corrupted the Ossianic dialogues with excesses of low comedy, for, he tells us, when "the opposition between saint and pagan descends to mere buffoonery," it is a sign that the poetry has been "adapted to the taste of the humbler folk into whose keeping the old tradition had passed."[22] Whenever Murphy touches the subject there is this tone of regret, with a hint of social snobbery behind it, which ignores the possibility that the "humbler folk" might have enriched the tradition with the infusion of comedy. The folk poets would naturally have sympathized with the scapegoat Oisín, looked back with him to the golden age of pagan freedom, and shared the comical old Celt's mockery of the cranky cleric's catalogue of thou-shalt-nots. Since it was aimed at a deserving target, the "mere buffoonery" might have been a necessary and fortunate descent (or was it something of an ascent?) into antic laughter.

Most Celtic scholars are disinclined to consider the comic or mock-heroic tradition as a valid one for the Ossianic dialogues. For example, Aodh de Blacam in *A First Book of Irish Literature* (1934) and Robin Flower in *The Irish Tradition* (1947), when they

discuss the Ossianic poetry, either ignore or dismiss its characteristically comic moods and themes. De Blacam was partly taken
in by Macpherson, whose fabricated versions he felt "did contain
broken, but curiously appealing echoes of the Ossianic poetry";
and it is therefore not surprising that he saw in the dialogues
between Oisín and Patrick only "the most beautiful nature
poems, moving lamentations, and sublime flights of heroic utterance."[23] Robin Flower placed most of his stress on the *Agallamh na Senorach*, and when he came briefly to the dialogues he
simply avoided a confrontation with the comedy by observing
vaguely that "the hero and the saint rail upon each other in good
set terms."[24] But his main concern is to rule out any hint of
tension in the poems, comic or irreverent, by insisting that the
arguments are innocuous and contain no criticism of the clergy:
"It is with the poets who composed and the peasants who repeat
the poems merely the delight in developing the implications of a
situation to their last extreme."[25] Since Flower does not tell us
what the "good set terms" are, or what the "implications of the
situation" might be, and what creates the "delight," we must
pretend that these aspects of the poetry are entirely gratuitous.

In most of the anthologies and commentaries on Celtic literature the dialogues between Oisín and Patrick are not mentioned
at all, or alluded to in a vague or superficial manner. Kathleen
Hoagland, in *1000 Years of Irish Poetry* (1947), devotes one section to the Ossianic cycle and tells us that this poetry expresses a
love of hunting and nature but also a "love of the humorous, of
the grotesque, and the bombastic."[26] How curious it is, then, that
she should not include a single example of humorous or grotesque Ossianic poetry; that she should include several passages
from the noncomic "Colloquy" and nothing from the "Dialogue"; and that she should tell us that "more good than ill came
from [Macpherson's] work."[27] Myles Dillon, in *Early Irish Literature* (1948), concentrates mostly on the "Colloquy" and dispenses
with the "Dialogue" in a few general remarks, though unlike
Robin Flower, he does point out the comic irreverence in the
ballad poems: "There is something here of the anticlerical
humour which inspires the fantastic 'Vision of Mac Con Glinne,'
which [Kuno] Meyer attributed, indeed, to the twelfth century,
and Brian Merriman's amazing 'Midnight Court,' written to-

wards the end of the eighteenth century."[28] These are important comparisons, but there Dillon leaves the issue, quoting one semisatiric Ossianic ballad, "The Blackbird of Derrycarn," without comment. In his anthology, *A Celtic Miscellany* (1951), Kenneth Hurlstone Jackson unequivocally states that Macpherson misrepresented Celtic literature as being exclusively mysterious and melancholy; but though he has a section on "Humour and Satire," in which he includes some passages from MacConglinne and Merriman, he completely ignores the humor of Oisín, which might have provided an appropriate corrective to Macpherson. Eleanor Knott devotes five pages of *Irish Classical Poetry* (1957) to the "Ossianic Poems," most of it about the "Colloquy," with only this frustrating allusion to the humor in the "Dialogue," as she moves on to more "serious" matters: "The dialogue poems are of special interest. The exchanges between Oisín and Patrick have a humorous tone, but there are also more serious and more dramatic dialogues."[29] Yet there is nothing more dramatic, and more comically serious, than those confrontations between pagan and saint. In their *Celtic Heritage* (1961), Alwyn and Brinley Rees mention the *Agallamh na Senorach* but, as one could almost predict by now, omit any reference to the *Agallamh Oisín agus Padraig*. Myles Dillon and Nora K. Chadwick, in *The Celtic Realms* (1967), tell us that the Fenian cycle, dating from the twelfth century, "coincided with the first appearance in Ireland of ballad poetry, and the Fenian ballad appears as a new literary form."[30] Nevertheless, they seem to have no time for the accompanying new form of irreverent humor, which was one of the main elements of the ballad dialogues, and they reduce the poetry to a series of adventure stories: "Fenian ballads became very popular, and the big collection known as *Duanaire Finn* has been made the subject of a special study by Gerard Murphy. Many of them are in the form of a dialogue between Oisín, son of Finn (MacPherson's 'Ossian'), and Saint Patrick, in which Oisín tells the saint stories about the adventures of the *fiana*, or Fenians."[31]

One notable yet limited exception to this general censorship of profane humor can be found in Vivian Mercier's *Irish Comic Tradition* (1962). Mercier concentrates on the mock-heroic tradition in what is the first important study of this material, for, as he rightly observes, there has been no comprehensive account of the comic tradition of Gaelic literature. He makes some valuable comments on the comic desecration of the father figure in the early poem, "The Quarrel between Finn and Oisín"; but, unfortunately, he has very little to say about the mainstream of mock-heroic and burlesque comedy in the Ossianic poetry, which he merely alludes to in several brief paragraphs. And strangely enough, he introduces with approval the hedging and frustrating passages from Robin Flower's *Irish Tradition*, which are quoted above. Furthermore, one does not know what to make of Mercier's apology in his Preface for having omitted a chapter on stage comedy, which means he has more or less ignored Irish drama, and then his concluding statement: "If the reader of this book does not find that his appreciation of Joyce and Beckett, Yeats and Synge, Shaw and O'Casey has been enriched and his understanding of them deepened, then I have failed in part of my self-imposed task."[32] Since he has by his own admission very little to say about comedy in the plays of Yeats, Synge, Shaw, O'Casey, and Beckett, the reader can only conclude there has been a considerable failure in this significant area. And there is a parallel failure to come to terms with the comedy in the Ossianic dialogues.

This general failure to cope with the mythic Oisín and the comic tension in the Ossianic poetry might be attributed to the fact that the emphasis of Celtic scholarship has been directed more often toward the Gaelic language than toward the literature. It was partly a matter of national pride and necessity in a subject nation that had to identify the cause of its political freedom with the revival of its native language, which had been ruthlessly suppressed by the British occupation of the country; however, this experience had helped to create a consequential gap between linguistic and literary studies. There has been no lack of outstanding scholars in allied fields of research during the past half century—one can call the roll of such distinguished men and women as Kuno Meyer, Standish Hayes O'Grady, Douglas Hyde, Eleanor Hull, Alfred Nutt, Eoin MacNeill, Osborne Bergin, Gerard Murphy, Robin Flower, Myles Dillon, T. F. O'Rahilly, Eleanor Knott—but it must be remembered that for the most part they turned their considerable insight and energy to important yet predominantly nonliterary disciplines. Indeed, it would take something of a Polonius to catalogue the emphasis of this scholarship: grammatical, philological, linguistical, textual, historical, bibliographical, not to forget Patriciological.

In 1945 the poet Austin Clarke revealed his impatience with what he called the myopic "Irish grammarians" when he became involved in an extended controversy with Dr. Osborne Bergin in a series of letters and reviews in the *Irish Times*. Clarke felt that the "grammarians" had been so intent on working with and in the Gaelic language that they had overlooked the important function of translations in the Irish literary tradition. At one point he stated: "Although much has been written in recent years concerning our literary revival, critics have been curiously lacking in perception. Few of them have realized that the movement has owed its inspiration to the tradition of translation and has been sustained by it."[33] To which Dr. Bergin replied in behalf of the insular specialists: "The reason why there is not more literary criticism of Gaelic poetry is simply the difficulty of the language, unknown as it is to almost all men of letters and their readers, and the complexity of the subject-matter, with its unfamiliar medieval atmosphere."[34] Clarke must have anticipated this claim of linguistic complexity and medieval difficulty, for earlier in the controversy, as if he were playing Oisín to Bergin's Patrick, he had set a trap for the doctor with this barbed jest: "The rest of Dr. Bergin's letter shows why there is scarcely any literary criticism of Gaelic poetry. When a timid literary man (like myself) dares to approach this preserve, grumbling grammarians and thin textualists try to scare him away with ogreish frowns and fee-faw-fummery. But this is pantomime month, so let us climb the beanstalk and see whether there is a giant up there or only a scholar on stilts."[35]

To borrow Clarke's analogy, it has been the purpose of this chapter to climb the Celtic beanstalk in order to illustrate that while there may be some bona fide giants up there, they are usually scholars on grammatical stilts when it comes to Ossianic poetry. With due respect for the difficulties of the Gaelic language, the poems became accessible in English over a hundred years ago, and many serviceable translations are available. There is no doubt that we need new translations, by artists, not scholars, such as the excellent short passages of Ossianic poetry translated by the late Frank O'Connor. And it is to be hoped that Irish poets of the stature of Thomas Kinsella, who in 1970 provided us with a magnificent translation of the *Táin Bo Cuailnge* ("The Cattle Raid of Cooley"), will offer us modern versions of the "Dialogues." Meanwhile it is possible and necessary to get at the heart of the hidden Oisín.

Oisín Revealed

The "rageous Ossean" of the ballad dialogues is a mock-heroic playboy of the pagan world fallen among Christians. There is a pervasive irony in his present condition as a blind old fool with intimations of grandeur and mortality. He is a rebellious prisoner who must create wild dreams of his past freedom; he is a romantic comedian who must assume the role of a pagan Christy Mahon. Patrick is only half right in calling him a ridiculous old fool, for he is young in his aspirations, wise in his folly, and, like Shakespeare's disreputable clowns, he consistently protests that though the puritanical Patrick be virtuous, there will still be cakes and ale for Oisín and all who believe in him. But the irony also turns in the other direction, for though Patrick is the virtuous ascetic, he cannot resist the great pleasure of listening to the worldly adventures of Oisín, urges his scribe to write them down for posterity, and sometimes seems to forget his primary mission of trying to convert and save the boisterous old pagan. When they return to fighting and Patrick becomes the fanatical proselytizer, he plays the unwise fool for Christianity's sake. Though they mock each other, they also need each other, like Falstaff and Prince Hal, like "Captain" Jack Boyle and Joxer Daly, like Gogo and Didi. Most of the time, however, Patrick is the straight man in the lively banter, so Oisín usually gets the best of the comic battles even if he is destined to lose the serious war between paganism and Christianity. The more Patrick ridicules the pagan way of life and argues for a future life in heaven, the more Oisín ridicules the Christian way of life and opts for the good old days on earth. The more Oisín opts for past glories, the more Patrick alternates between wanting to hear about them and wanting to save Oisín from them. The more Patrick listens and then threatens, the more Oisín alternately succumbs to and conquers his fears.

Is it possible, then, that the folk bards who wrote these poems might have been dramatizing the split in a single character, the two voices in the quarrel representing two contradictory attitudes of one wavering sensibility? If, as Yeats put it, "we make out of the quarrel with others, rhetoric, but out of the quarrel with ourselves, poetry,"[36] then the quarrel between Oisín and Patrick could be called Ireland's quarrel with herself. "Unlike the rhetoricians . . . we sing amid our uncertainty."[37] In this allegory of national characteristics, both of the uncertain voices, the pagan and the Patrician, are Ireland, Ireland's two dominating impulses, one drawn toward religious fervor, the other toward artistic imagination: Ireland's divine self versus Ireland's daimonic self. This concept of opposing selves, the given self and the antiself, might further be reinforced by Yeat's view that "each Daimon is drawn to whatever man or, if its nature is more general, to whatever nation it most differs from, and it shapes into its own image the antithetical dream of man or nation."[38] Perhaps the two realities, the given self and the dream self, can be found within the consciousness of one nation as well as one man. And, appropriately, Yeats was aware of the inherent irony in this quarrel and quest, for he was also "persuaded that the Daimon delivers and deceives us."[39] In these dialogue poems the process works in both directions, for Oisín and Patrick deceive and deliver each other.

When we turn from these implications of the situation to the situation itself, we find that the modes as well as the voices of the poetry are dual or split: the quarrels are dramatized in heroic and mock-heroic counterpoint. There is a double structure in the "Dialogue," one operating at a high or epic level, the other at a low or comic level. In the first structure, the saint begins by asking the old warrior-poet to sing his elegiac tales of the pagan past, and Oisín responds with glowing accounts of the life and death of the great Fenians; the heroic deeds of courage, courtesy, and generosity; the pleasures of eating and drinking and wooing; the fun of the hunt, the friendship of the hounds, the love of nature and poetry, the delight in the countryside and the blackbird's merry song. At this level the two men enjoy a common bond of vicarious experience, and they refer to each other as "noble Oisín" and "generous Patrick." Within this epic and romantic framework, however, there is a second structure in which both men are brought abruptly back to the present, a fifth-century Ireland in which all the Fenians, except Oisín, are dead and confined in a Christian hell, since Patrick and his priests now control the country. At any moment, even in the midst of a tale, Oisín might overhear the doleful prayers of the priests and feel alienated, or he might linger over the tragic fate of the Fenians and fly into a rage, or he might simply become ravenously hungry, and he breaks off his narrative, realizing he is a blind old scarecrow of an antihero, at the mercy of Patrick, who suddenly remembers that he must convert the angry pagan. Now the tone and the mode of the poem shift to the form of the flyting, and we are in the midst of a burlesque battle of insults and opposing views of life, with the men calling each other "miserable Oisín" and "Patrick of the crooked crozier." Oisín threatens to beat the heads off the clerics, and Patrick warns him to beat his own breast in submission or suffer the torment of eternal damnation. But Oisín, who feels he is already being tormented and damned by the new Christian life of self-mortification, refuses to renounce his old pagan life, and one gets the distinct impression that he believes Patrick's religion as well as his crozier is crooked.

Oisín's pagan alternative of a free and joyous life had its origins in the supernatural circumstances of his birth, and in the noble concept of freedom he inherited from his father and mother. According to the folk mythology, when the beautiful maiden Saba, who was to become his mother, rejected the advances of the Dark Druid of faeryland, she was transformed into a deer, and it was in this shape that she first encountered the Fenian chief Finn MacCool as he chased her during a hunt in the Sligo woods on Ben Bulben. Since Finn was the only charm that could bring her back to her natural form, she became a woman again when they met and they immediately fell in love. For a time they were great lovers and, as the legend has it, "their joy in each other was like that of the Immortals in the Land of Youth." But one day, while Finn and his warriors were away defending

Erin against foreign invaders, the jealous Dark Druid gained his revenge by changing Saba back into a deer. The brokenhearted Finn never saw her again, but one day while he was hunting on Ben Bulben he found a naked boy who had grown up in the forests and glens with his mother, a gentle deer, and so father and son were united. "Finn called his name Oisín (Little Fawn), and he became a warrior of fame, but far more famous for the songs and tales that he made; so that of all things to this day that are told of the Fianna of Erin men are wont to say: 'Thus sang the bard Oisín, son of Finn.'"[40]

Before Oisín met Patrick, he fell in love with the golden-haired Niamh (Nee-av), daughter of the king of Tir na nÓg, and he went with her to stay for three hundred years in the Land of Youth, where he had many idyllic and heroic adventures, among them the characteristic rescue of an imprisoned princess from a tyrannical Formorian giant. Champion of freedom that he was, Oisín eventually began to think of his own freedom—those three hundred years seemed like three weeks to him, but he was restless—and he longed to return to his native Erin and see his Fenian comrades again. But Niamh warned him that the price of freedom was very high, that if he left the land of eternal youth he would lose his strength and become old and blind as soon as he touched earth again. Furthermore, she told him that Ireland was no longer the country he had known, that the noble Fenians had been replaced by hordes of priests. Nevertheless, the Celtic quest for freedom runs throughout the Ossianic legend, and Oisín must abandon his happy bondage with Niamh and risk the homeward journey.

Michael Comyn, the eighteenth-century Gaelic poet, in his "Oisín in the Land of Youth," gives an account of Oisín's return, and he mentions the changes that have come to Ireland in this farewell warning by Niamh:

> 'Tis woe to me, Oisín, to see
> How thou canst be so anxious-souled
> About green Erin, changed for aye—
> For past's the day of the fian bold.
>
> In Erin green there's nought seen
> But priests full lean and troops of saints—
> Then Oisín, here's my kiss to thee,
> Our last, may be—my heart now faints![41]

Yeats had read the Ossianic Society's translation of the "Dialogues," and also the first English translation of Comyn's poem, on which he based much of his "Wanderings of Oisín"; and like Comyn, Yeats maintained the original second structure of protest against the loss of the free pagan life. In the following passage Yeats's Oisín compares life under the pagans and the priests:

> Then in that hall, lit by the dim sea-shine,
> We lay on skins of otters, and drank wine,
> Brewed by the sea-gods, from huge cups that lay
> Upon the lips of sea-gods in their day;
> And then on heaped-up skins of otters slept,
> And when the sun once more in saffron stept,
> Rolling his flagrant wheel out of the deep,
> We sang the loves and angers without sleep,
> And all exultant labours of the strong.
> But now the lying clerics murder song
> With barren words and flatteries of the weak.[42]

Yeats's Oisín can be as sensuous and irreverent as the traditional warrior-bard, and his Patrick never ceases to issue threats of damnation and rebuke the old hero for his "godless and passionate rage."

The Ossianic Society's literal translation of the *Agallamh Oisín agus Padraig* falls far below the high level of Yeats's poetry, but in its faithful rendering of the original work it contains the most passionate and comic rage of Oisín. Even though the boisterous old pagan is virtually Patrick's prisoner, he is a comic victim who is incapable of accepting defeat. There is often a humorous naiveté in Oisín's protests which neatly turns the laughter against him, as when he tries to argue reasonably that he might consider going to the Christian heaven on one fundamental condition: if he can take his favorite hound with him. But Patrick categorically denies this foolish request and Oisín categorically withdraws his magnanimous offer.

Sometimes it is possible to laugh with and at the incongruities in both men, the old pagan son and the young Christian father, even when they desecrate each other's gods. For example, Patrick says that his King of Heaven created the fields and the grass, something that Finn, the king of the Fenians, could never do. Oisín counters this boast with the reply that it was much wiser of Finn to use his energies for fighting and hunting, wooing and

playing games, than merely making grass and fields. They alternate between this sort of comic boasting and a more vigorous
form of mutual abuse. Nevertheless, it is in their moments of
humorous overstatement that Oisín and Patrick become more
interesting for their frailties. This is quite a comedown for Ireland's great saint, and a similar descent for her great Fenian
hero, but it is a significant descent into human fallibility that
appears to have made both characters more accessible to the
popular folk imagination. In the dual tone and structure of
these poems, at once epic and comic, the two men have survived
in Irish myth and folklore for at least eight centuries, and the
poems and tales continued to be sung and recited in the Gaelic-
speaking districts into the twentieth century.

Although the irreverent bards who wrote the poetry have tip-
ped their sympathies in the direction of Oisín's love of freedom
and the pleasures of this world, they may mock but they cannot
dismiss Patrick's call for a life of self-denial with the reward of
salvation in the next world. The mockery itself functions as a
compensatory way of accepting Patrick's ultimate victory and
living with the austere disciplines of Christianity. Furthermore,
since failure has always been a more common condition of life
than victory in fatalistic Irish experience, the scapegoat Oisín
must emerge as an extremely empathetic and comforting figure.

Oisín and Patrick sometimes try to suspend their comic abuse
and make some well-meaning attempts at reconciliation, but
their good intentions only backfire. When Patrick softens his
tactics and offers to forgive Oisín if he will submit to God, the
suspicious pagan threatens to make some clerical heads roll:

> *P.* I pity thy withered form,
> O Oisín! cease talking such silly words;
> Shameful it is for thee, I believe truly,
> Thy constant mockery of the son of God!
> *O.* O Patrick! were I devoid of sense,
> I would rid thy clerics of their heads;
> There would not be a crozier or white book,
> Or matins bell in thy church![43]

Oisín prefers to contrast the melodious songs of the blackbirds
and thrushes with the gloomy bells of the clergy; the love of
beautiful women with the practice of chastity; the hunting and

feasting with prayer and fasting; the playing of games and listening to bards with breast-beating and going to Mass; the magnanimity of the warmhearted Finn with the vindictiveness of Patrick and his hard God.

Oisín is provoked into making this last comparison when the desperate Patrick falsely declares that Finn is in bondage in hell "because he committed treachery and oppression." No one was ever more generous and freedom-loving than the noble Finn, Oisín replies, and there are innumerable examples in the legend to support his claim. The incredulous Oisín can't understand why Patrick's God should be the tyrannical master of man. Why would any just God want to put a great hero like Finn in hell? Why, he wants to know in his naive sense of fair play, can't God and Finn be equal and enlightened monarchs, like honorable warrior-chiefs? In order to resolve the argument, Oisin proposes a cosmic wrestling match between the champions of heaven and earth. Since Finn is in hell, Oisín chooses his son Oscar to represent the Fenians against God, and he warns Patrick to be respectful of the pagans or Oscar will beat him up too. In his comic innocence Oisín concedes that if God managed to bring Oscar down in a fair fight, his victory would mean that God was a strong fighter, but it would not mean that God and his priests were better men than Finn and the Fenians. Here is a brief sample of the argument about the farcical wrestling match:

> P. Misery attend thee, old man,
>   Who speakest the words of madness;
>   God is better for one hour,
>   Than all the Fians of Eire.
>
> O. O Patrick of the crooked crozier,
>   Who makes me that impertinent answer;
>   Thy crozier would be in atoms
>   Were Oscar present.
>
>   Were my son Oscar and God
>   Hand to hand on Cnoc-na-bh-Fiann,
>   If I saw my son down,
>   I would say that God was a strong man.
>
>   How could it be that God,
>   Or his clerics could be better men;
>   Than Fionn the chief king of the Fenians,
>   A generous man without a blemish?[44]

Repeatedly Oisín asks why Patrick and his God are not as generous as Finn and the Fenians. The pagan is now a helpless old man reduced to the frugal comfort of the saint's house, and he complains that the niggardly Patrick must be starving him as if he were a fasting priest. In one section of the poem called "The Chase of Loch Lein," Oisín recalls his herculean appetite and protests against Patrick's meager table:

> O. I often slept abroad on the hill,
>   Under grey dew, on the foliage of trees,
>   And I was not accustomed to a supperless bed
>   While there was a stag on yonder hill!
> P. Thou hast not a bed without food,
>   Thou gettest seven cakes of bread,
>   And a large roll of butter,
>   And a quarter of beef every day.
> O. I saw a berry of the rowan tree
>   Twice larger than thy roll;
>   I saw an ivy leaf
>   Larger and wider than thy cake of bread.
>   I saw a quarter of a blackbird
>   Which was larger than thy quarter of beef;
>   'Tis it that fills my soul with sadness,
>   To be in thy house thou poor wretch![45]

Oisín relies on his mock-heroic voice when he transforms such mundane matters as food into important issues, jesting about a clerical supper on a quarter of a blackbird. But even when he is in a heroic mood, in his account of the chase his sense of titanic proportion carries a comic force. For example, he pauses to call the role of the "melodious" Fenian hounds, naming 294 dogs in 120 lines. An imitation of the traditional epic catalogue of great names, this fantastic performance of ringing the changes on so many onomatopoetic canine titles is a stunt of mock-epic virtuosity, though not without some inevitable longeurs. Oisín, after all, is more human than heroic.

And precisely because he is more human than heroic, Oisín at the end of the poem may have won the argument but he has lost the fight for his pagan heritage. The myth may favor the Fenians, but history is on the side of the Christians. In the final confrontation, while Patrick is still crying "submit," it is Oisín who magnanimously makes an offer of typical pagan charity, suggesting that if it happened that God were in bondage, Finn would fight to liberate him. Oisín forgives God for making him suffer so much; but at the same time he adds a characteristically comic touch by claiming he must be one up on a God who would condemn him to live among the clerics, deprived of all his pagan pleasures, fourteen of which he promptly recounts for the un-amused Patrick. Oisín ends with another threat to make the clerical heads roll, and then utters a poignant lament for Finn and the lost Fenians, a cry that recalls Pegeen Mike's heartbreak-ing lament for her lost playboy. Here are the concluding stanzas:

P. Let us cease our comparison on both sides,
   Withered old man who are devoid of sense;
   Understand that God dwells in the heaven of degrees,
   And Fionn and his hosts are all in pain.

O. Great would be the shame for God,
   Not to release Fionn, from the shackles of pain;
   For if God himself were in bonds
   The chief would fight on his behalf.

   Fionn never suffered in his day
   Anyone to be in pain or difficulty;
   Without redeeming him, by silver or gold,
   By battle or fight, till he got the victory.

   It is a good claim for me on thy God
   To be among his clerics, as I am;
   Without food, without clothing or music,
   Without bestowing gold on bards.

   Without the cry of the hounds or of the horns,
   Without the guarding of harbours or coasts;
   For all that I have suffered for lack of food,
   I forgive heaven's King in my will.

   Without bathing, without hunting, without Fionn,
   Without courting generous women, without sport;
   Without sitting in my place, as was due,
   Without learning feats of agility or fighting.

P. Cease recounting them,
   O son of the king whose fame was great;
   Submit to Him who doeth all good,
   Stoop thy head, and bend thy knee.

   Strike thy breast and shed thy tear,
   Believe in Him who is above;
   Though thou are amazed at its being said,
   'Twas He gained victory over Fionn.

> *O.* O Patrick, were I without sense,
> I would take off the heads of thy clerics;
> There would not be a book or a crozier bright,
> Or matin bell left in thy church.
> Oisín said, sorrowful is my tale!
> The sound of thy lips is not sweet to me;
> I will cry my fill, but not for God,
> But for Fionn and the Fians not being alive![46]

Like many great clowns, Oisín carries within himself a profound sense of sorrow that only his comic spirit can temporarily
overcome. In Freudian terms, he is not prepared to pay the
price for Christian civilization and his discontent gives rise to his
rebellious laughter. His mockery of Patrick allows him to circumvent his pain by giving him the dreamlike impression that he
has retrieved what he has lost through the myth of his hidden
aspirations, aspirations sustained by the magic of poetry. Like
Yeats's defense of "The Cherry Tree Carol" and the plays of
Synge and O'Casey against clerical attack, Oisín's tragicomic defense "contains what a belief, tamed down to a formula shudders
at, something wild and ancient."[47]

Oisín and Synge and O'Casey

In 1899, the same year that Yeats and Lady Gregory were laying
the groundwork for the Abbey Theatre by establishing the Irish
Literary Theatre, Alfred Nutt, one of the few Celtic scholars
who saw the dramatic tension of the Ossianic dialogues as an
invaluable source of artistic inspiration, regretted that no
modern Irish writers had yet found a form to exploit that rich
material. But Nutt inadvertently anticipated and described what
was to become the mainstream of a native Irish drama when he
wrote: "The dialogues between Patrick and Ossian contain matter promising in the extreme, but there is lacking an artist capable of conceiving all that the contrast of ascetic Christianity and
Pagan joy of life implied, and seeking until he found the one
form of words adequate to the conception."[48] While there is only
an indirect line of descent from the Ossianic dialogues to the
plays of Synge and O'Casey, for example, it is apparent that
these two dramatists, and many of their creative countrymen,

fulfilled the dual aspect of Nutt's unwitting prophecy: they played infinite changes on the comic contrast between Christian asceticism and the pagan joy of life; and in their respective folk idioms they found a unique "form of words adequate to the conception."

Even though he did not consciously imitate them, O'Casey had the instinctive advantage of Synge's plays before him; Synge had the instinctive advantage of Lady Gregory's experiments with the Irish peasant idiom in front of him, though he did not consciously try to imitate it; and all of them were unaware, or unconsciously or mythically aware, that the guiding spirit of Oisín may have been hovering over them. The whole process of literary influence here must be viewed in metaphoric terms, as a happy occasion of indirect and fortuitous resonances emanating from a common source of inspiration. The voice of Oisín was heard again in the land in the mock-heroic characters of modern Irish drama. Patrick is holy Ireland's patron saint, but Oisín is the patron hero of her two finest modern dramatists, Synge and O'Casey.

Lady Gregory, who in her plays and translations of Celtic legends wrote in the peasant idiom that Synge was to develop to its highest artistic level, and who was to become O'Casey's closest friend and adviser at the Abbey Theatre, preserved many of the folk myths by recording versions of the Ossianic tales she had heard from the peasants in the west of Ireland. Although she was herself an aristocratic lady of the big house, she knew that the oral tradition of the country was the main source of the rich folk imagination, and she therefore justified her retention of the peasant idiom in her redaction of the legends: "I have found it more natural to tell the stories in the manner of the thatched houses, where I have heard so many legends of Finn and his friends, and Oisín and Patrick, and the Ever-Living Ones, and the Country of the Young, rather than in the manner of the slated houses, where I have never heard them."[49] She must have been acutely aware of the comic irreverence of Oisín, which was so popular with the peasants, for she recorded one particular version of the Oisín and Patrick dialogues that anticipates the sly and profane humor of the Synge and O'Casey characters. The highly amused narrator picks up the story after Oisín decided to leave the Land of Youth, in spite of Niamh's warning that Ireland was now overrun by hordes of priests, and upon his return fell from his horse while generously trying to help some men lift a heavy stone. As soon as his feet touched the earth he became a ridiculous old man at the mercy of St. Patrick, but it is clear from this passage that there is considerable wisdom in his comic folly:

> It was after Usheen fell from his horse, Saint Patrick began to instruct and convert him. And he asked where all his companions were, and Goll the champion of Ireland. And it is what Saint Patrick said that God had them all shut up in hell with the devil. And Usheen said, "If I could see them I would draw them out of that, and the devil with them and his whole forge." And Saint Patrick told him about Adam and Eve and how they were turned out and lost for eating the forbidden fruit, an apple he called it. And Usheen said, "Although God has all my friends shut up in hell, if I knew fruit was so scarce with him, and he to think so much of it, I'd have sent him seven carloads of it." It was very decent of Usheen to say that; he always had a very decent name for those sort of things. And Usheen said another thing to Patrick. He said, "Don't the blackbird and the thrush whistle very well, and don't they make their nests very nice, and they never got any instruction or teaching from God?" And what Patrick answered to that I don't know.[50]

This hilarious spectacle of the saintly Patrick beaten into silence by the crafty Oisín must have warmed the hearts of the Catholic peasants who needed this touch of irreverence to sustain their hidden pleasures as well as their open faith. Such comic blasphemies are a compensatory sign of belief, not disbelief; and they provide a mythic sense of dramatic irony that is often the lifeblood of literature in a conservative country. When Synge and O'Casey boldly went beyond Lady Gregory and brought this ironic folk imagination of the Ossianic dialogues to the stage of the Abbey Theatre, in their own characters if not in the actual personalities of Oisín and Patrick, few people realized, let alone appreciated, what was happening in Irish drama. Nevertheless, there was an unmistakable feeling among the more vigorous critics of the Abbey, in the protests of such nationalists as Arthur Griffith, that a dangerous pagan influence was invading the country.

For those insular critics who half-understood the plays of

Synge, the terms Protestantism, paganism, and satanism were often synonymous. Maurice Bourgeois and Daniel Corkery, for example, had no trouble recognizing the pagan spirit in Synge's plays, and they were both shocked by what they saw, rejecting it as an unfortunate and "un-Irish" aspect of his genius. Bourgeois even went so far as to suspect Synge's debt to the Ossianic dialogues, and he was appalled by this possibility. Objecting to the lack of "intense Catholic piety" in the plays, he concluded unhappily: "To Synge, the Irish peasant is a latter-day Pagan, on whose old-time heathendom the Christian faith has been artificially and superficially grafted."[51] Bourgeois also drew up a catalogue of "un-Irish elements throughout Synge's dramatic work," and at the top of the list were these two complaints: "Critics in general have no hesitancy in branding as un-Irish Synge's sardonic humour"; and "A more distinctly un-Irish element in Synge's plays is his non-religious view of life."[52]

What Bourgeois calls the pagan or "sardonic humour" in Synge's plays is clearly that barbarous element of antic comedy which lies at the core of his genius; and if that pervasive element were to be classified as "un-Irish," a large proportion of the sharp-witted Irish people, ordinary citizens as well as writers, would have to be drummed out of the country as impostors. And if, in order to satisfy not only Bourgeois but many latter-day critics of Synge and O'Casey, the "sardonic humour" in modern Irish drama, and in the literature in general, were to be removed, or diluted by the introduction of "intense Catholic piety," the result would probably lead to a literary disaster and an increase in the already thriving industry of devotional tracts.

Daniel Corkery, a more formidable critic who wrote twenty years later than Bourgeois and might have been expected to avoid his literary myopia, takes a relatively similar position and even relies on many quotations from Bourgeois to make his case against Synge as an Anglo-Irish or un-Irish dramatist who misrepresented and distorted the peasant character. Corkery often sounds like an implacable disciple of St. Patrick reading harsh sermons to the irresponsible disciples of Oisín. He is convinced that Synge is hopelessly and dangerously tainted by paganism, and therefore "bluntly insensitive to the finer spiritual values,"[53] by which he means the values of Irish Catholicism. And Corkery must have felt that the even more dangerous O'Casey was corrupted by the spirit of Satan as well as Oisín, for he often limits himself to sneering asides, as when, upon finding something distasteful in Synge, he will add, "It is like something one would expect to find in Sean O'Casey at his worst, or is it his best?"[54] At one point he accuses both dramatists of having insulted the Irish national and religious character, and he is so distressed by this libelous insult that he goes on to justify the notorious riots that broke up performances of *The Playboy* and *The Plough* at the Abbey Theatre:

> To sit among the audience in the Abbey Theatre when one of, say, Sean O'Casey's plays is on the stage, is to learn how true it is that the single blot is, *with great gaiety*, attributed to the whole people. To remain silent in the midst of that noisy gaiety, even to fling brickbats about, protesting against it, is, one thinks, to avoid the deeper vulgarity. . . . Religion and nationality are not separable in Ireland. If in any piece of work there occurs not only incidents which reflect, or seem to reflect, on the native Ireland, but also words and phrases which hurt the religious consciousness of that Ireland, then the offence of that piece of work is reckoned, in such periods, doubly gross, and not deserving of any fine consideration or afterthought. So was it with *The Playboy*.[55]

Apparently Irish Catholic nationalism can sometimes be so hypersensitive and humorless that even such a respected scholar and creative artist as Corkery must succumb to its Patrician intolerance, and in his own vindictive terms, he must fight comic vulgarity with pious vulgarity. It is significant that Corkery should be so particularly indignant about the "*great gaiety*" of the satiric laughter in the plays of Synge and O'Casey. Perhaps fanatical idealists have no time for the redemptive self-criticism of comedy. And the comic "blot" or "offence" need only be indirect, that is, merely "seem to reflect on the native Ireland"—for on this subject doubt is tantamount to guilt—to earn the automatic brickbats and ostracism. Thus it is not alone the plays of Synge and O'Casey but the controversies they provoked that recall the conflict between pagan and Christian values in the Ossianic dialogues, and the rancorous tones of St. Patrick are heard again in the land.

Critics such as Corkery may be right about the vulgarity of low comedy, but like Malvolio, they fall into puritanical error if they adopt a moralistic and rancorous tone when confronted by it. Antic Irish comedy unashamedly fulfills the triple meaning of the term "vulgar": it embodies "coarse manners and offends against refinement or good taste"; it embodies "the common or uneducated people"; it embodies "the vernacular tongue."[56] The rich vulgarity of this comic impulse is itself a vital aspect of the rebellious discontent of the humorously profane lower orders who are oppressed by the often superficial or hypocritical refinements of so-called good society. Furthermore, in the plays of Synge and O'Casey the antic comedy denies the sentimental expectation of poetic justice, since the wise fools in these works, like Oisín in the dialogues, are not censured or reformed in the end. Irish comedy is not Jonsonian comedy of humours or Bergsonian comedy of correction; it concentrates on revolt and liberation, not reformation and punishment.

Synge was determined to liberate his comic characters from the stereotypes of national idealism, and his tramps and tinkers reveal the "blot" of their irreverent freedom, just as his heroines openly burn with the repressed passion of Merriman's earthy women in *The Midnight Court*. The Tramp in his early play *In the Shadow of the Glen* (1904), an Ossianic vagabond poet, liberates young Nora Burke from the frustrations of a loveless marriage to a hard old man. Her "wheezing" husband pretends to be dead in the hope of trapping her, since he mistakenly suspects she already has the lover she so desperately yearns for. It is during the hilarity of the mock wake that Nora openly rebels against her churlish husband and turns her back on the sacrament of marriage—she is now not "afeard of beggar or bishop"—and decides to go off with the eloquent Tramp. He promises her a free life that celebrates, in the catalogue of bird songs and bright features, many of the pastoral and sensual pleasures of Oisín:

> Come along with me now, lady of the house, and it's not my blather you'll be hearing only, but you'll be hearing the herons crying out over the black lakes, and you'll be hearing the grouse, and the owls with them, and the larks and the big thrushes when the days are warm, and it's not the like of them you'll be hearing a talk of getting old like Peggy Cavanagh, and losing the hair off you, and the light of your eyes, but it's fine songs you'll be hearing when the sun goes up, and there'll be no old fellow wheezing the like of a sick sheep close to your ear.[57]

But then, in one of Synge's characteristically deflating shifts from the lyrical to the comical, a transition that shakes even while it sustains the Tramp's romantic aspirations, Nora accepts the offer with these playfully ironic remarks: "I'm thinking it's myself will be wheezing that time with lying down under the Heavens when the night is cold but you've a fine bit of talk, stranger, and it's with yourself I'll go."[58] Even the Tramp's self-mocking remark about his own "blather," in contrast to the idyll that follows, contributes to this counterpoint of idealism and irony in which the lyric and comic modes are played against each other. It is a similar technique of ironic deflation, with many variations in the game, that occurs in the Ossianic dialogue, as well as throughout the plays of Synge and O'Casey. Synge went on to use it even more extensively in his mock-heroic attitude toward the blind Douls in *The Well of the Saints* (1905), Christy Mahon in *The Playboy* (1907), and Mary Byrne in *The Tinker's Wedding* (1907).

It is no surprise that the clergy and the most faithful of their flock, because they attack or represent a threat to the pagan pleasures of the peasants and tinkers, become the targets of Synge's irreverent mockery, though he does not spare his sympathetic clowns from a parallel if less devastating laughter. The comic villains may be Bergsonian automatons or *alazons*, but the comic heroes and heroines are Ossianic fools or *eirons*. Martin and Mary Doul, the blind old fools in *The Well of the Saints*, are temporarily defeated by the adverse circumstances of the real world when the Saint restores their sight and thus destroys the dream world they had previously experienced through their heightened senses. One can't help thinking that God and his Saint, as well as the taunting Molly Byrne and Timmy the Smith, are part of this cruel trick played on the unfortunate Douls. "The Lord protect us from the saints of God!" is Mary's comic-ironic way of summing up the situation in a pregnant Irish bull, a loaded jest and lament. And in the central paradox of the play, the Douls manage to turn defeat into victory when they mock the miracle that restored their sight and choose to become blind and free again. Even though the Saint tells them about the wonders they will be able to see if they have their sight restored permanently, "the summer and the fine spring, and the places where the holy men of Ireland have built up churches to the Lord," Martin replies, in a typical Ossianic comparison, by describing pagan wonders greater than holy places: "Isn't it finer sights outselves had a while since and we sitting dark smelling the sweet beautiful smells do be rising in the warm nights and hearing the swift flying things racing in the air, till we'd be looking up in our own minds into a grand sky, and seeing lakes, and broadening rivers, and hills are waiting for the spade and plough."[59]

Finally, when the Saint appears again with his sacred bells and his can of holy water to complete the miracle, Martin shocks everyone by irreverently striking the can from the cleric's hand and stating defiantly: "Go on now, holy father, for if you're a fine saint itself, it's more sense is in a blind man, and more power maybe than you're thinking at all. Let you walk on now with your worn feet, and your welted knees, and your fasting, holy ways have left you with a big head on you and a thin pitiful arm."[60] Martin has a mythic sense of his own power, and by denying and desecrating the Saint he has committed his comic hubris without any fear of guilt. There is a risk in this choice, for Timmy says, as the blind Douls wander off to the warmer south, they may drown in the flooding rivers; but Martin gladly exchanges a dubious miracle for a precarious freedom.

Christy Mahon represents a life of precarious freedom to the repressed Pegeen Mike in *The Playboy*. Before she meets the mock patricide and potential playboy, she has longings similar to those of Nora Burke, since she is painfully aware of her imminent and loveless marriage to Shawn Koegh, the hapless local product of pious Catholicism. A cringing bumpkin who sees terrible sins lurking everywhere, Shawn lives in mortal fear of Father Reilly, whose name he repeats with almost hysterical frequency. When he is about to be confronted by the mysterious Christy, and he should be "protecting" Pegeen, he panics and calls to the saints Joseph, Patrick, Brigid, and James to save *him*. Pegeen's father tries to prevent Shawn's hasty exit, but he escapes screaming, "Leave me go, Michael James, leave me go, you old Pagan, leave me go or I'll get the curse of the priests on you, and of the scarlet-coated bishops of the courts of Rome."[61] The rebellious Oisín, whose pagan spirit seems to hover over this play, would have given Shawn a well-deserved knock on the head for his trouble, which, incidentally, is exactly what Pegeen does at the conclusion.

Besides this burlesque of the excesses of Catholic piety, what must have contributed to the riot against Synge was revealed in Bourgeois's main objection to the play as "a specimen of blasphemous neo-Paganism in view of the continual use of expressions referring to God and the Church, and the profane travesty on the sacrament of marriage."[62] The attacks, then, did not arise exclusively, as was commonly believed, from Christy's remarks about preferring Pegeen to "a drift of chosen females, standing in their shifts itself,"[63] which merely exposed the Victorian prudery of the Irish. The deeper indignation must have been provoked by the liberty Christy took with the Lord's name, as when, thinking about all the kisses he will squeeze on Pegeen's puckered lips, he feels "a kind of pity for the Lord God in all ages sitting lonesome in his golden chair."[64] This is precisely the kind of profane and innocently comic compassion that Oisín felt for poor God. And the blasphemous parallel is maintained as Christy, in his rapture over Pegeen, genuinely feels sorry for the Lord's holy men, those lonely and sexually repressed celibates in heaven and on earth: "If the mitred bishops seen you that time, they'd be the like of the holy prophets, I'm thinking, do be straining the bars of Paradise to lay eyes on the Lady Helen of Troy, and she abroad pacing back and forward with a nosegay in her golden shawl."[65]

In the context of the Ossianic rebellion against all paternal authority, as a reflection of the comic Oedipal conflict, all father figures in the play are mocked, whether it is Christy violently desecrating his father and the church fathers, Pegeen boldly defying her drunken father, or Shawn ridiculously venerating his Father Reilly. In the end the children are left to sort out their ironic victories and defeats. When Christy emerges as a truly liberated playboy and leaves "to go romancing through a romping lifetime from this hour to the dawning of the judgment day," Shawn feels it is indeed a judgment from God, and he tells Pegeen it is a miraculous victory for the church, Father Reilly, and the sacrament of marriage. But the heartbroken Pegeen, who in the crisis lost her nerve and her playboy, knows the truth.

In her rage and grief at having lacked the courage to follow Christy, as Nora Burke had followed the Tramp, she blasts the impervious Shawn with a wallop on the ear, and then breaks into "wild lamentations" over her loss of "the only Playboy of the Western World." The triumphant Christy Mahon is "master of all fights from now," and his pagan victory is a mythic defeat for Sean Koegh's holy Ireland, as well as for the repressed Pegeen Mike. Nevertheless, in a final irony, it should be noted that Christy has won and lost; he may have discovered himself, but he has also lost the only playgirl of the Western world.

Before turning to Synge's most profane comedy, *The Tinker's Wedding*, it should be pointed out that even in his two tragedies he exalts the higher wisdom of pagan life. In *Riders to the Sea* he establishes an antithesis between pagan stoicism and Catholic ritual in which the former emerges as the superior force; and in *Deirdre of the Sorrows* the star-crossed legendary lovers are confronted by betrayal and death only when they abandon their primitive freedom in exile and return to Ireland, to the hidden terror of paternal authority.

A comic defense of primitive freedom establishes the central action in *The Tinker's Wedding*, a work that was considered to be so blasphemous and anticlerical, even by Yeats and Lady Gregory, that it was never performed at the Abbey Theatre. It is unfortunate that this provocative tinker farce has been kept on ice, for it is one of Synge's liveliest works, an exuberant and randy example of antic Irish comedy. Synge must have found "satanic or barbarous sympathies" in the vagabond itinerants, for he was fascinated by their pagan spirit and outlaw habits, a reckless way of life that made them hardy, shrewd, irresponsible, and completely uninhibited in their pursuit of earthly pleasures. Again the sacrament of marriage with all its respectable restrictions touches off the hilarious conflict when a tinker couple who have been living together try unsuccessfully to become lawfully married by a priest. The man, Michael Byrne, is reluctant to go along with the plan, for priests, like the police, represent distasteful authority and restraint to him. But his uneasy woman, Sarah Casey, finally insists on an official church marriage because she doesn't want to become a "wicked heathen" like Mary Byrne, Michael's cheerfully dissolute mother. To no avail Mary reminds Sarah of the pitfalls of respectability and warns her that the ring on her finger and the blessing of the clergy will not prevent her from losing her beauty or help her keep her man. Sarah calls for the priest, but it is the mischievous Mary who dominates and determines the knockabout resolution of the conflict. She is the mistress of misrule who presides over the improvised revels.

When the reluctant priest arrives, the tipsy Mary, pitying the sober celibate, entertains him with her merry gab, a "wicked" song, and an offer to share a drink with him. Overcome with weariness, he relaxes, takes a drink, and is so taken in by Mary's half-genuine, half-ironic compassion that he begins to feel sorry for himself. In a profane parody and reversal of a confessional scene, *he* unburdens his heart to *her*, the priest purging himself before the pagan Mary, telling her about his hard life, dreading a visitation from his censorious bishop, saying Mass with a dry mouth and running east and west over his parish to hear the sins of his people. And this recital moves Mary to yet another display of her double-edged compassion: "It's distroyed you must be hearing the sins of the rural people on a fine spring."[66] Thus she absolves and damns him and herself in the same breath. The pagan mother and the Christian father are both mocked, but with sympathy rather than malice.

The mutual mockery continues even after the drink wears off. The priest turns mercenary and refuses to marry the tinkers unless he receives some money and a gallon can. The incorrigible Mary eventually steals the can and trades it for more liquor. In the farcical brawl that concludes the play, the priest threatens to go to the police, but the tinkers now unite against the common enemy, knock him in a ditch, and tie and gag him in a sack. Both sides are lampooned in the burlesque battle as the priest condemns himself as well as the tinkers with a curse, and the pagan itinerants escape to love and fight and drink another day. Oisín would have had much in common with these profane rogues.

In a spirit of comic rebellion that is strongly akin to the irreverent paganism of Synge's tinkers, the urban peasants of O'Casey's tragicomic Dublin and the pastoral clowns of his later comedies fight against all forms of authority and respectability—Irish as well as British, religious as well as nationalistic. Daniel Corkery's reasoning may be questionable but his conclusion is understandable' when he recoils from what he calls the "great and noisy gaiety" that emanates from the O'Casey characters. Chauvinistic Ireland was in no mood to accept the profanation of its sacred middle-class virtues, since O'Casey, like Synge, refused to pay even lip service to the stereotyped image of national piety. O'Casey's long-standing quarrel with Ireland's conservative Roman Catholic hierarchy was not a direct issue in his early plays, though, again like Synge, he had been attacked by clerical as well as nationalistic critics from the beginning of his career. His rogue's gallery of paycocks and parasites were close cousins to Synge's playboys and tinkers. Specifically, one can point to the wise folly of such resilient clowns as Seumas Shields and Mrs. Henderson in *The Shadow of a Gunman* (1923); "Captain" Boyle and Joxer Daly in *Juno and the Paycock* (1924); Fluther Good and Mrs. Gogan, Bessie Burgess and Rosie Redmond, The Covey and Uncle Peter in *The Plough and the Stars* (1926).

In such plays as *The Silver Tassie* (1928) and *Within the Gates* (1933), O'Casey had begun to dramatize the conflict between the Christian mortification of the flesh and the pagan joy of life, but in these works it was introduced along with the dominating themes of world war and economic depression. In *Purple Dust* (1940), however, which largely satirizes the reactionary aspects of British life, the Ossianic motif is invoked in a direct way. Besides laughing at the invading antiquarians from England, Stoke and Poges, the crafty Irish peasants, led by Jack O'Killigain and Philib O'Dempsey (the 2nd Workman), also tangle with Canon Creehewel, the parish priest who fears and tries to place a ban on "the lower inclinations of the people," specifically the pastoral revels of dancing and singing and loving. O'Dempsey, who looks and talks like "a wandherin' King" of Celtic Ireland, knows all the old legends, out of which he himself seems to have stepped, and the lives of the pagan heroes are so vivid to him that he sometimes sounds like Oisín remembering his father when he celebrates the deeds of Finn MacCool:

> That was in the days o' Finn MacCool, before his hair was scarred with a hint o' grey; the mighty Finn, I'm sayin', who stood as still as a stone in th' heart of a hill to hear the cry of a curlew over th'

cliffs o' Erris, the song of the blackbird, the cry o' the hounds
hotfoot afther a boundin' deer, the steady wail o' the waves
tumblin' in on a lonely shore; the mighty Finn who'd surrendher
an emperor's pomp for a place with the bards, and the gold o' the
King o' Greece for a night asleep be the sthream of Assaroe![67]

When Poges remarks that the great Finn is gone now, O'Dempsey answers sharply and mysteriously: "He's here for ever!
His halloo can be heard on the hills outside; his spear can be
seen with its point in the stars."[68] In the fantastic and prophetic
imagination of O'Casey's peasant, Finn and all the Ossianic
heroes, together with the more modern heroes such as Wolfe
Tone and Parnell, are still alive up in the enchanted hills, waiting
for the day when they will redeem Ireland from internal as well
as external oppressors. Later, after the sly peasants wreak comic
chaos on the purple dreams of Stoke and Poges, and after the
symbolic flood comes to bring a judgment on the Englishmen
for their boorish presumption, and the Canon for his puritanical
prohibitions, O'Killigain and O'Dempsey go off to join the immortal heroes in the safety of the hills, taking the two young
women with them. In his call to Avril, O'Killigain sounds very
like Synge's Tramp urging Nora to follow him into a life of
primitive joy:

> Come where the rain is heavy, where the frost frets, and where
> the sun is warm. Avril, pulse of me heart, listen to me, an' let
> longin' flood into your heart for the call of life. The young thorn-
> three withered away now, can awaken again, an' spread its fra-
> grance around us. Spit out what's here, an' come where love is fierce
> an' fond an' fruitful. Come, lass, where there's things to say an'
> things to do an' love at the endings![69]

Another aspect of that idyllic life in the enchanted hills, where
the glory of the Fenians remains alive, was revealed in O'Casey's
next play, *Red Roses for Me* (1942). In the dream-vision of the
third act the lyrical spirit of Oisín now contributes directly to the
miraculous transformation of Dublin. Again it must be pointed
out that this is not the only theme in the play, which deals with
the 1913 General Strike in Dublin; nevertheless, that prophetic
transformation scene, O'Casey's great hymn of joy, is the
centerpiece of the work, and significantly it unites, in a golden
dream, the values of Oisín and God in a harmony of paganism

and Christianity. This play brings together the lyric as well as the comic spirit of Celtic Ireland.

After a series of fiery and satiric brawls, between the strikers and the police, between a Fenian patriot and a Darwinian skeptic, between Catholic and Protestant neighbors, and a farcical debate on whether Patrick was a Catholic or a Protestant saint, the drab people of the tenements gather with Ayamonn Breydon on the banks of the Liffey. One of the young Catholic women, Finnoola, a symbolic Cathleen ni Houlihan, dressed as they all are in shabby black clothing, begins to dream of the richly colored garments of "Finn MacCool of th' golden hair, Goll MacMorna of th' big blows, Caoilte of th' flyin' feet, an' Oscar of th' invincible spear."[70] Later she laments that "Songs of Osheen and Sword of Oscar could do nothing to tire this city of its shame."[71] But at that point, as twilight is settling over the city of "poverty, penance, and pain," a streak of sunlight mysteriously breaks through the darkening sky and illumines the head of Ayamonn, making his face look like a mythic visage out of the Celtic past. During the "miracle" that follows, the brilliant light spreads over the whole city, bathing everything and everyone in rays of scarlet and gold, changing the black dresses of the women to rich shades of green.

Now the ecstatic Finnoola describes one of the women, and she might well be talking about the new Dublin: "She's glowin' like a song sung be Osheen himself, with the golden melody of his own harp helpin'!"[72] Ayamonn, shouting triumphantly, "Our city's in th' grip o' God!" then leads the people in a lyrical Ossianic ballad of celebration, followed by a spontaneous dance along the riverbanks as they offer their thanks to God and the Celtic heroes. But this prophetic fantasy is short-lived, and presently darkness returns to the city, where the unsuccessful strike is in progress. The people are bewildered, and one of the women complains, "For God's sake give over dwellin' on oul' songs sung by Osheen," and Finnoola tries to explain what happened: "Dhreamin' I musta been when I heard strange words in a city nearly smothered be stars, with God guidin' us along th' banks of a purple river, all of us clad in fresh garments, fit to make Osheen mad to sing a song of the revelry dancin' in an' out of God's own vision."[73] In the wild imagination of this woman, the lyrical Oisín was in a mad rage to offer the people his song of joy. That phrase of Finnoola's—"make Osheen mad to sing a song of the revelry"—is strikingly similar to the phrase in *Finnegans Wake,* where Joyce wishes to "make the Rageous Ossean, kneel and quaff a lyre!"[74] In both instances the bardic hero is exhorted to fill, even drown, the world with song. One is also tempted to consider the possibility that Joyce, who played all the verbal stops, might have created some significant anagrams in his "Ossean," not only for Finn's son "Osheen" again and Earwicker's poetic son "Shaun," but for his "Rageous" and lyrical fellow countryman, the bold "Sean O'."

In *Cock-a-Doodle Dandy* (1949) a pagan symbol of joy and song in the guise of a merry and miraculous chanticleer becomes the master of the revels. But in this play God's representatives, led by the Patrician Father Domineer, not only refuse to join the revelry but ban all singing and dancing in the village of Nyadnanave, which means Nest of Saints in Gaelic, and also contains the Joycean pun Nest of Knaves. The play presents a mock-heroic battle between the forces of free-hearted paganism and puritanical Irish Catholicism, and as in the Ossianic dialogue, no reconciliation is possible. Since the rancorous Father Domineer and his crew of comic villains, the old religious quack Shinaar and the village idiot One-Eyed Larry, equate paganism with Satanism, the "Demon" Cock and his young allies must be driven out of the land. Before they go into exile, however, the mischievous Cock, with the help of Robin Adair and all the young women, spreads hilarious havoc throughout the village. Michael Marthraun, the local gombeen man who sides with the priest in the fight against the inherent sinfulness of women, warns the sorely tempted Sailor Mahon: "Oh, man, your religion should tell you th' biggest fight th' holy saints ever had was with the temptation from good-lookin' women"; and to prove his case he recalls the dangerous effect his own daughter, a great friend of the Cock, has on holy objects: ". . . once I seen the statue of St. Crankarious standin' on his head to circumvent th' lurin' quality of her presence; an' another time, I seen th' image of our own St. Patrick makin' a skelp at her with his crozier; fallin' flat on his face, stunned when he missed!"[75] Patrick was certainly a "St. Crankarious" to Oisín, and the old pagan, who had a passion for beautiful women, as well as a stronge urge to give Patrick of the "crooked crozier" a knock on the head, would have enjoyed laughing at the irreverent spectacle of the two upended saints in O'Casey's lampoon of Nyadnanavery.

In his last two full-length plays, *The Bishop's Bonfire* (1955) and *The Drums of Father Ned* (1960), O'Casey was in a somewhat more conciliatory mood. He anticipated the ecumenical movement by creating some young clerics who are the spokesmen for a flexible Irish Catholicism that attempts to liberate itself from excessive pietism. In the first work, while the people of Ballyoonagh prepare to celebrate the return of their native son, Bishop Bill Mullarkey—he never appears on stage and the play might have been called "Waiting for Mullarkey"—one of the stiff-necked Canon's flock regrets that the festivities are interfering with the proper conduct of "mortification and prayer." To which Father Boheroe, the liberal young curate, replies: "Too much formal prayer, Rankin, sometimes makes a soul conceited; and merriment may be a way of worship."[76] Perhaps that final phrase effectively sums up the Ossianic motif in all these plays.

For Father Boheroe, all aspects of life are sacred, the singing and dancing no less than the praying, and he has two voluble allies in the Prodical and the Codger. Prodical, a Flutherian workman who has a constitutional fondness for liquor and freedom, leaves no doubt about the kind of life he wants: "Prodical Carranaun demands a wider world, Father Boheroe; a world where a man can roar his real opinions out."[77] Codger Sleehaun, an eighty-four-year-old itinerant handyman and wandering minstrel—he might be described as a composite figure of Synge's Tramp, the bardic Oisín, and the then septagenarian O'Casey himself—fights the joy killers with his nimble mother wit and his pastoral ballads. When the Canon attacks the Codger and his merry songs, Father Boheroe comes to his defense: "I wish I could put into my prayers the spirit he puts into his songs. I'm afraid, Monsignor, God listens more eagerly to the songs of the Codger than He does to our best prayers."[78] But in spite of their best efforts, the Codger, Prodical, and even Father Boheroe are forced to leave the village at the end of the play.

In his last full-length work, however, *The Drums of Father Ned*, punfully subtitled *A Mickrocosm of Ireland*, O'Casey is in his ripest good humor, and now he offers an alternative to exile in the spirit of the symbolic title figure, Father Ned. The life-affirming young priest is always offstage beating his prophetic drums, preparing for the celebration of the village Tostal, the traditional Irish spring festival. Besides his symbolic drums, which awaken the people to the promise of a new life, Father Ned also uses the emblems of the Celtic heroes for his pageant, especially a shield with the image of Angus the Young, the Celtic god of love, his harp and his four bright singing birds. While the older clergy and the politicians join forces against the "pagan" Tostaleers, no amount of tricks or threats can stop Father Ned, who has caught the imagination of the young people. When the Mayor, who believes that "Father Ned is a menace to th' town an' th' whole countryside," objects to all the singing and dancing because "our Blessed Lord never joined in a dance, never halted His work to sing a song," Nora McGilligan, one of Father Ned's allies, gives her version of what God might have done. An ecumenical voice of the new Cathleen Ni Houlihan, Nora says:

> If He didn't dance Himself, He must have watched the people at it, and, maybe, clapped His hands when they did it well. He must have often listened to the people singin', and been caught up with the rhythm of the gentle harp and psaltery, and His feet may have tapped the ground along with the gayer sthrokes of the tabor and the sound of the cymbals tinkling.[79]

Oisín would have had no quarrel with such a glorious handclapping and foot-tapping God. Unlike the archbishop of Dublin, whose displeasure with the play, even though he hadn't read it, led to its withdrawal from the Dublin Tostal in 1958, Oisín probably would have joined the parade of merry Christians dancing to the drums of Father Ned in O'Casey's comic ritual of celebration.

Chapter 3

THE COMIC DESECRATION OF
IRELAND'S HOUSEHOLD GODS

SHIELDS. I'm a Nationalist meself, right enough—a Nationalist right enough, but all the same—I'm a Nationalist right enough; I believe in the freedom of Ireland, an' that England has no right to be here, but I draw the line when I hear the gunmen blowin' about dyin' for the people, when it's the people that are dyin' for the gunmen! With all due respect to the gunmen, I don't want them to die for me.
>   —Sean O'Casey, *The Shadow of a Gunman*

DOBELLE. The birth of a Nation is no immaculate conception.
>   —Denis Johnston, *The Moon in the Yellow River*

LUKE. He was hard up for a cause that fought and died for this country. I'd as lief fight and die for Spike Island.
>   —George Shiels, *The New Gossoon*

PAT. You know, there are two sorts of gunmen, the earnest, religious-minded ones, like you, and the laughing boys. . . . Because it's not a natural thing for a man with a sense of humour to be playing with firearms and fighting. There must be something the matter with him.
>   —Brendan Behan, *The Hostage*

The Hagiography of Cathleen Ni Houlihan

The rebirth of a nation's literature, to extend the irony of Denis Johnston, is not an immaculate conception. It is a process of renewal that often grows out of tragic attrition and comic desecration, a civil strife of violent words and conflicting aspirations. The Irish literary renaissance that developed at the turn of the twentieth century was not the result of a predestined revelation of the Celtic mystique, whatever that sacred vision might be; it evolved against the grain of patriotic fervor as the nation's new literature arose from a seemingly irreconcilable struggle between political necessity and creative imagination.

Paradoxically, though Irish nationalism and literature had an urgent need of each other's vitality and vision, their leaders were from the start suspicious of their respective values and methods; they were sharply divided by the common goal of seeking to reassert the country's heritage and pride. On the nationalist side, the political spokesmen tried to establish a public cult to idealize and purify the national life; and on the literary side, the creative artists tried to express their personal views of the ideals and ironies of the national life. It was therefore inevitable that the artists would question and even mock many of the nationalist dogmas. Militant nationalism often seems at the point of winning the struggle, especially during a revolutionary period, when in the cause of national honor all the writers are urged to celebrate the proposition that every Irishman is a courageous patriot, every Irishwoman is a paragon of virtue, and an unquestioning love of country is the greatest glory. But even when they have been inspired by unimpeachable principles of revolutionary justice, such unalloyed attempts to canonize the national character in the name of the sanctified Cathleen Ni Houlihan ironically threaten to become the occasion of national hypocrisy. They also become the obvious target of those uncompromising writers who gain the final victory because they owe their Irish allegiance to what might be called the higher nationalism—the search for the truth about the people and the nation, the quintessential nature of their character and their world. What Yeats and Lady Gregory had in mind for their new theater movement was a cultural nationalism, not the chauvinistic nationalism that was to become one of the chief opponents of that theater.

After the death of Parnell in 1891 the movement for national independence and the literary renaissance naturally but only temporarily coincided, each force guiding and inspiring the other in the early days as they worked toward the liberation of the country from British domination. Nevertheless, it soon became evident that nationalism and literature were destined to collide with each other when they weren't colliding with Britain. The record of that internal collision can be found in the life and work of Ireland's major writers, Yeats and Joyce, Synge and O'Casey, four Irishmen who felt they had to desecrate the pieties of Cathleen Ni Houlihan in order to be truthfully Irish. They maintained their loyalty to the higher nationalism of artistic integrity. Perhaps what W. R. Rodgers once wrote about Synge effectively expresses the writer's responsibility to his nation: "A writer's first duty to his country is disloyalty, and Synge did his duty by Ireland in presenting her as he found her and not as she wished to be found."[1] Synge is one of the seminal figures, and this view of his constructive disloyalty no doubt has its roots in Yeats's comment on the genius of Synge and the way it exposed the gap that often exists between the artist and the nation: "When a country produces a man of genius he is never what it wants or believes it wants; he is always unlike its idea of itself."[2]

Synge had raised the whole issue in 1903 with his first play, *In the Shadow of the Glen,* an irreverent lampoon of idyllic peasant life that was completely at odds with the country's sentimental idea of itself. And Yeats was also early in the field. On the controversial occasion of that first performance of Synge's play, presented by Yeats's Irish National Theatre Society at Molesworth Hall on October 8, 1903, the company also performed the premiere of Yeats's new play, *The King's Threshold,* which could be described as an ironic comment on, perhaps even a recantation of his highly nationalistic play of the previous year, *Cathleen Ni Houlihan.* It was no surprise, then, that Synge and Yeats were accused of slandering Ireland by the nationalist critics, the self-appointed guardians of the country's honor, and were vehemently attacked by Arthur Griffith, one of the leading apostles of the new nationalism. Founder of Sinn Fein and later president of the Irish Free State government, the formidable Griffith launched the first of his unrelenting assaults against Synge and Yeats and the new theater movement. About Synge's play he wrote the following comment:

> The Irish National Theatre Society was ill-advised when it decided to give its imprimatur to such a play as "In a Wicklow Glen" [*In the Shadow of the Glen*]. The play has an Irish name, but it is no more Irish than the Decameron. It is a staging of a corrupt version of that world-wide libel on womankind—the "Widow of Ephesus," which was made current in Ireland by the hedge-schoolmaster. . . . Mr. Synge's play purports to attack "our Irish institution, the loveless marriage"—a reprehensible institution but not one peculiar to Ireland. We believe the loveless marriage is something of an institution in France and Germany and even in the superior country across the way, and, if we recollect our books, it was something of an institution in that nursery of the arts—ancient Greece. . . . Man and woman in rural Ireland, according to Mr. Synge, marry lacking love, and, as a consequence, the woman proves unfaithful. Mr. Synge never found that in Irish life.[3]

Well, hardly ever. There is unintentional humor in this quixotic defense of the purity of Irish womanhood, but Griffith was unable to see the humor in the play and disinclined to judge it as a work of art. According to his nationalistic idealism, the play was a profane and foreign influence, a dangerous libel against Irish women, and therefore false. Nor was he alone in holding this chauvinistic view, for the performance of the play was greeted by some hissing and a minor disturbance when three prominent members of the Theatre Society who were in the audience walked out in protest and resigned from the company. Dr. James H. Cousins, the Irish poet and critic who was present at the time, has described the motive for the walkout: "Maud Gonne, Maire Quinn and Dudley Digges left the hall in protest against what they regarded as a decadent intrusion where the inspiration of idealism rather than the down pull of realism was needed."[4] The Irish artist, therefore, was now a decadent intruder in his native land, and by these pure standards of uplifting behavior, a fabricated idealism was more palatable than the ironic realities of Irish life.

If the three protesters had remained in the hall to see the following performance of Yeats's new play, they would have been exposed to another shock. They had all acted in his *Cathleen Ni Houlihan* in 1902, with Maud Gonne in the title role of the regal Old Woman who exhorts the patriots of the 1798 Rising to die a martyr's death for Ireland—"They shall be remembered for ever." But now in *The King's Threshold* Yeats turned away from the sacred symbolism of Cathleen Ni Houlihan and created a martyred poet as "the inspiration of idealism," the higher idealism of art. Now the poet, not the patriot, was to be remembered for ever. The Celtic parable in this play is Yeats's manifesto in defense of the poet's great gift of lyric power and his ancient right of high honor in the state. When King Guaire, following the advice of his national councillors, the bishops and judges and soldiers, insults the poet Seanchan (Shanahan) by dismissing him from the state council—"it is against their dignity / For a mere man of words to sit amongst them"— Seanchan acts to uphold his traditional position by going on a hunger strike on the palace steps. Rejecting all attempts at compromise, he sacrifices his life for the belief that the arts must never be controlled or diminished by the state. At one point Seanchan offers his disciples a Dionysian vision of the poet's great gift of tragic joy, a vision that owes more to Nietzsche than to nationalism:

> And I would have all know that when all falls
> In ruin, poetry calls out in joy,
> Being the scattering hand, the bursting pod,

The victim's joy among the holy flame,
God's laughter at the shattering of the world.[5]

The later and major Yeats is prefigured in these apocalpytic lines. Only poetry—and, one might add, comedy—can transform the tragic patterns of life and triumph over them; it is a mythic process of aesthetic joy that Yeats later embodied in such poems as "Sailing to Byzantium" and "Lapis Lazuli," and in such a symbolic comedy as *The Player Queen;* it is a mythic process of aesthetic joy that Synge and O'Casey embodied in all their dark comedies. Perhaps, in an analogous burst of comic joy, God's laughter can be approximated by human laughter, particularly at the shattering of romantic or nationalistic illusions of the world.

Seanchan's fight for the absolute supremacy of poetry led Una Ellis-Fermor to make the following comment on Yeats's aesthetic: "It is a flaming exaltation of that vision which is the symbol of all spiritual knowledge and the gift of the spirit beside which all other values are disvalued. Poetry is either the root of life or it is nothing.... Even Brand himself never proclaimed more unflinchingly the doctrine of 'all or nothing.'"[6] It is only surprising that Ellis-Fermor, instead of looking to Ibsen's Brand for a parallel to Yeats's Seanchan, did not more appropriately turn to Ibsen's great Irish disciple, James Joyce; for Seanchan is a blood brother of Joyce and surely anticipates his martyred high priest and jester of art, Stephen Dedalus. More precisely, perhaps, the priority of kinship between Yeats and Joyce on the absolute supremacy of art should be reversed, with Joyce as the initiator of the principle. It was the young Joyce, disdainfully aloof from both the literary and the national movements in Ireland at the turn of the century, who, in "The Day of the Rabblement" in 1901, had warned Yeats not to allow the Irish theater to become corrupted by the new nationalism. In that prophetic essay the nineteen-year-old Joyce had written with his characteristic arrogance that "Mr. Yeats's treacherous instinct of adaptability must be blamed for his recent association with a platform from which even self-respect should have urged him to refrain."[7] By 1903, however, the disenchanted Yeats had finally abandoned the nationalist platform, cut himself off from Edward Martyn and

George Moore, who were grinding different axes, and as if in reply to Joyce, created his apocalyptic and Joycean Seanchan. In retrospect, it should be clear that Joyce in his "all or nothing" essay had defined the crux of the creative issue for all Irish artists, not only for a Seanchan and a Dedalus, who were destined to collide with the sacred Cathleen Ni Houlihan:

> If an artist courts the favor of the multitude he cannot escape the contagion of its fetichism and deliberate self-deception, and if he joins in a popular movement he does so at his own risk. Therefore, the Irish Literary Theatre by its surrender to the trolls has cut itself adrift from the line of advancement. Until he has freed himself from the mean influences about him—sodden enthusiasm and clever insinuation and every flattering influence of vanity and low ambition—no man is an artist at all.[8]

Fortunately, Yeats did not surrender to the fetichism of the nationalist trolls, who, if they had had their way, would have fulfilled the symbolism of The King's Threshold by placing literature in a subordinate and probably suppressed position in the new Sinn Fein Ireland. No less than Joyce or O'Casey, Yeats spent the rest of his life fighting for the freedom of the artist, rejecting the favor of the multitude, defending his independent theater from nationalist attacks and riots. Predictably, Arthur Griffith did not like The King's Threshold, mainly because his sympathies were with the villain of the piece, the autocratic King Guaire, and because he had no use for what he called the "selfish" poet who ridiculously and unreasonably was fighting the wrong battle against the wrong enemy. Yeats wrote a formal reply, "An Irish National Theatre and Three Sorts of Ignorance," which Griffith printed in the October 24, 1903, issue of his United Irishman, defending his theater, his play, and Synge. In this article Yeats identified his version of Irish trollism as the "obscurantist" attitude of the three main pressure groups in the country that had made it their mission to protect the national honor against the profane artist: the political, religious, and Gaelic language propagandists.[9] This time Yeats had anticipated Joyce and initiated the principle, for there is a similar manifesto in A Portrait of the Artist as a Young Man (1916), when Stephen Dedalus, in rejecting the arguments of the nationalistic Davin, also identifies the triple enemy of the artist: "When the soul of a man is born in this country there are nets flung at it to hold it back from flight. You talk to me of nationality, language, religion. I shall try to fly by those nets."[10]

So Griffith had flung up his nationalistic net, and he was joined by Maud Gonne, who, in the same issue of the *United Irishman* in which Yeats's article had appeared, issued her own warning to the poet. From the time she had played the role of Cathleen Ni Houlihan in his play she behaved as if she were Cathleen incarnate, and she now wrote: "Mr Yeats asks for freedom for the theatre, freedom even from patriotic captivity. I would ask for freedom for it from one thing more deadly than all else—freedom from the insidious and destructive tyranny of foreign influence."[11] But for Yeats and the major writers of Ireland, all of whom were at various times accused of bringing foreign or pagan influences into Irish literature, and later had their works banned on this account by the Censorship of Publications Board, the most insidious and destructive tyranny for the artist was "patriotic captivity," or any form of captivity that restricted artistic expression.

Several months after Yeats's article appeared, in a letter of January 2, 1904, to Lady Gregory, he wrote: "Did I tell you of my idea of challenging Griffith to debate with me in public our two policies—his that literature should be subordinate to nationalism, and mine that it must have its own ideal."[12] Unfortunately that public debate never materialized; nevertheless, the substance of the issue, literature vs. nationalism, runs throughout modern Irish literature, not only in the heroic stance of Yeats's Seanchan and Joyce's Dedalus but also in the mock-heroic antics of barbarous Irish comedy, particularly in the mendacious strutting of Synge's "playboys" and O'Casey's "paycocks," who in their irreverent behavior mock the hagiography of Cathleen Ni Houlihan. As a result Synge and O'Casey were more visibly controversial figures than Yeats and Joyce, and their works touched off violent demonstrations of protest in the Abbey Theatre; though this violence was probably due to the fact that the theater is a more public and more immediately provocative art than poetry and fiction, and comic desecration is a more openly recognizable sign of "disloyalty" than literary martyrdom. This is in no way meant to belittle the massive influence of Yeats as a chastizer of the Irish philistines, or the versatile power of the apostate Joyce. Far from being limited to the arrogant aesthetics of Stephen Dedalus, Joyce was a master of comic irreverence in all his works and took satiric pleasure in exposing the nationalistic follies of his countrymen; for example, in the Cyclops chapter of *Ulysses,* where Leopold Bloom plays the sensitive mock hero as farcical scapegoat tormented by the patriotic ranting of the boorish Citizen. But few Irishmen had the opportunity to read Joyce during his lifetime, when the unofficial censorship kept his books hidden from most of the people; and Yeats's unpopular verse plays, seldom produced at the Abbey, never achieved notoriety, since they were actually written to be performed in private drawing rooms for carefully chosen audiences of no more than fifty sympathetic listeners.

Although the British tyranny had over many centuries created the need for Irish nationalism, and by its harsh Penal Laws forbidding all written references to Ireland had forced the poets to invent such allegorical names as Cathleen Ni Houlihan, the Dark Rosaleen, and the Shan Van Vocht (the Poor Old Woman), the insidious pressure of British domination was replaced by the sentimental piety of Irish chauvinism. To such moralistic guardians of the household gods as Arthur Griffith and Maud Gonne, and their more militant counterparts now out in force across the land, Synge and O'Casey were guilty of slandering Ireland; but in the hindsight of history and the assessment of literary value, it is apparent that the two dramatists, though they are still regarded with suspicion or enmity by some of their diehard countrymen, were guilty only of presenting Ireland "as they found her and not as she wished to be found."

Synge found the Irish peasants in varying states of comic paralysis and repression, straining under the contradictory moods of frustration and wild fantasy, with nothing but their farcical despair and rebellious imagination to sustain their uncertain lives. O'Casey found the dispossessed urban peasants of the Dublin tenements caught in the crossfire of the War of Independence, from the Easter Rising of 1916 to the Civil War of 1922, with nothing but savage laughter and ironic profanations to sustain their expendable lives. Perhaps Synge and O'Casey had desecrated the national character initially by the very fact that they chose to write sympathetically as well as satirically about cowards, hypocrites, liars, drunkards, tinkers, tramps, braggarts, parasites, fishwives, and prostitutes, as well as an odd assortment of peasants, publicans, priests, pedlars, charwomen, carpenters, chicken butchers, bricklayers, poets, gunmen, hungry old men and women, and consumptive children. To such marginal people, living for the most part on sheer nerve and animal guile, the world of reality in early twentieth-century Ireland was something of a nightmare that might have driven them to madness or death more quickly than they could have died for their country. Their basic problems and needs were more personal than patriotic, their impulses and desires were more immediate than idealistic, and their only weapon for survival was their comic imagination, a resourceful display of mother wit and rhetoric that kept their tormentors off balance. It was only natural, then, that such characters could turn a deaf ear on any pious slogans about the national honor with the same instinct for self-preservation that inspired Falstaff to cock an irreverent finger at an honorable corpse on the battlefield.

From O'Casey's point of view, if the patriots were now the guardians of the national honor, the playwright had to be the guardian of the national honesty. No matter how noble the cause, violent death was a dirty business, and the attempt to die for one's country could bring out the worst as well as the best in people. In O'Casey's plays the sacred Cathleen Ni Houlihan is transformed into a ruthless old bitch with a gun whose fanaticism leads to the slaughter of innocent people. He therefore created his own symbol of Cathleen in the stoical mothers of the Dublin slums, in a Juno Boyle or a Bessie Burgess. O'Casey's greatest profanation came in *The Plough and the Stars,* where he cast an ironic eye on the Easter Rising itself, one of the most holy events of patriotic sacrifice in Irish history. It was no surprise, then, that the mixed praise and hostility that had greeted his previous plays now exploded into riots in the theater and provoked Yeats's famous "You have disgraced yourselves again" speech from the stage of the Abbey to the protesting audience.[13] For the outraged nationalists, however, O'Casey's disgrace was his refusal to venerate the heroism of 1916, and his identification of Cathleen Ni Houlihan with the ragged women of the slums rather than with the patriots.

Some of that disgrace is also evident in the satiric desecrations of Denis Johnston in *The Old Lady Says "No!"* (1929) and *The Moon in the Yellow River* (1931), two allegorical plays that ironically mock the national hagiography of Ireland. When the first play, originally titled *Shadowdance,* was rejected by the Abbey Theatre before its acceptance by the Gate Theatre, the manuscript was returned to Johnston with what was to become the new title scrawled upon it. Although it is usually assumed that Lady Gregory was the one who had said "No!," it is symbolically more fitting that the Old Lady should have been none other than Cathleen Ni Houlihan herself, since the play is a grotesquely comic parody of the romantic and patriotic Ireland that was dead and gone. As the Blind Man remarks ironically to the old hag who represents Cathleen Ni Houlihan, "Do you not know, woman, that this land belongs not to them that are on it, but to them that are under it."[14] All the dead heroes are profaned and parodied by their own patriotic rhetoric and by the cynical people of modern Dublin, now a "Strumpet City," who have become weary of their sacred martyrs.

The chief character in this play-within-a-play is an actor who, while rehearsing for the role of the bold Robert Emmet, the leader of the abortive Rising of 1803 who was executed by the British, accidentally receives a knock on the head and thereafter believes he is actually Emmet. The play dramatizes his phantasmagoric "shadowdance" through past and present Irish history, with ironic allusions to the noble sentiments of Parnell and Pearse and every scrap of romantic poetry and patriotic idealism that had once captured the sentimental imagination of the people. But now the people ignore or mock this ghostly and ridiculous figure of Emmet, dressed like an extravagant pantomime character in his white plumed hat, green tunic, white breeches, and Wellington boots with gold tassels. "I am Robert Emmet," he proclaims to everyone, and one flippant citizen asks him, "Any relation to Paddy Emmet of Clonakilty?"[15] Searching for his beloved Sarah Curran, he comes upon "Two Young Things" from Phibsboro, Lizzie and Katie, who take him for a

116   THE PROFANE BOOK OF IRISH COMEDY

National Forester in his regimentals, the fancy-dress uniform
worn by the absurd Peter Flynn in the second act of *The Plough
and the Stars*—the savage irony of that antiheroic work is often
reflected in Johnston's play—and Lizzie blasts him with a
flourish of mock-O'Casey lingo. The harsh facts of life in
modern Ireland are in conflict with Emmet's romantic patriotism, Johnston tells us in a comment on the play, "particularly so
back in 1926, when several years of intermittent and unromantic
civil war had soured us all a little towards the woes of Cathleen ni
Houlihan."[16] This jaundiced attitude toward the Old Woman—
"Me four bewtyful gre-in fields," she laments in a parody of the
lines from Yeats's play—is effectively illustrated by C. P. Curran's sharp observation:

> The Actor-Emmet in delirium in search of his stage love goes
> vainly seeking through one vertigo after another of his own and
> Dublin's folly the proper habitat of his sentimentalism. His face
> lights up at every echo of the old familiar songs and shibboleths
> and clouds at the sardonic reality. Dublin eddies in little
> whirlpools of vulgarity and violence casting up a spume of poetic
> and patriotic verbiage in the iris of which he dimly discerns the
> object of his search. He is deafened by the gross vernacular of the
> streets, the banalities of the drawing-room and the cant of the
> little artists. He is spun from one maelstrom of madness to
> another until his final release from the pit in which Dublin lies
> chained to its phantoms. The play is a brilliantly witty and power-
> ful onslaught on that expression of sentimentality in which, to the
> dramatist's mind, Dublin lies. Kathleen Ni Houlihan of the poets
> has become a vampire Hag of Beare.[17]

If *The Old Woman Says "No!"* has the savage irony of a Swiftian
satire on romantic patriotism, *The Moon in the Yellow River* has
the witty irony of a Shavian dialectic on political idealism. Although the latter work lacks the theatrical brilliance and symbolic virtuosity of the former, Johnston now moves in another if
less spectacular direction by imitating Shaw's trick of appearing
to take both sides, or many sides, in an argument—here the
extended dispute over the blowing up of the Power House.
Technically *The Moon in the Yellow River* is a conventional
drawing-room play, a discursive work that alternates between
comic talk and tragic action, the two elements commenting on
each other so farcically and poignantly that it could be called

Johnston's *Heartbreak House*. One of the main tensions in the play lies in the fact that the dramatist divides and disguises his loyalties among the three central characters and there is no easy way to resolve the conflict between them: Dobelle, the enlightened nihilist who suffers from a "satiric neurosis" and presides over his converted military fort like an incapacitated Captain Shotover who knows too much to act; Tausch, the practical humanist in charge of the hydroelectric Power House opposite the fort, who wants to use the energy of the machine to help Ireland and all humankind; Blake, the political dreamer and IRA officer who wants to destroy the Power House in the hope of saving his country from the deadly progress of blast furnaces and dynamos. In the tragicomic end they all lose the argument, and Dobelle's fort, Ireland, remains a house of heartbreak. "This is no country!" Tausch complains. "It is a damned Debating Society! Everybody will talk—talk—talk—"[18]

The debating society responds by holding a mock trial, and Blake, as an amused but determined judge, asks everyone to vote on the charge that Tausch and his Power House are a threat to Ireland's beautiful green fields: "Our German brother stands indicted before the Bar of this Court on the gravest of charges. He has outraged the sacred person of our beloved Mother— Kathleen-ni-Houlihan."[19] But while Tausch has been waiting for the final verdict, Mother Ireland has already been exposed to many comic outrages by the Irish themselves. When IRA men invade the fort to search for arms, young Willie Reilly, dressed in the gunman's traditional trench coat with a handkerchief mask on his face, ominously waves a revolver and orders everyone to put up his hands; but Agnes, the servant, immediately recognizes him as her son and deflates the dignity of the Republicans: "If I put up my hands, it'll be to take you across my knee and give you a good skelping where you'd least expect it."[20] Mother Ireland is no match for Mother Reilly. The gunman joke continues when it is discovered that the explosives that were to destroy the Power House were carelessly left in the rain overnight and are too damp to ignite; and various attempts to blow up or burn down the villainous dynamo are comically thwarted. Even Blake, the visionary and articulate IRA Commanding Officer who wins all the verbal battles, is thwarted and becomes a grotesque and tragic victim when he is shot by a Free State officer who was once his Republican friend. Blake had anticipated his sacrificial but inglorious fate when he quoted the symbolic Chinese poem that gives the play its title:

> And Li-Po
> Also died drunk.
> He tried to embrace a Moon
> In the Yellow River.[21]

So Blake's idealistic embrace of Cathleen Ni Houlihan turns out to be an illusory dream of an idyllic Ireland free from British domination and German dynamos. The disenchanted Dobelle sides with Blake and against Tausch because he is himself an engineer who has lost his faith in machines as a form of human progress. Heartbroken, Dobelle recognizes that idealism is not enough for Ireland, and he accepts the murder of his friend Blake with the comment "The birth of a Nation is no immaculate conception."[22] And it turns out to be a farcical misconception when two amiable buffoons with their homemade gun accidentally blow up the Power House. The only thing sacred at the end is Dobelle's rediscovered love for his daughter, a neglected thirteen-year-old girl who replaces Cathleen Ni Houlihan.

Perhaps Johnston had a sentimental change of heart twenty-seven years later, when he wrote his 1916 play, *The Scythe and the Sunset* (1958). In his preface to the play he points out that he intended his title to be "an obvious parody" of *The Plough and the Stars*, and that, unlike the pacifist and mock-heroic O'Casey, he was now determined to celebrate the sacrificial heroes of the Easter Rising. Johnston had apparently decided to write a sacred, not a profane, play:

> Neither in verbiage, plot nor sentiments does this play of mine presume to bear any relation to its magnificent predecessor. The only point in so titling it lies in the fact that *The Plough* is essentially a pacifist play, implying that if only man had "a titther o' sense," these outbreaks of destruction and bloodshed would never occur. As a quiet man who, nevertheless, is not a pacifist, I cannot accept the fact that, theatrically, Easter Week should remain indefinitely with only an anti-war comment, however fine. So also, it may be noticed that the mouthpiece for most of O'Casey's pacifism is provided by his women; whereas in actual fact the women of Ireland, ever since the Maud Gonne era, have

been the most vocal part of its militancy. If I can claim nothing else, I can at least point with some complacency to the fact that—when it comes to the point—both my women are killers.[23]

So are his men, killers and killed for the greater glory of Ireland. Thus the "quiet man" managed to write a disquieting play that confirms Patrick Pearse's belief that "bloodshed is a cleansing and sanctifying thing." Furthermore, Johnston does not try to hide the fact that his hero, Commandant Sean Tetley, echoes the "militant idealism of Pearse" and similarly goes off at the end to seek a martyr's death.

It is therefore surprising that Johnston should insist that his play is an "antimelodrama," since the messianic resolution has all the trappings of a patriotic melodrama. He takes great pains to convince us that "it is far from my intention in this play to debunk 1916," and he insists "we must agree that the affair, on the whole, was a humane and well-intentioned piece of gallantry."[24] It is precisely that high tone of gallantry which romanticizes the total effect of the play, and Johnston's contrary conclusion is not entirely convincing when he says: "I have described my play as an antimelodrama, which may require some explanation. Most plays about national uprisings are based upon an assumption that the embattled rebels are always romantic, and that the forces of oppression are totally in the wrong."[25] The problem is that in trying to avoid this simplistic conflict between the good rebels and the evil oppressors, Johnston has created a climate of gallantry for both sides in the Easter Rising. Not only has he presented his Irish rebels as well-intentioned amateur romantics, he has also characterized his British oppressors as well-intentioned professional romantics. Unfortunately, the Irish Commandant Tetley and the British Captain Palliser often sound like proper military gentlemen who might have stepped out of R. C. Sherriff's *Journey's End* (1928), that sentimental glorification of patriotic sacrifice, each of them eager to outdo the other in gestures of heroic martyrdom. Tetley wins yet Palliser does not lose, since, in Johnston's manipulated version of the Rising, we are presented with the fiction that the rebellion would not have achieved its ironic success if Palliser, who may be an officer in the British army but cannot forget that he is by birth an Anglo-Irishman, had not prevented an ignominious early surrender by the rebels and thus assured a noble death for Tetley. An accomodation is even contrived for Palliser's noble death at the final curtain when he refuses the chance to escape and is crushed in the ruined building. So both men die a soldier's death for Ireland, and this sanctification of bloodshed is nothing if not melodramatic.

If the patriotic impulse in this play is too fervent, the comic impulse is too benign. The comic characters are inevitably upstaged by the glory of the Rising, by the gallant gestures of Tetley and Palliser, and by the only jealousy of Emer, that prudish fanatic who in her frustrated love for Tetley would quite cheerfully prefer to see him stretched out dead for Ireland than alive in her arms. She certainly is a "killer." This frigid rebel virgin with a hot machine gun is Johnston's Cathleen Ni Houlihan now, and she is the nightmare antithesis of O'Casey's mock-heroic, brawling, loving, and bighearted Cathleen of the tenements.

In an attempt at a comic diversion, Johnston allows the mad Endymion to wander in and out from time to time with his pronouncements of wise folly, but this historical figure plays little more than a cardboard cutout role, like one of the HELYS sandwich-board men in *Ulysses*. Dr. MacCarthy might have served as a useful comic chorus character if he had something significant to say, beyond trying to maintain an innocuous level of amusement with his stale jokes about Trinity College and "neo-Thom-cats." There is really nothing for the good doctor to do except nurse the wounded, make brave journeys into the combat zone to deliver messages, and get drunk and read Blake's *Marriage of Heaven and Hell* with Palliser. In a mild parallel Sherriff's British officers bravely read *Alice in Wonderland* in the trenches while they wait for death. In another attempt at ironic humor, Johnston created Roisin and her boyfriend Mickser, an unsuccessful effort to copy the earthy Dubliners of O'Casey's world, but their comic outbursts are too transparent, their comic idiom is obviously contrived, and like everyone else in the play, they are perhaps too easily convinced that the beauty of the rebellion is not terrible at all.

The sporadic comedy and irony have no sustaining functions in the play. At the end, when Tetley is preparing to go out to die beautifully for what he calls "liberty," the smiling Palliser confronts him with one of the few antimelodramatic speeches in the play: "You don't give a damn about liberty. All you care about is a cause. All causes always let you down."[26] But this sharp observation comes too late and is never developed; in fact, it is immediately undermined by the bloodshed of Tetley's martyrdom and Palliser's own self-sacrifice. Perhaps it is Johnston's own commitment to the cause that lets him down as a dramatist. Unlike the corrosively comic and compassionate *Plough and the Stars, The Scythe and the Sunset* is a well-intentioned piece of gallantry. Therefore, to confront Johnston with his own paradox, the patriotic conception of his 1916 play may have been too immaculate.

The Contentious Comedy of Lady Gregory

Lady Gregory's comic quarrel with Cathleen Ni Houlihan was less profane and more sympathetic than the skeptical attitude of Synge and O'Casey, but she was similarly disinclined to glorify or sentimentalize the national character. In most of her comedies she exploited the Irish propensity for unresolved farcical argument in a series of knockabout flytings. Like Synge and O'Casey, she created a war of comic words in her brisk dialogue, a rhetorical aggression that allows her disputatious characters to survive in a rural world that offers few material or spiritual gratifications. It was probably no comfort to the guardians of the national honor that Lady Gregory, instead of exalting the allegorical Cathleen, preferred to imagine the two contentious old paupers in *The Workhouse Ward* (1908) as the most symbolic representation of Ireland, for in a note to the play she wrote:

> I sometimes think the two scolding paupers are a symbol of ourselves in Ireland—is fearr imreas na uaigneas—"it is better to be quarreling than to be lonesome." The Rajputs, that great fighting race, when they were told they had been brought under the Pax Britannica and must give up war, gave themselves to opium in its place, but Connacht has not yet planted its poppy gardens.[27]

Fortunately the Irish never succumbed to Pax Britannica or poppy seeds, and if they were never to know the pleasures of peace or opium, they were too cheerfully quarrelsome to be lonesome. The symbolic McInerney and Miskell, Lady Gregory's two bedridden paupers, are frustrated and angry clowns who, like Beckett's Gogo and Didi, cannot live with or without each other and would rather console themselves with wild arguments than separate. Gogo's opening and symbolic line, "Nothing to be done," appropriately describes the contentious state of comic paralysis for McInerney and Miskell. When Mrs. Honor Donohoe, McInerney's sister, who has just buried her husband, arrives with the offer to take her brother home, she comes as if from Godot to say she can rescue only one of the paupers—one of the thieves may have been saved. McInerney is ready to go, and he donates his precious pipe to his friend, with the promise of an ounce of tobacco from time to time. But the hunger for talk is more vital than the puff of tobacco to the despairing Miskell, who cries out: "Ah, what signifies tobacco? All that I am craving is the talk. There to be no one at all to say out to whatever thought might be rising in my innate mind! To be lying here and no conversible person in it would be the abomination of misery!"[28]

This desperate plea for the salvation of talk changes everything. Never one to tolerate the abominable misery of silence himself, and with an innate mind of his own bursting with contentious talk, the irate McInerney decides he cannot leave the workhouse unless the peevish Miskell goes with him. Confronted by such perverse loyalty, Mrs. Donohoe, belying her name, Honor, abandons and damns both men: "Let the two of you stop together, and the back of my hand to you. It is I will leave you there the same as God left the Jews!"[29] And they are indeed both like scapegoat Jews cast out of respectable Christian society into the tragicomic exile of the workhouse ward, abandoned but happy. McInerney's gesture of loyalty to his friend is short-lived, for they immediately return to the comfort of quarreling again. Instead of being grateful for McInerney's unexpected devotion, the carping Miskell mocks Mrs. Donohoe's offer of hospitality and belittles what he calls the "periwinkle" meals she would have given them if they were both rescued, all of which provokes McInerney to such anger that he threatens to use physical force. In a savage speech that recalls the comic wrath of Christy Mahon and indicates that even the seemingly gentle Lady Gregory could strike the Ossianic note of barbarous comedy when the dramatic situation demanded it, McInerney, a seventy-year-old decrepit playboy with illusions of liberating power, says that if he were sufficiently aroused he would desecrate and destroy his own parents as well as his friend: "Stop your impudence and your chat or it will be the worse for you. I'd bear with my own father and mother as any man would, but if they'd vex me I would give them the length of a rope as soon as another."[30]

Nevertheless, we know that the savagery of this speech is more rhetorical than real as McInerney continues to play the braggart "Captain" Boyle to Miskell's parasite Joxer Daly, and they curse each other in a mock battle of hot words and flying pillows. In the comic chaos of the conclusion, the farcical flyting reaches its peak as the stage directions read at the curtain, "They throw all within their reach at one another, mugs, prayer books, pipes, etc."[31] Nothing is sacred and nothing can be done. Like most of her best comedies, this play ends without any corrective moral, or a return to a golden mean, for Lady Gregory wisely resists the temptation to soften or sentimentalize her antic comedians. It would be a mistake to compare her unreconstructed clowns with the chastised comic automatons of Molière's plays and Bergson's theories, for we invariably laugh with as well as at their transgressions. In Irish comedy the function of the laughter is noncorrective, contrary to that punitive function defined in Bergson's classic essay Laughter: "Laughter is above all a corrective. Being intended to humiliate, it must make a painful impression on the person against whom it is directed. By laughter, society avenges itself for the liberties taken with it. It would fail in its object if it bore the stamp of sympathy or kindness."[32]

With the exception of her later "wonder" plays and her modified versions of Molière's plays written in the Kiltartan idiom of her native Galway, there is no sign of correction, humiliation, or pain inflicted on the characters in The Workhouse Ward or her other comedies. Lady Gregory therefore belongs in the main tradition of antic Irish comedy to the degree that her clowns are not punished or reformed. Society gains no revenge at their expense, and their anarchic liberties only elicit our sympathy for their precarious condition as animated underdogs.

Only briefly do we see the character of the patriot as underdog exposed to a successful conversion, when, for example, the police Sergeant has a change of heart in *The Rising of the Moon* (1907), which, like Yeats's early *Cathleen Ni Houlihan,* was Lady Gregory's sentimental and atypical concession to the hagiography of Irish nationalism. More characteristically, her old miser in *Damer's Gold* (1912) is fortunately converted the wrong way, for instead of being gulled or humiliated like Molière's Harpagon, Damer manages to outwit his even more greedy relatives and, with the help of young Simon, decides to relive his youth by spending all his money on pleasure: the eccentric mock miser becomes a lively old playboy in the end. So conversions are really incompatible with the antic spirit of freedom that pervades such comedies. Again, in *The Jackdaw* (1907), Joseph Nestor's ingenious solution to Mrs. Broderick's financial dilemma whips up the townspeople of Cloon into a frenzy of bird-catching mischief, and there is no way to measure out rewards or punishments for such hilarious anarchy. Nestor's wisdom becomes Nestor's folly, and all the contentious culprits can only hide from the fumbling arm of the law.

Lady Gregory's comic characters seldom speak well of each other, but she never treats them with scorn or humiliating censure. She was the aristocratic Protestant lady of the big house who loved the Catholic peasants of Galway for their humanizing follies, and though she was a widow in her fifties when she launched her career as a playwright, during her remaining thirty years of writing she taught herself to use their comic energy and anarchy as the main source of her dramatic inspiration. Yeats and O'Casey, perhaps her two most significant writer friends, have recorded some illuminating comments on her vital contribution to the Irish theater. Yeats stressed the "purity" and sympathy of her comedy: "Lady Gregory alone writes out of a spirit of pure comedy, and laughs without bitterness and with no thought but to laugh. She has a perfect sympathy with her characters, even with the worst of them, and when the curtain goes down we are so far from the mood of judgment that we do not even know that we have condoned many sins."[33]

Perhaps those comic sins we have unconsciously condoned are sins only in the cold eyes of the repressed Irish Christians, for O'Casey saw in her a tempering of that Celtic Christianity with a mischievous pagan spirit when he described Lady Gregory's appearance and character as a unique combination of Christ and Puck, yet another fusion of Patrick and Oisín in the Irish temperament, in Irish drama: "Her face was a rugged one, hardy as that of a peasant, curiously lit with an odd dignity, and softened with a careless touch of humour in the bright eyes and the curving wrinkles crowding around the corners of the firm little mouth. She looked like an old, elegant nun of a new order, a blend of the Lord Jesus Christ and of Puck, an order that Ireland had never known before, and wasn't likely to know again for a long time to come."[34]

That careless and bright humor which moved beyond moral judgment was Lady Gregory's liberating insight as an artist. She did not see comic folly as a sin. Even when some of her defeated characters recognize their ridiculous transgressions in the end, like the two chimney sweeps, Darby and Taig, in *The Bogie Men* (1912), they are quite beyond Bergson's corrective humiliation. Without realizing it, the two sweepers have been waiting for each other as a potential savior, until their bubbles burst. This deceptive game of "waiting" for someone who doesn't come or something that doesn't happen occurs often in Irish comedy. After all their inflated illusions and arguments are exposed, after the "bogie men" scare each other, the defeated but unreconstructed Darby remarks philosophically: "And we nothing at all after but two chimney sweepers and two harmless drifty lads."[35] They come to nothing because like all antic clowns they are in their lowly state nothing but Shakespeare's unaccommodated men; they are free to drift into new follies, new illusions, new arguments and adventures, like the wandering Douls in *The Well of the Saints*, like the contentious Fluther and The Covey in *The Plough and the Stars*, "drifty lads" outside the paths of orthodox society, which is always the chief enemy of the wise fool.

Orthodox society and its repressive pieties are opposed and mocked by comic illusions in *Hyacinth Halvey* (1905). The title hero of the play is something of a harmless Shawn Keogh who desperately tries to become a dangerous Christy Mahon, but he is defeated by the gullible people of Cloon who are determined to make him a saint. The play is therefore a comic desecration of saintliness; it mocks the psychological need to exalt excessive virtue in spite of the fallibility of ordinary human beings. The mock-heroic quest for a savior in Synge's *Playboy* is reversed in Lady Gregory's *Hyacinth Halvey*, for whereas his irreverent Mayo peasants have a compulsion to create an outlaw hero to romanticize the attraction of sin, her pious Galway peasants have a compulsion to create a saintly hero to romanticize the attraction of virtue. In Synge's play the wages of sin finally lead to an excess of petty virtue; in Lady Gregory's play the wages of virtue finally lead to an excess of petty sin.

So the helpless Hyacinth is forced to commit some terrible "crimes" in the hope of liberating himself from the embarrassment of following the path of virtue. In a note to the play Lady Gregory says she discovered the theme quite by accident one day when she overheard some malicious gossip about a well-dressed man in the stalls of the Abbey Theatre and wondered if "extreme respectability might not now and again be felt as a burden."[36] In that burden of respectability she had touched one of the main conflicts of knockabout comedy. Extreme respectability does indeed become a heavy burden to bear in her play since the whole town of Cloon is convinced that Hyacinth, the new Sub-Sanitary Inspector, is a paragon of virtue: his very name and his high-sounding position shine with emanations of purity. In truth, however, he is another "harmless drifty lad," and so inept that his mother's cousin had to concoct the batch of glowing testimonials to his spotless character as the only means of persuading anyone to give him a job. So the inflated Hyacinth is himself to blame, along with the extremely gullible people of the town, for his saintly predicament as a sacred son of Cathleen Ni Houlihan, "devoted to the highest ideals of his Mother-land . . . a splendid exponent of the purity of the race,"[37] to quote from the fabrications of the mendacious mother's cousin.

Of course no one believes Hyacinth when he protests, "I am not as harmless as you think"; and in desperation he confides in Fardy Farrell, the dim-witted telegraph boy who is later accused of some of Hyacinth's "crimes." One wonderfully antic scene between Hyacinth and Fardy, which is worthy of Synge at his best form—and it should be pointed out that Lady Gregory wrote her play two years before the *Playboy*—vividly illustrates the need to desecrate the saintly image of respectability:

Fardy. There's not one in the town but will know before morning that you are the next thing to an earthly saint.

Hyacinth (stamping). I'll stop their mouths. I'll show them I can be a terror for badness. I'll do some injury. I'll commit some crime. The first thing I'll do I'll go and get drunk. If I never did it before I'll do it now. I'll get drunk—then I'll make an assault—I tell you I'd think as little of taking a life as blowing out a candle.

Fardy. If you get drunk you are done for. Sure that will be held up after as an excuse for any breaking of the law.

Hyacinth. I will break the law. Drunk or sober I'll break it. I'll do something that will have no excuse. What would you say is the worst crime that any man can do?

Fardy. I don't know. I heard the Sergeant saying one time it was to obstruct the police in the discharge of their duty—

Hyacinth. That won't do. It's a patriot I would be then, worse than before, with my picture in the weeklies. It's a red crime I must commit that will make all respectable people quit minding me. What can I do? Search your mind now.

Fardy. It's what I heard the old people saying there could be no worse crime than to steal a sheep—

Hyacinth. I'll steal a sheep—or a cow—or a horse—if that will leave me the way I was before.[38]

Thus poor Hyacinth longs to be the shiftless way he was before he was canonized; and the only fate worse than sainthood would be for him to obstruct the police and become known as a patriot. In the ironic terms of this comic revelation, then, Hyacinth mocks and rejects two of the most sacred figures in Ireland, the saint and the patriot. The only alternative open to him is to act on Fardy's absurd notion of a "red crime," and he steals what turns out to be Quirke's illegal sheep. Beginning with this petty crime, all of Hyacinth's "crimes" backfire and only make him appear to be more noble according to the quaint morality of Cloon. Since Quirke the butcher has regularly been dealing in "unwholesome" meat, he is saved from arrest because Hyacinth has stolen and hidden the evidence. And when Hyacinth next steals some money from the church poor box and tries to confess, he is admired as "a walking saint" for acting to save the reprehensible but innocent Fardy. Despite all his attempts to outrage the respectable people, Hyacinth is chaired triumphantly through the street as a savior by the townspeople, who apparently need a saint more than they need the truth. This one-act farce is therefore a wild lampoon of the vicarious pursuit of salvation as well as sainthood.

There are several remaining ironies. While Hyacinth recoils from the burden of respectability and tries unsuccessfully to break the law, the most respectable citizens of the town, the postmistress and the butcher, are surreptitious lawbreakers. And when Hyacinth is rewarded for stealing a sheep by being asked to substitute for the detained government lecturer on moral development and give the scheduled talk, "The Building of Character," he appeals to Fardy with "a hoarse laugh": "Why didn't you tell me, the time you advised me to steal a sheep, that in this town it would qualify a man to go preaching, and the priest in the chair looking on."[39] The comic irony of this speech is reminiscent of Christy Mahon's remark, when he realizes he has been richly rewarded for committing patricide, that he was foolish not to have killed his father years ago.

The parallel to Synge is also evident in *Spreading the News* (1904), which is constructed around the gallows humor of a mock death, the "killing" and comic "resurrection" of Jack Smith, somewhat in the farcical manner of the "slain" and "risen" Old Mahon in the *Playboy*. The action of the play occurs during a fair as a new magistrate appears, an absurdly consequential Dickensian judge who has come to reform a peaceful little town that he suspects is ripe with disorder and crime. As if not to disappoint the old fool, the town gossips and rumormongers, ably led by the deaf apple pedlar Mrs. Tarpey, inadvertently "spread the news" that a terrible crime has indeed been committed by the one man least likely to resort to violence, the timid Bartley Fallon. A precursor of the modern absurd antihero, and somewhat like Epihodov of the "two-and-twenty misfortunes" in Chekhov's *Cherry Orchard* (1904), the perpetually and comically morbid Bartley courts misfortune and happens to be obsessed with the idea of death, chiefly his own. His main pleasure in life seems to come from brooding about death, from dwelling on the macabre conditions under which his body might be discovered. For example, he is convinced that his wife will be buried before him, and he will then die alone and forgotten: "And the cat itself may be gone straying through the country, and the mice squealing on the quilt."[40] But a comedy of errors and misunderstandings, accelerated by Mrs. Tarpey's deafness and the rampant credulity of the tongue-wagging townspeople, soon transform the harmless Bartley into a suspected murderer, even though his overbearing wife has accurately described him as her "nice quiet little man."

Taken into police custody by the triumphant Magistrate, Bartley is accused of having committed a crime of passion in order to run away with Jack Smith's wife, and everyone, including Bartley's wife, turns against him, most of all the "murdered" Jack Smith himself, who suddenly appears in full health and fury. Confronted by the ludicrous discovery that he has been killed, and feeling highly insulted that the deed has been done by "a pleasant sort of a scarecrow," Smith compounds the gallows humor with an Irish bull: "I'll break the head of any man that will find my dead body."[41] In the end the rumormongering folly of the townspeople is outdone by the pompous Magistrate, who promptly proves that "the law is a ass" by arresting Jack Smith as well as Bartley and deciding to take both men to the scene of the nonexistent crime to confront them with the body of the real Jack Smith. In his lugubrious parting thought, Bartley can only lament that the real Jack Smith will surely reverse the game and murder *him* now.

In this hilarious game of mock murder Lady Gregory may not be up to the brutal comedy and gaudy rhetoric of Synge, but she has nevertheless constructed a one-act masterpiece of gallows humor with a remarkable economy of theatrical tricks and a disinclination to allow any of her characters to run away with the farcical scenes. Ensemble playing with fun for everyone is the key to her dramatic design. Synge, and even more O'Casey, often resorts to a superabundance of farcical episodes and heightened language, with virtuoso comic arias for some of the leading clowns, but there is not a superfluous action, not a wasted word, not a redundant character in all of Lady Gregory's brilliantly conceived one-act comedies. She relies on a single incident to spark the dramatic fire, and the contentious misunderstandings that grow out of it open up the comic frailties of all her characters. The eccentric people of her mythical village of Cloon force each other to invent their protective disguises and illusions, which can be admired for their unconscious ingenuity, even though their petty follies must inevitably lead to the comic hubris of farcical defeat. But it is a comedy of errors without punishment.

Like all Irish dramatists, Lady Gregory was intrigued by the humorous aspects of defeat and saw something attractive in her comic victims. Sympathetically as well as satirically she has described the prevailing Irish frailty as "our incorrigible genius for myth-making"[42]—a self-defeating yet self-liberating trait that has universal implications even if it is distinctly Irish. By "myth-making" she meant a paradoxical impulse that is illusory but necessary because, in the Freudian sense of myth or dream, it seeks to circumvent the dull or repressive obstacles of daily life. In her one-act plays the act of comic circumvention can release an incorrigible energy of fabrication that transforms a Hyacinth Halvey into a pseudosaint or a Bartley Fallon into a pseudomurderer. Under slightly different circumstances that same incorrigible energy can release myths or hidden images that transform ordinary dullards into comic dreamers.

The myths may be impossible to fulfill but they sustain and comfort the absurd dreamers, which is the case in one of Lady Gregory's best and favorite full-length comedies, *The Image* (1909). Because she could suspend moral judgment in her comedies, she was able to laugh at yet empathize with her frustrated mythmakers. In a note to the play she tries to explain her fascination for those defeated dreamers and even finds a spiritual strength in their futile hopes: "But if the dreamer had never tried to tell the dream that had come across to him, even though to 'betray his secret to the multitude' must shatter his own perfect vision, the world would grow clogged and dull with the weight of flesh and clay. And so we must say 'God love you' to the Image-makers, for do we not live by the shining of those scattered fragments of their dreams?"[43]

As a theorist Lady Gregory may come close to sentimentalizing her dreamers with this "God love you" embrace, but as a dramatist in the play itself she concentrates on antiheroic laughter and achieves a controlled sympathy without cloying sentiment. Fortunately, she must have realized that comedy can relieve "the weight of flesh and clay" more effectively than the bubble of romantic aspiration; that no dream is so sacred that it cannot be mocked without malice. All the characters in this play are "image-makers," and whether they soar high or low, they are destined to be defeated in a series of comic-Icarus crashes. Their farcical return to earth denies them their dreams but not the stubborn need to go on dreaming. Led by Thomas Coppinger, the stonecutter, many of the people are waiting for a hero to come, a savior who will somehow give them a sign of mysterious hope or the promise of immortality. But their waiting never becomes more than a mock quest, since the hero never arrives because he exists only in their image-making minds. When Coppinger's wife, whose dream is to emigrate and find salvation in America, laughs at her husband's wild dream of carving a headstone of a hero for posterity, he replies in a prophetic tone that will be ridiculed throughout the play: "Some thing will come to pass. Some great man might come wanting a monument that would put up my name for ever. Some man so great his death would put away laughter in Ireland."[44]

Some unusual and absurd events do come to pass in this little Munster town, but no man, alive or dead, is great enough to put away laughter in Ireland. As the image-makers become more cloquent in their fantasies, the laughter of defeat grows more pervasive. Malachi Naughton, an illiterate and strange "mountainy man" with a barbarous imagination, tries to fulfill Coppinger's prophecy by using a piece of driftwood to invent a great hero for the town. It has been a night of "signs and wonders" for Malachi, a dark night of miracles when the cock crowed prematurely, when two fighting whales washed up on the strand, when his straying goat found the sacred relic from the sea, a board on which Mrs. Coppinger read for him the mysterious name of Hugh O'Lorrha. This parody of supernatural symbolism does not deter the dreamers. At first the men argue over whether they should make their heroic statue for a proper patriot, for Brian Boru, Daniel O'Connell, or Parnell, but Malachi soon convinces them that the fabulous Hugh O'Lorrha must be celebrated as "the champion of Ireland." They decide to build their statue with the money they hope to get from the oil of the whales, and the authorities in Dublin confirm the plan to have Coppinger carve the great monument. When they are unable to discover any specific information about the life or exploits of O'Lorrha, they try to humor Peggy Mahon, the old midwife who knows everything worth remembering, in the hope that she may help them give birth to their imaginary hero. But mad Peggy is so full of her own image of preparing for the day when she will go to meet her dead husband, "one of the fair-haired boys of Heaven," that she can only laugh at the dreamers who mock her dream: "Ha, Ha! Ye are defeated, and ye earned defeat!"[45]

Everyone in the play is open to the ridicule of defeat. When the Dublin authorities send down a conventional picture of an orator that is to serve as the pattern for Coppinger's statue of the nebulous Hugh O'Lorrha, Malachi violently rejects this literal interpretation of the fantastic hero in his mind. For him there is a great gap between a stereotyped picture and a sacred image of one of the fair-haired boys of Heaven, to draw an analogy to Synge's Mayo peasants. With his "terrible scissors of a tongue," Malachi lashes out at the picture and the men in a barbarous flyting that vividly illustrates Lady Gregory's special gift for contentious comedy:

> Be off out of that you unnatural creature, or it is I will twist your mouth round to your poll! I'll blacken the teeth of you and whiten the eyes of you! It is your brain I will be putting out through the windows of your head! If I had but a rod in my hand it's soon I would make you limber! It is powder I will make of your bones and will turn them to fine ashes! It is myself is well able to tear you to flitters and to part your limbs asunder! Be going now before I'll break you in thirty halves. To be putting such an appearance and such an insult on my darling man! The devil skelp the whole of ye! My bitter curse upon the spot ye had planned out for to be putting up a thing the very spit of yourselves, and ugly out of measure![46]

There is a dark tone of heartbreak under the laughter here, and neither Synge nor O'Casey could have written a more effective speech on the anguish of comic defeat. And like those two playwrights, Lady Gregory characteristically avoids the danger of sentimentality inherent in the frustration of dreams by maintaining and concluding on a wild note of ironic farce. Malachi's sacred board predictably turns out to be a piece of driftwood from a wrecked ship named the *Hugh O'Lorrha*. And while the Munster men have been arguing about their nonexistent hero,

the neighboring Connacht men have drawn off the whale oil
that was to pay for the statue. Meanwhile the gullible authorities
have organized a ceremony to dedicate the spot for the monument, and during the third act the noise of the gathering crowd
is heard offstage, and the band is playing in honor of the hero
"that never was in it at all." Darby Costello, the philosophical
seaweed hawker who had originally wanted to build the status
for Parnell in spite of the objections of the clergy, tries to console
Thomas Coppinger with the comic wisdom that there must be
some comfort in failure. Perhaps all Irish comedians are shrewd
fatalists who have learned to live with defeat on the ironic terms
that Costello defines:

> Let you not fret, Thomas. There did no badness of misfortune
> ever come upon Ireland but someone was the better of it. You not
> to go shape the image, there is no person can say, it is to mis-shape
> it you did. Let you comfort yourself this time, for it is likely you
> would have failed doing the job.[47]

This comic rationalization may be the making of another
dream, yet there can be no permanent defeat for such clever
temporizers, and no end of their image-making. At the final
curtain, as the band moves in closer playing "O'Donnell Abu!"
and shouts of "Hi! for Hugh O'Lorrha!" are heard, the image of
the hero is desecrated and the image-makers run away in hilarious confusion, in order to live to dream another day, God love
them and laugh at them. For Eugene O'Neill's characters the
pipe dreaming is an illusory trap that leads to the tragic paralysis
of lost hope; for Lady Gregory's characters the image-making is
an illusory game that leads to the comic paralysis of suspended
hope.

As an extension of her ironic attitude toward idealism, *The
Image* is in its three tightly constructed acts a darker and more
profound comedy than her early short farces, and it stands out
as the most effective treatment of the antiheroic theme that appears in so many of her works. In one of her later "wonder"
plays, *Aristotle's Bellows* (1921), excessive idealism is again
mocked when a folk philosopher, the "cranky" Conan, sets out
to reform the people of Ireland with the magic of Aristotle's
enchanted bellows. In Irish folklore the Greek philosopher,
familiarly known as "Harry," appears as a figure of fun and

ridicule who is too wise for his own good. Similarly, then, the wise Conan is comically thwarted in all his attempts to save Ireland, for all his idealistic changes turn out for the worst. When some of the ambitious peasants get hold of his bellows and invoke the blast of its miraculous power, the farcical results are reminiscent of the legend of the sorcerer's apprentice. But for all this potentially rich comedy, Lady Gregory is less successful in this play because the single stratagem of the bellows is too limited to fill out the repetitive three acts, and because she chooses to be didactic as well as lighthearted, since in the convention of the fable that the play illustrates the laughter must point to a simplistic moral: beware of cranky idealists in a hurry to reform humankind.

Although there is no Bergsonian humiliation, Conan himself is finally converted from a "crabbed fault-finder" into a complaisant jester. Furthermore, presiding over the comic revels are two Puckish chorus Cats who supernaturally control the magic bellows and spell out the moral that human folly will remain in spite of all changes:

> *1st Cat.* We did well leaving the bellows for that foolish Human to see what he can do. There is great sport before us and behind.
>
> *2nd Cat.* The best I ever saw since the Jesters went out from Tara.
>
> *1st Cat.* They to be giving themselves high notions and to be looking down on Cats!
>
> *2nd Cat.* Ha, Ha, Ha, the folly and the craziness of men! To see him changing them from one thing to the next, as if they wouldn't be a two-legged laughing stock whatever way they would change.[48]

This may be a charming if commonplace game of laughing at the foolish mortals, but Lady Gregory's comedy is more effective when her unreconstructed characters revel in their follies than when her heavenly Cats moralize about them. It is well to remember that like all her "wonder" plays, especially *The Dragon* (1919), *Aristotle's Bellows* was written in the fairy-tale spirit of the Christmas pantomimes, and on this level of innocent entertainment it serves its modest purpose. When Lady Gregory becomes didactic in these plays, the only conversion she can accept is a sentimental "change of heart," which was her alternate title for *The Dragon*. For all this delightful flummery, however, there are

still many fine examples of contentious comedy in these Kiltartan fantasies; in Conan's peevish battles with his forgetful
mother and lazy sister in *Aristotle's Bellows;* in the lively flytings
between the henpecked King and his shrewish Queen, the scolding Sibby and her masquerading son Taig, in *The Dragon.*

Perhaps the most appropriate stage direction for all the comedies occurs in *The Wrens* (1914), in which the appearance of
William and Margy Hevenor, the Strolling Singers whose farcical arguments indirectly lead to the defeat and dissolution of the
Irish parliament, is noted in a simple phrase: "Enter Hevenor
and Margy, disputing." Like McInerney and Miskell, Martin and
Mary Doul, "Captain" Boyle and Joxer, Gogo and Didi, the disputatious Hevenor and Margy are Lady Gregory's "symbol of
ourselves in Ireland—'it is better to be quarreling than to be
lonesome.'" The paradoxical pleasure of contentiousness may
be the only abiding comfort of alienated comedians, who invariably "enter, disputing."

The Barbarous and Benign Comedy of George Shiels

George Shiels is a sheep in wolf's clothing in the theater who
does his best work when his wild disguise hides his simple heart.
He is a dramatist of conflicting impulses because he is equally
capable of creating barbarous and benign comedy, antic laughter that shakes the foundations of society and sentimental de-
nouements that restore and sanctify those foundations. Most of
his characters "enter, disputing," but after they have indulged
their comic contentiousness and rebellion in a variety of hilarious situations, they have to pull in their horns when Shiels melodramatically decides to solve their previously irreconcilable dis-
putes at the eleventh hour and rescue them from their eccentric
follies. But on those occasions when he is able to resist or even
mock that unmistakable streak of bourgeois benignity in his nature, he can be a richly inventive and entertaining artist of comic
desecration.

Perhaps Shiels's dilemma was that he was too prolific and too
popular for his own good. Over a period of twenty-seven years,
from 1921 to 1948, he wrote twenty-two plays for the Abbey
Theatre, most of them successful at the box office but only a half

dozen or so of exceptional artistic merit. During those years he saw only one of his plays performed, when the Abbey players were touring in Belfast, for he was confined to a wheelchair for all of his adult life, having been crippled as a young man in a railway accident in Canada. He returned to his native Ballymoney, Co. Antrim, where he had been born in 1886, and he was thirty-six years old when, with no previous experience in the theater, he began his career as a playwright, working at it steadily until his death in 1949. His most popular if not his best work, *The Rugged Path*, ran for a then unprecedented twelve weeks at the Abbey, and many of his plays, especially such an effective comedy as *The New Gossoon*, were often revived. He earned the dubious honor of being the most prolific writer of what has become known as the stereotyped Abbey "kitchen comedy," that genial and folksy play about rural Ireland which presented a home-grown version of the stage Irishman as an amiable and sentimental rustic, a harmless bumpkin who amused audiences and distressed critics for many years. There is therefore some justice in Peter Kavanagh's description of Shiels as "the great vulgarizing influence on the Abbey Theatre during the late 1920s and all through the 1930s."[49] Like most critics of Shiels, however, who are convinced that his popularity breeds contempt, Kavanagh, completely overlooking the most significant plays and Shiels's important contribution to the development of Irish comedy, unjustly puts him down as nothing more than a superficial writer: "Shiels was a dramatic journalist rather than a playwright. His work proved vastly amusing to audiences interested only in the superficialities of life. Any subject was good enough; many of his plays had really no subject at all. There was never any danger of his offending the crowd, and everyone was satisfied except those interested in genuine comedy."[50]

There are endless arguments about what makes comedy "genuine," and Kavanagh holds with those apprehensive critics who insist that farce is the "impure" element that undermines it, especially the low comedy of Shiels. The pejorative term usually invoked is "mere" farce, though there is nothing "mere" about the efficacious laughter of farce or low comedy when it mocks and deflates whatever is excessively sacred in society; and it is this element of low comic profanation that defines the genuine and palpable subject of Shiels's best comedies. Robert Hogan, who does recognize many of Shiels's dramatic achievements, nevertheless ignores the symbolic qualities in some of the plays and substitutes the term "asinine" for "mere" in describing the farce of Shiels: "Almost totally realistic, his plays range from asinine farce to adroit and wryly thoughtful dramas."[51] But there is nothing "asinine" about his first play, *Bedmates* (1921), a symbolic farce on the subjugation of Ireland that for its knock-about virtuosity can be compared favorably with the one-act comedies of Lady Gregory and O'Casey, contrary to Andrew E. Malone's statement that "beyond the fact that it provoked laughter there was nothing very notable in it."[52]

The three tramps in *Bedmates* who want to spend the night in Molly Swan's overcrowded doss house are two Irish ragmen and a cockney thimblerigger from Whitechapel; but they are also symbolic representations of the historical conflict between Ireland and England. After Pius Kelly, a high-spirited Catholic ragman from southern Ireland, and his friend Andrew Riddle, a nervous Protestant ragman from Northern Ireland, have arranged with Molly to share the last available bed, Bertie Smith, the shifty English con man, schemes to take Pius's place in the allegorical bed. Bertie, the comic and historical villain who plays the traditional British game of divide and conquer, decides on a plan to separate the two Irishmen: "These Irish 'ooligans are easier fooled than ruled, that's wat I see."[53] So while Pius is out drinking in a pub, Bertie forges a seditious document, surreptitiously places it in Pius's bag, and then helps the credulous Riddle discover it, "a Fenian plot to destroy the British Empire and burn all Ulster Loyalists at the stake."[54] Terrified by this disclosure of a perfidious "Popish Plot," Riddle allows Bertie to get into the bed with him while they wait for the return of the merry and unsuspecting Pius. When he arrives and realizes that England and Ulster have conspired against him, the outraged Pius identifies the allegory: "It's the story av Ireland come to life in a lodging-house; seven hundred years' history cut down to man's size."[55]

In a prophetic jest about the partition of Ireland, which separated the twenty-six counties of the Free State from six of Ulster's nine counties in 1922, a year after the play was performed,

Bertie urges Riddle to get a saw and cut the bed in half. This is too much for Pius, who threatens to kill the Englishman if he doesn't clear out and allow the two Irishmen to settle their own differences, which originally had been manufactured by the outsider. The farcical resolution completes the political parable in the end when Bertie is chased away and the two uneasy bedmates are finally reunited in their beleaguered bed. It is ironic as well as a sign of Shiels's exceptional insight that well over fifty years after its initial performance this allegorical farce remains such a durable and relevant work in the context of the tragic violence in Northern Ireland. And no doubt that initial performance was enhanced by the fact that the unknown young actor who played the leading role of Pius Kelly was Barry Fitzgerald. Subsequently, Fitzgerald and F. J. McCormick, the two finest comic actors in Abbey history, went on to create their most memorable roles in the comedies of Shiels and the tragicomedies of O'Casey. Fitzgerald was Paul Twyning, McCormick was Professor Tim; McCormick was Rabit Hamil in *The New Gossoon,* Fitzgerald was Mike Duddy in *Mountain Dew;* Fitzgerald was Dick Cartney and McCormick was Harry Kevney in *Cartney and Kevney;* McCormick was Felix Grogan and Fitzgerald was Paddy Grogan in *Grogan and the Ferret.* And they probably gave their greatest performances when Fitzgerald played "Captain" Boyle and Fluther Good, and McCormick played Seumas Shields and Joxer Daly in O'Casey's plays.

But the benign comedy of Shiels often gravitates toward sentimental conversions and therefore lacks the integrity and barbarous irony of O'Casey's dark comedy. O'Casey never cheats by trying to "civilize" or clean up such corrosive clowns as Boyle and Joxer. Shiels may come close to these profane rogues with his Pius Kelly, Dick Cartney, Rabit Hamil, and Felix Grogan, but he is just as likely to provide his shaughrauns or clever tramps with more bark than bite and disguise their noble hearts with a rough exterior of comic rhetoric, as he does with the title characters in *Paul Twyning* (1922) and *Professor Tim* (1925). In these two companion pieces Shiels uses his itinerant heroes as resourceful matchmakers in his favorite game of matrimonial farce in rural Ireland. Paul Twyning, a meddling tramp plasterer from Dublin turned loose in a Northern Irish village, sets out to repair James

Deegan's family affairs as well as the walls of his farmhouse. The plot is as predictable as it is amusing and in the inconsequential end love conquers a variety of parental obstacles. Deegan is a tyrannous farmer of seventy-five who has forced most of his children to emigrate to "Philadelphy" when they refused to give him blind obedience, and now he offers the same fate to his timid and terrified son Dan unless he marries the overaged and overdressed returned Yank, Daisy Mullan. A gray-haired "lad" of forty himself, the bumbling Dan is about to choose emigration because he prefers to marry the young Rose M'Gothigan rather than the "Ould Daisy Mullan, that could be my granny!" It is a lightweight version of the incident in the *Playboy* when Old Mahon attempts to force his son Christy to marry the old Widow Casey who had suckled him. The mythologized Christy liberates himself, but the mundane Dan requires the expert help of the ubiquitous Paul Twyning for his liberation. Taking advantage of the fact that the rural Irish are notoriously litigious, Twyning encourages Rose's equally domineering father, Denis, to sue Deegan for breach of promise, since Dan had given Rose a "conversation lozenger," a peppermint sweet containing some doggerel verse about undying love and marriage. While the fathers fight, the children tremble, until Twyning urges the reluctant Dan to fight for his love and freedom. Unable to rise to rebellious patricide, Dan threatens to destroy his prospective father-in-law in a mock-heroic scene that characterizes the farcical fun of Shiels:

> *Paul.* Now, Dan! Let the whole world see how you can defend your sweetheart. That blackthorn isn't an ornament, it's for practical purposes. Spit on the end of it and it's loaded.
> *Dan* (beside Rose draws the stick). I'm in flames, but I'll defend my own Rose to the death! I'll have to fight the Black and Indians in Philadelphy, and I may as well practise a bit at home. Now, Denis, I daar you!
> *Paul* (laughs). Emancipated! Behold Dan Deegan emancipated!
> *Denis* (going to Rose). Come on, gerril—
> *Paul.* Now, Dan Quixote, let him have it!
> *Dan* (with a flourish). Keep back! or, by all that's holy, I'll split you to the chin![56]

In this play the comedy of Shiels goes no further than this rhetorical profanation of parental authority and the quixotic

emancipation of Dan Deegan. The miraculous resolution elimi-
nates all conflict when the intractable fathers suddenly become
enlightened through intimidation, the emancipated lovers get
married, and even Paul Twyning himself unaccountably decides
to marry the brash Daisy and go off to Philadelphia with her.
There are seldom any ironies or loose ends at the conclusion of a
Shiels melodrama. This neat mixture of sentimental love and
comic spice is repeated even more blatantly in *Professor Tim,*
where the vagrant Tim only pretends to be a "poisonous prodigal" and finally turns out to be a wealthy and respectable professor who reforms a domineering mother and rescues a pair of
thwarted young lovers. Sean O'Casey was at the Abbey Theatre
on the opening night of this play, and the next day, in a letter to
Lady Gregory, he recorded his impressions, which effectively
expose the benign formula of Shiels's comedy-melodrama:

> "Professor Tim" was played to a crowded house, and appar-
> ently, thoroughly enjoyed by all. Parts of the play are very amus-
> ing indeed, & the acting was excellent—particularly the work of
> Barry Fitzgerald, Sally Allgood & F. J. McCormack. The play
> itself is, I think, a poor one, but it would be absurd to try to
> criticise the obvious innocency of the work.
>
> George Shiels is very fond of fashioning hearts of gold & hearts
> of silver, & here & there, a heart of oak, & one or two even
> labouring to be deceitful above all things, & desperately wicked,
> but then eventually become the broken & contrite hearts that
> no-one dare despise, and those who do not get a crown, at least
> will get a palm branch.
>
> I always feel panic-stricken & frantic to run for shelter when he
> starts at the end of his plays to bomb us with conversions, and
> seals all his characters with his own funny seal of righteousness.
>
> It's really terrible when you look into it.[57]

Fortunately there is no need to look very far into the transparent
machinery of this too-well-made play in which all comic misunderstandings are forgiven and every character wins a palm
branch or crown, especially the golden-hearted Professor Tim.
    Irish comedy at its best does not accommodate itself success-
fully to the imposed righteousness of happy endings, for its antic
laughter cuts deeper than the conventional theme of love and
marriage, the commonplace tale of romantic lovers thwarted
and then united. Irish comedy springs most effectively out of

rebellion and discord rather than romance and harmony; it concentrates on the wise folly of the rude mechanicals rather than the frivolous misunderstandings of the heartsick nymphs and shepherds. Somehow George Shiels must have been aware of this important distinction when he wrote his next play, perhaps his best work, *Cartney and Kevney* (1927), his most comic profanation of all that is sacred and superficial in middle-class life. In his seedy antiheroes, Dick Cartney and Harry Kevney, Shiels created two outrageously rude and high-class tramps who, as unconscionable parasites, are the comic enemies of society in a provincial Irish town. All notions of respectability and responsibility are anathema to them, for they would rather rot in their slothful ease than commit the cardinal sin of going to work. They are both, by Kevney's apt descriptions of Cartney, shining examples of "cowardice in excelsis," "psychological curiosities," "degenerates," and "freaks." With such remarkably profane credentials they must take their place in the mainstream of barbarous Irish comedy.

Dick Cartney, a flabby-faced drone who shuffles about perpetually in a shabby dressing gown and slippers, looking "like an old midwife," has not worked since he was sacked from his job as a bank clerk seven years ago, for the "mis-management" of seven thousand pounds, and even though he has a wife and three small children whom he cannot support, he has gone on living off his irate creditors with amiable indifference. He prefers to write hundreds of his famous begging letters asking for donations, loans he can never repay, and jobs he does not want. He owes four years' rent, and he has not even stepped outside of his house in five years. By his own admission he is physically afraid of work and would gladly go on enjoying seven more years of comfortable disgrace if his wife, his relations, and his creditors were not now conspiring to end his reign of indolence. Harry Kevney, his brother-in-law and partner in disgrace, is an ex-captain who served in the First World War and has for three years been living with the Cartneys and sharing with them an army pension to which he is not entitled, and which he is about to lose because his indignant father has informed the authorities that the claim for the pension is fraudulent. They are both ingenious failures who manage to remain likable in their stratagems for survival as genteel parasites, and they may even be enviable in their comic desecration of the Protestant work ethic. Perhaps Kevney's clever comments on Cartney accurately sum up the repulsion and attraction of such blithely self-indulgent folly:

> He that loves the danger shall perish in it. And he that loves safety shall rot in it. That's you, Cartney. You love everything that's soft and cosy. Your flabby face suggests an old easy-chair, an old lounge, an old featherbed. You're as selfish as a gluttonous baby, and as cunning as an old harlot. You're the living, breathing allegory of Indolence. But we all love you, Cartney.[58]

Kevney himself may not be a big, fat, lovable, spoiled baby like Cartney, but he is equally gluttonous and cunning and indolent. He is the brains of the partnership in successful failure, and as the drawing-room wit who is the occasion of laughter in himself as well as others he enjoys his frailties as much as those of his farcical friend. He insists that he can be just as selfish and dissolute as Cartney; he refuses to be reformed by a pious old maid, and he displays a refreshing sense of self-disparagement when he cheerfully accepts the blame for his disgrace: "I went rotten. That's all. Potatoes and onions and other vegetables go rotten, and man . . . No, the poor war's blamed for everything. 'Twas myself. I wasn't the right stuff to begin with, and the war found it out."[59]

Like his irresponsible friend, however, Kevney is an engaging rotter, and together they form an unholy alliance against the respectable world. Calamity strikes early in the first act when against Kevney's advice Cartney applies for and is offered a job as a bookkeeper in a paper mill, and they spend the rest of the play trying to avoid the balancing of the books. "Weren't you a great ass, Cartney," says Captain Kevney, with the comic wisdom of O'Casey's "Captain" Boyle, "to apply for a job so near to home? Sure, you might have known there was a big risk of you getting it."[60] When Cartney's longsuffering wife, Maud, suggests that they send for a motor car to drive him off to the job immediately, he appeals to his friend in desperation:

> It's transportation, Harry! It's the old press gang back again. Whipped away in a motor without a moment's notice—Oh, my stars, such merciless treatment! Harry, do something. Suggest

something. Don't let this outrage be carried out under your very nose.... Harry, this is a horrible ending. Going to be a mill-worker. Richard Gerald Joseph Cartney, a paper mill-worker! Judgment of God, how has this poor mortal offended you![61]

This burlesque of self-righteous indignation in an incurable parasite is only the horrible beginning of the revels for a middle-class clown who would rather quit than fight. Cartney may have acted as a brave rebel originally when he chose to marry without the consent of his father and Maud's father, but after seven years of determined failure he can only resort to comic subterfuge for survival. In the tradition of the *miles gloriosus,* however, he has not been too artful in his deceits, for everyone is aware of his self-dramatizing charades, and his furious landlord, Mr. Petrie, exposes his profane credentials with dire accusations and threats:

> You don't want work. You never wanted work. You low, mean, lazy son-of-a-prig, you'd rather beg than work. You've bled me white. You've bled the whole town white. You'd rob Heaven. (*Menacing him.*) Besides four years' rent you owe me sixty pounds of borrowed cash. If you don't take this job and get out of my house—as sure as Heaven, I'll murder you! I will—I'll murder you![62]

Even the threat of murder cannot drive Cartney to work, and in his stalling tactics he resorts to the mock-heroic protection of gallows humor when he pleads with Kevney to honor a last request by giving the condemned criminal a stiff drink before he mounts the scaffold. But the taste of whiskey only gives him the false courage of trying to escape from the job by hiding in the back kitchen, a ridiculous maneuver that nevertheless gains him a three-day reprieve from the mortal threat of work. While Cartney waits for the job or the bailiff to descend upon him, Kevney's illegal pension is suddenly stopped, and now both men, surrounded by the bourgeois enemy, decide to kneel and take a mock-military oath never to yield:

> *Cartney.* Repeat after me, Harry: To stand or fall together.
> *Kevney.* To stand or fall together.
> *Cartney.* To present a united front to the enemy.
> *Kevney.* To present a united front to the enemy.
> *Cartney.* Never to yield.

Kevney. Never to yield.
Cartney. Till Victory crowns our efforts.
Kevney. Till Victory crowns our efforts.
Cartney. We swear.
Kevney. We swear.
(*They stand up. Cartney looks almost heroic.*)
Cartney. There! You know now whether we've begun a new life or not. Let the storm roar. We defy it. Decrees? A fig for decrees! Landlord, spirit-grocer, huxters of all denominations—damn the whole lot! They thought to crush me, to break my spirit, to disgrace me. But they reckoned without Kevney. My ally, my commander! (*Expands his chest.*) As giants we await the onslaught.[63]

These puffed-up giants are only disarmed middle-class warriors and their bravado soon evaporates. With their backs to the wall and all avenues of escape cut off by creditors and relatives, the alliance is broken when Cartney chooses dubious reformation and Kevney chooses tainted exile. In the end Shiels creates one of his typical miracles when the two hard fathers, Old Cartney and Felix Kevney, experience a change of heart, though their errant sons try to enjoy the last laugh. Cartney is saved when his wealthy father agrees to adopt the whole family and take them into his big house, and in a parasite's parody of rebirth, which is conveniently motivated by the realization that he has at last been liberated from the terror of work, Cartney celebrates his expedient reformation with one of his rhetorical flourishes:

Hark! the transformation has come! I know it. I feel it. The heart is beating like an anvil, and the pulses are playing a strange tune. (*Rushing across to Old Cartney.*) Father, shake hands with a new son, a new man. (*Grabs his hand.*) Your voice has touched the lost chord. Give me one other chance. I'll be a credit to the old name—My stars, I feel emanicpated, regenerated, redeemed![64]

The mock moral of the tale may be that it pays to be a parasite. But Shiels softens this profane outcome by invoking Kevney's self-respect in the other half of the resolution. When his forgiving father tries to give him a fresh start, Kevney, amused by the unlikely spectacle of a redeemed Cartney but disinclined to repeat it, says no: "If you want to help me, leave me alone. Unlike Cartney, I can't be born again. They're putting Cartney back on the bottle, and teething rings, but I've lost my milk teeth once for all."[65] So when Shiels decides to drop the other shoe it turns out to be an ironic but moral one: Cartney's redemptive folly leads to Kevney's unrepentant wisdom. He is a failure, Kevney tells his father, because he has been affronted by the materialistic success of his respectable brothers; and he would rather choose to fail on his own terms than succeed on someone else's. He must emigrate to England now, he says, to redeem himself before he can be redeemed by others. Never one to overlook the concession of comedy to romance, Shiels gives Kevney a curtain speech to the patient woman who still loves him, Nora Denny, which presumably is meant to restore the somewhat shaken pillars of society:

> Nora, I've already told you that I won't be rescued like Cartney, or taught to work, or messed about. I'm going away for six months or a year—to recover a little of my self-respect. At the end of that time—if you still want me—I'll come back and marry you.[66]

The almost noble Kevney here is unrepentant yet reconstructed, and he sounds like a proper Anglo-Irish gentleman, in contrast to the repentant yet unreconstructed Cartney, who acts like an improper Irish jackeen. Perhaps Shiels is having it both ways in this play by complementing Cartney's allegory of indolence with Kevney's allegory of independence. It is a clever contrivance aimed at offering something to everyone. Nevertheless, the jackeen easily steals the play from the gentleman, for the dramatic success lies not so much in the straight-man intelligence of Kevney as in the irreverent clowning of Cartney. In the final analysis, the Harry Kevneys are the benign heroes of romantic comedy, but the Dick Cartneys are the barbarous antiheroes of antic Irish comedy.

In his next play, *Mountain Dew* (1929), Shiels seemed to be marking time and merely rehearsing for his following and far superior *New Gossoon* (1930). Both plays deal with the protest against the hardships of life in rural Ireland, though *Mountain Dew* is a kitchen melodrama that dodges and sentimentalizes the conflict, whereas *The New Gossoon* is a kitchen comedy that confronts and sentimentalizes the conflict. In the earlier play Brian Mulvenna robs seven thousand pounds from a bank in a desperate attempt to save his family and friends who are starving on the land. In spite of the efforts of the local people to protect the criminal, a popular theme in Ireland which Shiels developed in some later plays, Brian is caught and sent to prison, but before he goes he has this gritty scene with his sweetheart, Tess Moylen:

> *Brian.* This country has no future—at least this part of it. They're dug in here for another hundred years—the last refuge of ignorance and stupidity and slavery.
>
> *Tess.* Ireland was all right three days ago, Brian. It's yourself has changed in the meantime. When a decent Irishman commits a crime he starts blaming the country—
>
> *Brian.* Ah, hell! quit talking like a copybook—Can a man live on mountain-air and keep the Commandments? If they won't let us work in our own country, like human beings, I'm going to rob and steal. An Englishman or a Scotchman wouldn't stand for it. Is the fool Irishman to let himself be plundered and bulldozed from the cradle to the grave and remain a saint? I'll be damned if I stand for it.[67]

This is a promising collision between the damned and decent voices of Ireland, yet nothing comes of it because Brian is promptly hauled off to prison, or because Shiels simply lost interest in it. Brian makes another brief appearance at the end of the play when he escapes, comes back in the disguise of a priest to find and return the money he stole, and prepares to marry Tess without another thought about the "ignorance and stupidity and slavery" that originally provoked him. Meanwhile the main action of this rather muddled play is divided between the other two plots, the tragic fate of Henry Moylen, the distiller of illegal "mountain dew" who dies at the end of the second act, and the comic fate of Mike Duddy, the grotesque old farmer who unsuccessfully woos Tess's thirty-year-old sister, Anna. A seventy-year-old flamboyant mountain goat of a man, Duddy is a hilariously aggressive lover whose comic defeat provides most of the vitality and fun in the play. All the Duddys are wild geriatric comedians, for his ninety-five-year-old mother and seventy-odd-year-old sister Kate never cease fighting with each other and the world in their attempts to prevent the marriage of their darling "prodigal boy." One is reminded of Lady Gregory's view of the salvation of contentious Ireland—"It is better to be quarreling than to be lonesome"—when Duddy justifies the pugnacious nature of his ancient mother and sister: "That's what keeps her young. Herself and Kate snarl and fight from morning to night, but that's only for practice."[68] If Shiels had concentrated on the Duddys, the play might have achieved a more effective unity, as well as a comic life of its own to parallel the work of Lady Gregory.

Comedy is restored to its dominant position in *The New Gossoon*, one of Shiels's most deservedly popular plays, which successfully dramatizes the inevitable collision between rebellious youth and conservative age in rural Ireland. Young Luke Cary speaks and acts for the new breed of disillusioned gossoons who refuse to live by the old virtues of unquestioning obedience and back-breaking work. But instead of robbing a bank like Brian Mulvenna, Luke only steals some sheep from his mother's farm in order to buy a motor bike to liberate himself from the drudgery of farm labor by racing wildly around the countryside. Since he is an angry but not too clever young man, his rebellion is limited to noise and petty "sins," such as defying his mother, gambling on greyhounds, and flirting with country girls at dances. He is a comically flawed and ineffectual hero who knows what is wrong but can't do anything about it, beyond making himself a nuisance and menace to his mother and neighbors and any livestock that happen to stray on to the road as he races by on his motor bike, the symbol of his protest and freedom. Like his terrified mother, his stern uncle Peter is shocked by the new breed of youth and warns that the temptations of Satan have invaded Ireland and destroyed the old values:

> This country's going to hell at a hundred miles an hour! Petrol and pictures and potheen and jazz and doles and buses and bare legs and all sorts of foreign rascalities. You and I were content to toil and moil for a living, but the new breed wants to be well paid, well fed, and idle.[69]

This quaint notion of toiling and moiling contentedly in an agrarian Ireland of nineteenth-century hardships was to survive for the next generation in Eamon de Valera's dream of "frugal comfort" for his people, and it was to be exposed to savage mockery in all of O'Casey's later pastoral comedies. Shiels is satisfied to laugh at it without bitterness, and to soften the impact of his mild protest, he adds his usual mixture of matrimonial farce. When Luke is not rebelling against his mother and uncle, he fights and flirts with his sweetheart, Sally, daughter of Rabit Hamil, the comic rogue of a poacher who possesses all the barbarous guile and wisdom that might have truly liberated the callow Luke. Sally, who has inherited her father's sharp tongue and wit, is something of a high-spirited Pegeen Mike who is determined to control and win Luke on her own terms; and she gains her victory in the end since Luke is only an immature playboy who needs a mythic image of his potentialities more than he needs a motor bike. "I like fighting with men," Sally says, and she has good reason to enjoy the game, since she makes up her own rules and usually wins. Luke's mother, Ellen, on the other hand, a respectable woman who plays by the rules of propriety and snobbery, hopes to control her son by marrying him off to some decent girl; and she is shocked when it appears that Sally might be the girl, for she considers the Hamils to be no better than tinkers or "vermin." But respectability is discredited when, after the Hamils are accused of being dishonest, Luke confesses his own dishonesty and reveals his mother's culpability in provoking his misdeeds: "I've stolen sheep myself, and money too. I'd to steal eggs and sell them to get cigarettes and petrol. She only give me sixpence on Saturday night, and a shilling at Christmas. Isn't that meaner than stealing?"[70]

Luke may be a playboy without a mythology, but he has the indignation and the ability to articulate the grievances of his generation. It was the generation born too late to become intoxicated by the fanaticism of national sacrifice—death and glory for the honor of Cathleen Ni Houlihan during the 1916–22 "troubles." It was the generation that refused to respond to the romantic call for sacrifice on the land; and when the moralizing Uncle Peter strikes that sacred chord of the national idealism by urging Luke to work hard and take "pride in the land," the new gossoon replies:

> But I've none. I take no pride in drudgery. All that poetry about the young Irishman's passion for the red soil is bunk. If the damned thing can't afford a decent living without tearing our guts out day and night—then it's only slavery, and should be worked by Chinamen.[71]

This desecration of agrarian idealism is also a reply to the same people who had earlier attacked Synge for his farcical and unflattering characterization of Irish country life. In an explanation of why Maud Gonne and Dudley Digges had walked out in protest against *In the Shadow of the Glen* in 1903, Padraic Colum wrote: "They felt the play let the Irish country people down. In those days it was an article of faith that the country people were the heart, soul and voice of Ireland."[72] Now Shiels was questioning that article of faith because, according to Luke Cary, the country people themselves had been let down by the harsh and inhuman conditions on the land. Colum himself had posed this conflict in his early popular Abbey play, *The Land* (1905), but he took the side of the agrarian idealists who were full of poetic passion for the red soil. Toward the end of his play, when some of the farmer's sons become disillusioned and decide to emigrate, one of the young men who remains on the land proclaims this rousing curtain speech to his people and the audience and the nation:

> "Men of Ballyhillduff," you might say, "Stay on the land, and you'll be saved body and soul; you'll be saved in the man and in the nation. The nation, men of Ballyhillduff, do you ever think of it at all? Do you ever think of the Irish nation that is waiting all this time to be born?"[73]

The chauvinistic Uncle Peter touches the same raw nerve of the national pride, and when he responds to Luke's disillusionment by invoking the memory of the men who fought and died for the Irish nation, the collision between the profane and pious voices of Ireland, Oisín and Patrick all over again, comes to a head:

> *Luke.* He was hard up for a cause that fought and died for this country. I'd as lief fight and die for Spike Island.
> *Peter.* When you get the farm you shouldn't waste your time growing oats and potatoes—you should grow petrol and potheen, and motor-bicycles and leather helmets—
> *Luke.* And old men. It's an ideal country for growing old men. They can live on a diet of legends about Brian Boru and the Big Wind.
> *Peter.* It's better than a diet of greyhounds and Black African dances.
> *Luke.* If 'twasn't that 'twould be something else. Everything in this country is a mortal sin. It's a mortal sin to keep a greyhound, or a motor-bike. It's a mortal sin to go to a dance, or smoke a cigarette.

It's a mortal sin to speak to a girl after sunset—I don't know how the population of this country was over eight millions—at the time it was so holy, and no motor-bikes.[74]

When the argument comes round to repressed sex, the fate of Ireland shifts to matrimonial farce and the fun of sorting out the various couples. Rabit Hamil, who is about to lose his housekeeping daughter to Luke, temporarily proposes marriage to Mag Kehoe, the Carys' gossiping and complaining servant girl, who talks as hard as she works: "The man that freed the blacks in America should be President of Ireland."[75] But since Rabit was interested only in her life's savings, he decides to sacrifice the love of material reward and remain a liberated poacher rather than an enslaved husband. Ned Shay, the upright farm laborer who has run the farm for twenty years for the widowed Ellen Cary, is too shy to propose to her, but the meddling Peter, who has advice for everyone, urges him to ask for her hand. Peter is a richly drawn character, full of comic contradictions and eccentricities, and if he can't understand Luke, he can provoke Ned into marriage: "Lord above, such a wooden man! Such a frosted turnip! It's no wonder you're just where you started. A fine woman going to loss before your eyes—If you'd been with Eve in the Garden of Eden, you'd be there yet."[76] Meanwhile Sally has been a scheming Eve who knows that love without marriage cannot tame the savage beast. But since all the fight goes out of Luke when he becomes a lovesick swain, he is a willing victim for matrimony in what suddenly and sentimentally turns out to be the best of all possible agrarian worlds. If Shiels raises more issues than he resolves in this play, it is mainly because he allows the barbarous edge of the comedy to be blunted by the traditional machinery of romance. Only the untamed Rabit Hamil escapes the benign embrace because, as one of Shiels's most artful rogues, he rejects holy matrimony and respectability, refuses to be civilized, and therefore retains his comic freedom.

Since there are no young or old lovers to be wedded and bedded properly or improperly in *Grogan and the Ferret* (1933), Shiels is able to concentrate entirely on comic roguery and folly in one of his liveliest farces. This play is constructed with a music-hall simplicity that calls for a succession of loosely connected comic episodes in which the knockabout characters strive to abuse and outwit each other. Felix Grogan and his neighbor Miss Hatty have been fighting for forty years, the now bankrupt publican who has enjoyed a life of ostentatious disrepute and the eavesdropping "ferret" of a scandalmongering old maid who sees and hears and disapproves of everything associated with Grogan and his dissolute friends. Grogan is described as "a big old giant of a man, battered up with pains and hard drinking, and leaning on a stick,"[77] a comic ruin of a "bankrope" who has been sleeping in a horse box in his decaying stable since he lost all his possessions. He has been surviving illegally on an old-age pension that keeps him and his cronies in drink, but in the latest skirmish Miss Hatty discovers he is only sixty-seven instead of seventy and informs the authorities, who have just decided to revoke the pension. The main action of the play is centered around Grogan's attempt to avenge himself at Miss Hatty's expense and keep out of the workhouse by regaining his pension. Miss Hatty, whose head keeps popping up over the garden wall to ferret out the latest rumors and counterstratagems, is determined to get rid of her seedy neighbor, and her moralistic judgment of him is perhaps the best testimonial to his unimpeachable status as a barbarous clown: "What could you expect? After a long life of drinking, thieving, and fighting—what could you expect? The man was a born savage, a menace in any civilized community. How he escaped the gallows is a miracle."[78]

How he escapes from Miss Hatty is a greater miracle. Meanwhile he is comforted and abetted by his clever parasite of a servant and drinking companion, "a picturesque toper" who always refers to himself in the third person as "P. Blakes" and has lived through what he calls "The Rise and Fall of the Grogan Empire." Blakes plays a convincing Joxer to Grogan's conniving "Captain" Boyle, and they are joined in mischief by the patriotic John Byrne and his nephew Fred. Byrne's grocer's shop is the meeting place for Grogan's gang, and it is rightly called "John Byrne's Parliament" because it is there that debates are regularly held to plan the end of the tyranny of Miss Hatty against Grogan and the British government against Ireland. While Grogan anticipates the Rise and Fall of the Hatty Empire, Byrne considers the Rise and Fall of the British Empire. And Fred Byrne, who has just come back from Africa and sounds like an expert on the

Rise and Fall of the Black Empires, warns the puritanical Miss Hatty that the Irish are no different from any other people when it comes to crusades of respectability and reform: "Any person who attempts to reform a native—whether here or in Africa—is a plain lunatic."[79]

Unusual for Shiels, there is not an ounce of sentimentality in this play, since the antic comedians are all beyond pathos and often discredit each other with derisive laughter. Until the scheme for dealing with Miss Hatty is worked out, the argument over Grogan's future is narrowed down to going to live in Scotland with his daughter or going to live on a farm with his brother Paddy. But Paddy's mountainy wife drives a hard bargain and will take Grogan in only if he can pay for his keep out of the pension he no longer has. Amid the comic haggling over the nonexistent money, Paddy, always in mortal fear of his shrew of a wife, who is ready to skin Grogan for a few shillings, tries to assert his tainted courage by attacking the shifty and vulnerable Blakes: "Moses, if ye speak back to me, I'll split your skull wi' the stick! Shure the wurl knows you're only an ould sot—would steal the cross off an ass."[80] In the spirit of the flyting, the rhetoric of skull splitting, more than the deed, is a favorite pastime in rural Ireland. But "John Byrne's Parliament" has been in session and Fred has come up with a solution to avoid violence and save all faces. He has pulled some strings in Dublin to reinstate Grogan's pension so that he can go to live with his brother Paddy, having first convinced Miss Hatty that if she doesn't try to block the pension again, she has seen the last of Grogan. Since the contentious Grogan and Miss Hatty both feel victorious and "exit, disputing," it is a happy ending with good riddance all round and without any melodramatic conversions.

In a number of his later plays Shiels became more interested in crime than in comedy, and in defending the household gods of law and order he had to minimize the profane and antic laughter to such an extent that his crime plays cannot be called comedies at all. It is also possible that his comic well was running dry. In a benign melodrama such as *The Jail-Bird* (1936), a miscarriage of justice is put right when Dan Farran, returning to his village in disguise after serving a prison term for a crime he didn't commit, is befriended by a kindly widow until the real criminal is discovered and Dan's innocence is proclaimed, after which he marries the good widow and all's well. What can one do with such heartwarming platitudes but shed tears over them, feel panic-stricken and run for shelter, or ignore the whole thing as a miscarriage of drama? There is some improvement in the quality of the melodrama in *The Rugged Path* (1940) and its sequel, *The Summit* (1941), where the theme is murder and the unwritten code that brands as an informer anyone who dares to help the police catch the criminal. It is a grim business that does not accommodate itself to comedy, though Shiels allows himself the indulgence of creating one of his clever vagabonds in the tinker Marcy. At the end of the first play an intimidated Irish jury refuses to convict Peter Dolis of the murder that everyone knows he committed, and the Tansey family who "informed" on him are left to the vengeance of the malevolent Dolis family; but this is such a sinister ending that Shiels was prepared with a sequel in which the whole community unites to banish the murderer and reassert the supremacy of law and order.

Shiels is not much of a thinker in the theater, and when he does try to become "thoughtful" in his problem plays he is not very "adroit" or "wry," and he is certainly not very comical. He was not an innovator in the theater, for in technique he was a conservative naturalist, never experimented with new forms, and ventured into the area of comic symbolism only in his first play, *Bedmates*. In latter years he was preoccupied with the vindication and rehabilitation of former prisoners and the triumph of justice, all of them commendable concerns, but they represented the decline of his dramatic and comic talent. "Let right be done!" is a noble sentiment, as Terence Rattigan has demonstrated with proper Victorian optimism; but for fatalistic Irishmen whose country had been exposed to 700 years of British injustice, there were at least 700 reasons to suspect that right would not be done in Ireland. The situation cried out for political or comical rebellion, both of which apparently the aging Shiels, perhaps confined too long to chronic illness in a Northern Ireland village, failed to understand.

The Barbarous and Profane Comedy of Brendan Behan

Brendan Behan was a radical anarchist in the theater who experimented freely and even recklessly with the episodic structure of drama, and who in the tradition of O'Casey's tragicomic knockabout concentrated on the barbarous rituals of political and comical rebellion in his plays. There is a rich texture of mythic profanation in Behan's uninhibited desecration of Ireland's household gods, for his comic characters abundantly illustrate in their fabulous posture the view held by Freud and Lévi-Strauss that "myths express unconscious wishes which are somehow inconsistent with conscious experience."[81] In Behan's works the world of experience creates obstacles of restraint that must be mocked and undermined by his antic comedians, who are the self-appointed spokesmen for the unconscious wishes of the Irish folk imagination, an imagination that Yeats had described as "wild and ancient." Behan, in his own instinctive way, understood and dramatized the Freudian concept of comic circumvention: the sharp edge of his knockabout laughter represents "a rebellion against authority, a liberation from its pressure."[82] That wild act of comic liberation involves a structural as well as a thematic rebellion, for in *Borstal Boy* (1958), his unqualified masterpiece of autobiographical writing, as well as in his plays, *The Quare Fellow* (1954), *The Hostage* (1958), and the posthumous *Richard's Cork Leg* (1972), he circumvents and profanes all authority with an ironic technique that might be called the music-hall principle of comic diversion.

Music-hall comedy is a loosely organized catchall of knockabout routines composed of gags and pratfalls, parodies and burlesques, songs and dances, all of which are calculated to divert an audience from the serious business of life; and those routines often function as a profane commentary on the serious business. The ironic connection between the serious main plot and the farcical subplot was a popular device in many Elizabethan plays, as we know, for example, from the antics of Wagner in *Dr. Faustus* and the drunken Porter in *Macbeth*. But in Irish comedy, especially the plays of O'Casey, Beckett, and Behan, that Elizabethan structure is inverted because the farcical subplots, largely composed of episodic music-hall routines, dominate the stage, while the serious main plots, dealing with civil war, metaphysical speculation, and executions, run their secondary yet significant course offstage. This structural inversion defines the uniquely open and contingent form of *The Quare Fellow* and

The Hostage, since Behan creates his music-hall diversions in order to entertain his audience while the serious business develops fitfully yet organically in the wings, until he gradually moves it to the center of the stage from time to time, finally allowing it to merge with the antic routines with a tragicomic jolt. And even that jolt is inverted and mocked by gallows humor when the prisoners argue and toss for the sacrificial quare fellow's letters, and when the dead hostage is resurrected and sings a jesting song. These comic diversions underscore the tragic horror, for Behan is of course on Christ's side even as he winks at the Passion with a last laugh.

In a reply to some critics who had objected to what they believed to be the gratuitous laughter and disjointed form of *The Hostage,* Behan defended his dramatic methods in a forthright statement that could be applied to all his works:

> I wrote the play very quickly—in about twelve days or so. I wrote it in Irish and it was first put on in Irish in Dublin. I saw the rehearsals of this version and while I admire the producer, Frank Dermody, tremendously, his idea of a play is not my idea of a play. I don't say that his is inferior to mine or that mine is inferior to his—it just so happens that I don't agree with him. He's of the school of Abbey Theatre naturalism of which I am not a pupil. Joan Littlewood, I found, suited my requirements exactly. She has the same views on the theatre that I have, which is that the music hall is the thing to aim at for to amuse people and any time they get bored, divert them with a song or a dance. I've always though T. S. Eliot wasn't far wrong when he said that the main problem of the dramatist today was to keep his audience amused; and that while they were laughing their heads off, you could be up to any bloody thing behind their backs; and it was what you were doing behind their bloody backs that made your play great.[83]

So behind their backs and under their laughter Behan the jester was building up an indictment of the hypocrisy and fanaticism that warped people's minds, and the noble reasons they gave for the ignoble ways they exploited and killed each other. This was hardly a new indictment, since variations of it had long provided the main thesis of naturalistic literature since Zola. Behan, however, was in revolt against naturalism as well as society, and what made his plays "great" or memorable was not so much the unorthodox ingredients as the outrageous way they were mixed and measured out: take a superabundance of comic diversions well spiced with song and dance and a minimum of serious plot, add a ton of anarchic knockabout to an ounce of righteous indignation, a barrel of antic irreverence to a teaspoon of morality, then attach a slow farcical fuse, sit back, and wait, laughing. If most uninhibited audiences entered into the spirit and fun of Behan's revels more enthusiastically than some middle-class critics, part of the reason may be found in T. S. Eliot's observations:

> With the decay of the music-hall, with the encroachment of the cheap and rapid-breeding cinema, the lower classes will tend to drop into the same state of protoplasm as the bourgeoise. The working man who went to the music-hall and saw Marie Lloyd and joined in the chorus was himself performing part of the act; he was engaged in that collaboration of the audience with the artist which is necessary in all art and most obviously in dramatic art.[84]

On some notorious occasions during performances of *The Hostage* in London and New York, Behan himself suddenly appeared on stage briefly and became part of the singing and dancing in an unprecedented collaboration between the dramatist, the actors, and the audience. The irrepressible Behan may have stepped over the line of artistic objectivity, but his merry indulgence must have been prompted by the music-hall spirit of fun, as well as the excess of spirits he had probably consumed, and this wild behavior should not prevent us from realizing that in his writing he was a serious comic artist with his own unique idea of a play.

When Behan's idea of a play led to his quarrel with Frank Dermody over the music-hall diversions in *The Hostage,* the dispute was somewhat similar to O'Casey's quarrel with Yeats over the experimental form of *The Silver Tassie.* Both dramatists were determined to break away from the structural stereotypes of Abbey Theatre naturalism, the predictable form of the well-made play, which O'Casey had already done in *The Plough and the Stars,* though Yeats and his directors could not see this, and which Behan had already done in *The Quare Fellow,* though Dermody and many critics could not see this. O'Casey was distressed by the dictatorial Yeats because he suspected that his new methods as well as his play had been rejected; but thirty years later Behan could be magnanimous with the powerless Dermody because he knew that his new methods and his play had been performed successfully. On both occasions, however, the limitations of middle-class naturalism had been exposed by two dramatists from the working-class north side of Dublin who had learned much of their craft from the free form of the music-hall theater, unorthodox dramatists who had their own ideas of a loosely structured play with song and dance and a wild mixture of comedy and tragedy. O'Casey later wrote *Purple Dust* (1940), *Cock-a-Doodle Dandy* (1949), and *The Drums of Father Ned* (1960), all of them antic comedies with dark overtones of satiric vision and pastoral symbolism in which he fully exploited the music-hall principle of high spirit and low comedy. Behan unfortunately died in 1964 at the age of forty-one, too soon to fulfill his dramatic genius, which nevertheless rests securely on the extraordinary achievements in *The Quare Fellow* and *The Hostage*.

Those achievements have often been questioned, representatively by two very intelligent Irish and American critics, Kevin Casey and Robert Brustein, who offer some concessions of praise but basically object to Behan's plays because he breaks the "rules" of drama. Perhaps too much intelligence can be a dangerous thing, especially if it interferes with the willing suspension of disbelief in the free-wheeling form of music-hall-inspired drama. Like many critics, Casey prefers *The Quare Fellow* to *The Hostage*, though he rigorously measures both of these unconventional plays by what he calls the "conventional discipline" and conventional "machinery" of dramatic construction:

> In "The Quare Fellow" a maximum amount of bizarre comedy is extracted from a hauntingly tragic situation. In "The Hostage" a maximum of farce is loaded into a situation which, under the strain, collapses into something that is neither comic nor tragic. Although "The Quare Fellow" is entirely devoid of the machinery which is generally thought to be essential for dramatic construction, it does move, with a strong degree of inevitability, towards its climax. . . . They represent, of course, a perfectly valid approach to the theatre but if variety is to be the object of the exercise, it should be balanced by some degree of conventional discipline. Control, in "The Hostage" is hidden in the wings: irrelevancy is the key-note of the proceedings and the piece, although theatrically effective within its own limitations, is by no means as good as "The Quare Fellow."[85]

These comments are tainted by the sort of scholastic carping that demands that all plays must conform to a preconceived pattern of "control," a formal structure and discipline the precise nature of which Casey does not identify and few critics, from neo-Aristotelians to neo-Marxists and neutrals, can agree upon. It is safe to say only that historically all innovations in art have been criticized by precisely those formalistic old standards from which the new art seeks to liberate itself.

In a review of *The Hostage* Robert Brustein continued Casey's exercise in academic strictures by deducing that Behan's drama lacked an "organizing principle" as well as "dramatic logic," though of course he failed to identify which principles of dramatic organization and logic he had in mind. First Brustein tried to be fair by holding Behan up as "a welcome presence in our sanctimonious times," but then he put him down as an impure and totally disorganized example of what he called "the destructive Libido":

> Behan is waging total war on all social institutions excepting brothels and distilleries. But though destructive Libido can be the source of a lot of fun, it is hardly an organizing principle, so the author's assault on order leaves his play almost totally lacking in dramatic logic. Its substance is taped together with burlesque routines, Irish reels, barroom ballads, and outrageous gags (some old, some new, some borrowed, but all "blue"), while its scarecrow plot is just a convenient appendage on which to hang a string of blasphemous howlers.[86]

Some unenthusiastic Irish critics had made the same complaint about *The Quare Fellow* when it was first produced by Alan Simpson and Carolyn Swift in Dublin at the Pike Theatre in 1954 and after its production by Joan Littlewood in London at the Theatre Royal in 1956, charging that it was only "a stringing together of music-hall sketches."[87] The prim people who are unamused by "mere" farce usually complain about "mere" music hall. It is not a foregone conclusion that a dramatist who writes a farcical play in an episodic music-hall form is "merely" having fun—though he certainly is entertaining his audience with his wild antics as well as arranging some surprises and jolts behind their backs—or that in rejecting the structural proprieties of the well-made play he must end up with a badly made play. Farce is not formless, it only seems that way, for there is reason in mischief as well as madness, as Eric Bentley points out in his wise discussion on farce. Bentley insists that "every form of drama has its rendezvous with madness," and that "in farce chance ceases to seem chance, and mischief has method in its madness":

> Our colloquial use and abuse of words is always full of meaning, and what we mean when we say of some non-theatrical phenomenon, "It's a farce," or "It's absolutely farcical," throws light back on the theatrical phenomenon. We mean: farce is absurd; but not only that, farce is a veritable structure of absurdities. Here the operative word is *structure*, for normally we think of absurdities as amorphous. It is only in such a syndrome as paranoia that we find reason in the madness: the absurdities which we would be inclined to call stupid are connected in a way we cannot but consider the reverse of stupid. There is an ingenious and complex set of interrelationships.[88]

It may therefore be possible to say that farce is controlled by an ingenious and complex structure of interrelated absurdities; and that the chain-reaction process that unites those absurdities functions like the cause-and-effect syndrome of paranoia, or comic reason in madness. Delusions of grandeur are of course endemic to farcical characters, as we know from the paranoiac fantasies of such diverse figures as the Chaplin and Buster Keaton tramps, Laurel and Hardy, W. C. Fields and Harpo Marx; Falstaff, Leopold Bloom, Christy Mahon, Roger Carmody, "Captain" Boyle, Dick Cartney, Gogo and Didi, Dunlavin and Monsewer: their delusions grow out of their insecurities, which create the need for mad dreams that tentatively protect them from the terrible constraints of the supposedly sane world. For all these reasons, and for what Freud called the psychic process by which tendentious or desecrating jokes allow people to circumvent the obstacles of society and achieve a gratification of forbidden wishes—for all these subversive games of laughter, the low comedy of farce is perhaps the most irresistible art form; it provides an open structure of compensatory absurdities, a mad fantasy of vicarious freedom for discredited or dispossessed clowns, for the tramps, prevaricators, cowards, parasites, cuckolds, and prisoners of antic Irish comedy.

Consider, for example, some of the compensatory absurdities of Dunlavin and Neighbour in *The Quare Fellow,* and the connections between their comic rituals of survival and the mad prison

world that in the name of retributive sanity is about to execute
the quare fellow. Dunlavin and Neighbour represent only one of
many episodic subplots that rotate around and dominate the
main plot of the execution, inverting and mocking that terrible
deed because this is the only way people can go on living and
waiting in the shadow of the gallows. It is the classic example of
how gallows humor functions as the chief diversion in a play
about gallows tragedy. Only the laughter makes the tragedy
bearable. While they laugh and wait, then, Dunlavin and
Neighbour and their cell mates conduct their absurd revels. At
the beginning of the play Dunlavin is preparing a special
sideshow, tidying up his cell, polishing his enamel chamber pot,
and hanging up his holy pictures in the expectation of obtaining
favors from "Holy" Healey, the official from the Department of
Justice who always visits the prison before a hanging:

> I have to do me funny half-hour for Holy Healey.... I have to
> hang up my holy pictures and think up a few funny remarks for
> him. God, what Jimmie O'Dea is getting thousands for I've to do
> for a pair of old socks and a ticket for the Prisoners' Aid.[89]

Dunlavin's continuous entertainment for everyone is indeed
parallel to the jokes and antics of Jimmie O'Dea, Dublin's most
popluar music-hall comedian. When a sexual deviate is placed in
an adjoining cell, Dunlavin's sense of propriety is outraged and
he protests that he would rather be next to "a decent murderer"
than "a bloody sex mechanic"; and when they have to fall in to
see the doctor, Dunlavin calls to the deviate: "Hey, come out and
get gelded."[90] The sex jokes become blasphemous when
everyone rushes to the windows to watch the female prisoners
hanging up their laundry in the exercise yard, a spectacle that
the men irreverently call "the May procession," an allusion to the
annual devotion to the Virgin Mary. This prompts Dunlavin and
Neighbour, dirty old men who are now beyond the sexual
mechanics of any persuasion, to create their own procession of
venerable prostitutes, a devotional roll call of fond memories of
the women they have known: Meena La Bloom, May Oblong,
Lottie L'Estrange, Cork Annie, Lady Limerick, Julia Rice, and
the Goofy One. Some of the younger men boast about what they
could do to the women prisoners, and, as they leave dancing the
samba with their cleaning brushes, they mockingly condemn the

old men to prayer and Bible reading. But this "disrespectful" attitude encourages Neighbour and Dunlavin to recall the many times they were comforted by the Bible:

> *Neighbour.* Many's the time the Bible was a consolation to a fellow all alone in the old cell. The lovely thin paper with a bit of mattress coir in it, if you could get a match or a bit of tinder or any class of light, was as good a smoke as ever I tasted. Am I right, Dunlavin?
>
> *Dunlavin.* Damn the lie, Neighbour. The first twelve months I done, I smoked my way half-way through the book of Genesis and three inches of my mattress. When the Free State came in we were afraid of our life they were going to change the mattresses for feather beds. And you couldn't smoke feathers, not, be God, if they were rolled in the Song of Solomon itself. But sure, thanks to God, the Free State didn't change anything more than the badge on the warders' caps.[91]

This allusion to the Irish Free State government broadens the scope of the jest, for many people felt they would be living in clover and sleeping in fine feather beds once the Irish drove the British out and governed themselves. But Dunlavin's irony implies that the rosy promises of a changed life in Ireland amounted to nothing more than the change of the badge on the warders' caps; and the Irish government went about hanging its condemned prisoners as cheerfully as the British government had done when it was in power with a different badge on the caps. Dunlavin therefore has little faith in the Irish government and its civil service bureaucracy, of which "Holy" Healey exemplifies the educated and secret drinker who in his official piety is too close to God for God's good. As a result Dunlavin wants to protect God as well as himself from such hypocritical time servers who do the devil's work while they look condescendingly upon God as if He were a naive civil service department head fresh from the bog who needs the patronizing support of His allied departments. Dunlavin explains it to Neighbour:

> The likes of Healey would take a sup all right, but being a high-up civil servant, he wouldn't drink under his own name. You'd see the likes of Healey nourishing themselves with balls of malt, at eleven in the morning, in little back snugs round Merrion Row. The barman would lose his job if he so much as breathed their name. It'd be "Mr. H. wants a drop of water but not too much."

"Yes, Mr. O." "No, sir, Mr. Mac wasn't in this morning." "Yes, Mr. D. Fine morning; it will be a lovely day if it doesn't snow." Educated drinking, you know. Even a bit of chat about God at an odd time, so as you'd think God was in another department, but not long off the Bog, and they was doing Him a good turn to be talking well about Him.[92]

Immediately after this speech Dunlavin gives us a farcical example of the *uneducated* drinking habits reserved for the prisoners when he steals some swallows from the bottle of methylated spirits that Warder Regan is rubbing on Dunlavin's supposedly rheumatic leg. It is a game that Dunlavin and Neighbour play regularly, but this time the sly Dunlavin is too full of himself to share a drink with the miserable Neighbour as the two men go through their hilarious Boyle-and-Joxer routine. They are interrupted when "Holy" Healey finally appears to offer his officious bromides to the prisoners, and to check the details of the hanging with Regan. Here at the end of the first act the horror of the main plot breaks through the compensatory comedy as Regan, the only voice of conscience among the prison officials, assures Healey that the quare fellow's neck will be "properly broken in the morning," then shakes Healey with another twist of gallows humor:

> *Healey.* Well, we have one consolation, Regan, the condemned man gets the priest and the sacraments, more than his victim got maybe. I venture to suggest that some of them die holier deaths than if they had finished their natural span.
> *Warder Regan.* We can't advertise "Commit a murder and die a happy death," sir. We'd have them all at it. They take religion very seriously in this country.[93]

But Healey with his characteristic misunderstanding of the religious attitudes of the prisoners gives his pious sermon and one of his holy pictures to Silvertop, the condemned man just reprieved from the gallows, who responds by trying unsuccessfully to hang himself at the end of the act. It is a grim rehearsal of what awaits the quare fellow. As the curtain falls, "the old triangle goes jingle jangle," and Regan tries to comfort the shaken Healey: "It's a soft job, sir, between hangings."[94]

It's a soft play, between hangings, for this is Behan's characteristic method of entertaining and shaking his audience, using gallows humor to withhold the terror until the moment of truth draws near; and even then the violence of institutional killing is reflected through the subterfuge of comic irony. Since Behan was clearly determined not to allow his play to become a naturalistic debate on the transparent evil of capital punishment, it is pointless for some critics to object on the old naturalistic assumption that "the first act was really nothing but an over-blown exposition scene."[95] The open and inverted structure of Act I does not develop through the expository machinery of the traditional play of ideas, but through a series of entertainments and delayed shocks, which continue in the remaining two acts.

In the second act, as a contrast to such hardened old come-dians as Dunlavin and Neighbour, we find another subplot in the two young innocents with Kerry accents from the same is-land off the west coast of Ireland, the Irish-speaking Prisoner C, and a new warder named Crimmin, who have no humor or experience to protect them from the shadow of the gallows. While these new men worry about the execution for all of us, Neighbour bets Dunlavin his Sunday bacon that there will be no last-minute reprieve for the quare fellow; and Prisoner E, a bookie, "acts as if he were a tick-tack man at the races" by taking side bets on the bacon. As nerves become raw the comic conten-tiousness increases. All the prisoners argue about the quare fellow's fate, and in spelling out the gruesome details of his deed of fratricide they subvert Prisoner C's sentimental attitude to-ward the condemned man. Prisoner A, "a hard case," pointedly reminds everyone of the crime: "Begod, he's not being topped for nothing—to cut his own brother up and butcher him like a pig."[96] But for the men this knowledge does not alter the fact that the government will now compound the crime by butchering the quare fellow. And Regan, who is sickened by both crimes, quietly tries to calm the trembling Crimmin by absolving the imported British Hangman, an amusing and impersonal publi-can who moonlights as an executioner: "Himself has no more to do with it than you or I or the people that pay us, and that's every man or woman that pays taxes or votes in elections. If they don't like it, they needn't have it."[97]

This biting comment points the finger of guilt directly at the people in the audience, who gradually realize that the understated tragic theme has been breaking through the overstated comic subplots. In the third act even the warders become contentious when Regan gets into an argument with the Chief Warder and repeats the charge: "I think the whole show should be put on in Croke Park; after all, it's at the public expense and they let it go on. They should have something more for their money than a bit of paper stuck up on the gate."[98] At this point a variety of "shows" are in progress as the world inside and outside the prison approaches knockabout hysteria: the pipe-tapping Morse code system has been increasing in volume and frenzy since the beginning of the last act; a riotous crowd outside the walls can be heard protesting and singing; the tipsy Hangman and his hymn-singing assistant are preparing the gallows in a mood of unconscious humor that qualifies their cockney reverence; Mickser gives a horse-race announcer's account of the final preparations as the clock strikes the fatal hour; the prisoners let loose a ferocious howling; Crimmin faints and is carried away as the deed is done; Neighbour reminds Dunlavin that he has lost his Sunday bacon, and Dunlavin cheerfully replies that he has lost nothing since his stomach is bad and the doctor has put him on a milk diet; and at the final curtain, to the accompaniment of the "old triangle" ballad, three prisoners toss for the right to sell the quare fellow's letters to the Sunday papers, in an ironic allusion to the soldiers who gambled for the seamless robe of Christ.

It is finished. The quare fellow dies for all of us, but if he is not a sacred figure, his life represents something sacred that is inhumanly violated. Behan has wisely understated this theme because his play is more than an indictment of capital punishment; it is a profane celebration of the sanctity of life. He has allowed a shocked audience to enjoy the spectacle they should despise because he felt that we could accommodate ourselves to the reality of such a terrible deed only through the antic rituals of low comedy. Cathartically as well as dramatically, such terror demands such comedy.

This extravagant exploitation of the music-hall principle of comic diversion is treated with even greater freedom, if less tension, in *The Hostage,* another open-structured gallows entertainment about waiting for an execution. Again the threat of violent death demands the compensation of wild laughter. Like all writers of profane Irish comedy, Behan understood the universal efficacy of Freud's comic circumvention strategy: "By making our enemy small, inferior, despicable or comic, we achieve in a roundabout way the enjoyment of overcoming him."[99] This is of course one of the most enduring gratifications of comic desecration: he who laughs feels superior, he who is laughed at feels inferior. This time the sacred "enemies" are excessive Irish nationalism and religiosity, both of which created the repressive climate of fanatical patriotism and puritanism so prevalent in modern Ireland. In the broader sense, however, all the political and religious pieties associated with both side of the Anglo-Irish "troubles" are desecrated in the play, since the pompous John Bull is just as ridiculous as the sentimental Cathleen Ni Houlihan. Masters and martyrs are equally vulnerable to comic exposure, the pathetic Captains and Kings of England, the Holy Joes and Horse Protestants of Ireland—the RCs and the C of E, the I.R.A. and the R.A.F., and for good measure the F.B.I. and the perpetrators of the H-Bomb.

Some people in Ireland, such as Ulick O'Connor, feel that this play is a betrayal of Behan's republican as well as his artistic principles, since he was in his youth a member of the I.R.A. and served two prison terms for political offenses. But as a man and artist Behan was one of his own "laughing boys" whose sense of humor and humanity made it difficult for him to accept the fighting and dying for Ireland without a skeptical and profane point of view: "This is nineteen-fifty-eight, and the days of the heroes is over this thirty-five years past. Long over, finished and done with. The I.R.A. and the War of Independence are as dead—as dead as the Charleston."[100] Behan identifies himself with the gallant old I.R.A. of Michael Collins, the original "Laughing Boy" of the War of Independence, in contrast to the new breed of fanatical puritan-patriots, such as the I.R.A. Officer in the play, the "Holy Joe" who is a total teetotaler: no drinking, no smoking, no sex, and above all no laughter. When the irreverent Pat, the sly caretaker of the brothel who claims he lost a leg fighting with the old I.R.A., confronts the officer of the new breed, the contentious issue becomes clear:

> *Officer.* This is no laughing matter, you idiot.
> *Pat* (to audience). You know, there are two sorts of gunmen, the earnest, religious-minded ones, like you, and the laughing boys.
> *Officer.* Like you.

> *Pat.* Well, you know in the time of the troubles it was always the laughing boys who were the most handy with a skit.
> *Officer.* Why?
> *Pat.* Because it's not a natural thing for a man with a sense of humour to be playing with firearms and fighting. There must be something the matter with him.[101]

There must be something the matter with everyone in the play except Pat and Meg, Teresa and Leslie, the old and young couples of experience and innocence, who are the only characters that do not pretend to be anything other than what they are, a brothel caretaker and his madame and two naive orphans. All the other characters are involved in political, religious, and sexual masquerades. The central metaphor of the play as a brothel world of illusions in a time of rebellion can be compared to Genet's "House of Illusions" in *The Balcony* (1956). The simulated masquerades that Irma, the madame in Genet's play, blasphemously calls "the liturgies of the brothel" have their parallels in Behan's play, although Behan has more comedy and compassion than Genet, and less Artaudian cruelty. Behan's blithely cracked Monsewer, the mad owner of the brothel who thinks all the girls and their clients are working for the nationalist cause, is an Irish-speaking Anglo-Irish Oxonian masquerading in kilts and playing the war pipes as a buffoon of a fanatical I.R.A. commander. The religious hypocrites and homosexuals, led by Mulleady, turn out to be secret police in disguise; and when the police raid the house at the end, the diehard patriots, led by the I.R.A. Officer and his men, disguise themselves as whores and flee ingloriously from the battle. Heroism and religion in Ireland are thoroughly discredited. In a world of such corrupted idealism, Meg and Pat speak the ironic language of reality:

> *Meg.* Pound notes is the best religion in the world.
> *Pat.* And the best politics.[102]

The Irish Teresa and the cockney Leslie speak the ironic language of innocence on Anglo-Irish politics when they talk about Monsewer's decision to leave England and fight for Ireland:

> *Teresa.* Anyway, he left your lot and come over and fought for Ireland anyway.
> *Soldier.* What did he want to do that for? Was somebody doing something to Ireland?

Teresa. Wasn't England, for hundreds of years?

Soldier. That was donkeys years ago. Anyway, everybody was doing something to someone in those days.[103]

and on Anglo-Irish religion when they talk about their childhood experiences in their orphanages:

Teresa. We were not allowed to take off our clothes at all. You see, Leslie, even when we had our baths on Saturday nights they put shifts on the girls, even the little ones four or five years old.

Soldier. Did they?

Teresa. What did you have?

Soldier. Oh no, we never had anything like that. I mean, in our place we had all showers and we were sloshing water over each other and blokes shouting and screeching and making a row—it was smashing. Best night of the week, it was.

Teresa. Our best time was the procession we had for the Blessed Virgin on May Day—

Soldier. Procession for who?

Teresa. Shame on you, the Blessed Virgin. Anyone would think you were a Protestant.

Soldier. I am, girl.

Teresa. Oh, excuse me.

Soldier. That's all right. Never think about it myself.[104]

This is an ingenuous account of the differences between Cathleen Ni Houlihan and John Bull, and Behan often hides his art in such innocent ironies. Meanwhile, as the suspense of imminent death mounts, he breaks the tension with irreverent songs and wild dances and asides to the audience, in a kind of Brechtian "alienation" process. Under these diversionary antics the suspense continues to build up gradually, almost leisurely but irrevocably to a jolt at the end of each act. And almost in spite of the alienating antics, or in effective contrast with them, the sympathy for Teresa and Leslie increases, just as it does for Grusha and Simon, the innocent young lovers in *The Caucasian Chalk Circle,* in spite of Brecht's alienating techniques. For both playwrights, laughter and song and love are enduring impulses in a brutalized world at war.

At the conclusion of their "mixed infants" scene Teresa and Leslie, who have only their love for comfort in this loveless world, get into bed together, after Teresa symbolically places her religious medal around his neck, to honor and protect him, as if he were King of the May, and after they ritualistically sing the Dublin children's street-rhyme ballad on marriage, "I Will Give You a Golden Ball," to sanctify their love. This was a very difficult episode for many Irishmen to accept, as Ulick O'Connor indicates in his objections to the play, on religious as well as political grounds. He is distressed by what he calls this cheap exploitation of "lust" and goes back to the earlier Irish version of the play for untainted innocence:

> Leslie the soldier and Teresa the maid know nothing of the world. They are both orphans. She has just left a convent where she had been reared by nuns. He has been brought up in an institution in Macclesfield. It is their innocence which produces the catharsis. In *An Giall* they are two flower children baffled by violence, understanding love but not lust. . . . The love treatment has been changed in the West End version so that the soldier has become a hardened sexual athlete, while Teresa is an experienced colleen who will hit the sack at the wink of an eyelid. They are no longer remote from what is going on about them.[105]

This rather moralistic objection overlooks Behan's basic point, that the Teresas and Leslies of the world cannot remain remote from the terrible things that are going on around them. Behind our backs this knockabout entertainment gradually concentrates on the loss of innocence, the loss of love, the loss of life. Teresa not only loves Leslie, she knows that he is a "quare fellow" doomed to die as an innocent hostage for the Belfast martyr, and she offers up her innocence for genuine love, for something that in her childlike mind is finally higher than narrow patriotism and repressive religion. How can she and Leslie remain pure "flower children" in that beleaguered brothel world of hypocrisies and imminent death? It is no "wink of an eyelid" that brings Teresa to bed with Leslie; and since he has discovered he loves her, too, and only her, he can hardly be called "a hardened sexual athlete" when he accepts her sanctified medal and her love. If it is anything it is a profoundly moving as well as an amusing example of gallows love, deathbed love, not "lust." The profanation is blessed. And when the catharsis comes at the end, it is tragicomic, not sentimental, because Behan is wise enough to write a sharp entertainment, not a sermon on Irish purity. After Leslie is accidentally shot during the confusion of the police raid, after Teresa keens her poignant lament over his body, the dead

Leslie suddenly comes back to life in a comic resurrection as he jumps up and sings a parody of the familiar passage in the First Epistle of St. Paul to the Corinthians, 15:55: "O death, where is thy sting? O grave, where is thy victory?" Just as John Gay rescues Macheath from the gallows with a laugh at the end of *The Beggar's Opera* (1728), Behan rescues the doomed Leslie with a comic flourish:

> The bells of hell
> Go ting-a-ling-a-ling
> For you but not for me.
> Oh death where is thy
> Sting-a-ling-a-ling
> Or grave thy victory?[106]

So the art of gallows humor is an improvement on life, and the comic catharsis that accompanies this delightful shock is a Freudian victory of the psyche due to Leslie's miraculous circumvention of death. Suddenly the sorrow and pity that flooded the nervous system have been released and replaced by laughter and joy. Martin Grotjahn has appropriately described the psychological and dramatic pleasure that accompany such a curtain scene: "In humor, especially in Freud's favorite 'gallows' humor, energy is saved from the repressing emotions: I do not need to pity the condemned criminal because he is strong, he can take it, he does not need my pity. He is stronger than his fate and possibly stronger than reality."[107]

In the light of this psychic victory it may be possible to say that the character who acts out of a profound or even capricious sense of comic profanation is temporarily stronger than his fate, whether he is a condemned criminal or hostage, or simply someone condemned to the repression of a living death: his desecrating laughter makes him stronger than the reality that might have subjugated or destroyed him. Freud himself once called this comic victory the "grandeur of humour" which results in a magnanimous conquest of despair. In a discussion of gallows humor he offers as an illustration the rogue who, while being led to his execution on a Monday morning, remarks ironically: "Well, this week's beginning nicely." Then Freud explains what he means by the "grandeur" of such humor:

> The case was the same when the rogue on his way to execution asked for a scarf for his bare throat so as not to catch cold—an

otherwise laudable precaution but one which, in view of what lay in store so shortly for the neck, was remarkably superfluous and unimportant. It must be confessed that there is something like magnanimity in this *blague,* in the man's tenacious hold upon his customary self and his disregard of what might overthrow that self and drive it to despair. This kind of grandeur of humour appears unmistakably in cases in which our admiration is not inhibited by the circumstances of the humourous person.[108]

Dunlavin and Neighbour express this redemptive "grandeur of humour" for the doomed "quare fellow," for all the imprisoned or condemned men and women everywhere. Pat and Meg, Teresa and Leslie express it for themselves and for all the victims of "the terrible beauty" and the terrible reality of patriotic crusades. The bawdy and mock-heroic characters in Behan's fragmentary *Richard's Cork Leg* express it in all their graveyard profanations, which abound in such throwaway lines as the "Immaculate Contraception"; "Lourdes—Haemorrhage of Bad Taste"; "An honest God's the noblest work of man."[109] Behan himself as the young delinquent narrator of *Borstal Boy* expresses it as effectively as any of his dramatic characters, that magnanimous gesture of comic grandeur which assures us that his literary *persona* is always stronger than his imprisoned fate. Only the real-life Behan, who impulsively burned himself out at the age of forty-one, was unable to achieve the comic grandeur and resurrection of Leslie and the Borstal boy.

In the end Behan's artistic role as a dramatist was more successful and more enduring that his public role as a playboy. The legend of his carousing life, which he invented and performed with such merry and self-destructive abandon, should not blind us to the fact that he was a deliberate and dedicated artist whose extravagant instincts for drama were incredibly moving and hilarious. As a man Behan was the ultimate "quare fellow," a great-hearted figure of a clown who was determined to laugh his way through a life that he sensed had to be lived magnanimously in the shadow of his premature death.

Chapter 4

MANNERS AND MORALS

IN IRISH COMEDY

BROADBENT. But he spoke—he behaved just like an Irishman.

DOYLE. Like an Irishman! Is it possible that you dont know that all this top-o-the-morning and broth-of-a-boy and more-power-to-your-elbow business is as peculiar to England as the Albert Hall concerts of Irish music are? No Irishman ever talks like that in Ireland, or ever did, or ever will. But when a thoroughly worthless Irishman comes to England, and finds the whole place full of romantic duffers like you, who will let him loaf and drink and sponge and brag as long as he flatters your sense of moral superiority by playing the fool and degrading himself and his country, he soon learns the antics that take you in. He picks them up at the theatre or the music hall.
    —Bernard Shaw, *John Bull's Other Island*

MRS. KELLY. Conn nivir did an honest day's work in his life—but dhrinkin', an' fishin', an' shootin', an' sportin', and love-makin'.

MOYA. Sure, that's how the quality pass their lives.

MRS. KELLY. That's it. A poor man who spoorts the sowl of a gentleman is called a blackguard.
    —Dion Boucicault, *The Shaughraun*

Stereotypes and Archetypes of the Stage Irishman

When Larry Doyle mocked Tom Broadbent's quaint notion of the typical Irishman in *John Bull's Other Island* (1904), he was exposing the stereotype of the stage Irishman that had flourished in the English theater for four centuries. Shaw was also reminding us that, in the patronizing manner of the stage Englishman such as Broadbent, all Irishmen are stage Irishmen. It is apparent throughout the play that Tim Haffigan, the British-born Irish parasite who speaks and behaves "just like an Irishman," is a parody of an Irishman created for the purpose of amusing and flattering the inflated British ego. Centuries of condescension had corrupted the pompous master as well as the foolish slave, since it takes the frailty of a Broadbent to bring out the folly of a Haffigan. When he enters fawning at the heels of Broadbent, Tim is described by Shaw in the vivid but stock image of the engratiating Irish buffoon:

> Haffigan is a stunted, shortnecked, smallheaded man of about 30, with a small bullet head, a red nose, and furtive eyes. He is dressed in seedy black, almost clerically, and might be a tenth-rate schoolmaster ruined by drink. He hastens to shake Broadbent's hand with a show of reckless geniality and high spirits, helped out by a rollicking stage brogue. This is perhaps a comfort to himself, as he is secretly pursued by the horrors of incipient delirium tremens.[1]

This recognizable stereotype is reinforced by many examples of the overripe Haffigan blarney, a catalogue of stage-Irish clichés that quickly betray the theatrical caricature of the insecure Celt: "More power to your elbow! an may your shadda never be less! for youre the broth of a boy intirely. An how can I help you? Command me to the last dhrop o me blood."[2]

If Tim Haffigan represents the stereotypical stage Irishman who degrades himself and his native country by playing the dialect buffoon for the diversion of the Anglo-Saxons, there is also an archetypal stage Irishman who protects himself and his native country by playing the wise fool for the amusement of the Celts. This second and more formidable figure, a nimble and cunning stage Irishman, is a resourceful clown who in his dramatic ancestry goes back to the parasite-slave of ancient Greek and Roman comedy. Furthermore, the parasite-slave seldom appeared without his coconspirator in knockabout comedy, the braggart-warrior. Both of these traditional figures were recreated by O'Casey with remarkable resemblances to the original characters in those two Dublin "butties" in *Juno and the Paycock,* "Captain" Jack Boyle and Joxer Daly. Such stereotypes as Haffigan are rigid buffoons who illustrate Bergson's theory of comic automatism; they are comic *alazons* who are punished by the satiric laughter they provoke. Such archetypes as Boyle and Joxer, on the other hand, are resilient clowns who illustrate Freud's theory of comic circumvention; they are comic *eirons* who mitigate censure, using their wise folly to entertain us by undermining the restraints of a hostile world.

Although Plautus is usually given credit for creating the originals of Boyle and Joxer in the blustering Pyrgopolynices and the crafty Artotrogus of the *Miles Gloriosus* in the second century B.C., one can find earlier counterparts in the fourth century B.C., in the Greek satyr plays of Sophocles and Euripides, in the pompous Polyphemus and the clever Silenus.[3] Down through the centuries they have remained perennial figures of fun and comic invention, for in various disguises they continued to reappear in the medieval *fabliaux* and cycle plays, in Elizabethan and Restoration comedy, in eighteenth- and nineteenth-century drama and fiction. And they have been very much with us in the twentieth century, not only in Irish comedy but in the cinema tramps of Charlie Chaplin and Buster Keaton.

The braggart-warrior as stage Irishman made one of his earliest if brief appearances as Captain Mackmorrice in Shakespeare's *Henry V* (1599), and thereafter he became the stock figure of ridicule, the roaring and blundering soldier-Celt with his predictable equipment of blarney, bulls, and brogue. In the eighteenth century he was appropriately named O'Blunder and O'Trigger by the two Sheridans. Thomas Sheridan, a Dublin actor and sometime playwright, the father of Richard Brinsley, wrote a popular play while he was still a student at Trinity College, *Captain O'Blunder, or, The Brave Irishman* (1738), in which he anticipated his son's famous "malapropisms" by having the title hero attribute his recruiting sergeant's knowledge of horses to the fact that "he was manured to it from his cradle."[4] There are even some distinct signs that Sheridan's brash captain might possess the comic eloquence of a mock playboy when, in a speech that anticipates Christy Mahon's "It's Pegeen I'm seeking only, and what'd I care if you brought me a drift of chosen females, standing in their shifts itself maybe, from this place to the Eastern World,"[5] O'Blunder chooses his beloved Lucy in the following manner: "She's as fair as an image in Leislip, Egypt, I mean . . . give me this lady's lily-white hand, and I'll take her stark-naked, without a penny of money in her pocket, but the cloaths upon her back."[6]

The playboys and paycocks of Synge and O'Casey can similarly resort to mock-heroic hyperbole, but there is in them a self-preserving shrewdness that enables them to avoid the obvious buffoonery in O'Blunder, or the demeaning stereotype that was so prevalent in such typical eighteenth-century braggart stage Irishmen as Sir Callaghan O'Brallaghan in Charles Macklin's *Love à la Mode* (1760), Major O'Flaherty in Richard Cumberland's *West Indian* (1771), Sir Lucius O'Trigger in Richard Brinsley Sheridan's *Rivals* (1775), Captain Kilmallock in George Coleman's *Mountaineers* (1794), and Captain O'Curragh in Thomas Morton's *Zorinski* (1795). In most instances this stage-Irish soldier or sailor was a strutting fool full of military conceits and whiskey, or a scatterbrained country squire full of equestrian metaphors and bravado, with a total disregard for law or logic. Above all he was a grotesque "Oirish" primitive manufactured for the amusement of John Bull.

A more attractive and sympathetic version of this braggart, together with his partner, the alert parasite-slave or clever peasant, often appeared in eighteenth- and nineteenth-century Irish fiction, for example, in Maria Edgeworth's *Castle Rackrent* (1800), William Carleton's *Traits and Stories of the Irish Peasantry* (1830–33), Samuel Lover's *Rory O'More* (1837), and Charles Lever's *Jack Hinton* (1842). The popular Lover and Lever tended to vulgarize their Irish clowns with predictable if highly amusing routines and stage-Irish rhetoric, while the artistic Edgeworth and Carleton created more subtle and complex comic characters, such as the sly retainer Thady Quirk in *Castle Rackrent*, who sits in ironic judgment on his decadent masters, and the incorrigible Felim O'Toole and Denis O'Shaughnessy in *Traits and Stories of the Irish Peasantry*, two of many rich Carleton rogues in this classic work whose hilarious antics combine the brash and shrewd traits of the braggart and peasant in a single character.

It remained for Dion Boucicault, however, to bring the consummate Irish rogue as combined braggart and crafty peasant into the nineteenth-century theater and prepare the way for the modern revitalization of the stage Irishman as mock hero in the works of Synge, Fitzmaurice, O'Casey, and Behan; nor should Joyce's memorable Simon Dedalus be left out of this group. Boucicault may have lacked the literary genius of a Carleton, but as a resourceful playwright, actor, and producer with a highly developed sense of comic style and theatrical genius, he took the vulgar buffoonery out of the stage Irishman and made him an attractive and articulate clown who dominated the stage. This character had previously been a subordinate figure of ridicule, like Major O'Flaherty or Sir Lucius O'Trigger, consigned to one of many subplots, but now Boucicault moved him up to the main plot as the central character or comic catalyst.

Nevertheless, the benign conventions of Boucicault's nineteenth-century theater demanded that his comic-rogue hero should be linked to a romantic love plot and a happy ending, whereas there was to be little romance and no reconciliation of lovers in marriage in the barbarous conventions of twentieth-century antic Irish comedy. The romantic element defines the genteel manners and morals of love in Boucicault's plays as the

idealization of reality that one usually finds in traditional comedy. Like the lovesick and temporarily distressed young couples
in Shakespeare's comedies, though without their eloquence,
Boucicault's heroes and heroines must be alternately thwarted
and redeemed by love, which finally dispenses rewards and
punishments all round. Therefore, even the comic hero Conn
and his clever peasant sweetheart Moya in *The Shaughraun*, like
the proper gentleman and lady, Robert Ffolliott and Arte
O'Neal, must be united by the conventions of romantic love.
Oscar Wilde's Miss Prism would have been shocked by the wild
antics of Conn, but she might have recovered her composure
sufficiently to recognize that the poetic justice of the happy ending illustrated her reassuring concept of literature: "The good
ended happily, and the bad unhappily. That is what Fiction
means." Now such a sophisticated writer as H. B. Charlton
functions at a much higher level of literary criticism than the
simplistic Miss Prism, yet his elevated view of Shakespeare's
romantic comedy in the following passage would have comforted her:

> Rosalind, Viola, and, to a lesser extent, Beatrice, are Shake-
> speare's images of the best way to love. They, and the men in
> whom they inspire love, are Shakespeare's representation of the
> office of love to lift mankind to a richer life. So, by the entry into
> it of love, not only has the world of these comedies become a
> bigger world: the men and women who inhabit it have become
> finer and richer representatives of human nature. They have
> entered into the possession of spiritual endowments which, if
> hitherto suspected to exist at all, had either been distrusted as
> dangerous or had become moribund through desuetude. They
> have claimed the intuitive, the sub-conscious, and the emotional
> as instruments by which personality may bring itself into a fuller
> consciousness and a completer harmony with the realities of exis-
> tence. They have left Theseus far behind; they have also out-
> grown Falstaff.[7]

This highly idealized and heroic view of love and fine ladies is
an admirable if somewhat too exalted attitude, and it becomes
necessarily stereotyped in such lesser dramatists as Boucicault. It
is in Boucicault's comic plots, however, that the noble ladies, as
well as the ethereal Theseus, are left far behind, while the lively
knockabout of Falstaff flourishes and is never outgrown. It is in

those low comic antics of an conniving Conn that we find some sources of the barbarous clowning that was eventually to be developed into a fine art in modern Irish comedy. No small thanks to Boucicault, then, such dramatists as Synge and O'Casey were able to create a mock-heroic way of laughing at the excessive idealizations of human nature, which oppress and intimidate ordinary mortals. The sublimating laughter released by this realization may serve as a reminder, when we happen to overhear the organ music of a Charlton, that the wild and discordant notes of low comedy can also reverberate at a high level of consciousness—consciousness particularly of our comic fallibility and the need to deflate what Freud called the celestial models of perfect behavior that unnerve many of us.

When celestial women become the touchstones of virtue and truth, it may be time to shake their pedestals by remembering that Crazy Jane and Molly Bloom, the Widow Quin and Rosie Redmond, Mary Byrne and Bessie Burgess reflected their own affirmation of life, which called for a reassessment of the idealized Irishwoman. Traditionally she may have been a sentimentalization of the longsuffering and noble Mother Machree, who was a secularized version of Cathleen Ni Houlihan, or the equally stereotyped beautiful colleen with red shawl and bare feet, playing the harp, both of them idealized images that were too sacred for laughter and therefore couldn't be found in modern Irish comedy, where love is usually thwarted or irrelevant. Idealistic love can be a major theme in Irish ballads, or in Irish tragedy, as in the powerful Deirdre legend, but it seldom has much importance in antic comedy because ordinary Irishmen seem disinclined to endure the elaborate rituals of courtship and sex, possibly, as Stanislaus Joyce claimed, because of the Jansenist influence of the church and the emotional indifference of the men:

> Love gets a cold welcome in Ireland unless it is obedient to priestly control before marriage, and, through the confessional, after marriage too. Unmarried mothers had better be dead than alive in the greenest of isles. If it is known that there has been intercourse between the couple before marriage it is remembered against them as long as they live. Irishmen seem to marry for prosaic reasons or to get it over, and are faithful rather than devoted husbands. In Ireland, more than elsewhere, the hen-

pecked husband is a rarity and a laughing-stock. For the most
part, women do not interest Irishmen except as streetwalkers and
housekeepers. . . . This indifference or concealed hostility of
Irishmen to women is reflected in the character of their women.
It would be interesting to determine whether the coldness,
bigotry, and absolute lack of romanticism of Irish women are
innate or unconsciously desired by the males of the race; for, in
the last analysis, women are always blamed by men for being just
what men themselves have made them.[8]

If Stanislaus took a hard view of love in Ireland, he identified
the enemy and prescribed the need for a revival of the comic
rebellion by Irishwomen that had been rumbling intermittently
since Brian Merriman's *Cúirt an Mheán Oíche* (*The Midnight
Court*, c. 1780), which, significantly, could be read without hin-
drance in its original Irish version under the Republic of Eire
but was judged to be so salacious in twentieth-century English
translations that it was banned by the government censorship
board. Needless to say, it was an all-male board, acting on the
unspoken wishes of a celibate clergy. Merriman's flock of earthy
young women, who were frustrated by that chaste clergy and the
grim prospect of January-and-May marriages, should be recognized as archetypal women, as distinct from the idealized
stereotypes, for they are part of the direct link between Eve, the
Wife of Bath, the Widow Quin, Pegeen Mike, Molly Bloom,
Crazy Jane, and the nubile young women in O'Casey's later
comedies. Nevertheless, in a country where the hard puritanism
of St. Patrick had consistently repressed the easy hedonism of
Oisín, these women were destined to seek their natural pleasures
in secrecy or go on suffering in silence under the tyranny of a
chauvinistic male clergy that led to sexual indifference. As a
consequence, it should be no surprise that romance and sex are
either submerged or scandalized in modern mock-heroic Irish
comedy. Furthermore, any anti-idealistic or sensuous characters
in the plays, beginning with Synge, were to be condemned as
vulgar stage Irishwomen by the hypersensitive guardians of
manners and morals in Ireland.

Many high-minded and self-appointed guardians such as Ar-
thur Griffith, who was later to become the first president of the
Republic, protested from the start that the shameless Nora
Burke in Synge's *In the Shadow of the Glen* was not only a terrible

slur on Irish womanhood but an alien and therefore impure
influence, completely ignoring the fact that Nora was as honest
and Irish as Merriman's frustrated young woman in her provocation to leave her wheezing and indifferent old husband. Synge
could easily have found the native theme of his play in any
number of passages in *The Midnight Court,* such as the following
lines, which sharply illustrate a loveless January–May marriage
similar to Nora's:

> A starved old gelding, blind and lamed
> And a twenty-year-old with her parts untamed.
> It wasn't her fault if things went wrong
> She closed her eyes and held her tongue;
> She was no ignorant girl from school
> To whine for her mother and play the fool
> But a competent bedmate smooth and warm
> Who cushioned him like a sheaf of corn.
> Line by line she bade him linger
> With gummy lips and a groping finger,
> Gripping his thighs in a wild embrace
> Rubbing her brush from knee to waist
> Stripping him bare to the cold night air,
> Everything done with love and care.
> But she'd nothing to show for all her labour;
> There wasn't a jump in the old deceiver,
> And all I could say would give no notion
> Of that poor distracted girl's emotion,
> Her knees cocked up and the bedposts shaking,
> Chattering teeth and sinews aching,
> While she sobbed and tossed through a joyless night
> And gave it up with the morning light.[9]

There is no hope of a return to an ideal state or golden mean
that never existed in this mock-pastoral world, a world so typical
of Irish comedy with the sharp element of despair that characteristically accompanies the laughter. Unlike Merriman's high
and dry young bride, Nora Burke may have an alternative when
she finally abandons her old gelding and goes off with the
eloquent young Tramp, but this desperate move is more of an
uncertain release than a sentimental happy ending; and, in fact,
to most devout Irish people it must have been considered a
blasphemous deed to mock and break the marriage vow in this
reckless way.

The men even more than the women in Synge's plays were

often criticized for being too irreverent and vulgar, and therefore too stage Irish. Such disreputable braggarts as Christy Mahon and Martin Doul were thought to be too outrageous in their eloquent departures from social and religious proprieties. In his study of the stage Irishman, G. C. Duggan observed that Synge, as a product of Yeats's new and controversial theater, was guilty of pseudo-Irish excesses: "Synge has some characters which, in their own way, are as unreal as any Stage Irishman. Before the printer's ink was well dry on the plays written for the Irish National Theatre, other writers, as quick to take offense at what they regarded as a slight on their fellow-countrymen as John Mitchel in earlier days, were labelling Synge's peasants with their occasional blasphemous utterance as being 'The Stage Irishman of the Pseudo-Celtic drama.'"[10] This common criticism that the characters in Irish drama should be more *real* was actually a demand that they should be more *ideal*, a tendency that is always evident in the Catholic nationalism of such writers as Daniel Corkery; and Maurice Bourgeois early betrayed this plea for greater idealization in art with his dubious claim that the stage Irishman had been eliminated from the Irish theater as a result of a new ethical and patriotic consciousness: "In brief, the stage Irishman has been banned simply because Ireland has at last awakened to a sense of her ethical dignity, to patriotic self-consciousness."[11]

Irish literature, however, and particularly comedy, has always taken a skeptical view of ethical or patriotic sermons on national idealism because such overly virtuous attitudes are often attempts to limit laughter as well as artistic freedom by pretending that native joys and follies do not exist. This conflict raises a central aspect of the difference between moralistic and artistic priorities, as another and earlier Irishman, Oliver Goldsmith, pointed out in his article in the *Westminster Magazine* in December 1772, appropriately titled "An Essay on the Theatre: A Comparison between Laughing and Sentimental Comedy." Goldsmith saw the theatrical dilemma accurately as a choice between high sentiment and low comedy, and, of course, like Synge more than a century later, he defended the freedom and necessity of laughter, so brilliantly illustrated in his own *She Stoops to Conquer* (1773), in contrast to pious sentiment, so tediously illustrated by such plays as Richard Steele's *Conscious Lovers* (1722). The liberated and clownish Tony Lumpkin helped prepare the way for Conn the Shaughraun and Christy Mahon, Fluther Good and Dunlavin. In his essay Goldsmith warned that the new sentimental dramatists were beginning to dominate the stage with their tracts on virtue in imitation of Steele and threatening to banish laughter from the theater:

> Humor at present seems to be departing from the stage, and it will soon happen that our comic players will have nothing left but a fine coat and a song. It depends upon the audience whether they will drive those poor merry creatures from the stage, or sit at a play as gloomy as at the Tabernacle. It is not easy to recover an art when once lost; and it will be a just punishment, that when, by our being too fastidious, we have banished humor from the stage, we should ourselves be deprived of the art of laughing.[12]

Synge was also very much aware of the danger of banishing the clowns with their merry humor when he wrote in the Preface to *The Tinker's Wedding:* "Of the things which nourish the imagination humour is one of the most needful, and it is dangerous to limit or destroy it."[13] O'Casey was also acutely aware of the danger of limiting or banishing laughter when he wrote in his essay on "The Power of Laughter: Weapon against Evil": "A laugh is a great natural stimulator, a pushful entry into life; and once we can laugh, we can live. It is a hilarious declaration made by man that life is worth living."[14]

The Playboys and the Paycocks of Boucicault

Unlike Synge and O'Casey, who were influenced by his creation of the comic-rogue hero, Dion Boucicault always insisted on poetic justice in his plays. His comedies were usually melodramatic reversals of the unfortunate struggle for Irish freedom from British misrule, for if eighteenth- and nineteenth-century history showed a record of unbroken Irish defeats, a pattern of vicarious comic victories could be found in the plays, victories contrived by the clever clown who was Boucicault's significant embodiment of the braggart and parasite in one consummate character, the *shaughraun* or vagabond. Like Dickens, that master of comedy and melodrama, Boucicault didn't allow his sentimental resolutions to undermine his ripe comedy; and if he lacked the literary genius of Dickens, he compensated for it with his theatrical genius. He was the complete comedian in the theater.

Modern Irish comedy reached its full glory in the early decades of the twentieth century at the Abbey Theatre, but it had its origins in the nineteenth-century plays of Boucicault. While it is evident that Yeats and Lady Gregory founded a great theater in 1904 which provided the occasion and inspiration for a native Irish drama written in English, the two finest comic dramatists of the Abbey, Synge and O'Casey, owed a deep and prior debt to the popular Irish comedies that Boucicault wrote, *The Colleen Bawn* (1860), *Arrah-na-Pogue* (1864), *The Shaughraun* (1874). To give full credit to the Abbey, and to the dramatists themselves, the influence of Boucicault alone could not have produced a Synge or an O'Casey; nevertheless, it is doubtful whether they would have created their unique "playboys" and "paycocks" in quite the attractively barbarous manner that they did if they had not developed an early enthusiasm for Boucicault's comic rogues.

Yet Boucicault, until some recent revivals of his plays in Dublin and London, was long neglected and maligned as a purveyor of Victorian melodrama. In large measure he was himself responsible for this fate, for he suffered from the limitations of his own talent as well as those of the time in which he lived. He was one of the most popular and prolific of Victorian dramatists, having written or adapted over 150 plays during his fifty-odd years in the theater, from 1838 to 1890, very few of which have survived in the modern repertoire. But perhaps there are some significant connections in the fact that the Dublin-born Boucicault, who borrowed so freely from the works of such early Irish dramatists as Congreve, Farquhar, Goldsmith, and Sheridan, should have provided some direct and indirect sources of inspiration for such later Irish dramatists as Wilde, Shaw, Synge, O'Casey, and Behan. Thus, while one cannot call him an outstanding figure—his achievements were more theatrical than literary, and the drama demands distinction in both fields—it is necessary to consider not only his limitations but those enduring qualities of his theatrical and comic genius which have continued to appeal to modern Irish dramatists and audiences.

Boucicault wrote in what might loosely be called the tradition of comic melodrama, but he was far from a traditional dramatist. He saw the drama as a mixed or impure form of entertainment, a combination of comedy and melodrama, farce and burlesque, song and sentiment, sensational and Gothic stage effects. In this respect he seems to have anticipated the modern dramatist's irreverent attitude toward the rigid or academic modes of drama, even if he was largely Victorian in his treatment of the mixed forms. There was nothing Victorian, however, in his practical reaction to those pseudo-Aristotelian critics who objected to his disregard of the so-called unities of the drama when he replied in an article: "The essence of a rule is its necessity; it must be reasonable, and always in the right. The unities of time and place do not seem to be reasonable, and have been violated with impunity, therefore are not always in the right. The liberty of imagination should not be sacrificed to arbitrary restrictions and traditions that lead to dullness and formality. Art is not a church; it is the philosophy of pleasure."[15] Obviously Boucicault agreed with Goldsmith's view that the theater was Liberty Hall and a place for entertainment, not a gloomy tabernacle for the dissemination of morality or a tedious occasion for critical formalism. At other times he insisted that audiences did not want pure forms, especially "pure comedy," whatever that was supposed to be; and in defending his own kind of heretical pleasure play he invariably assumed that purity was a quality audiences demanded in heroines, not comedy. He was shrewd in anticipating the unsophisticated tastes of the popular audiences of the nineteenth century, and he devoted a vigorous lifetime to giving the people what he believed they wanted—an extravaganza of melodramatic plots, broadly comic characters, and music-hall exuberance. Nevertheless, in giving the Victorians what they wanted, he became the victim as well as the champion of popular taste in the theater.

At the peak of his limited genius, however, Boucicault developed the comic persona of the Irish rogue-hero, the combined braggart-warrior and parasite-slave of Greek and Roman comedy, for as freely mixed creations of folly and wisdom his comic characters form the prototype of Synge's peasants and O'Casey's Dubliners. In the mid-nineteenth century, when Boucicault not only created but acted the role of the comic Irish vagabond—the *shaughraun,* literally, the wanderer—the stage Irishman had long been a recognizable caricature in English drama. This buffoon was merely a figure of ridicule, the absurd Irishman making a fool of himself among his betters, the British. Boucicault altered this trite image by making his comic Irishman the clever and attractive central character in a play set in Ireland, in which the absurd Englishman or Anglo-Irishman makes a fool of himself among his betters, the Irish. His hero is the archetypal wise fool who is the occasion of hilarity in others as well as natural wit and humor in himself. He can be a blathering rascal and cheerful liar, a profligate playboy and strutting paycock who cavorts outside the ordinary restraints of society, a picaresque clown who ultimately rights all wrongs with his instinctive sense of justice. It is in his creation of this distinctly Irish yet universally comic character—as Myles-na-Coppaleen, Shaun the Post, or Conn the Shaughraun—that Boucicault finally transcends the Victorian world. And it is part of this triumph that much of antic Irish comedy as we know it today has its orgins in the theater of Boucicault.

Born in Dublin in 1820, on the north side of the city, within a short distance of the birthplace of Sheridan, O'Casey, and Behan, Boucicault spent his first ten years in Ireland and then was sent to England, where he eventually launched his career as dramatist and actor at the age of eighteen. In 1838 in Brighton he appeared in his own play, *A Legend of the Devil's Dyke,* a comedy-melodrama that contained many of the popular ingredients that illustrate Boucicault's strengths and weaknesses in the theater. The melodramatic plot, so characteristic of nineteenth-century theater, revolves about a mysterious will and the villainous attempts of an army deserter to deprive the upright hero and hapless heroine of their inheritance and happiness. The merry antics of the comic plot, however, in which three rude mechanicals make a mockery of their aristocratic betters, reveal Boucicault's masterful talent for comic invention and almost redeem the play. Teddy Rodent, the comic lead played by Boucicault, who has been making his fortune as a rat catcher in London, comes back to the country to marry the servant girl Bessy, only to discover that there are just as many rats in the country as in the city. In a parody of the melodramatic plot, Teddy and Bessy, with the bumpkin of a footman named Tim Terrier, dress up as a fashionable trio and crash the gala ball, with the resourceful Teddy masquerading as Bessy's wealthy aunt. In the comedy of errors that follows—as if in anticipation of something out of *Charley's Aunt* or the Marx Brothers— the matronly Teddy baits his trap so seductively that he catches a fortune-hunting fop, while the proper hero and heroine are busy catching the villainous army deserter.

Though Boucicault wrote the part of Teddy in a cockney idiom, he wisely played it as an Irishman; but either way, it indicates his early facility with comic characterization and knockabout farce. Furthermore, it is apparent that he was serving his apprenticeship under the influence of the comic masters. There are many echoes from Goldsmith and Sheridan in the play, for the prankish Teddy Rodent is partly modeled after Tony Lumpkin, and all the rustics use vivid colloquial speech and malapropisms that suggest the comic spirit of such plays as *She Stoops to Conquer* and *The Rivals.* Still there are also many signs of Boucicault's own theatrical inspiration in his first play—a remarkable achievement for a young man of eighteen—in the comic vitality of the whole work, in the clever tricks and masquerades he creates for his brash clown-hero, and in his dedication to exuberant fun as the main impetus for his drama.

Three years later, in 1841, he scored his first hit in London with *London Assurance,* a play written in the same spirit but in a slightly different form, a combination comedy of manners and farce in the tradition of Congreve and Farquhar. In the typical Restoration attitude, Boucicault's aloof heroine, Grace Harkaway, decides to "dwindle into a wife," and in trying to cure Charles Courtly of his blithe assurance, somewhat like Congreve's Mrs. Millimant, confronts him with an affectation of indifference: "I have many employments—this week I devote to study and various amusements—the following week to repentence, perhaps."[16] Since it is his own father, Sir Harcourt Courtly, that she intends to marry and repent of, Charles and his parasite friend Dazzle conceive a counterplan, a "beaux' stratagem" whereby he will go to the country to woo Grace in the disguise of a Mr. Hamilton. When he is almost trapped in this farcical masquerade, however, Charles is forced to "kill" the poor Hamilton, just as Wilde's Jack Worthing later has to dispose of his similarly convenient fiction, Mr. Bunbury. The lively plot is complicated through five acts of comic cross-purpose by a host of familiar *eiron* and *alazon* characters, and the play is probably the best comedy in English since Farquhar. In recent years it has finally been revived with remarkable and well-deserved success in London and New York.

Boucicault's early triumph with *London Assurance* was premature. On the apparent assumption that he had found a new formula in the old comedies, he promptly wrote a half-dozen similar plays and most of them were failures. At least two, however, deserved a better fate, *A Lover by Proxy* and *The Irish Heiress,* both written in 1842. Besides being a witty farce, *A Lover by Proxy* is of special interest because it seems to have anticipated Oscar Wilde's *Importance of Being Earnest* (1895), since it has in Harry Lawless and Peter Blushington a pair of highly amusing idle gentlemen very like Jack Worthing and Algernon Moncrieff, and in its garden scenes some striking parallels with Wilde's play, even to the inclusion of Miss Penelope Prude, who possesses the chaste views of a Miss Prism and the overbearing presence of a lesser Lady Bracknell. The other play, *The Irish Heiress,* which unfortunately closed after only two performances, is nevertheless a delightful comedy, with the added attraction of Boucicault's first Irish comic heroine, Norah Merrion. She is an Irish country girl of native wit and freshness that fairly sparkles when she is turned loose among the fashionable lords and ladies of London. No doubt the play's sentimental machinery of secret documents and discoveries is not as effective as the farcical game of disguises and deceptions, but it was predictably on moralistic and realistic grounds that the Victorian critics attacked the play. The reviewer in *The Times,* who had praised *London Assurance* while objecting to what he called its lack of proper morality and realism—he had disapproved of "the utter absurdities that are committed by the characters, such as no human being would perpetrate"[17]—condemned *The Irish Heiress* outright in similar terms. He protested that the clever Norah was not a "lady," that "the goodness of her heart was not effectively displayed, and her simplicity was little more than barbarous."[18]

To call for proper realism and reject absurdities is to reject the inherent exaggeration and distortion of comedy. To call for simple virtue and reject "barbarous" manners is to reject the inherent primitive and irreverent spirit of Irish comedy. Perhaps the British guardians of manners and morals, with their plea for more idealized goodness and simplicity and their rejection of native shrewdness as something too "barbarous"—the choice of the taboo word is inadvertently accurate—were similar to their Irish counterparts, whose high-minded view of the national character later led to riots in the Abbey Theatre. Lacking the courage as well as the genius of Synge and O'Casey, Boucicault must have been chastened by the rebuke of the *Times* reviewer, for he spent the next two decades writing and adapting the typical melodramas, softened by a proper expression of noble sentiments, which are usually associated with his name.

At the age of forty, however, when Boucicault was nearing the peak of his career in the theater, he finally decided to write his first play exclusively about his native Ireland, *The Colleen Bawn* (1860), which now gave him an opportunity to prove that he was not only a theatrical showman but a dramatist of considerable talent. Even though he borrowed the story from Gerald Griffin's *Collegians* (1829), a popular novel that had been based on an actual murder case in Limerick, he modified the theme to suit his own spectacular purposes. Griffin had created a vivid and accurate picture of the customs and social conflicts in eighteenth-century rural Ireland, but his characters were mostly set down in single dimensions of virtue and vice; and throughout the book he consistently called attention to the moral lessons to be drawn from the fate of the people. Hardress Cregan, the hard-riding country gentleman as hero-villain, who is so dominated and spoiled by an overindulgent mother that he seems to drift into crime, is condemned to suffer the agonies of remorse on a convict ship. His mother becomes a penitent of her church and devotes her life to "austere and humiliating works of piety." And the two "noble" characters, Kyrle Daly and Anne Chute, marry and turn to a life of religious devotion. In the end Griffin trusts that the reader not only has been amused but has learned "the avoidance of evil, or the pursuit of good."

Wilde's Miss Prism might have been satisfied with such a resolution. Not Boucicault. Since in melodrama it follows as natur-

ally as the night the day that evil must fall and good must rise, he
had no need to lecture his audience on this solemn subject and
was therefore free to concentrate on the knockabout amusement. Taking only the climax of Griffin's interminable plot, and
drawing on a variety of other sources as well as his own fertile
imagination, he created a less realistic Ireland but one with more
vital and memorable characters—an Ireland of unforgettable
comedy and romance, in the folk spirit of the popular ballads.
He found the name for his play in the well-known ballad "Willy
Reilly" or "Willy Reilly and the Colleen Bawn"—on which
William Carleton had also based his comic novel *Willy Reilly and
His Dear Colleen Bawn* (1855)—the ballad in which Willy's brave
sweetheart comes to his rescue when her father imprisons him
for stealing the love of "the colleen bawn" (the blonde or fair-
haired girl). In another popular hedge-school love ballad, "The
Colleen Rua," he may have found the name for his second
heroine, Anne Chute, who is known in the play as "The Colleen
Ruadh" (pronounced "rua" or ru-ah, and meaning the red-
haired girl). He certainly knew and used the ballad and novel
Rory O'More (1837), both written by Samuel Lover, for he had
played the role of Rory in a dramatization of the novel during
his early years as an actor in Brighton. In this comic ballad, the
courting Rory wins his coy mistress, Kathleen Bawn, by kissing
her nine times.

It was probably the mirth-provoking Rory of Lover's novel
who served as the model for Boucicault's rogue-hero Myles-na-
Coppaleen, only a minor figure in Griffin's novel, now transformed into the main comic character in *The Colleen Bawn*.
Lover's picaresque novel—which was also to provide some of the
background plot for *Arrah-na-Pogue*—gives an anecdotal account of Rory's hilarious misadventures on the road, in Dublin
and Paris, during the Rising of 1798. A sly clown of a peasant
adrift in the big world, Rory outwits or outruns soldiers and
police, publicans and bullies—"You impidint vagabone of the
world," he shouts from a safe distance at a Dublin jackeen, "You
dirty thief o' the world," phrases that might accurately describe
Rory himself, and the newly created Myles. The novel has a
scene in which the rebels meet in an old smuggler's cave under
an ancient ruin by a river, and this may well have suggested to

Boucicault the water cave where Myles keeps his whiskey still. Further parallels can be noted in a whiskey-punch episode in a pub, and in the trial scene at the end of the book, when Rory, in danger of being hanged for killing a man, is saved as the supposedly murdered man appears at the crucial moment, just as Father Tom enters with the supposedly murdered Colleen Bawn in time to save the imprisoned Cregan.

Another minor Irish novelist of the nineteenth century, Charles Lever, who shared a wide popularity with Lover, wrote a number of comic novels that might have provided material for Boucicault, especially his *Jack Hinton* (1842), in which there are two significant secondary characters; one is the jovial Irish priest called Father Tom, who in name and personality is very close to Boucicault's priest; and the other, Tipperary Joe, is a shrewd tramp with a quick tongue and a special interest in horses who could be a double for Myles-na-Coppaleen. In Griffin's novel Myles was an undeveloped character, a crafty mountaineer who owned hundreds of wild ponies, hence his name, Myles-of-the-Ponies.

Even when one accounts for these various sources of influence, however, the total could not in itself add up to a play. It took the unique talent and theatrical experience of a Boucicault to reshape this raw material, to organize it as an integrated and swift-moving plot with the carefully timed suspense of melodrama, with the interwoven comedy of errors and disguises, and then to develop the crackling dialogue and distinctive traits that give his characters their energy and gaiety. It is especially his control of wit and farce that redeems the ill-conceived hero and heroine of Griffin's novel, except for Hardress Cregan, who, while he may now be a more credible lover, still comes over as a stiff-necked stage Anglo-Irishman. Yet it was Boucicault's intention to laugh at Cregan's gentlemanly inhibitions, his prudish distaste for tobacco and whiskey, and most particularly in those scenes when the exuberant Eily, trying with great pains to play the Galatea to his proper Pygmalion, keeps falling back into her unladylike peasant dialect, like an earlier version of Eliza Doolittle.

Boucicault was even more successful with his second heroine, the high-spirited Anne Chute, who recalls the earlier Norah

Merrion. Anne's well-aimed arrows of comic simile are matched only by the inimitable Myles, and the two of them are so adept at impaling their victims on the figurative jest that their aggressive wit becomes one of the most effective techniques in the play: the use of laughter to deflate much of the sentimentality that arises from the melodramatic plot. There are of course many occasions when the melodrama dominates the action of the play, for the harum-scarum story it tells is a romantic thriller. The use of sudden surprises to whip up excitement and tighten the suspense is a common convention in drama; but since Boucicault is out to make the most of both worlds, he continually allows his Celtic comedians to deflate the tension, as if he were winking at his audience lest in their apprehension they draw too near the edge of their seats. Actually, much of the melodramatic machinery of asides, misunderstandings, and the mortgage is treated with comic levity. In the music-hall manner, Myles often shares his jokes with the audience. The misdirected schemes of the ingratiating Danny Mann usually become immobilized in the drollery of his self-intoxicating rhetoric.

At last Boucicault seemed to have found the confidence to enjoy a good-natured laugh at the expense of the romantic melodrama that he himself had made so popular. As if in anticipation of the technique that was to become standard practice in the silent films of a Charlie Chaplin or a Harold Lloyd, he combined farce with melodrama in such a way that, for all the "hair-raising" suspense and "death-defying" deeds, the comic tone produced something close to mock melodrama. There is also a predominant theme in the play, developed through the character and behavior of Myles-na-Coppaleen, that could only be considered subversive by Victorian standards of manners and morals. For all his amiability, Myles is a lazy lying tramp, beyond any hope of reform, a horse thief and ex-convict, a poacher and operator of an illegal whiskey still who thumbs his nose at all authority—in short, an irresponsible rogue who is the complete antithesis of Victorian respectability. And yet this may have been one of the reasons he became such a popular hero, for he gave the inhibited Victorians a chance to find vicarious release from the solemn and righteous standards by which they tried to live. In this barbarous Irishman they obviously saw what Boucicault intended them to see, a romantic vagabond whose freedom from the restraints of society made him a better and more natural man than the effete gentlemen of an urban civilization. He has the universal traits of the irreverent clown who plays the wise fool at the expense of pompous authority.

In creating this comic rebel, therefore, Boucicault, that most typical of Victorian playwrights, may have transcended his time. He was to transcend it again in two more highly successful Irish plays. In 1864 he repeated his triumph as playwright, actor, and director with *Arrah-na-Pogue,* a comic melodrama loosely based on the Rising of 1798, with patriotic and farcical echoes from *Rory O'More,* though he was really imitating himself more than Lover. In this play, however, the comic vitality is often but not always overshadowed by the sentimental themes of thwarted love and patriotism. Instead of being a reckless vagabond, Shaun the Post, the comic hero, is a fairly respectable mailman, and only too eager to marry his Arrah-na-Pogue (Arrah of the Kiss) and become a properly domesticated husband. Neither of the two heroines, Arrah and Fanny, who devote much of their energy to weeping and self-sacrifice, have anything like the playful spirit and bold humor of the Colleen Bawn and Anne Chute. As for Beamish MacCoul, the romanticized Irish rebel, he is so earnestly occupied with his melodramatic adventures of trying to escape from the British authorities and be caught by his everloving Fanny that one can only put him down as a dashing hero with little besides dash.

Nevertheless, the play has many redeeming features. It is only after Shaun is hauled off to prison and treated like a subversive rogue that he fortunately begins to act like one, resorting to such a display of guile and comic bravado that the play quickly comes alive with spontaneous mirth. The jail scenes between Shaun and the obliging sergeant are excellent low comedy. And Boucicault never wrote a better scene than the trial at the end of the second act, in which the clever Shaun makes a mockery of the court, tying the law and the British major into knots with his sly and unconventional testimony. He is encouraged in this hilarious game by a crowd of cheering and jeering peasants, and he receives some unexpected help from that proud and magniloquent Irishman, the O'Grady. This scene is so effective that

Bernard Shaw paid Boucicault the compliment of copying it for the trial scene in *The Devil's Disciple* (1897).

Something further must be said about that colorful character, Colonel O'Grady, as one of the memorable aspects of the play. Known as "the O'Grady," since he is the head of an ancient Irish family, he is an eccentric nobleman, generous and impulsive, always ready to defend Shaun and the oppressed peasants in his trenchant and comic style. When the police want to search Arrah, over Shaun's protest that he'll brain the first man who touches her, the O'Grady's sense of honor is aroused and he goes Shaun one better by reverting to the earthy brogue and direct action: "Be the powers, I'd have brained him first and warned him afterwards."[19] In one of his more reflective moments, however, he makes the most incisive speech in the play, after the appropriately named Major Coffin tries to justify his role of hanging judge on the grounds of his "principle and firm conviction," and the O'Grady comments ironically:

> There goes a kind-hearted gentleman, who would cut more throats on principle and firm conviction than another blackguard would sacrifice to the worst passions of his nature. If there be one thing that misleads a man more than another thing, it is having a firm conviction about anything.[20]

This is precisely the kind of skeptical wisdom one might expect from Shaw's General Burgoyne, or his Caesar, for it became a typical Shavian attitude toward senseless bloodshed. It is also a view shared by O'Casey, who expressed it with acute irony in all his antiwar plays; for example, through the sardonic Seumas Shields in *The Shadow of a Gunman*, the tragic Juno Boyle in *Juno and the Paycock*, and the tragicomic Harry Heegan in *The Silver Tassie*.

So Boucicault had made a penetrating comment on human folly, but he seldom allowed himself the luxury of such digressions into profundity. During the next decade he was to turn out over twenty of his routine farces and melodramas, until in 1874 he wrote, directed, and acted in the best of his Irish plays, *The Shaughraun*. Again he borrowed from himself, repeating most of the comic and romantic techniques of *The Colleen Bawn* and *Arrah-na-Pogue,* and improving them. In the role of Conn the Shaughraun, closely modeled after Myles and Shaun, he created the nonpareil of his comic-rogue heroes. Again Irish lovers and patriots spin the opéra bouffe plot, with Conn, acting as the clown ex machina, inevitably launching his inspired pranks or ingenious yarns to save the day, and the play. And again Boucicault turned to recent Irish history, in a very general manner, using the activities of the Fenian Brotherhood, a revolutionary secret society that carried out a series of abortive raids against the British during the late 1860s. If any playwright had dared to treat this incendiary subject seriously in 1874, he and his play would certainly have been suppressed as an incitement to riot. But the lighthearted Boucicault, though he was vocally an ardent Irish nationalist and even wrote a letter to Disraeli demanding the release of the Fenian prisoners, was concerned only with an incitement to fun in his play. He completely romanticized his Fenian rebel, Robert Ffolliott, and the whole play is too full of harmless entertainment to be taken as anything more than a Celtic version of Ruritania. And since Boucicault played the role of Conn in a slightly modified Tony Lumpkin costume, and Conn imitates some of the wild Tony's rustic pranks, the comic spirit of Goldsmith's Liberty Hall lives again in this play.

In its intricate and melodramatic plot, or many plots, this play is even more fantastic and farcical than Boucicault's previous Irish works, with its Fenian rebel on the run, a police spy in league with the British soldiers and an Irish Squireen, the inevitable threat of a mortgage foreclosure, separated lovers, secret letters, a brave Irish priest, a forlorn Irish mother, a Monte Cristo prison escape, mystery ships, a series of multiple chases over the bogs and cliffs of Sligo, gunshots and falling bodies, the offstage mongrel named Tatthers who is more intelligent than most of the people and performs the heroics of a Rin-Tin-Tin, a Puckish rogue hero with an inexhaustible supply of tricks, and the gallows humor of a mock wake. It all adds up to a hilariously incredible mixture of whirlwind melodrama and merry Celtic moonshine. And as before, Boucicault is most Victorian in his treatment of those thwarted sentimentalists, Robert Ffolliott and Arte O'Neal, but least Victorian in his farcical treatment of the disreputable Conn and the crafty peasants.

Conn the Shaughraun, "the soul of every fair, the life of every funeral, the first fiddle at all weddings and patterns,"[21] stirs up such a wave of irreverent humor that the stock responses of melodrama are often inundated by laughter. When those two familiar symbols of sentiment and piety, his mother and his priest, try to bring him back to respectability, he responds with the guile of an Irish Huckleberry Finn and cheerfully refuses to be "sivilized"; and he convinces us that he is, like the unreconstructed Huck, a better man in his primitive freedom than the proper Christians who behave prudently. There is an instinctive nobility in him, for there are no limits to which he will not go to save someone from tyranny, as when he stows away to far-off Australia to "poach" Ffolliott out of prison; but he considers it nothing less than tyranny for anyone to try to save him from sin.

Nothing is sacred to Conn except his freedom, and the love of Moya, which he wins on his own terms. Even that supposedly inviolable concept of Victorian and/or Irish motherhood becomes one of his prime targets. He plays so many practical jokes on his poor peasant mother that the "Mother Machree" image is reduced to mock melodrama, especially in the wake scene, when he pretends to be dead. His mother is a hardy old woman who likes a bit of fun herself, yet she despairs over the fact that he lives only for pleasure and often ends up in the shebeen or the jail. She warns Moya that he is nothing but a lazy blackguard: "Conn nivir did an honest day's work in his life—but dhrinkin', an' fishin', an' shootin', an' sportin', and love-makin'." But the shrewd Moya, who doesn't want a "dacent" and respectable husband, only loves him the more for his pleasant vices, and she replies as a well-trained pupil of Conn's: "Sure, that's how the quality pass their lives."[22]

Besides emulating the quality of a playboy, Conn is also a vainglorious paycock who finds sheer delight in telling fantastic lies, the bigger the better, for telling the truth is too dull and virtuous for a fellow of his rich imagination. More important, as we know from Falstaff and "Captain" Boyle, lies are not only a form of amusement but a method of defense, therefore one of Conn's favorite tricks for protecting himself from the pressures of respectable people. There are many examples of his protective mendacity: his roundabout explanation to his mother of how he happened to steal Squire Foly's horse; his tall excuse to Father Dolan of how he came to break his sworn oath to stay sober when he got drunk at Tim O'Maley's wake; his swaggering jest at his mother's illiteracy in the letter scene, even though he cannot read himself.[23] And most brilliant of all, his fabrication of his own wake, in the midst of which Conn the corpse sits up unobserved among the tippling mourners, steals a drink from the whiskey jug, and utters an aside to the audience: "It's a mighty pleasant thing to die like this, once in a way, and hear all the good things said about ye afther you're dead and gone, when they can do you no good."[24] Boucicault is a master of the characteristically absurd and shrewd Irish bull. The gallows humor of the mock-wake scene is quite common in Irish balladry and folklore, and although one can find many farcical parallels, for instance, by looking back to such a popular ballad as "Finnegan's Wake," or ahead to such a play as Synge's *In the Shadow of the Glen,* Boucicault's handling of the situation is by any comparison an outstanding piece of comic invention. Conn is the liveliest and most resourceful corpse that ever was stretched, for as Moya explains it in a sly bull: "Surely, if he hadn't been murdhered, he couldn't have saved us."[25] He saved them all, he saved himself, and he saved Boucicault.

The Benign Manners of Robinson and Boyle

There are no rogue heroes, no sharp ironies, no dark shadows in the benign light comedy of Lennox Robinson. On at least one occasion he indicated that he half understood the direction that the mainstream of Irish comedy had taken when he wrote in his autobiography: "To write a tragedy in terms of comedy is to write the perfect play and I feel that some day Brinsley Macnamara may achieve this most difficult thing."[26] He was wrong about Macnamara, who never achieved anything more ambitious in the theater than his mildly farcical kitchen comedy *Look at the Heffernans!* (1926), though Robinson might have been thinking about his satirical and controversial novel *The Valley of the Squinting Windows* (1919); and if he was right in his description of the perfect Irish play as a tragedy written in the terms of comedy, he had failed to realize as late as 1942 that Synge and Fitzmaurice and O'Casey had already created that unique type of modern tragicomedy or dark comedy. It was a kind of barbarous comedy that was beyond Robinson.

He was a competent and predictable playwright who seldom

deviated from his formula of safe and simple entertainment. Denis Geoghegan, the title character in his first and most successful comedy, *The Whiteheaded Boy* (1916), might appear to possess some of the reckless traits of a playboy or rogue-hero. He is an idle and flamboyant country boy wasting his time and his family's money in Dublin, where he lives for pleasure and plays the horses instead of applying himself to his studies to become a doctor at Trinity College, and he has just returned to his local village in apparent disgrace after having failed the final examinations for the third time. In spite of his transgressions, however, he has no genuine desire to be a playboy, for he is his mother's whiteheaded or favorite boy, and she insists on forgiving him and treating him like a returning hero. It is the doting mother who has spoiled the child and therefore should be the comic villain of the piece, like Goldsmith's Mrs. Hardcastle; but in this instance, as in all the Robinson comedies, there are no villains, comic or otherwise; and the heroes, such as they are, regardless of their tentative deviations from the golden mean, are all redeemable and must be conveniently restored to the contented family fold. Denis is really too respectable and conscientious at heart to be a playboy or a rogue, so he finally settles down and accepts the contrived offer to be a manager of a shop, marries the sweet girl he loves, and lives happily ever after.

There are no profanations and no clowns in the romantic comedies of Lennox Robinson. In fact, it would be safe to say that the quaint middle-class world of rural Ireland in his plays is seldom disturbed by barbarous or irreverent characters. It is a world of benign manners where the innocent excesses of maternal domination and filial ingratitude are easily put right by sentimentalized good sense. It is a world of provincial stability where moral doubts are never raised, not even with levity or laughter. Presided over by matronly women, it is a comfortable world that has no need for primitive jesters or grotesque paycocks, a domesticated milieu in which gentle laughter is touched off by inconsequential tremors: innocuous stratagems and misunderstandings, naive illusions and awakenings, frustrated and reconciled lovers. Because of their forgivable frailties, all the characters are so basically good that they must be rewarded with the poetic justice they deserve. The result is a type

of genteel village comedy that had a certain popularity but was
not in the mainstream of antic Irish comedy; though it should be
pointed out that the Abbey Theatre, during its lean years in the
generation after the rejection of O'Casey and the death of Lady
Gregory and Yeats, had to survive on an undistinguished surfeit
of this front-parlor and back-kitchen comedy of benign manners.

Robinson had superimposed a tone of anecdotal whimsy on
The Whiteheaded Boy by adopting a folksy narrator's voice in the
stage directions that smacks of amateur theatricals, and even
though these intimate asides are picked up only in a reading of
the text, their sentimental aura hangs over the play like a thick
syrup that will not pour. Robinson's quaint persona sounds more
like a stage-Irish maiden aunt than the onstage Yankee narrator
that Thornton Wilder was later to use with overbearing success
in *Our Town*. Everyone is coddled by the narrator's gossipy
forbearance—liberally sprinkled with effusive sighs and smirks,
and trite "whishts" and "begobs"—so that in the end Robinson
has transformed all misunderstandings into a heart-warming
display of homely virtues. Perhaps the characters are treated
with too much sympathy for effective satire and too much sentimentality for effective comedy. Nevertheless, it is in those
moments when Robinson puts a damper on the glow of sentiment that he creates some highly amusing situations. For example, when George, the head of the family, threatens to deport
the seemingly profligate Denis to hard labor in Canada, John
Duffy, the father of Denis's sweetheart, sees the threat as an
attempt to prevent the marriage and warns that he will sue the
Geoghegans for breach of promise. The counterthreat touches
off a series of wild lies about Denis's prospects which eventually
suggest that he will become a Canadian "railway king" or a
tramp, none of which Duffy believes, as the fabricated Denis
goes from rags to riches to rags. It is likely that this merry game
of multiplying lies owes a debt to a similar situation in Lady
Gregory's *Jackdaw*. As another extension of the theme of
thwarted lovers, Robinson avoids the farcical rebellion of a
January–May marriage by setting up a proper January–January
marriage between the angry Mr. Duffy and Denis's scheming
Aunt Ellen. This middle-aged romance provokes more fun and

laughter than the thwarted young lovers, since the hardheaded
Duffy, who has a soft heart, extracts hush money from all the
Geoghegans on the promise of dropping his lawsuit, even from
Aunt Ellen, who allows herself to be gently blackmailed into
love, until he almost explodes with joy:

> *Duffy.* Cripes! I'd like to get drunk, I'd like to pull the house
> down, I'd like to go bawling singing through the streets of Bal-
> lycolman!
> *Aunt Ellen.* I hope you'll do nothing of the kind, a respectable
> man like you, with a grown daughter and a wife interred.[27]

True to form, respectability always conquers wild impulses in
this play, and, in fact, it is the main pattern of behavior in most
of Robinson's comedies, in *Crabbed Youth and Age* (1922), *The
Far-Off Hills* (1928), and *Drama at Inish* (1933). Although the
restraining influence of respectability resolves all problems in
The Whiteheaded Boy, Robinson wants us to believe he had a more
serious purpose in writing the play. In the Preface to his next
play, *The Lost Leader* (1918), his ill-conceived tragedy about the
collapse of Parnell and the sad fate of Ireland, in which he
developed the hypothesis that the great leader may have lost his
battle with scandal but somehow managed to go on living secretly as Lucius Lenihan in the west of Ireland until 1917, he
claimed that his previous light comedy carried a political allegory: "*The Whiteheaded Boy* is political from beginning to end,
though I don't suppose six people have recognized the fact."[28] A
painstaking search will reveal that there are some scattered references in the play to Ireland's independence; for example,
Aunt Ellen, who is in favor of the farmers' cooperative movement, says in Act I that "Co-operation . . . will be the salvation of
Ireland"; the talk about the enforced emigration of Denis to
Canada in Act II illustrates a major problem for young
Irishmen; and in Act III, when Denis refuses to go to Canada
because, as he says, "I only want to be able to do what I like with
my life—to be free," Mr. Duffy replies, "Free?—Bedad, isn't he
like old Ireland asking for freedom, and we're like the fools of
Englishmen offering him every bloody thing except the one
thing."[29] It would strain credulity to accept the notion that the
mildly profligate and suddenly awakened Denis is supposed to
symbolize exploited Ireland, and all the other people in Bal-

lycolman symbolize oppressive England. Robinson must have been extremely naive about the complexities of the Irish dilemma if he felt that those brief and isolated comments in his genteel play could add up to a political allegory, which never develops as he resolves his simplistic conflict between the respectable old Ireland and the romantic new Ireland with a series of happy compromises that conveniently offer money and marriage to the old and young couples.

Robinson is on safer ground when he avoids Irish politics and concentrates on his provincial politics of domineering mothers and confused children. This motif is evident in all his popular Abbey plays. In *Crabbed Youth and Age,* the overbearing Mrs. Swan proves to be wiser and more attractive than her three innocent daughters. This slight little parlor comedy was originally titled *The Revolt of the Swans,* but since the formidable mother so easily outwits the girls in a coy game of romance that could hardly be called a revolt, the play might more appropriately have been called *The Reign of Mrs. Swan.* In *The Far-Off Hills* we see another and more successful variation of Robinson's favorite parent–child situation, this time in the Clancy family: the widower Patrick and his three young daughters. Marian, the eldest, who is planning to become a nun, controls and represses the whole family as the surrogate mother, or better, mother superior. She constantly scolds her two fun-loving sisters, Ducky and Pet, and inhibits her father so much that he has to resort to secret relief sessions with his two old cronies, when they drink and discuss the lurid stories in *The News of the World.* Marian insists that he should read the respectable *Observer.* Stratagems for potential marriages strain the melodramatic plot as Ducky and Pet scheme to get their father married so that a new mother, Susie Tynan, will then replace the repressive Marian; but Marian suddenly changes her mind about becoming a nun and unaccountably proposes to the lugubrious Howard Mahoney, a superfluous character brought on only for some easy little laughs, who fortunately rejects her; Susie's nephew Pierce then proposes to Marian and she accepts him. It is the garrulous and capricious maid, Ellen, who regularly falls in and out of love, and has just abandoned her fiancé for a new fellow she hasn't met yet, who spells out the platitude that can be applied to everyone in the play: " 'Tis the far-off hills are green."[30]

Robinson's plots may be complicated with coincidences but his world is very simple: all the frailties are curable, all the people are gently chided and rewarded. The characters in all his comedies are afflicted with domestic illusions that can be put right with a truism: be satisfied with what you are and what you have. The same can be said of perhaps his best play, *Drama at Inish*, which in editions published outside of Ireland appeared under the title *Is Life Worth Living?* The answer is a resounding yes, if one lets sleeping dogs lie and avoids turning over any flat stones, to apply the relevant truisms. This play is Robinson's defense of his provincial world, now set in the small seaside town of Inish, which is invaded by a touring repertory company from sophisticated Dublin that arrives to perform a summer season of "intellectual" plays by Ibsen and Strindberg, Chekhov and Tolstoy, in an attempt to bring culture to the country people of Ireland. The result is nearly disastrous and often hilarious. At first Robinson seems to be having a good laugh at the expense of the ignorant locals, but in the end he approves of their natural innocence, which saves them from the terrible dangers of culture. He is much more mockingly satiric in his treatment of the overripe thespians from the big city, Hector de la Mare and Constance Constantia, who affect the grand theatrical manner and openly condescend to the philistines of Inish.

As soon as the serious continental plays are performed, the bored but once happy people are transformed into suffering creatures who begin to imitate art by exposing their hidden frustrations and wounds. In the obligatory mother vs. child scene, the frivolous Annie Twohig and her now Chekhovian son Eddie argue about the first of a series of mock-suicide attempts in the town, this one unsuccessful because the suddenly miserable young couple didn't have enough money to put in the coin-box gas meter when it ran out. They were right to try to kiss and die, Eddie announces melodramatically to his shocked mother:

> *Annie.* Eddie, that's wicked, shameful talk. Where's your religion—and your common sense?
> *Eddie.* Oh, common sense be hanged! Is life worth living?[31]

As always in the benign comedy of Robinson, religion and common sense must eventually prevail, though he cleverly ex-

ploits the temporary outbreak of farcical violence among the
culturally enlightened natives of Inish. Suffering now becomes
an occasion for outrageous public behavior, and the rate of
suicide attempts increases the rate of laughter. In despair Jim
Clancy throws himself off the pier: "Was he drowned dead?"
"No, ma'm. Bruised. The tide was out." Dejected because his
sweetheart keeps turning him down, the impressionable Eddie,
stirred up by Ibsen and Chekhov, also leaps into the sea, but he
happens to be such a good swimmer he is incapable of drowning.
Enter his mother to the rescue, after he emerges from the sea
full of water and foolishness. The mothers in Robinson's comedies may be domineering creatures, but they are always treated
with extreme sympathy because they know how to identify and
fight the enemy. Annie Twohig explains the whole problem of
bedeviled Inish to the culpable actors, who have finally been
sacked and replaced by a harmless circus, when she resorts to
what could be called the reliable flat-stone theory of life:

> I remember saying the morning you came—God forgive me—
> that we were blue-mouldy here for want of a good scandal or two;
> well, it seems there were lots of scandalous things going on in the
> town that no one knew anything of except the parties concerned.
> We were all more or less happy and comfortable, good-tempered
> and jolly—until these plays began to put ideas into our heads. We
> got suspicious of our neighbours and of our own families. The
> young people got asking themselves, "Is life worth living?" . . . Did
> you ever see a big stone in a field, Mr. de la Mare? . . . You might
> be sitting by it, idle-like, some sunny afternoon, and then for no
> reason at all you'd turn it over. And what would you see? Worms.
> Little beetles that'd run this way and that, horrible little creepies
> that'd make your stomach turn, and you'd put the stone back as
> quick as you could, or you'd run away.[32]

At the final curtain, after the question in the play's sometime
title has been answered with a resounding yes, Annie's husband,
after consultation with the priest about the decision to dismiss
the actors, announces, "We've put back the old stone." No more
Ibsenite worms and Chekhovian beetles for Inish. It is not a very
profound view of life, nor is it very flattering to the simple-
minded people of rural Ireland, who are unintentionally
satirized for their provincialism, but it resolves the comic conflict
and sums up Robinson's concept of benign comedy.

If Robinson too easily forgives all his characters for their innocent follies, William Boyle, the civil servant and part-time writer
who was one of the earliest playwrights for the Abbey Theatre,
wrote several popular comedies in which the central character
carries one dominating trait to excess, for which comic transgression he is ridiculed and corrected. In his first and most
promising work, *The Eloquent Dempsy* (1906), Boyle began with a
colorful hero who is a potential comic rogue, but then he pro-
ceeded to sentimentalize and reform him. Jeremiah Dempsy is
an ambitious publican, grocer, and county councillor whose
"eloquence" is his dissembling habit of telling people what he
thinks they want to hear in his attempt to sell more whiskey and
get reelected to public office. As a result he is invariably on the
verge of making everyone very happy or very furious. Although
there are many comical possibilities in this situation, they are
only partially fulfilled. And once more it is a wise and good
woman who diverts the direction of the play from comedy to
common sense. It is Dempsy's devoted wife who sees through his
trickery and even plots to expose him in order to save him, and it
is she who reveals the soft spot that takes the bite out of the
laughter, especially in one of her explicit speeches that assures
us once again that life is worth living:

> You're like Lanna Macree's dog—a piece of the road with every-
> body.... You'll go anywhere and subscribe to anything if they'll
> only let you make a speech about it. (*Dempsy protests by a gesture.*)
> Jerry, you're a rag on every bush, fluttering to every wind that
> blows; and (*tenderly*) if you weren't the best husband and the best
> father that ever broke the bread of life, I'd say you were the
> biggest rascal in the whole of Ireland.[33]

That deadly touch of tenderness gives the comic game away
and the rascal proves to be so harmless that a barbarous possibility is shifted to a benign reality. There is no room for a Pelagian
heresy in this promise of a compensating heaven for the wayward Dempsy. Virtue must triumph when, as a result of his
wife's well-intentioned scheming, Dempsy is defeated in the elec-
tion and retires from public life to live quietly and happily on a
farm with his dear wife. Like Robinson, Boyle couldn't resist
softening and oversimplifying his comic figures. His play is a
type of transparent and tractable comedy that illustrates a mild

form of Bergsonian automatism that is too readily curable. Above all, Boyle lacked an ironic and sustaining point of view, perhaps something that approximated the comic irony of an O'Casey in his ambivalent attitude toward the rascally "Captain" Boyle and Joxer Daly who are at the same time seen as irrepressible and reprehensible, or heretically comic and therefore beyond any hope of tender reformation.

Another indication of Boyle's limitations can be illustrated in his *Family Failing* (1912), in which the single flaw of family laziness becomes the main source of comic frailty and redemption. Dominic and Joe, the slothful or "Do-nothing Donnellys," have allowed their farm to fall into heavy debt and near ruin, until their Uncle Robert returns from America with the hint that he might bail them out with his reputed great wealth. The moralizing Robert is actually penniless, but his sermons on the glory of the work ethic, plus his pretended promise of money, suddenly inspire Dominic to work hard for the first time in his life and save the farm as well as himself in yet another benign transformation, and thus the "family failing" is conquered. It is of course a manufactured ending, and a gross oversimplification of life and comedy.

Robinson and Boyle served a useful purpose in providing the early Abbey Theatre with much-needed plays for the company's repertoire, but it should be apparent that they didn't discover any native themes or reveal any dramatic insights that could contribute to a significant tradition of Irish comedy.

The Barbarous Morals of Shaw and Carroll

At the reluctant invitation of Yeats, Shaw tried to provide a play for the early Abbey Theatre, and the result, *John Bull's Other Island* (1904), though it had to be rejected because the modest little theater company could not cast or stage it, deserves a significant place in the tradition of Irish comedy. The only Irish play that Shaw wrote, it has many elements of the irreverent joking and ironic humor that are so typical of barbarous comedy, as well as a number of mock-heroic characters who illustrate the Pelagian or uniquely Irish heresy of comic autonomy, which in Shavian terms could also be described as the liberating spirit of the comic life force. There are no conventional heroes and no villains at all in this antiromantic comedy, unless mother Ireland herself, the intractable Cathleen Ni Houlihan, can once again serve as the villainous old sow who symbolically devours or frustrates all the Irish characters. One might have anticipated that the British Tom Broadbent should have been the villain of the piece, but such an obvious concession to Irish nationalism would have carried with it the melodramatic machinery to undermine Shaw's unique dramatic strategy of characteristically mocking all sides of the conflict in his game of comic cross-purposes. So the nominal enemy Broadbent must share a central position with the disenchanted Irishmen Larry Doyle and Father Keegan, all of them, three in one and one in three, mock heroes who represent aspects of Shaw's ambivalent attitude toward the Irish question at the turn of the century. Perhaps Keegan speaks for all three, and for Shaw, when he says, "My way of joking is to tell the truth. It's the funniest joke in the world."[34]

The unamused Yeats was undoubtedly relieved about the expedient rejection because he considered the play to be too didactic and tainted by naturalistic Ibsenism, and therefore not appropriate for his poetic theater. For his part, Shaw, like Joyce, was an avowed Ibsenite and therefore skeptical about the pre-Raphaelite Yeats's theater, dedicated to the "cultic twalette"—as Joyce laughingly called it—of legendary and romantic Ireland. Shaw had intentionally set out to mock the Ireland of legend and romance in his play, and if he was a disciple of Ibsen in his apparent pursuit of truth, he also projected a broadly comic spirit that was calculated to provoke more ironic laughter than naturalistic dogma. Actually, the enigmatic truth about Ireland is hidden in a variety of Shavian jokes; in the blundering common sense of Broadbent, in the sardonic sermons of Doyle, and in the apocalyptic visions of Keegan. Most profoundly, however, it is in the prophecies of the mad Father Keegan that we find the symbolic and impossible truth; "Saint" Peter, the rock of Rosscullen, and the ostracized fool as defrocked priest who is one of the most poetic and visionary characters Shaw created. The best and last joke comes when we realize that Keegan's wild dream of a new secular trinity is finally and hopelessly the thematic heart of the play: an Irish trinity of church and state and people—"It is a godhead in which all life is human and all humanity divine: three in one and one in three. It is, in short, the dream of a madman."[35]

It is one of those rare instances when Shaw allowed the poetry of drama to take precedence over propaganda, and so he concentrates on the comedy of defeat as the isolated Keegan remains magnificently mad and mockingly untriumphant at the end. Keegan has the saintly vision of Shaw's Joan without the vindicating glory of her beatitude. He is the village jester or sublime fool of the play. As a failed priest he is a mock-heroic figure, a failed saint without miracles or martyrdom, without any disciples in Rosscullen except, ironically, for an animated grasshopper and a half-witted Patsy Farrell, though Shaw may have hoped that some loyal Keeganites might one day emerge in modern Ireland. In light of the violent course of twentieth-century Irish history, however, that would have to remain a vain hope, one Shavian joke that is still untrue, similar to his wild forecast in the Preface of the play that the Irish Catholic church would probably liberate itself from Rome when the Irish nation liberated itself from England.[36]

What this means is that the comedy of the play is more convincing than any of Shaw's propaganda; or that his comic-ironic view of Ireland is more dramatic than didactic. Shaw's comic point of view is established at the beginning in the farcical scene between Tom Broadbent and Tim Haffigan, the pompous Anglo-Saxon who sounds like a stage Englishman, and the pseudo-Celt who sounds like a stage Irishman. This alliance of fools is promptly exposed when Larry Doyle, speaking as an ironic chorus voice, as he often does, scolds Broadbent:

> But when a thoroughly worthless Irishman comes to England, and finds the whole place full of romantic duffers like you, who will let him loaf and drink and sponge and brag as long as he flatters your sense of moral superiority by playing the fool and degrading himself and his country, he soon learns the antics that take you in.[37]

To learn the antics of the master–slave game is the main purpose of the clown's self-deprecating masquerade. But while romantic duffers like Broadbent encourage stage-Irish parasites like Haffigan to play the fool for fools in England, native Irishmen, according to the sardonic Doyle, suffer from another and more incisive form of folly, which in his most important speech in the play he calls the curse of dreaming, though some farcical ironies will later temper these hard judgments:

> Oh, the dreaming! the dreaming! the torturing, heart-scalding, never satisfying dreaming, dreaming, dreaming, dreaming! [*Savagely*] No debauchery that ever coarsened and brutalized an Englishman can take the worth and usefulness out of him like that dreaming. An Irishman's imagination never lets him alone, never convinces him, never satisfies him; but it makes him that he cant face reality nor deal with it nor handle it nor conquer it. . . .
>
> If you want to interest him in Ireland youve got to call the unfortunate island Kathleen ni Houlihan and pretend she's a little old woman. It saves thinking. It saves working. It saves everything except imagination, imagination, imagination; and imagination's such a torture that you cant bear it without whisky. . . .
>
> And all the while there goes on a horrible, senseless, mischievous laughter. When youre young, you exchange vile stories with them; and as youre too futile to be able to help or cheer them, you chaff and sneer and taunt them for not doing the things you darent do yourself. And all the time you laugh! laugh! laugh! eternal derision, eternal envy, eternal folly, eternal fouling and staining and degrading, until, when you come at last to a country where men take a question seriously and give a serious answer to it, you deride them for having no sense of humor, and plume yourself on your own worthlessness as if it made you better than them.[38]

Shaw betrays his own distress in this devastating speech, but he was seldom more brilliantly diagnostic and tragicomic than he is in this dramatic assessment of the Irish malaise of frustrated dreaming and savage laughing. There is no sharper revelation of this barbarous knowledge that haunts the imaginative Irishman and exposes the ironic sense in his seemingly senseless laughter: it provides the only way to go on living in an unlivable world. There are no serious answers; there are only defensive jokes. Fortunately Shaw was a comic genius as well as a puritan preacher, so that he could have it both ways by being seriously didactic and wildly satiric. He could therefore laugh with as well as at his stricken clowns by providing an abundance of vivid jokes that illustrate the liberating Irish folly of psychic release through prevarication and self-deprecation. If there is an element of damnation as well as salvation in that type of dark Irish humor, it might be called making the best of a bad situation. Joyce called the Irish situation a state of "paralysis," O'Casey called it a world of "chassis," and Beckett said there was "nothing to be done" about it. Nothing except survival games of mischievous laughter and gallows humor, as Shaw illustrates in his play. Freud and Eric Bentley have wisely reminded us that one can only grin and bear it, because only the grinning makes it bearable.

As civil engineers who plan to develop the land by building a hotel and golf links as a tourist haven to save Rosscullen from stagnation, Doyle and Broadbent never stop fighting and grinning at each other, as well as at all the local eccentrics. On the other hand, Father Keegan, as an uncivil engineer of human souls who hopes to develop his private dream of an Irish heaven on earth, challenges everyone, and he begins his mission by chatting and grinning with a lowly grasshopper. Many of the jokes in the play are based on comic insect and animal imagery— grasshopper and caterpillar, ass and pig—a little bestiary that provides a series of Shavian fables on human frailty. On his first entrance, before we know who he is and what to expect from him, the white-haired fifty-year-old Keegan, with "the face of a young saint" and "a brogue which is the jocular assumption of a gentleman," appears in friendly conversation with the grasshopper as they debate whether Ireland is heaven or purgatory or hell. An example of this clever dialogue should indicate the wide range of Shaw's comic artistry and show how effectively he can play with fine profanations of holy Ireland:

> The Man [encouragingly] Thats right. I suppose now youve come out to make yourself miserable be admyerin the sunset?
> The Grasshopper [sadly] X.X.
> The Man. Aye, youre a thrue Irish grasshopper.
> The Grasshopper [loudly] X.X.X.
> The Man. Three cheers for ould Ireland, is it? That helps you to face out the misery and the poverty and the torment, doesnt it?
> The Grasshopper [plaintively] X.X.
> The Man. Ah, it's no use, me poor little friend. If you could jump as far as a kangaroo you couldnt jump away from your own heart an its punishment. You can only look at Heaven from here: you cant reach it. There! [pointing with his stick to the sunset] thats the gate o glory, isnt it?
> The Grasshopper [assenting] X.X.

The Man. Sure it's the wise grasshopper yar to know that. But tell
me this, Misther Unworldly Wiseman: Why does the sight of
Heaven wring your heart an mine as the sight of holy wather
wrings the heart o the divil? What wickedness have you done to
bring that curse on you? Here! where you jumpin to? Wheres
your manners to go skyrocketin like that out o the box in the
middle o your confession [*he threatens it with his stick*]?
The Grasshopper [*penitently*] X.
The Man [*lowering the stick*] I accept your apology; but dont do it
again. And now tell me one thing before I let you go home to bed.
Which would you say this country was: hell or purgatory?
The Grasshopper. X.
The Man. Hell! Faith I'm afraid youre right. I wondher what you
and me did when we were alive to get sent here.[39]

In this irreverent ritual of mock confession a spoiled priest is
symbolically shriving the people of Ireland, represented by a
penitential grasshopper who had the misfortune to find itself in
hell in Rosscullen. Sentimental cheers and prayers and sunsets
can no longer soften the misery and poverty and torment of life
in holy Ireland. Only mischievous laughter can appease that
trinty of woes. The play is a comic allegory about the certain
damnation and doubtful salvation of Ireland. When Doyle
realizes that Broadbent's hotel scheme for saving Rosscullen will
probably mean yet another conquest and exploitation of Cathleen Ni Houlihan by John Bull, he resorts to his caterpillar fable
to explain the efficient folly of the English national character:

> The world is as full of fools as a tree is full of leaves. Well, the
> Englishman does what the caterpillar does. He instinctively makes
> himself like a fool, and eats up all the real fools at his ease while
> his enemies let him alone and laugh at him for being a fool like
> the rest. Oh, nature is cunning! cunning![40]

When Keegan realizes that Broadbent's extended plan for saving Rosscullen includes his standing for the local seat in parliament, the mock saint damns the Englishman with faint praise by
deciding it might be the better part of wisdom to vote for an
efficient English devil than a mindless Irish patriot. But Broadbent is reluctant to accept this dubious flattery, so Keegan shifts
to a more mundane analogy and calls him an English ass, pin-
ning the tail on him with the following testimonial:

You may take it without offence from a madman who calls the ass
his brother—and a very honest, useful and faithful brother, too.
The ass, sir, is the most efficient of beasts, matter-of-fact, hardy,
friendly when you treat him as a fellow-creature, stubborn when
you abuse him, ridiculous only in love, which sets him braying,
and in politics, which move him to roll about in the public road
and raise a dust about nothing. Can you deny these qualities and
habits in yourself, sir?[41]

Broadbent good-humoredly accepts this satiric portrait of
himself, since, in yet another of Shaw's mischievous jokes, the
foolish Anglo-Saxon has begun to conquer the even more
foolish Celts. As Keegan indicates, Broadbent has in a recent fit
of brashness been braying his love successfully to Nora Reilly,
the local "heiress" with a fortune of forty pounds per annum as
her chief claim to fame; and as a result of his newly discovered
political ambition he has just been the cause of the hilarious
slaughter of Matt Haffigan's pig in the crowded main street of
Rosscullen on market day. That farcical killing, a wildly knockabout example of gallows humor, is probably the most exciting
thing that ever happened in the town, and, as if in anticipation
of the mythmaking patricide of Christy Mahon in Synge's
Playboy, the pigicide of Broadbent leads to his transformation
from fool to folk hero. Up to the moment he volunteers to
deliver Matt's pig in his motor car, as an exaggerated gesture of
goodwill that unpredictably turns into a comic miracle, Broadbent has been a laughable curiosity in Ireland, and a special
target of ridicule by Doyle and Keegan. But the bored people of
Shaw's Rosscullen, like the frustrated people of Synge's Mayo,
welcome the mock killer as something of a playboy-savior and
celebrate his exploits as an epic adventure of merriment. Doyle
and Keegan may be skeptical about it all, but the exuberant
Barney Doran, who has already told the spectacular story three
times and is aching to tell it again, sets the tone for the mock-
heroic final act: "Doran is reeling in an ecstasy of mischievous
mirth which has infected all his friends. They are screaming with
laughter, doubled up, leaning on the furniture and against the
walls, shouting, screeching, crying."[42] The comic imagination of
the Irish, then, contrary to Doyle's view of it as a terrible trait of
self-torture, functions as a liberating instinct of escape from

grim reality. Keegan disapproves but recognizes the compensatory process of gallows humor: "There is danger, destruction, torment! What more do we need to make us merry? Go on, Barney: the last drops are not squeezed from the story yet."[43]

As the faithful recorder of the comic epic, Barney doesn't need encouragement to describe once more Broadbent's wild ride and crash in the center of the town, unable to stop because the frightened pig bolted away from Patsy Farrell and landed in Broadbent's lap with its tail caught under the foot brake before it made its fatal bacon leap in front of the car. After that, in Barney's words, "dhere was little left for me or anywan else to go over except wid a knife an fork." Barney and Keegan offer the comical obsequies:

> Doran [*reflectively*] He has the divil's own luck, that Englishman, annyway; for hwen they picked him up he hadnt a scratch on him, barrn hwat the pig did to his cloes. Patsy had two fingers out o jynt; but the smith pulled them sthraight for him. Oh, you never heard such a hullaballoo as there was. There was Molly cryin Me chaney, me beautyful chaney! n oul Matt shoutin Me pig, me pig! n the polus takin the number o the car, n not a man in town able to speak for laughin—
>
> Keegan [*with intense emphasis*] It is hell: it is hell. Nowhere else could such a scene be a burst of happiness for the people.[44]

It was one of Mark Twain's barbarous jokes, as well as Shaw's, that there is humor and happiness in hell, not in heaven. In spite of the comic lamentations of Keegan and Doyle, Rosscullen has been transformed into a happy hell with its mock wake for a pig, a Joycean "funferall"—a fun-for-all and funeral. When the battle-scarred Broadbent staggers in, he is welcomed as a conquering hero, an ironic reversal that encourages him to play the braggart-warrior and deliver a pompous electioneering speech that is greeted with such hearty cheers that he is practically assured of winning the parliamentary seat. Unlike Synge, Shaw doesn't allow the people to reject the mock hero they have created, but, nevertheless, Broadbent's victory is partially discredited. He is recognized as a tainted or proxy hero, an efficient stage Englishman who may be the lesser of all impractical Irish alternatives.

In the ironic resolution of the play, as so often happens in Shavian comedy, the winners sound like losers and the losers sound like winners. Only Keegan, the mad saint, is in a tentative state of grace now, though he has won nothing except the ostracized freedom to go on dreaming his noble but impossible dream of a divine humanity. His is the presiding and prophetic voice at the final curtain, and he speaks for Shaw when he defends the dreams and jokes of the play: "Every dream is a prophecy: every jest is an earnest in the womb of Time."[45] In the more immediate time of the play, the fate of Rosscullen belongs in the hands of Broadbent and Doyle as partners in the syndicate that will build the golfing hotel to save the town, though Keegan doesn't see that as salvation. In an attempt to mediate between the two partners, Keegan sardonically sums up the Shavian view of the Englishman and Irishman: "Standing here between you the Englishman, so clever in your foolishness, and this Irishman, so foolish in his cleverness, I cannot in my ignorance be sure which of you is the more deeply damned."[46]

In the end we are left with a perspective of enlightened folly and damnation, in the melodramatic fatalism of Doyle and the consequential optimism of Broadbent, in the mad prophecies and dreams of Keegan. It is a dark and uncertain conclusion for a comedy because Shaw finds little hope in the paternalism of England or the romanticism of Ireland. Even love, the reassuringly happy convention of comedy, is deflated in the love triangle of Doyle and Broadbent and Nora Reilly. After eighteen years of self-exile from Ireland, Doyle has lost all his illusions about modest little Nora, whom he offers up to the impressionable Broadbent as cheerfully as Professor Higgins bequeaths Eliza Doolittle to Freddie. Shaw makes it very clear that his thirty-six-year-old heroine is no romantic stage-Irish colleen, for he describes her as "a slight weak woman in a pretty muslin dress (her best)," an undistinguished spinster of frail and delicate charm who is quite commonplace to the Irish if attractive to outsiders. She is almost painfully discredited when Shaw looks at her through the eyes of Broadbent and Doyle and concludes: "For Tom Broadbent therefore, an attractive woman, whom he would even call ethereal. To Larry Doyle, an everyday woman fit only for the eighteenth century, helpless, useless, almost sexless, an invalid without the excuse of disease, an incarnation of everything in Ireland that drove him out of it."[47]

This antiromantic view of Nora indicates that she is one of the rare Shavian women who is almost devoid of the life force, that unique gift of creative imagination that in this play is bestowed only on Keegan. But if an antiromantic tone dominates much of the comedy, again it might be said that Shaw, the comic puritan, in one of his typical jokes, tries to have it both ways by making the visionary Keegan something of a Blakean romantic. When Shaw says No to a corrupting way of life, he invariably offers his own Yes to an idealistic alternative; and in this instance only the marriage of an earthly heaven and a happy hell in the womb of time could lead to a new Jerusalem in Ireland. Keegan, therefore, implicitly pursues his mad dream under the redemptive motto of Blake: "If the fool would persist in his folly he would become wise."[48]

The wise fools in O'Casey's later pastoral comedies also dream about a new Jerusalem in Ireland, especially in *Purple Dust* (1940), which could be called a knockabout version of *John Bull's Other Island*. Unlike the vegetarian Shaw, however, the randy O'Casey doesn't exclude red-blooded romantic love from his earthly Celtic paradise, and his satiric defeat of John Bull is more devastating than Shaw's clever game of English and Irish folly, but the two dramatists share a comic vision of damnation and salvation in Ireland. In O'Casey's play the stage Englshmen Stoke and Poges are outwitted and routed by a band of barbarous Irish clowns, who are inspired by the visionary Philib O'Dempsey, the 2nd Workman, with his wild Celtic and Blakean dreams that establish his kinship with Peter Keegan.

There are many wise fools in the melodramatic plays of Paul Vincent Carroll, and his most memorable characters are often foolishly wise priests who, unlike the stern and wrathful St. Patrick, have an affinity for exotic Spain or the self-indulgent ease of Oisín, and they resort to guile and wit in guiding their eccentric people. Partially influenced by Ibsen and Shaw, Carroll allows some of his rebellious schoolmasters and sentient young women to stand alone as courageous enemies of the people, or to reject the common path and emerge as symbolic figures who dream of an idealized Ireland that might have been a comfort to Peter Keegan. Although there are unmistakable signs of an irreverent and sometimes barbarously comic attitude toward narrowly Catholic Ireland in his plays, Carroll can also dilute the force of the laughter in his unexpectedly pious and benign resolutions. The daring and expedient Carroll tends to hedge all his bets. In a contradictory rather than complementary manner, unlike the paradoxical Shaw, Carroll tries to have it both ways alternately, rather than ironically; for even though he appeals directly to the enlightened spirit of the pagan Oisín and the symbolic Niamh in *The White Steed* (1939), he also imposes a Christian resolution, and he has already been chastened and consoled by the Catholic spirit of the nation through the saintly Brigid in *Shadow and Substance* (1937).

These two plays represent his most successful work and also reveal his most characteristic strengths and weaknesses as a dramatist. Carroll's acute understanding of the people of provincial Louth provides him with an abundance of comic portraits for his minor characters, but his main characters, who are drawn with equally vivid comic strokes, must also carry an extra burden of Irish symbolism that clogs the plays with heavy meanings that can become more abstract than dramatic. *Shadow and Substance* is prefaced with an epigraph that sets up the triangular symbolism that links the three central figures: "A legend connected with St. Brigid relates how, in order to escape the attentions of persistent suitors, she disfigured the loveliness of her face at Faughart, her birthplace, near Dundalk, Ireland."[49] The innocent servant girl of Canon Skerritt, Brigid is the martyred saint of the play, and her two suitors in the allegory are the conservative Canon and the radical schoolmaster O'Flingsley. Three in one and one in three, they represent a trinity of Irish faith, dogma, and progress that cannot be reconciled. At the end of the play there is a faint hope that the men's complicity in Brigid's death might compel them to join forces in honor of her sacrifice, but it remains doubtful whether the spirit of Brigid is strong enough to achieve such a unity of purpose in a divided Ireland.

When the play opened in New York in 1938, Carroll commented on the symbolic conflict in a manner that offers no possibility of a reconciliation: "The rebel schoolmaster and the

Canon represent the conflicting forces that crush Brigid (the spirit of the nation) between them."[50] As the devout and vulnerable spirit of the nation, the gentle Brigid lacks the awesome stature of the traditional Cathleen Ni Houlihan, who demands blood sacrifice from her patriotic countrymen. She is a wise fool whose simple faith is based on universal love and humility, but this naive wisdom is too fragile to save the tormented Irish. Again we are confronted by the recurring theme of damnation and salvation in Ireland, and Carroll often takes a comic approach to the potentially tragic condition, as he does in the opening scene between Brigid and O'Flingsley. The schoolmaster is described as an alert young man of "passion and pride . . . bright in manner, and has a pleasing sense of humor." By contrast, Brigid is described as a backward and antiheroic heroine, something of an unconscious jester who is wiser than she knows: "Brigid is small, possibly a little stupid-looking, with large eyes; neat, but not to any degree Quakerish. She is obviously not mentally outstanding, but capable of deep affection, and pleasing in her person."[51] Brigid is an other-worldly being who hears voices, and in telling O'Flingsley about her miraculous conversations with St. Brigid, she carries her saintly experiences lightly and cheerfully: "I'm used to her now. She is always smilin', smilin' and in great humour, as if she was enjoyin' makin' me happy. It's lovely that she's not sour like a nun at the convent school, or like a priest in the box."[52]

Joy and laughter and love radiate from her half-stupid countenance, and yet she can stun the schoolmaster and the Canon with the uncanny insights that St. Brigid reveals to her. At this early point no one knows yet about the secret book O'Flingsley has written as a satiric exposure of the reactionary and inept clergy, but Brigid already knows the truth and says: "She told me you had a secret. . . . She said—a dark secret, and that you were a blunderer, but that God loved blunderers because they were the children of Peter."[53] Then she astounds him again when, with equal perception, she sums up St. Brigid's view of the Canon: "She said that there was great holiness in him, but that his pride would need the tears of a hundred just men and the soul of a child, to soften it."[54] Both men are transfixed in these shrewd revelations, and thereafter they can only fulfill the saintly prophecies and contribute their rash blundering and their intense pride to the destruction of the naive saint. Add the vicious folly of the vigilante curates Father Corr and Father Kirwan, and the situation has all the ingredients of a moving melodrama. The play is often comic and eventually tragic, but it is not a tragedy, unless it is Ireland's tragedy. Brigid is a sacrificial victim, not a tragic heroine. The cause of her death must be found in the blind folly of others, not in any conscious act of her own overweening pride. She is not the bold peasant girl of Lorraine playing Saint Joan for France and the world; she is the wise village idiot of Louth unwittingly playing Cassandra for Ireland. She is a pure and guiltless spirit.

The guilty and central figure of the play is the proud Canon Skerritt, who reigns over his parish like an enlightened and amusing despot. One of the most Shavian characters outside of a Shaw play, he is Carroll's finest achievement, a superhero with feet of clay who dominates all the action and generates the comic and tragic motifs. It is he that provokes O'Flingsley, who in turn provokes the curates, whose mob then accidentally causes the death of Brigid. We should despise him and yet we must admire him as a distinguished man of many parts and powerful convictions who is beset by comic-ironic contraries: he is a reactionary Irish clergyman with romantic Spanish memories and refined tastes; he is a classical and cultural enthusiast surrounded by the vulgarity and hooliganism of the Sacred Heart Confraternity; he is a lordly man of infinite wit and irony who cannot see the simple humor and wisdom of the lowly Brigid. Until her melodramatic death at the end of the play, he emerges as a rare breed of *miles gloriosus,* an intellectual and subtle braggart who justifies his inflated image of himself with attractive arrogance and a-plomb.

When the curates present the Canon with a gift from the Women's Confraternity, a gaudy oleograph of the Sacred Heart, in order to counteract what they consider to be the outrageously "secular" paintings that adorn the walls of his living room— reproductions of masterpieces by Velazquez, Murillo, El Greco, Da Vinci, and Raphael—he recoils in horror from "the nightmarish conception of some uncouth vulgarian." He then proceeds to read them all an ironic sermon about the extent to which cheap religiosity has corrupted genuine religious art and ethics—"they have taken away our aesthetic sense and given us in exchange a rather spurious ethical sense, and as you can see here—(*He points to picture*) they deal with a whitewash brush in terms of the divine. Yet you stand aghast when I point it out to you—when I refuse to allow barbarians to impose on me their vulgar conception of Christ and His Saints." And then he concludes with a righteous blast that must have sounded like blasphemy to his stunned listeners: "If, for a moment, I felt our Redeemer's heart was akin to that monstrosity on the wall, I should go back to Socrates, and be a pagan."[55]

One cannot be blamed for suspecting that the refreshingly irreverent Canon might be more at home with the creative disciples of Oisín than the vulgarized sheep of St. Patrick. This is one of Carroll's ironic jokes that runs throughout the play. It is unfortunate that the Canon doesn't understand Brigid's simple visions as shrewdly as he judges whitewashed religiosity in art. But perhaps his insubstantial attempt to understand and save the shadowy Brigid is really beyond the capability of anyone in Ireland, for she is more than an unusual girl of simple faith, as Carroll points out directly and symbolically. More than she or anyone realizes, she is herself Ireland, the unfulfilled and innocent spirit of the nation. Perhaps she is too innocent, too idealistically and impractically conceived. Her tragic fate, the fate of Ireland, cannot be redeemed by the humbling of a canon, a schoolmaster, or two curates. The proud Canon spends most of his time engaged in witty and satiric contests with his insensitive parishioners, and his frustration emerges from his stubborn encounters with O'Flingsley and Brigid, especially when Brigid's fate is taken out of his hands at the end. In the narrow eyes of the Confraternity members, whom he considers to be the barbarians who are corrupting the holy faith, he must seem to be a barbarously irreverent priest; and he is in his ironic complexities a unique figure, a tragicomic clergyman who occupies a special status in Irish comedy, a sophisticated jester who is finally defeated in his proud attempt to go on living in an unlivable parish.

In his next play, *The White Steed*, Carroll created another type of unique figure whose comic lineage owes more to O'Casey

than to Shaw, a sly old priest as the unsophisticated parish jester
who is able to rise out of his defeat. Canon Matt Lavelle is a more
broadly comic and sentimentalized character than the more
aloof and formidable Canon Skerritt, and he is directly associated with the Ossianic symbolism of freedom that is perhaps
overambitiously intended to unify the play. Again Carroll sets
up an epigraph to explain his symbolic theme:

> This play is symbolically based on the old pre-Christian tale of
> Ossian, the son of Finn, who was taken away by the lovely Niam
> on her white steed to the Land of Youth. Returning 300 years
> later in search of Finn, he finds all the great heroes dead, and the
> land swarming with priests and the little black men. One day he
> contemptuously leans down from the white steed and hurls into
> the air a flag of marble that one hundred of the little men are
> vainly trying to raise, but in doing so, he smashes the saddle-
> girdle, and as his feet touch the earth, he withers miserably
> away.[56]

It is difficult to maintain these allegorical relationships
throughout the play because the wild pagan spirit of Ossian, or
Oisín, cannot easily be integrated with the benign Christianity of
Canon Lavelle. There are at first some surface parallels. Like the
disillusioned and disabled Oisín of Celtic legend, who suddenly
grew old and impotent when he returned to Ireland and fell
from the white steed of invincible youth and power while trying
to help the people raise a heavy stone, the once active and beloved Canon has suffered a stroke while trying to help a friend
fix a fence and is now confined to a wheelchair in his parochial
house in the little seaside village of Lurcan, in county Louth.
Nevertheless, it strains credulity to identify the Canon with the
Oisín who returned from a 300-year sojourn in Tir na nOg, the
Land of Youth, with the beautiful Niamh (Nee-av), only to discover that the great Fenians had been replaced by the new Christian priests and their frightened little dark people of no courage
or hope, the Firbolgs, who were overrunning Ireland. Lurcan
has now been overrun by Father Shaughnessy, the new vigilante
priest who has replaced the ailing Canon and is turning the
villagers into little dark people of fear and hatred. Furthermore,
the Canon must share the Ossianic affinities with Nora Fintry,
the symbolic Niamh of the play, the martyred librarian who has
been sacked by Father Shaughnessy and beaten up by his

vigilance committee for keeping blasphemous books on the library shelves. The main action of the play centers around the attempt to liberate Lurcan from what the schoolmaster calls "the new clerical fascism."

If the paralyzed Canon is something less than a mythical Oisín, the martyred Nora is something more than an idyllic Niamh. She is a militant young woman who, unlike the innocent Brigid, refuses to become a sacrificial lamb and decides to fight against the clerical opposition of Father Shaughnessy. Instead of having religious visions, she has heroic dreams about the pagan Niamh and her white steed, the liberating steed that becomes in the imagination of Nora a symbol of the Celtic power and courage that inspired Oisín and Cuchulain to accomplish great deeds of honor. Nora is convinced that it will take such courageous deeds to save Lurcan and Ireland now. Denis Dillon, the frightened schoolmaster who loves her but lacks the fearless blundering of O'Flingsley, wishes he had the strength to join her in the struggle against Father Shaughnessy. He calls to her: "Lift me on your white steed, Nora." To which she replies: "Every man, Denis, must lift himself on the white steed."[57] Thus, for Nora, who is a liberated Ibsenite woman with a Shavian life force, everyone has his own daimonic white steed of vital power that always waits to be harnessed and ridden into battle against the forces of darkness.

The paralyzed Canon Matt may be unable to mount his white steed, but he has the guile of the comic daimon and folk imagination to help him expose the malicious folly of the Vigilance Committee. When Father Shaughnessy accuses him of being a blundering old fool, the Canon replies pointedly: "I am what Christ cautioned us to be, as simple as a dove, but as wise as a serpent."[58] It may tie a knot in Carroll's pagan symbolism, but it makes more consistent sense that the sly old Canon should use the vital power or white steed of Christ rather than Oisín. He considers Father Shaughnessy to be a Calvinistic aberration in the Catholic church and declares his own principles with this quaint wisdom that concludes with a mock-heroic gesture:

> I am human enough to want, like all ordinary people, a little sugar in my tea, a little soda in my whiskey, a wee bit of coaxing in my dogma and a hot bottle in my bed on a frosty night. I hate

anything in the raw, from raw poteen to raw men like Calvin, whom I'd have strangled out of a sense of decency to the humanity Christ died for.[59]

Canon Matt is a benign and barbarous old codger who often sounds like a half-rehabilitated Fluther Good in a Roman collar, but unlike the ironic O'Casey, Carroll cannot resist sentimentalizing his clerical jester. The play moves inevitably toward a melodramatic happy ending, and it is a Christian, not an Ossianic, miracle that allows the Canon to rise out of his wheelchair at the eleventh hour and walk with canes to confront and defeat Father Shaughnessy and the Vigilance Committee. He is ably assisted by the flinty Inspector Toomey, who in another minor miracle of timing appears at the crucial moment and threatens to arrest Father Shaughnessy and his unruly mob. Carroll inconsistently resolves the conflict in a very reverent manner that owes nothing to the daimonic spirit of Oisín and the white steed, by resorting to the restraining power of the village establishment, police and priest, to restore civil law and clerical order. The rebellious Nora and the now courageous Denis are appeased by the Canon's victory and they settle for a future life together draining and tilling her father's farm. It is not a very heroic prospect. Some final lip service is paid to the glory of Celtic Ireland when Nora claims that she has "been born out of warriors, poets, saints and heroes"; when the Canon encourages Denis to go to her: "her white steed has not come down the centuries for nothing." But this symbolism is not enhanced by the simplistic ending with the Canon's reassurance that the fighting is over and all's well in Lurcan, followed by his comforting prayer to the Blessed Virgin at the final curtain: "Well, Holy Mother, we're used to these little mountain storms, but, sure, the mountains remain. We needn't be afraid, need we now?"[60] The dramatic storm has been overcome so easily that we begin to wonder if it really was that serious from the start. And perhaps we should place our faith in the mercy of the Blessed Virgin rather than the white steed of Oisín, which would be a valid theme for a different kind of symbolic play.

Carroll wrote a number of less ambitious and mildly amusing comedies, and one early play, *Coggerers* (1934), should be examined briefly here because it is a work of political symbolism, a one-act tragicomic fantasy about the 1916 Rising which calls for a comparison with O'Casey's *Plough and the Stars*. The diehard nationalists who rioted against O'Casey's play would have roared their approval of Carroll's patriotic homage to Cathleen Ni Houlihan. The mock-heroic heroine, Mrs. Galgoogley, is an earthy old Dublin charwoman. While working in a city library on Easter Monday she carries on some lively comic banter with the animated busts of five famous Irish martyrs: John Mitchel, Lord Edward Fitzgerald, Wolfe Tone, Robert Emmet, and Parnell. They are the "coggerers" or conspirators (from the Gaelic *cogarnach*—Carroll later changed the title to *The Conspirators*), and they sense that there is a smell of gunpowder in the air on that fateful day.

For the first three-quarters of the play, before the Rising begins, the coggerers argue and joke among themselves and with Mrs. Galgoogley, who dusts their heads and amuses them with a comic "come-all-ye" ballad about dear dirty Dublin. When the mild-mannered librarian, Eamon O'Curry, appears briefly on his way to join the Rising—he is wearing a Volunteer's uniform and guns under his overcoat—he asks the charwoman if she noticed anything unusual about the look of the city when she came to work that morning, and she replies: "Look? Sure, jist as it always looks—like a woman paradin' in all her finery, but a dirty house at home. That's Dublin."[61] But dirty Dublin is to be different on this day, after which it will be changed utterly by bloodshed and martyrdom. In the last ten minutes of the play the comic mood changes suddenly when the sound of gunfire is at last heard in the street, and Emmet proudly tells Mrs. Galgoogley that her young son Oweneen is now at the barricades in Stephen's Green. Her first impulse is to lash out savagely at the stony martyrs in a speech of furious accusation that reminds us of Nora Clitheroe and sounds as if she might have been at home in O'Casey's Dublin trilogy. "Yous knew this was comin' and yous wouldn't tell me! Yous villains and cut-throats and stinkin' coggerers! I that always had the wee word for yous and the wipe of me duster, when the patent leather people passed yous and the high men with big books. And did I not sing for yous the song of the greedy oul' bitch that yous all died for." She then tells them she is determined to protect and save her son rather than allow them to take him as another sacrificial hero, and she concludes by cursing them and Cathleen Ni Houlihan: "My seven curses on yous and my seven curses on the oul' bitch yous died the death for."[62]

She has no sooner finished than her son staggers in mortally wounded, crying and shivering from the pain, and he dies in her arms without a word about his beautiful sacrifice for Ireland. The terrible moment is ripe for a Mrs. Tancred or Juno Boyle to keen over her son's bullet-riddled body, but before Mrs. Galgoogley can get beyond another outburst against the villainous coggerers and the bitch Cathleen, the bold Robert Emmet interrupts and changes the mood of the play with a stock response of patriotic fervor: "Slut! I'm ashamed of you! What kind of talk is that for the mother of a proud hero? You should lift up your heart and be proud."[63] Parnell then makes a brief attempt to question "this dying with honor with a bullet in your guts," but the other martyrs shout him down and convince the poor mother that her son will now have a special place of glory beside them. All too quickly she puts aside her grief and asks innocently, "(*with pathetic eagerness*) Do yous want him? Honest now, do yous?" To which they all reply, "Put him amongst us. He is ours now. We claim him." And she says humbly, "Aye then—he's yours."[64] Earlier, when she was barbarously comic and furiously tragic, Mrs. Galgoogley was a dominant and richly impulsive character, but now that she is suddenly humbled and pathetically patriotic, Carroll rubs away her colorful complexities in order to make her a benign symbol of noble Irish motherhood. The play comes to its melodramatic conclusion with Emmet "oratorically" forbidding anyone to shed tears for the heroic men who died for Ireland, and he reaches his highest cadenzas at the curtain: "And there is the music of Liberty! Listen! (*From without come the rapid reports of rifles and revolvers and the spitting of Thompson guns*) The symphony of Freedom, gentlemen! What notes on a thundering scale! What grand crescendos! What immortal musicians!"[65]

One is tempted to say that there is something slightly sickening about this murderous music played for the liberation of Cathleen Ni Houlihan; but perhaps it should simply be put down as Carroll's artistic lapse, his inspirational sop to the bloodthirsty patriots, the only audience that could be moved by such a hagiagraphical allegory. Skeptics might do well to turn to O'Casey's *Plough and the Stars* for tragicomic consolation, especially the mock-heroic second act, when the mesmerized patriots are exposed to grim irony as they abandon their families and prepare to die because Ireland is greater than a mother or a wife; and when the Falstaffian Fluther Good, instead of preparing to die for his country, embraces the prostitute Rosie Redmond as she sings a bawdy song and they go off to spend the night together.

What mock crescendos! What irreverent and mortal musicians!

Chapter 5

THE VICTORY OF COMIC DEFEAT

THE Playboy's real name is Synge; and the famous libel on Ireland (and who is Ireland that she should not be libelled as other countries are by their great comedians?) was the truth about the world.

—G. B. Shaw

MR. O'CASEY is a master of knockabout in this very serious and honourable sense—that he discerns the principle of disintegration in even the most complacent solidities, and activates it to their explosion. This is the energy of his theatre, the triumph of the principle of knockabout in situation, in all its elements and on all its planes, from the furniture to the highest centres.

—Samuel Beckett

Comedy and Failure

It is the function of all great comedians to libel their countries, to libel the intimidating world, as Shaw pointed out in his defense of Synge. Their libel is based on their comic desecration of whatever becomes too sacred and therefore too repressive in society, and it is sustained by the cheerful and eloquent way their jester characters thrive on their protective masquerades as outcasts or failed men and women. In Irish comedy the gadfly clowns take comfort from their condition of farcical defeat because it liberates them from the terrible burden of responsibility and respectability. Successful men the world over are so busy straining and striving that they have little time for the ironic truths that are hidden in the laughter of failure. There is no room for comedy in the work ethic, and theater audiences may well consist of people who are seeking a vicarious escape from the specter of the sacred job. Some nervous governments grudgingly recognize the need to provide an emotional release for their regimented people, as William Empson revealed in his observation about the function of comedy in Russia: "I believe the Soviet Government in its early days paid two clowns, Bim and Bom, to say as jokes the things everybody else would have been shot for saying."[1]

In Ireland the comic libelers are neither paid nor shot, they are greeted with riots in the theater, they are exposed to official and unofficial censorship for insulting the national character. Perhaps the following comment on a report in the Dail sums up the Irish government's attitude toward its greatest dramatists, whose fame rests largely on their mock-heroic jester characters: "In April 1933, De Valera, the new Prime Minister, informed the Dail that he had told the [Abbey] Theatre's directors that certain plays (by which he meant those of Synge and O'Casey) would damage the good name of Ireland."[2] It is a sad joke that the libelous playboys and paycocks, like the irreverent Falstaffs, must be rejected by chastened kings and pinchbeck prime ministers. It must be fairly obvious, however, that Ireland only damaged its good name when it tried to reject or suppress its Celtic Bims and Boms, who have nevertheless managed to prevail even though many of them have been denigrated and silenced from time to time.

Clowns always affirm by denying, rise by falling, lament by laughing. As figures of farcicial defeat, Irish clowns are forced to live in the immaterial Berkeleyan world of the unrestricted senses, a private world of perceptions and instincts, a fantastic world of comic fictions in which their creative imagination can transform material defeat into spiritual victory. They question all pious verities and stock responses, they subvert all platitudes about the honor of servile and respectable behavior. They laugh in order to liberate. Most of the characters in Irish comedy are therefore the fortunate victims of failure, outcasts with the gift of redemptive laughter, as we can see, in varying degrees, in the plays of Synge and Yeats, Lady Gregory and Shaw, Fitzmaurice and O'Casey, Johnston and Shiels, Behan and Beckett. Synge is the crucial figure in this comic mythology of mockery and survival. Nora Burke in *In the Shadow of the Glen* is a tragicomic woman whose failure as a wife forces her to desecrate a January–May marriage and pursue a risky adventure with a knight-errant tramp. Sarah Casey in *The Tinker's Wedding* is a disconsolate young tinker woman whose failure to negotiate a proper church marriage saves her from the terrors of respectability. Martin Doul in *The Well of the Saints* is an irascible old blind man whose failure to accept the miracle of sight allows him to retain his poetic imagination and escape from the cruel world of sighted people. Christy Mahon in *The Playboy of the Western World* is a repressed little peasant whose failure to murder his father ironically creates his playboy mythology and saves him from his wretched self and the hypocrisies of Mayo people.

There is an unworldly and impractical streak in all of Synge's darkly comic characters which sets them apart from conventional or normal people. They must go their own unpredictable and unorthodox ways, and their impracticable aspirations are poetic reminders of humankind's atavistic power. They are among the first and unique comic primitives in modern drama. They are so barbarous and grotesque that their appearance on the Abbey stage early in the century was more of an outrage than a triumph. Although Yeats and Lady Gregory were very sympathetic to Synge's work, they suspected that it would create hostility among Irish audiences and tried unsuccessfully to soften the rough cutting edge of his comedy. Willie and Frank Fay, the actors who were the first and most faithful interpreters of Synge's plays, often urged him to revise his eccentric characters and make them more normal and tractable in their language and habits. Fortunately, however, Synge resisted all attempts to make him civilize his clowns. While *The Well of the Saints* was in rehearsal in 1904, he complained in a letter to Lady Gregory that Frank Fay, who was playing the Saint, objected specifically on nationalistic and religious grounds that the play was an alien and dangerous influence in Ireland: "The difficulty is that F.F. is dead against my play. . . . He says my work is only addressed to the blasé town-dwelling theatre-goers, that as long as we play that sort of work we are only doing what Antoine does in Paris and doing it worse, that he wants a National Theatre that will draw the people etc. etc. etc. He's got Brian Boru on the brain it seems. I do not know whether all this is his own feeling only—in which case it is of no consequence—or whether there is a Neo-patriotic-Catholic clique growing that might be serious."[3] This turned out to be a very prophetic anticipation of the "Neo-patriotic-Catholic cliques" that had St. Patrick as well as Brian Boru on the brain and later rioted in the Abbey against *The Playboy* and *The Plough*.

Yeats, who tried to be more diplomatic than Frank Fay, wrote a letter to Synge on August 21, 1904, after watching a rehearsal

of *The Well of the Saints,* in which he raised a minor point about
an echo from *King Lear,* and then suggested some deletions in
the dialogue: "But I do think it is of some importance that you
should cross out a number of the Almighty Gods. I do not object
to them on the ground that they are likely to shock people but
because the phrase occurs so often that it may weary and irritate
the ear."[4] It is really doubtful whether he was objecting on
aesthetic rather than religious considerations, for later in the
letter he identifies the source of his concern when he mentions
that Fay "is very anxious to reduce the number of God Almi-
ghtys." By actual count, "God Almighty" and "Almighty God" are
mentioned thirteen times in the play, and there are as many as
fifty-four references to God, in such expressions as "God forgive
you" and "God help you." If this repetition of the deity's name
seems excessive, it nevertheless serves a specific function that
stresses the ironic and intentionally satiric tone of a play that is
after all a mock-miracle comedy. The thematic function is to
mock not God but rather those people who are excessively familiar with him in their ostentatious and mechanical piety, and to
sympathize with the unfortunate Douls who are tormented by
the miraclemongers. "The Lord protect us from the saints of
God" is Mary Doul's very apt and comic-ironic lament.

Synge rightly refused to make any alterations to suit the fears
of Yeats and the Fays. He said he would rewrite any passage in
order to improve it artistically, but he wouldn't change the language of his characters to make it conform to proper or decent
speech. In a letter to Willie Fay in which he defended the religious attitudes of his characters, Synge made his stand for fair-
ness and artistic integrity: "You understand my position: I am
quite ready to avoid hurting people's feelings needlessly, but I will
not falsify what I believe to be true for anybody. If one began
that where would it end? I would rather drop play-writing al-
together."[5] O'Casey took a similarly uncompromising stand
twenty years later when some of the Abbey actors wanted to
change what they considered to be the indelicate language in
The Plough and the Stars. Lennox Robinson had pointed out a
number of passages in the play which had "irritated or shocked
some of the members of the Caste"—mainly F. J. McCormick
and Eileen Crowe—but O'Casey, like Synge, refused to make

any alterations and made his stand: "The play itself is (in my opinion) a deadly compromise with the actual; it has been further modified by the Directors but I draw the line at a Vigilance Committee of the Actors." The directors, Yeats and Lady Gregory and Robinson, had already persuaded him, against his better judgment, to omit Rosie Redmond's bawdy song at the end of Act II. Now, apparently, Robinson had erroneously, or deceitfully, told O'Casey that Synge had willingly made changes to accommodate the objections of the actors, and O'Casey replied: "I am sorry, but I'm not Synge; not even, I'm afraid, a reincarnation. Besides, things have happened since Synge: the war has shaken some of the respectability out of the heart of man." Thus, in spite of Robinson's misleading comments about Synge, O'Casey sounded very much like Synge in his absolute refusal to conform to respectability, and especially in his concluding remarks: "As I have said, these things have been deeply pondered, and under the circumstances, and to avoid further trouble, I prefer to withdraw the play entirely."[6]

Although Yeats as a director of the Abbey had to endure many pressures and was forced to make some minor compromises with temperamental actors from time to time, he was no apologist for respectability and fought many notable battles for the artistic integrity of his playwrights, especially Synge and O'Casey. He associated Synge with the great tradition of Shakespeare, as he stated in his Preface to the first edition of *The Well of the Saints* in 1905, a tradition he associated with writers who "had abundant, resonant, beautiful, laughing, living speech,"[7] a unique characteristic of dramatic language that could also be attributed to O'Casey. In Irish comedy generally the characters are endowed with a superabundance of vivid and strong speech because they live in an impermanent world of tragicomic crises and imminent defeats, and they must compensate for their material failures with a glorious excess of rich and giddy language that somehow helps to make life bearable. It is in his Preface to *The Well of the Saints* that Yeats considers the grotesque characters of Synge in relation to the outward defeat and inward victory of their dreams in a life full of ironic impossibilities: "Mr. Synge, indeed, sets before us ugly, deformed or sinful people, but his people, moved by no practical ambition, are driven by a dream of that impossible life. That we may feel how intensely his Woman of the Glen dreams of days that shall be entirely alive, she that is 'a hard woman to please' must spend her days between a sour-faced old husband, a man who goes mad upon the hills, a craven lad and a drunken tramp; and those two blind people in *The Well of the Saints* are so transformed by the dream that they choose blindness rather than reality."[8]

All of Synge's comic characters are defeated in reality but not in their impossible dreams, though it would be misleading to exaggerate the extent of their triumphs, which are invariably hedged by ironies that make them accept illusions for realities and prevent any sentimentalization of their condition. Yeats was right to stress their rejection of all practical ambition, though it should be noted that when he speaks of their frailties, their ugliness and deformity and sinfulness, these pejorative terms represent the view of respectable society and must be qualified in the context of the plays. There is a paradoxical attraction in their ugliness and deformity and sinfulness, all of which are only the rough and natural blemishes of their marginal and frustrated living conditions; and none of this roughness is as damning as the acquired hypocrisies and deceits of the normal people in the plays. What passes as the sinfulness of the clowns is actually the release of their repressed anger and passion. Yeats understood the impossibility of the trapped and dreamy Nora Burke's choices in *In the Shadow of the Glen,* confronted as she is by the loss of the mad Patch Darcy, and her impulsive decision to go off with the Tramp, whom Yeats dismisses with the term "drunken," with no reference to the fact that he is mainly drunk with romantic eloquence, which may be temporarily seductive but is no permanent solution to her dilemma. As for the isolated Douls in *The Well of the Saints,* especially the gullible and misguided Martin, it is better to be a blind and defeated outcast, in the imperceptive eyes of the uncharitable villagers, than to become converted to that malicious and normal world of reality. The earthy old Mary Byrne in *The Tinker's Wedding* helps Sarah Casey make a similar choice when, with the inadvertent help of the mercenary priest, she persuades her to remain a sinful but free tinker woman and avoid the pitfalls of a respectable marriage.

Christy Mahon in *The Playboy of the Western World* also avoids the pitfalls of respectability and marriage, but for different reasons and in a different situation. Although he shares the ugliness, deformity, and sinfulness of Synge's typically grotesque comic characters, he is a mock hero whose impossible dream of freedom through patricide alternately fails and succeeds, succeeds and fails. Without intending to become a heroic liberator in the eyes of the repressed Mayo people, he grows out of his early wretchedness and assumes the mythic role of a daring playboy and *miles gloriosus*. Even after he has been miraculously transformed into a figure of superhuman proportions, he can paradoxically be heroic and hysterical, eloquent and insecure, proud and foolish. And the ironies and reversals of fortune proliferate throughout the play. If he had been strong enough to kill his father the first time, Christy might have been able to marry Pegeen Mike, or the Widow Quin, and live happily ever after with either of them, though he preferred Pegeen, who preferred him. If he had been strong and mad enough to kill his father the second time, or even the third time, he would have been betrayed to the police by the disillusioned people who, like Pegeen, know the difference between "a gallous story and a dirty deed," and were prepared to turn him in when they thought the killing had taken place in their own backyard. Reality is always the enemy in Synge's plays, in all Irish comedy, and the only alternative, for the villains of Mayo as well as for the outcast Christy, is the wild dream of an impossible life.

Christy's dream is constantly being won and lost as the specter of his murdered father keeps haunting him in the midst of all his victories. And just when ignominious defeat seems inevitable, after the unpredictable people of Mayo forsake their dream of reflected glory and revert to their repressed and law-abiding ways, Christy is suddenly resurrected. He now realizes that his heroic self is accessible to him without their sublimated mythologizing. The mock savior, Christ-y, cannot save anyone but himself; and this is a deflation as well as an elevation. So even his final victory contains the irony of failure, for in the end he is more and less than a playboy hero: he has overcome the tyranny of his father and the hypocrisy of Mayo, but he has let down the side by failing in his attempt at patricide and allowing reality to destroy the people's dreams. Furthermore, if Pegeen has lost her nerve and her man, Christy has lost his passion and his only playgirl of the Western world.

This latter defeat, the irreparable loss of Pegeen, is usually overlooked at the final curtain as she laments her own heartbreaking loss of her only playboy, after he goes "romancing through a romping lifetime from this hour to the dawning of the judgment day."[9] But these words reflect the vainglorious as well as the triumphant Christy, for his exuberant bragging is the beginning of another impossible dream. Unless he can find a high-spirited girl like Pegeen to love, which seems unlikely now, there won't be much genuine romancing for him. He has a similarly hyperbolic and unlikely notion of his future relationship with his resurrected father. Old Mahon may be so pleased about the transformation of his son from fool to hero that he is willing to overlook the attempted patricide, but it is questionable whether he will go along with Christy's rosy version of the future and play the heathen slave to his son's gallant captain: "Go with you, is it? I will then, like a gallant captain with his heathen slave. Go on now and I'll see you from this day stewing my oatmeal and washing my spuds, for I'm master of all fights from now."[10] These domestic observations do not promise a very romantic or exciting future for the gallant captain, to be feasting on stewed oatmeal and spuds, even if these modest meals are now to be prepared by the father instead of the son. Christy may be a new man, but he will still be the same preening paycock of a *miles gloriosus*. He may never become a frightened Shawn Keogh, which might have been his fate if he hadn't "killed" his father and been transformed into a playboy; but it is quite possible that he might grow into a reckless and raging man like his father and escape from reality by staying drunk for weeks on end, as he described Old Mahon to Pegeen, "rising up in the red dawn, or before it maybe, and going out into the yard as naked as an ash tree in the moon of May, and shying clods again the visage of the stars."[11] Short of acting out such a spectacularly absurd sight, another of the limited options open to Christy would be that like

Pegeen's father, Michael James, he could get "paralatic" drunk at wakes and lie "stretched out retching speechless on the holy stones";[12] or he could end up in gallows-humor gossip like Jimmy Farrell and Philly Cullen, talking about having fun with black and yellow skulls in blue jars, or playing with skeleton bones in the graveyard to pass the boredom of the day.

It is pertinent to bear such comically deflating possibilities in mind for the presumptuous Christy, for although he seems to be the most victorious of all the defeated characters in Irish comedy, he is nevertheless consistently mocked throughout the play, especially when he puffs himself up with too much vanity and bragging. Even those three very nubile women, Pegeen and the Widow Quin and Sara Tansey, who are all fascinated and sexually aroused by his playboy antics, also laugh at his mock-heroic posturing and quickly abandon him when his father arrives and threatens retribution, though the eager Widow is inclined to take him on even as a fraudulent hero. Christy's worst moments come when the people attack him for destroying the impossible dream they created in his mythic transformation, and the tragicomic tone of the play darkens as the tainted hero suddenly cowers in desperation like a terrified animal: "And must I go back into my torment, is it, or run off like a vagabond straying through the Unions with the dusts of August making mudstains in the gullet of my throat, or the winds of March blowing on me till I'd take an oath I felt them making whistles of my ribs within?"[13] As a further humiliation, Sara takes off one of her petticoats and, with the help of the Widow, tries to put it and her shawl on Christy to allow him to escape disguised as a woman. But it is too late for such farcical melodramatics. After he has returned from "killing" his father a second time, the bitterly disillusioned Pegeen orders the men to put a rope around his neck in preparation for his hanging by the police, and Christy, groveling on the floor, cries out hysterically: "Cut the rope, Pegeen, and I'll quit the lot of you and live from this out like the madmen of Keel, eating muck and green weeds, on the faces of the cliffs."[14]

Like Macheath's mock-heroic rescue at the eleventh hour in *The Beggar's Opera,* Christy's reprieve from death comes when his father returns for a third time, and in the gallows humor of a farcical salvation, certain defeat is changed into uncertain victory. The villainy of Mayo has turned Christy into "a likely gaffer in the end of all." And in the end of all it must also be said that there is still a good deal of the cowardly gaffer and strutting paycock in the temporarily redeemed playboy, even though he is not as profligate a character as O'Casey's supreme paycock, the mendacious "Captain" Boyle, whose boozy dreams of glory are self-defeating as well as hilariously impossible. For playboys and paycocks the inevitable conditions of crisis and "chassis" are often self-inflicted, since pipe dreams and pratfalls are common occurrences for such accident-prone comedians, who create their own illusory victories and comforting defeats. These characters live in an impermanent and improvised world in which they must fall and rise and fall again in a cyclical pattern of comic reversals. They are continually up and down but never out.

What the mock-heroic characters of Synge and O'Casey, and indeed all Irish clowns, have in common, then, is that they are constantly exposed to a process of comic discrediting that maintains our sympathy for their frailties at the same time that it reduces them to ridicule without reformation. It is a process of comic humiliation that brings them abruptly down to the leveling earth when they overreach their playboy or paycock masquerades. It is a dramatic technique of comic discrediting that is anti-idealistic in its purpose and prevents the playwright as well as the audience from succumbing to sentimentality through excessive admiration of the characters. When Shakespeare was eventually confronted by that danger of excessive admiration of Falstaff, the ultimate playboy-paycock whose comic failures became too attractive, he felt he had to abandon and kill off his greatest clown. The Irish playwrights, however, dealing with clowns of memorable yet less formidable dimensions, settle for the efficacy of comic discrediting. Falstaff was always discredited, too, but unfortunately Shakespeare was finally more concerned about history than comedy and saw his great clown as a potential danger to the state. Apparently the Russians decided to eliminate their Bims and Boms for similar reasons. Nevertheless, most modern playwrights are wisely content to indulge and discredit their clowns, to let them go on living and laughing as they gain their comic victories in defeat. So Chekhov indulged and discredited his Lopakins and Vanyas; Brecht his Azdaks and Macheaths; and in Irish comedy, Synge his Martin Douls and Christy Mahons; Lady Gregory her Hyacinths and Bartleys; Shaw his Keegans and Doolittles; O'Casey his Boyles and Fluthers; Fitzmaurice his Roger Carmodys and Jaymony Shanahans; Shiels his Cartneys and Kevneys; Behan his Dunlavins and Pats; Beckett his Gogos and Didis. Synge and O'Casey took a similar view of their second bananas, the Michael James Flahertys and Philly Cullens and Jimmy Farrells; the Adolphus Grigsons and Joxers, the Coveys and Uncle Peters. And they used the same process of comic discrediting to expose the warts on their liberated women clowns, the Mary Byrnes and Widow Quins, the Bessie Burgesses and Rosie Redmonds.

Synge and O'Casey also used an ironic method of ending their plays on an anticlimactic note that partially deflects the audience's attention from the main action so that there are no melodramatic tableaux or happy solutions at the final curtain, no taint of sentimentality or heroics. There is no moral, no attempt to read a sermon on the wisdom of restraint or virtue, no chastisement of comic or profane excesses. In all of Synge's comedies the main characters, the outcasts, gain an ironic victory in defeat, but since they are pariahs who refuse to conform to the mores of normal society, they must be driven away so that the final joke leaves the world in possession of the conventional people or comic villains who lack the vision and courage to defy the system. After Nora Burke goes off defiantly with the Tramp at the conclusion of *In the Shadow of the Glen,* the two men who rejected her, her cranky old husband, Dan, and the shrinking young Michael Dara, sit down in a nice cozy way to enjoy a quiet drink together without vindictiveness or even a thought about the faithless wife. They are now only nominal villains, suddenly humanized in their shared loneliness, powerfully thirsty after the ordeal with Nora, which they do not mention, and the play ends antiheroically with their improvised camaraderie as they become yet another variation of the defeated couples who try to come to terms with their comic frustrations in Irish drama.

The blind Martin and Mary Doul in *The Well of the Saints* are perhaps the most frustrated and liberated couple who must reject the Saint's supernatural powers and create their own miracle of insight. Again at the final curtain we are not allowed to dwell too long on their victory in defeat as they go off stubbornly to face the spring floods and perilous freedom, for Synge brings us back to the nominal villains in the normal world where preparations are under way for the marriage of the tainted couple, Molly Byrne and Timmy the smith, by the deflated Saint. Somewhat similarly, when the deflated Priest is released from the sack and utters his Latin malediction at the end of *The Tinker's Wedding*, the unrepentant tinkers, Mary and Sarah and Michael, run away to follow their irresponsible and free way of life. In another typical Synge conclusion, the victorious tinkers are suddenly routed, and they leave the Priest, another nominal villain, "master of the situation," a farcical and empty situation that discredits his victory. Michael, in his last speech as he leaves, is full of the same kind of comic bravado that characterized the departing and romping Christy Mahon, and he says: "We'll have a great time drinking that bit with the trampers on the green of Clash."[15] But again Synge is too ironic and skeptical to grant his clowns a romantic escape: the retreating tinkers have almost snatched defeat from the jaws of victory.

In his endings O'Casey goes further than Synge with the sudden shocks of comic irony and antiromanticism. The plays of the Dublin trilogy all end badly for the braggart clowns, even though they all manage to endure, for in their tainted victories of sheer survival they affirm the life force yet are discredited even more ironically than Synge's characters. O'Casey's comic characters live in a more dangerous world than the repressed pastoral milieu of Synge's plays, an urban world of poverty and disease and war, and their instinctive ability to remain alive and laugh in the midst of violent death constitutes their limited victory in defeat. Gallows humor again: it is only the grinning that makes it possible for them to bear it. After Minnie Powell sacrifices herself to save Davoren and Shields, the two inflated shadow men in *The Shadow of a Gunman,* the broken Davoren makes a painful speech about his guilt, but the clownish Shields, who has no time for moral judgments, confronts death with the humor of an ironic shrug when he delivers the anticlimactic curtain speech: "I knew something ud come of the tappin' on the wall!"[16]

Tragedy is cut even more sharply by comedy in *Juno and the Paycock,* where one of the most effective endings in modern drama yokes the two genres together in a violent counterpoint of opposites. After Juno has delivered her elegiac appeal to the Virgin Mary for her dead son and all the sons of the world who are slaughtered by their fellow men, the two dissolute clowns appear for the finale. Defeated, drunk, and discredited, Boyle and Joxer take over the empty stage for their barbarously comic duet. In a grotesque parody of homage to the tainted Cathleen Ni Houlihan, which anticipates Gogo and Didi's mock homage to the tainted Mister Godot, O'Casey's clowns play out their corrosive version of the braggart-warrior and parasite-slave routine as the world around them collapses in a state of "chassis." Perhaps this ironic conclusion is less a victory in defeat than a mock triumph of comic bravura over tragic reality. If, as T. S. Eliot claimed, humankind cannot bear too much reality, it is all the more necessary to resort to such savage laughter, as O'Casey and Beckett realized, such gallows humor in the midst of such despair. This essential correspondence between inevitable tragedy and irrepressible comedy is maintained throughout most of O'Casey's plays, as well as in his endings, and this vital relationship cannot be broken. In one unfortunate production of *Juno,* however, it was flagrantly destroyed when the final scene between Boyle and Joxer was eliminated and the play ended abruptly with Juno's tragic speech.[17]

It would have been similarly unfortunate if *The Plough and the Stars* had concluded with the dying Bessie Burgess and the mad Nora Clitheroe; but O'Casey knew that he had to establish some comic-ironic counterpoint to the main tragic action. He sets up the final curtain scene, therefore, by shifting the focus to the nominal villains, the British soldiers, who now are not villains at all but only a comically detached cockney couple, Sergeant Tinley and Corporal Stoddart, sharing a cozy cup of tea that the mad Nora has prepared for her dead husband. "What abaht a cup of scald?" Their mundane words contrast sharply with the terrible events of destruction and death, as the heavy shelling of Dublin is heard offstage, the red glare of the burning city can be seen through the window, and the enemy soldiers calmly sip their tea and sing, "Keep the 'owme fires burning."

Several moments earlier Fluther had clashed with these two cockney soldiers, who accused the Irish insurgents of sniping from rooftops and not fighting fair. The heavily armed and superior numbers of British troops may be winning the war in the streets, but the bold Fluther wins the battle of words when he replies with the rhetorical weapon of the disarmed clown: "Fight fair! A few hundhred scrawls o' chaps with a couple o' guns an' Rosary beads, again' a hundhred thousand thrained men with horse, fut, an' artillery—an' he wants us to fight fair! D'ye want us to come out in our skins an' throw stones?"[18] After this defiant speech, however, when the Sergeant and Corporal roughly round up all the men in the house for detention, the Irish comedians are necessarily deflated as they go off. Fluther's parting shot as he leaves reminds us that while he may be able to use words as formidable weapons of comic survival, he remains an antiheroic if wise fool, a discredited if colorful braggart-warrior to the end: "Jasus, you an' your guns! Leave them down, an' I'd beat th' two of yous without sweating!"[19] It is indeed a wise and calculating fool who knows when his gratuitous boasting might deflate but not hurt him. Such comic defeats can sustain the illusion of comic victory.

In some of his later plays in which he makes a direct protest against the unjust conditions of modern life, O'Casey resorts to his typical broad laughter along the way, but he tends to become solemn and symbolic at the ending, where he withholds his comic-ironic view, allowing such martyred figures as Jannice in *Within the Gates,* Jack in *The Star Turns Red,* and Ayamonn in *Red Roses for Me* to fulfill their tragic destiny. At the conclusion of *Red Roses,* however, he does rely on such comically discredited characters as the parsimonious Brennan and the grumbling Samuel, two crotchety old clowns, to play against the tragic action with some gritty laughter and elegiac song. In *The Silver Tassie* there are two tragically martyred figures, Harry Heegan and Teddy Foran, but the conclusion shifts ironically away from them to the singing and dancing couples, the nominal villains, and it is the quaint and slightly addled Mrs. Foran who delivers the curtain speech in a comically detached manner, somewhat like the cockney soldiers at the end of *The Plough,* that rubs absurdly against the tragic events: "It's a terrible pity Harry was too weak to stay an' sing his song, for there's nothing I love more than the ukelele's tinkle, tinkle in the night-time."[20]

The pastoral comedies, such as *Purple Dust, Cock-a-Doodle Dandy, The Bishop's Bonfire,* and *The Drums of Father Ned,* end with wild celebrations of singing and dancing, with the invocation of apocalyptic floods, bonfires, and drums, or with the exile of the comic rebels, who, like Synge's escaping outcasts, go off in search of a perilous freedom. There are some dark and repressive forces at work in these fantastic and prophetic comedies, but though the threat of defeat is always present, O'Casey's rustic clowns and jesters go off to live and laugh another day.

Comedy and History

When he rejected *The Silver Tassie* in 1928, Yeats urged O'Casey to purify his art by ignoring such historical events as the Great War in his plays: "The whole history of the world must be reduced to wallpaper in front of which the characters must pose and speak."[21] This strange advice must have struck O'Casey as an incredible contradiction, since he had already turned directly to Irish history and the War of Independence for the main theme and structure of his first three plays, all of which, of course, the earlier Yeats had praised and defended from attack. Everything O'Casey had written and went on to write, including his monumental autobiography, his books of essays, and even his voluminous letters, was pointedly related to the tragicomic nightmare of history, from which some people might try to hide but no one could ultimately escape. Yeats had urged O'Casey to seek a mystical art form, a nonhistorical purification through the fire of the dramatic action; however, the dramatic fire of war and suffering in O'Casey's plays creates its own ritual of purification; it blazes with historical images of compassion and comedy that deny any relevance to Yeats's isolated world of wallpaper. Even Yeats ignored his own advice in one of his last and best plays, *Purgatory* (1939), in which he introduces violent historical events and images in order to condemn what he feels are the corruptive elements of modern history; and he doesn't try to reduce those dark forces to a pure pattern of dramatic wallpaper. Nevertheless, it was O'Casey, almost alone among Irish playwrights, who confronted the ironies of history with a tragicomic point of view that defended the innocent victims of war and questioned all sacred notions of death and glory for the love of holy Ireland.

Sacred events in Irish history have sometimes been celebrated in works of comic profanation by Ireland's disenchanted writers, but in 1966, for example, the fiftieth anniversary of the Easter Rising, no literary or theatrical confrontations were allowed to desecrate the patriotic genuflections in honor of the 1916 martyrs. The Abbey Theatre, which under the leadership of Yeats and Lady Gregory had rocked the nation as well as the cradle of Irish genius by staging plays that were skeptical about the hagiography of Cathleen Ni Houlihan, now paid its silent respect to the hallowed occasion by agreeing not to perform any plays by the irreverent O'Casey, particularly the best and most notorious 1916 play in its repertoire, *The Plough and the Stars,* which in 1926 had provoked a nationalist riot in the theater. Forty years after its first production O'Casey's play was still considered in some high quarters to be an insult to the national honor. Rosie Redmond was one of the chief offenders in *The Plough,* and her comic-ironic attitude, indeed, her very presence as a prostitute on a Dublin stage in the midst of the preparations for the Rising, provided a profane comment on the sacred offstage words of Patrick Pearse when she lamented the lack of available clients: "They're all in a holy mood. Th' solemn-lookin' dials on th' whole o' them an' they marchin' to th' meetin'. You'd think they were th' glorious company of th' saints, an, th' noble army of martyrs thrampin' through th' sthreets of paradise. They're all thinkin' of higher things than a girl's garthers."[22]

Now Dublin was in a holy mood again, and perhaps it was expedient, if regrettable, that Rosie and O'Casey's other rude mechanicals had to be banished from the Abbey stage during the 1966 commemoration, for in the name of historical and artistic accuracy their real-life counterparts were very much in evidence in the city in 1966 as well as 1916. Tim Pat Coogan, a shrewd Dublin journalist and author who was not likely to be intimidated by sacred Irish occasions, has explained the absence of O'Casey's play in the following earthy manner:

> Few writers ever kicked their country's most cherished beliefs so
> firmly in the national testicles, so accurately and so often. In view

of the fact that the blood-obsessed chauvinist (The Speaker) of
"The Plough and the Stars" was Padraig Pearse it was no wonder
that the last outraged residue of this injured pride led the National Committee, set up to commemorate the 50th Anniversary
of the 1916 Rising, to "ask" the Abbey, dependent on State funds,
to refrain from desecrating the occasion by staging a play by Sean
during the anniversary celebration.[23]

The self-appointed guardians of the national pride, Coogan also
remarked, invariably respond to antinationalist criticism "with
an air of injured patriotism. An attitude of 'How dare you hit me
now with Cathleen Ni Houlihan in my arms.'"[24] Throughout
most of his eighty-four controversial years, the spectacle of his
sentimental countrymen in a holy embrace with Mother Ireland
was usually enough to provoke O'Casey's most comic desecrations.

O'Casey knew that his working-class integrity as well as the
artistic honesty of The Plough demanded that diehard
nationalism be seen through the ironic eyes of the Dublin poor,
who in their tenement hell could find little salvation in the
militaristic rhetoric of Pearse. In spite of this necessary disen-
chantment, however, O'Casey had an ambivalent attitude toward Pearse the man: he damned the chauvinistic sin but not the
mortal sinner. He had great admiration for Pearse as a creative
teacher and significant educational reformer, and in June 1913
he had helped organize the publicity for Pearse's cultural
pageant in Jones's Road (now Croke Park), based on the Celtic
legend of the Táin Bo Cuailnge ("The Cattle Raid of Cooley").
But he had to modify this admiration several months later when
the fallible Pearse, who could at times be insensitive to the needs
and loyalties of labor, was accused of strikebreaking for continuing to use the "black" trams during the General Strike and Lock-
out. Nevertheless, when O'Casey looked back in anger and admiration in the third volume of his autobiography in 1945, he
wrote a powerful tribute to the martyred Pearse. He indicated
that as a skeptical Irishman he could celebrate as well as desecrate his country's history when he remembered the cultural and
spiritual heritage of Pearse as rebel poet and Catholic teacher:

> Ah! Patrick Pearse, you were a man, a poet, with a mind simple as
> a daisy, brilliant as a daffodil; and like these, you came before the

swallow dared, and took the Irish minds of March with beauty. A catholic with whom the roughest unbeliever could be safely silent, not for shame, but out of respect for your gallant and urging soul; a catholic who almost made one see that Ireland's blue sky was Brigid's poplin shawl; that the moon and stars were under Mary's feet, the Virgin-born on her breast, stretching out little leal hands that were to guide to a Father's home the long-banished children of Eve.[25]

For all this lyrical and ecumenical belief by one who considred himself to be a rough unbeliever, a decade after O'Casey's death few nationalists were willing to forgive him and understand his profanation of Pearse and the Republican martyrs in *The Plough*. Michael McInerney has recorded the fact that even such a generally respected Republican socialist as Peadar O'Donnell, who knew O'Casey in the early days in Dublin and recognized his genius, remained bitter about the antinationalism in his plays, and as late as 1974—O'Casey died in 1964—could not even think about *The Plough* without a feeling of nausea:

> O'Donnell has some of that bitter vision many Republicans have toward Sean O'Casey. He says that he knew O'Casey as a cranky man rather than a revolutionary. He lived through a period of history when "resistance was the theme of the people in Dublin from 1913 onwards particularly, yet O'Casey's characters showed none of this. He was a great dramatist and will be remembered long after I am forgotten as a literateur. A great dramatist he was, and his plays are very good theatrically, yet his plays do not excite or stimulate me. His *Plough and the Stars* I find nauseating. There is no character in the play from whom any revolutionary action could proceed."[26]

Of course it was part of O'Casey's intention to nauseate the diehard nationalists; and it was historically and artistically valid, if politically distressing to such men as O'Donnell, to recognize that no revolutionary action could proceed from such mock-heroic characters as Fluther Good and the Covey and Peter Flynn, or, for that matter, from Donal Davoren and Seumas Shields, "Captain" Boyle and Joxer Daly, Juno Boyle and Bessie Burgess and all the tenement women in the Dublin trilogy. When O'Casey did explore revolutionary themes and techniques in some of his later pastoral comedies, he was scrupulously non-patriotic, when he wasn't openly mock patriotic; he created his own unique rebels, mythical creatures and irreverent folk characters, not revolutionary nationalists. To the hilarious accompaniment of apocalyptic dance and drumbeat, rather than Cathleen Ni Houlihan's "Faith of our Fathers," he created his comic redeemers in the guise of a Dionysian Cock and a visionary Father Ned. No doubt these fabulous and mythic figures who celebrate an idyllic life in a future Ireland would also have nauseated such militant nationalists as O'Donnell for different reasons, though they have largely been spared this further distress since *Cock-a-Doodle Dandy* didn't reach the Abbey Theatre stage until 1975, seventeen years after it was written, and *The Drums of Father Ned,* rejected by the Dublin Theatre Festival, has never been performed by the Abbey Theatre.

The official and unofficial banning of O'Casey's works in his native land is another story that has been told elsewhere. The more immediate issue raised by O'Donnell and the nauseated nationalists concerns the credibility of the exclusively Republican interpretation of the Easter Rising as a sacred and therefore inviolable event that must not be exposed to comic irreverence. In recent years this Republican dogma has been questioned by some Irish historians, but this ironic or revisionist view, which was first dramatized in *The Plough and the Stars,* was also banned at the time of the 1966 commemoration, when a provocative essay by the Reverend Father Francis Shaw, S.J., was refused publication. Professor of early and medieval history at U.C.D., Father Shaw had submitted his pioneering work, "The Canon of Irish History—A Challenge," to *Studies* in time for the anniversary issue on the Rising, but, like the directors of the Abbey Theatre, who silently suppressed the revival of any O'Casey play, the editors of the magazine apparently decided it would be impolitic to publish it at that time. The essay finally appeared in *Studies* in 1972, unfortunately two years after Father Shaw's death.

Basing his argument on religious as well as political factors, Father Shaw charged that the Republican concept of national blood sacrifice as the only means of redeeming and liberating Ireland was blasphemous, as well as dubious, claiming that the "equation of the patriot with Christ is in conflict with the whole

Christian tradition and, indeed, with the explicit teaching of Christ."[27] Even though the conservative hierarchy of the Irish Catholic church had consistently supported British authority in the past, perhaps because the bishops were opposed to any revolutionary action that might threaten their dominant position in the country, Father Shaw as an individual cleric was arguing from the principles of Catholic faith, not institutional expediency. Furthermore, as a historian he was rejecting the inviolability of the diehard Republican canon of Irish history, the prevalent assumption that anyone who questioned the chauvinistic motives of 1916 was either a fool or a traitor:

> The canon of history of which I speak stamps the generation of 1916 as nationally degenerate, a generation in need of redemption by the shedding of blood. It honours one group of Irishmen by denying honour to others whose merit is not less. In effect it teaches that only the Fenians and the separatists had the good of their country at heart, that all others were either deluded or in one degree or another sold to the enemy. This canon moulds the broad course of Irish history to a narrow pre-conceived pattern; it tells a story which is false and without foundation. It asks us to praise in others what we do not esteem or accept in ourselves. It condemns as being anti-Irish all who do not profess extremist nationalist doctrine, though it never explains how it is possible to be judged to be against your own people when the views you hold are those which they overwhelmingly support. This canon is more concerned with the labels and trappings of national politics than with the substance which wisely-used political action can bring. It sets more store on what people profess themselves to be than on what they are.[28]

Father Shaw then concentrates his attack on the "labels and trappings" of the Republican cause as they appear in the writings and speeches of Pearse in order to illustrate how his "Messianic view of nationalism is connected with the unqualified glorification of blood-shedding and war."[29] Forty years earlier O'Casey had anticipated Father Shaw's feeling of horror by using the original words of Pearse for his offstage Speaker in the second act of *The Plough*. While the Figure of Pearse stands outside the pub urging the people to fight and give their lives for Ireland in a ritualistic frenzy of blood sacrifice that directly links the martyrdom of the patriots with the martyrdom of Christ, the tenement dwellers inside the pub are busy getting drunk and fighting with each other in a series of ridiculous brawls that mock the holiness of Pearse's call to arms:

> Bloodshed is a cleansing and sanctifying thing, and the nation that regards it as the final horror has lost its manhood.
> The old heart of the earth needed to be warmed with the red wine of the battlefields. . . . Such august homage was never offered to God as this: the homage of millions of lives given gladly for love of country. We must be ready to pour out the same red wine in the same glorious sacrifice, for without shedding blood there is no redemption!
> Heroism has come back to the earth. War is a terrible thing, but war is not an evil thing. People in Ireland dread war because they do not know it. Ireland has not known the exhilaration of war for over a hundred years. When war comes to Ireland she must welcome it as she would welcome the Angel of God![30]

Throughout Act II these sacred and terrifying words of Pearse interrupt the action, only to be overwhelmed and desecrated by the farcical squabbling of dirty Dublin's wise fools. Fluther Good finds something "derogatory" in everyone and he fights with the absurd Uncle Peter rigged out in the fancy-dress costume of the harmless National Foresters, with the fanatically Marxist Covey and the militantly Protestant Bessie Burgess; Bessie also attacks everyone and gets into a hair-pulling battle with Ginnie Gogan over illegitimacy and respectability; the Covey "twarts an' torments" Peter and struggles to defend his proletarian and prudish honor from Rosie's solicitations. And Ginnie Gogan, whose quaint predilection for gallows humor is awakened whenever anyone talks about dying for Ireland, offers a melodramatic parody of the sacrificial patriots when she visualizes the unlikely Peter in his fancy masquerade hanging heroically at the end of a rope:

> The Foresthers' is a gorgeous dhress! I don't think I've seen nicer, mind you in a pantomime.—Th' loveliest part of th' dhress, I think, is th' osthriches plume.—When yous are goin' along, an' I see them wavin' an' noddin' an' waggin', I seem to be lookin' at each of yous hangin' at the end of a rope, your eyes bulgin' an' your legs twistin' an' jerkin', gaspin' and gaspin' for breath while yous are thryin' to die for Ireland![31]

At the end of the act the local patriots arc determined to fulfill the martyrdom of Pearse's words, but they sound as if they are going to act out the grotesque pantomime of Ginnie Gogan's words. The scene is heavy with irony as the men, "mesmerized by the frenzy of the speeches," transfer their loyalties from life with their mothers and wives to death for Cathleen Ni Houlihan:

> *Clitheroe.* You have a mother, Langon.
> *Lieut. Langon.* Ireland is greater than a mother.
> *Capt. Brennan.* You have a wife, Clitheroe.
> *Clitheroe.* Ireland is greater than a wife.[32]

O'Casey was sickened by the spectacle because the mesmerized men had made the abstract symbol of Ireland greater than their faith in common humanity. Father Shaw was sickened because they had succumbed to Pearse's blasphemous usurpation of the sacrifice of Christ and in the process made their allegiance to Cathleen Ni Houlihan greater than their Catholic faith.

Since Pearse had also made Cu Chulainn his idealized symbol of the mythic Irish patriot who fought and died for his country, Father Shaw pointed out that Pearse had actually distorted and sentimentalized the character and deeds of the famous Celtic hero, whose statue was to be erected in the G.P.O. in Dublin as a memorial to the men of 1916. This demythologizing of Cu Chulainn is an extension of Father Shaw's attempt to de-mythologize the Easter Rising:

> About Cu Chulainn we know a little more. We know that when he came to Eamhain Macha [the capital of Ulster] at the age of seven he terrified both boys and adults by the violence of his behaviour. The unhappy warrior who was rash enough to call him in the morning died suddenly: Cu Chulainn split his head open with the flick of his wrist. He had bad moods, really bad ones, when he became a killer.... One other observation may be made. For Pearse, Cu Chulainn was the image of the patriotic soldier heroi-cally giving his life for his country. In so far as Cu Chulainn may be regarded as a historic and human figure—and Pearse himself expressed his doubts about this in *The Story of a Success* ... —the old epic tells us that he was not fighting for his country or indeed for the part of it in which he was born. He was fighting for the Ulaid [Ulster] against the other four provinces of Ireland, and the old text tells us that he died, standing upright, "facing his enemies, the men of Ireland."[33]

These ironic reminders—that the great Cu Chulainn was more of a sinner than a saint, that he was a violent and moody warrior who could often be a vindictive and brutal killer, that he was actually fighting against his countrymen rather than for the unification of Ireland—these sobering thoughts cast some doubt on the Republican mythology that deified him as the noblest of all the martyred patriots. By contrast, Yeats's Cu Chulainn (Cuchulain), a private, not a patriotic, icon, is a construct of the poet's daimonic antiself rather than an emblem of nationalistic heroism; he is a tragic figure of courageous and passionate excesses who is out of place in "this filthy modern tide." There is really no significant connection between Oliver Sheppard's second-rate statue of the idealized Cu Chulainn in the G.P.O. and the resonant persona of Cu Chulainn that Yeats created in many poems and plays. Among other disparities, what is involved is the irreconcilable difference between chauvinism and imagination, between the patriotic and poetic impulses.

It must have been a poetic rather than a patriotic impulse that originally inspired the Celtic legends about Cu Chulainn, for there is evidence to indicate that the anonymous writers of the early epics, especially those who dealt with Cu Chulainn, were often cynical about heroism and, like O'Casey, were more interested in profane entertainment than in sacred causes. Father Shaw reminds us "that Pearse took Cu Chulainn very seriously and that for him the great old Irish epic which tells the story of Cu Chulainn was almost a sacred book"; and then he goes on to raise questions about that sacredness by quoting a Latin colophon that a Gaelic scribe had copied into the version of the *Táin* in the twelfth-century Book of Leinster, which Father Shaw translates as follows: ". . . but I who have written this history, or better fable, I do not believe some of it. A certain portion may be attributed to the deceits of the devil, some part of it is a poet's invention, some of it seems to be probable, some not, and some of it is but for the entertainment of fools."[34] If we can believe this skeptical and bemused scribe, the heroic exploits in Pearse's sacred book, and the sacred book of many nationalistic Irishmen, were the improbable and irreverent invention of some poets with a sharp sense of irony and comedy. More fabulous than historical, Cu Chulainn undoubtedly represented a symbol of the heroic aspirations of the early and modern Celts, but his extravagant deeds were not to be taken too literally. If those deeds were to become a code for patriots, they were also an entertainment for fools, the common people who loved a fantastic yarn and were not averse to the devil's imaginative deceits and conceits. Like the medieval ballad dialogues between Oisín and St. Patrick, the legends of Cu Chulainn reveal an artistic dialectic between the heroic and the mock heroic, the sacred and the profane. Father Shaw goes on to support the view that Vivian Mercier and other scholars of Celtic literature have presented, that the comic-ironic mode has always been one of the main traditions of the Irish literary experience:

> The tendency to be at least mildly cynical about the heroic is surely a Gaelic characteristic. The remarkable colophon to the Táin which I have cited has been interpreted as a clerical reaction to a secular tale, but that is not convincing. We have from about the same time in Irish the splendid composition—this time neither mild nor brief—*Aisling Meic Conglinne* in which is brilliantly satirized the heroic in both secular and ecclesiastical literature, and this satire is almost certainly the work of a cleric. That this trait is not dead is well known to anyone familiar with the type of comment likely to be heard in the crowd at a Dublin political, or socio-political, meeting today.[35]

One might add that this predominantly mock-heroic Irish trait is also recognizable to anyone who is familiar with early Gaelic poetry and prose, or the wide range of work represented by such writers as Swift, Merriman, Edgeworth, Griffin, Carleton, Wilde, Moore, Joyce, Yeats, Gogarty, Synge, Lady Gregory, Shaw, Fitzmaurice, O'Casey, Shiels, James Stephens, Denis Johnston, Frank O'Connor, Sean O'Faolain, Flann O'Brien, Austin Clarke, Patrick Kavanagh, Brendan Behan, Samuel Beckett, Brian Moore, John B. Keane, Hugh Leonard, Thomas Murphy, James Plunkett, and many others. It has been suggested by Herbert Howarth, in *The Irish Writers: Literature and Nationalism, 1880–1940* (1958), that the Irish writers were always striving to write a sacred book; but there is strong and copious evidence to suggest the contrary, that for centuries most of them were determined to write a profane book.

The comic profanations in Irish literature are a liberating impulse that mocks whatever is too sacred, any authority, whether

British or Irish, political or religious, which has become too holy or hypocritical, too stagnant or repressive, in relation to the complex realities and hopes of Irish life. In his last full-length play, for example, *The Drums of Father Ned,* published when he was in his eightieth year, O'Casey wrote a "Prerumble" as a satiric introduction in which he symbolizes some of the tragicomic aspects of modern Irish history. Like all his later pastoral comedies and his autobiography, the play presents some variations on the political theme that preoccupied him through the latter part of his life: the ironic twist of historical events in which Pearse's middle-class Rising led to De Valera's conservative shopkeepers' Republic rather than to Connolly's socialist workers' Republic. As O'Casey wrote in his autobiography, laughing at Yeats's aphoristic view of 1916, "A Terrible Beauty is Borneo."

The main action of the play is set in rural Ireland in the late 1950s, but the prophetic "Prerumble" takes place a generation earlier, during the time of "the Troubles," the Civil War that broke out in 1922 between the Free Staters and the Republicans. Some Black and Tan soldiers have captured two Irishmen, McGilligan and Binnington, the comic *alazons* who represent the opposing political sides and hate each other as ferociously as they hate the British. In his typical ironic manner, O'Casey looks both ways by exposing the brutality of the Black and Tans and the stupidity of the Republican McGilligan and the Free State Binnington, who represent the bitter harvest of 1916 and 1922: the fanatical McGilligan, who piously invokes the Republican name of "Poor Paudrig Pearse," and the fanatical Binnington, who piously keeps a picture of the Free State martyr Michael Collins in his house. Although they were born in the same year, the same town, the same street, went to the same churches and schools, courted and married sisters, McGilligan and Binnington prefer to die rather than make peace with each other, the "ditch-worm" vs. the "dung-beetle." The only common ground they have is their contact in the business world, for they are local merchants who act as profiteering gombeen men, and in spite of their political vendetta, their only sacred slogan now in De Valera's bourgeois Ireland is "business is business." At first the Black and Tan officer orders them to shake hands or be shot, and when they refuse, the soldiers fire wildly at them in mock anger. When one of the Tans seriously threatens to shoot them, the officer shrewdly prevents the execution: "No, you fool! Can't you see that these two rats will do more harm to Ireland living than they'll ever do to Ireland dead?"[36]

This prophetic remark becomes a central theme in the main action of the play and defines one of the dilemmas of modern Irish history: fanatical Irishmen cannot live with each other but they can live with Mammon. In his pastoral alternative, the positive aspect of his ironic theme, the proletarian O'Casey is more mystical than Marxist—his God is a Joycean "shout in the street," the festive street of the Tostal celebration where the visionary Father Ned beats his hallelujah drum and prepares to lead the enlightened rustics away from the fanaticism and materialism of McGilligan and Binnington toward a Christian-socialist version of the Celtic promised land. The mythical Father Ned probably would have delighted the historical Father Shaw, as well as the symbolic Father Keegan in Barnard Shaw's *John Bull's Other Island;* for O'Casey's play is an attempt to fulfill the mad dream of Father Keegan, "three in one and one in three," where church and state and people are finally united. It is clear in *The Drums of Father Ned* that O'Casey had never lost his faith in a worker's republic, a synthesis of the values of Christianity and socialism, though he feared that Ireland had lost that faith. And he traced that loss of faith back to the abandonment of James Connolly's socialist dream for Ireland.

As early as 1919, when he wrote his first book, *The Story of the Irish Citizen Army,* O'Casey had argued that the socialist ideals of Connolly had been swallowed up by the patriotic fervor of nationalism, before as well as after the Easter Rising. He even went so far as to claim that Connolly himself may have been partly to blame for this unfortunate situation because he courted and joined forces with the nationalists, many of whom had been antagonistic or indifferent to the socialist cause of labor during the 1913 General Strike. Since O'Casey had resigned in protest from his position as secretary of the Irish Citizen Army in 1914 over a dispute between the socialist Citizen Army and the nationalist Irish Volunteers—he suspected that the nationalists might dominate and absorb the socialists, as in fact they did—he had a special reason to lament the decline of socialism as an active force in Irish history. Perhaps it was inevitable that the emotional appeal of middle-class nationalism would triumph over the rational appeal of working-class socialism; but O'Casey was convinced that the outcome of the conflict was apparent after Jim Larkin went to America in 1914 to raise funds for the Irish labor movement, passing the leadership of the Citizen Army and labor on to Connolly.

In all his writings and speeches Connolly had been the most eloquent voice in articulating the principles of a socialist workers' republic for Ireland, in his regular newspaper articles and in such classic works as *Labour, Nationality and Religion* (1910) and *Labour in Irish History* (1910). While he may have lacked the personal dynamism of Larkin, known as the Tarzan of Labor, Connolly was able to stir the minds of the people with his brilliant analysis of the economic and social disasters in Irish life. In view of the grim circumstances, he was convinced that only socialism could save the Irish people and the world from further suffering. Nevertheless, O'Casey believed that he had detected a significant shift in Connolly's views after 1914 as he moved closer to the nationalists:

> It is difficult to understand the almost revolutionary change that was manifesting itself in Connolly's nature. The Labour movement seemed to be regarded by him as a decrescent force, while the essence of Nationalism began to assume the finest elements of his nature. His articles that now appeared in the *Workers' Republic* with consistent regularity, the speeches that he delivered at various demonstrations and assemblies, all proclaimed that Jim Connolly had stepped from the narrow byway of Irish Socialism on to the broad and crowded highway of Irish Nationalism. The vision of the suffering world's humanity was shadowed by the nearer oppression of his own people, and in a few brief months pressed into a hidden corner of his soul the accumulated thoughts of a lifetime and opened his broad heart to ideas that altered the entire trend of his being. The high creed of Irish Nationalism became his daily rosary, while the higher creed of international humanity that had so long bubbled from his eloquent lips was silent for ever, and Irish Labour had lost a leader.[37]

O'Casey's point was that the Irish labor movement had lost a leader before, not after, the Rising; and that after the Rising "Connolly was no more an Irish Socialist martyr than Robert

Emmet, P. H. Pearse, or Theobald Wolfe Tone."[38] It was painfully ironic that in his brave death Connolly and his great legacy
of socialist belief should have been taken over by the antilabor
nationalists. The imperialist occupation of Ireland, not the
capitalist exploitation of Ireland, had become the dominant
issue for future generations, although both should have been
the common enemy of the people:

> A further indication of the singular change in Jim Connolly's
> ideas, and of his determined attachment to the principles enunci-
> ated by Sinn Fein and the Irish Volunteers, which were, in many
> instances, directly contrary to his life-long teaching of Socialism,
> was the fixing on the frontage of Liberty Hall a scroll on which
> was written the inscription: "We serve neither King nor Kaiser—
> but Ireland." His speeches and his writings had long indicated his
> new trend of thought, and his actions now proclaimed trumpet-
> tongued that the appeal of Caitlin Ni hUllachain—"If anyone
> would give me help, he must give me himself, he must give me
> all"—was in his ears a louder cry than the appeal of the Inter-
> nationale, which years of contemplative thought had almost writ-
> ten in letters of fire upon his broad and noble soul.[39]

Perhaps it is not too difficult to understand why Connolly had
shifted his lifelong loyalties from socialism to nationalism, or
tried unsuccessfully to combine the two forces; why he decided
to stress the immediate enemy of British imperialism rather than
the long-range enemy of world capitalism. He was an Irishman
before he was anything else, and his "trumpet-tongued" dedication to Cathleen Ni Houlihan had predictably if paradoxically
become the new emblem on "his broad and noble soul." O'Casey
had struck the telltale chord of patriotism with that haunting
line from Yeats's early and superficial nationalistic play about
the uncompromising Cathleen—"he must give me all." Connolly
himself struck the same note when, as he lay seriously wounded
after the Rising had been defeated, shortly before his execution,
he remarked to his daughter Nora: "The Socialists will never
understand why I am here. They all forget that I am an
Irishman."[40] Connolly had not forgotten that he was also a socialist, but apparently he believed that he could best support the
cause of Irish socialism by fighting and dying for Irish
nationalism.

It turned out to be a noble delusion. Even though the views of

Marx, Lenin, and Trotsky supported Connolly's belief that nationalism and socialism should be complementary forces in a colonial nation such as Ireland, the nationalist Rising led to the eclipse of Irish socialism. Two months after the Rising, Trotsky commented that "the experience of the Irish national uprising is over . . . the historic role of the Irish proletariat is just beginning."[41] Unfortunately, however, Irish history has recorded a reversal of this pattern: the submergence of the Irish proletariat and the perpetuation of the nationalist cause; and more, the unimpeded survival of capitalism in Ireland. As a final irony, it is sad to relate that Connolly's visionary socialist principles have remained unfruitful in Ireland. His memory is celebrated by a number of conflicting republican and labor groups that in political lip service try to make him more narrowly nationalist or more narrowly socialist, and as a result his formidable creed remains suspended between the two irreconcilable forces that he himself was unable to unite. Father Shaw felt that Pearse's martyrdom blasphemed against the Christian faith; O'Casey felt that Connolly's martyrdom blasphemed against the socialist faith. For O'Casey the dramatist these failures made it necessary that he take a comic-ironic approach to the disillusionment of Irish history.

According to O'Casey, only one figure emerged from the Rising as a genuine martyr for humanity, and that was the high-spirited Francis Sheehy-Skeffington, the university friend of Joyce, ardent socialist, champion of women's rights, and militant pacifist, who ironically campaigned against the fighting but was senselessly and brutally executed by an insane British army officer. A year before the Rising, in a desperate attempt to prevent it, Sheehy-Skeffington wrote an open letter in the *Irish Citizen* addressed to Thomas MacDonagh, like Pearse a rebel poet who became one of the leaders of the Rising but did not suffer from Pearse's messianic complex, urging him to turn away from the "militarist and de-humanizing" path of nationalism. The idealistic and compassionate MacDonagh had stated at a Women's Protest Meeting, organized by Sheehy-Skeffington, that he stood for the freedom of women as well as men, and that he hoped it would not be necessary to resort to war to gain that freedom. He insisted he was a man of peace, and in some embarrassment referred to his "disgusting" duty as an instructor of bayonet fighting during military training for the Irish Volunteers. In his letter Sheehy-Skeffington pointed out that such training could lead only to war, not peace, and he pleaded with MacDonagh to consider the terrible consequences:

> Are not the bulk of the Irish Volunteers animated by the old, bad tradition that war is a glorious thing, that there is something "manly" about going out prepared to kill your fellow-man, something cowardly about a desire to see one's end accomplished without bloodshed? Will not this sentiment be inevitably fostered by the insensible growth of a military organization? ... But a few weeks ago I heard a friend, who is also a Volunteer, speaking from the same platform as me, win plaudits by saying that the hills of Ireland would be crimsoned with blood rather than that the partition of Ireland should be allowed. That is the spirit that I dread. I am opposed to partition; but partition could be defeated at too dear a price.... I want to see the manhood of Ireland no longer hypnotised by the glamour of "glory of arms," no longer blind to the horrors of organised murder.[42]

It is apparent that Sheehy-Skeffington had the militaristic rhetoric of Pearse in mind here, the patriotic appeal to Irish manhood for the glorious shedding of blood; and his jingoistic friend who wanted the hills of Ireland to be crimsoned with blood sounds very like Pearse. His prophetic comments on the attempt to defeat partition and the price of "organized murder" should have a special relevance for devastated Northern Ireland in the 1970s and 1980s. In his pacifist plea he was reacting precisely as O'Casey did several years later when in his Dublin trilogy he mocked the glory of war and blood scarifice and stressed his sympathy for his suffering women characters. The colorful red-bearded and knickerbockered figure of Sheehy-Skeffington was a familiar quixotic sight in Dublin, though O'Casey had known him from personal contact when they served together in 1914 as officials in the Irish Citizen Army, and no doubt must have read and admired the open letter to MacDonagh. As socialists, pacifists, and feminists, the two men shared a humanistic idealism for Ireland, and O'Casey paid the following tribute to Sheehy-Skeffington's memory three years after his tragic death:

> Unwept, except by a few, unhonoured and unsung—for no National Society or Club has gratefully deigned to be called by his name—yet the ideas of Sheehy-Skeffington, like the tiny mustard

254 THE PROFANE BOOK OF IRISH COMEDY

seed today, will possibly grow into a tree that will afford shade and rest to many souls overheated with the stress and toil of barren politics. He was the living antithesis of the Easter Insurrection: a spirit of peace enveloped in the flame and rage and hatred of the contending elements, absolutely free from all its terrifying madness; and yet he was a purified soul of revolt against not only one nation's injustice to another, but he was also the soul of revolt against man's inhumanity to man. And in this blazing pyre of national differences his beautiful nature, as far as this world is concerned, was consumed, leaving behind a hallowed and inspiring memory of the perfect love that casteth out fear, against which there can be no law.

In Sheehy-Skeffington, and not in Connolly, fell the first martyr to Irish Socialism, for he linked Ireland not only with the little nations struggling for self-expression, but with the world's Humanity struggling for a higher life.[43]

If the dynamic Jim Larkin was for O'Casey the living antithesis of capitalism and his symbolic "Prometheus Hibernica," the noble Sheehy-Skeffington as the living antithesis of blood sacrifice might have been his surrogate Prince of Peace.

O'Casey remains a controversial figure in Ireland today, and it is not likely that many of his nationalist countrymen would sympathize with his stirring tribute to the memory of a courageous socialist-pacifist-feminist-humanist. Nevertheless, Sheehy-Skeffington's impressive if unpopular ideals were kept alive through the years by O'Casey and a number of passionate disciples; by his remarkable widow, Hanna Sheehy-Skeffington; by their distinguished son and senator, Owen; by their brilliantly articulate nephew, Conor Cruise O'Brien; and by a small band of enlightened historians and citizens. It was therefore particularly ironic that Mrs. Sheehy-Skeffington should have been one of the leaders of the group of nationalists that rioted in the Abbey Theatre against *The Plough* in 1926. Although she shared most of her husband's progressive ideas, they would certainly have disagreed about the Rising and O'Casey's treatment of it in his play. On the evidence of his letter to MacDonagh, he would in all probability have praised that pacifist and mock-heroic work. And since she was an ardent defender of the Rising and its idealized martyrs, she, as Maud Gonne had done in her objections to the mock-heroic plays of Synge, predictably invoked the spirit of Cathleen Ni Houlihan in her indignant charge that O'Casey's play was an unforgivable insult to the national honor.

The full account of her attack and O'Casey's defense, in a series of letters they exchanged in the press, and in their public debate on the issue, is recorded in *The Letters of Sean O'Casey* (vol. 1, 1975). Subsequently, they reconciled their dispute out of mutual respect for each other, and by sharing their devotion to the memory of her great husband, whose beautiful spirit of peace and universal brotherhood could in this rare instance overcome the emotional appeal of the melodramatic sow, Cathleen Ni Houlihan. Mrs. Hanna may have been a strong-willed patriot, but she was also a Sheehy-Skeffington, and her original protest against O'Casey's play was gradually softened and remained free from O'Donnell's nausea.

Politically humiliated for centuries, frustrated so often in their abortive attempts to assert their national identity, the Irish have always found it difficult to resist that eternal embrace with Cathleen Ni Houlihan. But many noble Irishmen have resisted. And it is unreasonable if understandable that any honest skeptic who says no to the Old Lady immediately becomes the occasion of nationalistic protest or nausea.

Some recent political critics, such as Seamus Deane, and neoclassical critics, such as William Irwin Thompson,[44] are reluctant to recognize the comic-ironic humanity in O'Casey's *Plough* and misjudge the play as a failed political tragedy. They demand high tragedy at the barricades and feel cheated when they find low comedy in the tenements. For such disappointed critics, as well as for nauseated Irish patriots, all of whom seem to resent O'Casey's tragicomic denial of noble expectations, there may be an inevitable moral: those who refuse to laugh at past historical follies tend to repeat them.

Shaw's Father Keegan understood the relationship between history and comedy when he said: "My way of joking is to tell the truth. It's the funniest joke in the world."[45] It should therefore be no surprise that writers in Ireland have so consistently chosen to profane the national pieties; and this artistic truth is one of the funniest jokes in Irish history.

The Comic Denial of Expectations

Irish comedy is based on what might be called an oxymoronic view of life: losers can be winners; vices can be virtues; folly can be wisdom. This paradoxical approach to dramatic laughter thrives on contradictions and exaggerations that allow the comic characters to insulate themselves from the inevitable villainies of the world, as well as from their own palpable frailties. Antiheroic Irish clowns must therefore rely on a resourceful bag of survival strategems—disguises and subterfuges, prevarications and mendacities, verbal extravagance and aggression—because their awareness of imminent defeat demands a counterstrategy of masked bravado in order to keep the enemy, the overbearing and respectable world, off balance by creating an illusion of victory. It is a necessary illusion for self-preservation with which most audiences of predictably repressed or normally unheroic people can readily empathize. While this average audience is pleasurably surprised or even shocked, it must also be exposed to a reversal of ordinary expectations before it can freely revel with the comic conspirators in their victorious defeats. This unpredictable game of oxymoron functions like the calculated illogic of a Celtic bull: it is pregnant with mirth, with the barbarous laughter that is created out of the collision of antithetical impulses. It is the oxymoronic laughter that is released by a Christy Mahon, the braggart "playboy" and mock patricide who loses and wins only to survive as a comic outcast; by a "Captain" Boyle, the braggart "paycock" and mock father who wins and loses only to survive in comic desolation.

Our ordinary expectations about the comic fate of Christy and the "Captain" are constantly shaken and even reversed throughout the course of the plays. Such ironic dramatists as Synge and O'Casey continually exploit the fluctuating ground of uncertain expectation where the audience is prepared for one thing and then suddenly presented with another, often its opposite. Since the audience naturally brings to the theater all its conditioned or conventional attitudes toward human behavior, the unconventional dramatist contrives to arrange the action on stage so that these stock responses are mocked or denied. It is very likely, therefore, that Synge and O'Casey had instinctively anticipated Brecht's theory of alienation with their own comic version of this concept, in which the audience is temporarily alienated or liberated from its baggage of received ideas and preconditioned feelings by a cathartic denial of expectations. In the suspended and fictive reality that exists in a darkened theater, there is something delightfully outrageous in the comic rejection of one's habitual or predictable assumptions about what will happen next. T. S. Eliot took a more moderate yet very relevant approach to this technique of dramatic dissociation when, in discussing his own plays, he wrote: "And finally, I tried to keep in mind that in a play, from time to time, something should happen; that the audience should be kept in the constant expectation that something is going to happen; and that, when it does happen, it should be different, but not too different, from what the audience had been led to expect."[46]

This denial of expectations is usually more sudden and more violent than Eliot allows, if not in his own plays, in Elizabethan drama, and particularly in Irish comedy, where the audience must continually adjust itself to the unexpected reversals in a dramatized world, as distinct from the workaday world, where commonplace distinctions between vice and virtue are suspended; a mythic world where anarchic freedom always challenges repressive authority; a comic world where unreconstructed clowns swear by Sir Toby's classic rebuke to Malvolio: "Dost thou think, because thou art virtuous, there shall be no more cakes and ale?" If, as is likely, most people secretly share this desire to desecrate the household gods of respectability but understandably lack the courage to act on it, they can find a gratification of their forbidden wishes in the irreverent Shakespearean and Irish clowns. By contrast, in benign or conventional comedy, in the works of a Colley Cibber or a Richard Steele, a James Barrie or even a Lennox Robinson, an audience's expectations of virtue rewarded are confirmed, not denied, when all follies are corrected, all misunderstandings are put right, and, to the eternal faith of the Miss Prisms of the proper world, "the good end happily and the bad unhappily." In the barbarous or unpredictable world of Irish comedy, on the other hand, follies may be indulged or mocked but usually go uncorrected, misunderstandings remain unresolved, and the seemingly bad or irresponsible clowns are only rescued from the narrow paths of virtue.

Christy Mahon and "Captain" Boyle, like Falstaff and Sir Toby, are wise fools for our sake. They remind us of our own

frailties and help take the sting out of them through the therapy
of irreverent laughter. They are like Blake's fool who must persist in his folly in order to become wise. Enid Welsford said many
fine things about the wisdom of comic folly, but she did not
realize that her illuminating remarks about the archetypal fool
provide a special insight into the emotional affinities that draw
audiences to the antiheroic clowns of Irish drama:

> The Fool is an unabashed glutton and coward and knave, he
> is—as we say—a *natural;* we laugh at him and enjoy a pleasant
> sense of superiority; he looks at us oddly and we suspect that he is
> our *alter ego;* he winks at us and we are delighted at the discovery
> that we also are gluttons and cowards and knaves. The rouge has
> freed us from shame. More than that, he has persuaded us that
> wasted affection, thwarted ambition, latent guilt are mere delu-
> sions to be laughed away. For how can we feel spiritual pain if we
> are only animals?[47]

It is precisely his animal instincts, his barbarous impulses, that
save the wise fool or Irish clown from spiritual pain. For the
audience, too, for all of us who are ready to admit it, as well as
for those enlightened rogues who act as our grotesque surro-
gates, it is difficult to feel guilty while laughing at the liberating
vices of unashamedly natural men and women. Perhaps, therefore, the following distinction might be made between tragic
knowledge and comic knowledge: the noble hero of high
tragedy discovers that he was wrong to commit the deeds condemned by his society and is redeemed by the knowledge of his
painful transgression; the mock hero of low comedy discovers
that he was right to commit the deeds condemned by his society
and is redeemed by the knowledge of his painless aggression.
This paradigm of the genres suggests the typical denial of expectations we find in Blake's necessary contraries: tragic hubris
damns; comic hubris saves.

Here, too, in this ironic release of comic knowledge, there is a
thematic reversal that is inherent in the victory of comic defeat.
It is the unexpected condition of comedy that Santayana described when he called attention to "the mishaps, the expedients,
the merry solutions of comedy, in which everybody acknowl-
edges himself beaten and deceived, yet is the happier for the
unexpected posture of affairs."[48] Martin Doul, one of Synge's

representative wise fools in *The Well of the Saints,* must be deceived and beaten before he and his unbeautiful wife can finally opt for the unexpected and oxymoronic condition of blind freedom. All of Synge's frustrated tramps and wives, tinkers and playboys, must be comically ostracized before they can go out in search of their uncertain liberty. All of O'Casey's braggart "paycocks" in the Dublin trilogy, Shields and Boyle and Fluther, must be comically discredited and isolated in their final moments of dubious triumph; and all the irreverent women who follow the natural impulses cf the yea-saying Cock in the later plays must be beaten into symbolic exile before they can dare to seek their perilous freedom.

Along with this thematic reversal of comic misfortune, there is a structural and a verbal denial of expectations in barbarous Irish comedy. The structural joke involves an inversion of the traditional order of main plot and subplot, so that in this unexpected form the subplot and its comic supernumeraries become the central focus, while the action of the main plot is now consigned to a secondary position and often occurs offstage. Like O'Casey, Synge concentrates on the lower orders and outcasts of the usual subplot for his central characters. The full impact of the structural inversion, however, is even more strikingly revealed in the works of O'Casey and Beckett, in the various ways they deflate and deny the traditional heroic plot. Since the dramatic situation in *Gunman* and *Juno* and *Plough, Godot* and *Endgame* and *Krapp,* is dominated by grotesque clowns, the once noble or military figures of potentially tragic stature, now hidden in the wings, fighting at the barricades or refusing to appear, are mocked structurally as well as thematically. James Agate must have been aware of this reversal of expectations when, in his review of the London premiere of O'Casey's second play in 1925, he wrote:

> *Juno and the Paycock* is as much a tragedy as *Macbeth,* but it is a tragedy taking place in the porter's family. Mr. O'Casey's extraordinary knowledge of English taste—that he wrote his play for the Abbey Theatre, Dublin, is not going to be allowed to disturb my argument—is shown by the fact that the tragic element in it occupies at the most some twenty minutes, and that for the remaining two hours and a half the piece is given up to gorgeous and incredible fooling.[49]

Agate's significant estimate of the disproportionate time allotted to the comedy in contrast to the tragedy is characteristic not only of O'Casey's plays but of those dark comedies of Synge, Fitzmaurice, Behan, and Beckett. The general condition of life in these works may be tragic, but the pervasive energy of the central figures is comic, the ominous mood is tempered with gallows humor, and the form is therefore tragicomic, which is another denial of expectations. Aristotle had more to say about tragedy than comedy, but in one of his brief generalizations he tells us that "Comedy aims at representing men as worse, Tragedy as better than actual life."[50] If mock-heroic Irish clowns who trace their lineage back to Shakespeare's drunken Porter, and then further back to the braggart warriors and parasite-slaves of Greek and Roman comedy, naturally lack the elevated stature necessary for tragedy, they may be said to possess the tragicomic dimensions of characters who are at once worse *and* better than actual life. In a disordered modern world in which the dignity of actual life has too often been discredited, their comic worse may well be better; and that is another ironic reversal of expectations.

Furthermore, Agate was also right in insisting that the impure taste of English and Irish audiences demands an excess of "gorgeous and incredible fooling" in the theater, even in the midst of what should be a tragedy. It is a phenomenon that once more reminds us of our psychic need to grin in order to bear the pain of existence. It may also be a modern phenomenon that helps to explain the impulsive need to create comic subplots that dominate and diminish the tragic main plots.

What William Empson once said about the function of the tragicomic double plot in English drama expands the insight of Agate and has a particular relevance for Irish drama. Empson justified the seemingly careless and loosely structured Elizabethan play as a convenient and necessary departure from the neoclassical preference for a tightly ordered single-plot form. He defended the commodious double plot in the following manner:

> It is an easy-going device, often used simply to fill out a play, and has an obvious effect in the Elizabethans of making you feel the play deals with life as a whole, with any one who comes onto the

street the scene so often represents; this may be why criticism has not taken it seriously when it deserved to be. Just because of this carelessness much can be put into it; to those who miss the connections the thing still seems sensible, and queer connections can be insinuated powerfully and unobtrusively; especially if they fit with ideas the audience already has at the back of its mind. The old quarrel about tragi-comedy, which deals with part of the question, shows that the drama of England has always at its best had a certain looseness of structure; one might almost say that the English drama did not outlive the double plot.[51]

Empson also describes this loose double-plot structure as part of the "'tragic king—comic people' convention" so characteristically illustrated in Shakespeare's work, notably in the *Henry IV* plays. By comparison modern Irish drama also did not outlive the loose form of the double plot; in fact, the Irish dramatists, unlike the English, went on to deflate the main plot and elevate the subplot so that the comic tail now wagged the tragic dog. It should therefore be stressed that those "queer connections" between tragedy and comedy are insinuated most powerfully and obtrusively in Irish drama. The Elizabethans often allowed their clowns to mock their heroes—it was part of the necessary education of such erring heroes as Lear to be ridiculed by their wise fools—but ultimately the heroes had to have the last anguished words and dominated the tragic scene. The modern Irish dramatists, however, writing out of a comic suspicion of tragic heroism that had festered through many centuries of famine and exploitation, frustrated hopes for nationhood, and the sacrificial rhetoric of abortive insurrections, not only encouraged their clowns to profane their heroes but insisted that the clowns should have the first and last foolish words. The would-be Irish heroes, who are usually dying bravely or blindly offstage, strutting or making bloodthirsty speeches when they appear onstage, learn nothing from their alter-ego clowns. In the Irish version of the double plot, then, the rude mechanicals or "comic people" who come onto the street take over the main plot, while the "tragic king" or his surrogate warriors, now fighting for Cathleen Ni Houlihan against John Bull, are shunted into the subplot. This plot reversal is Ireland's painful laugh at itself as well as at England.

Some modern English dramatists, such as Harold Pinter, later picked up the plot-inversion technique in such tragicomic plays as *The Dumb Waiter* and *The Birthday Party,* where the comic outcasts take over the central action and the tragic menace of the demoted main plot appears ominously onstage or hovers in the wings; and Tom Stoppard probably achieved the most brilliant tragicomic reversal of the *Hamlet* structure in his *Rosencrantz and Guildenstern Are Dead.* There are many variations of this structural inversion in the plays of Genet, Ionesco, and Brecht, for example, in *The Caucasian Chalk Circle,* where the comic Azdak plot dominates and redeems the heroic Grusha plot.

Above all, however, the thematic joke of structural inversion is a uniquely Irish denial of heroic expectations. In his remarks on the tentative nature of the setting and characters in *Waiting for Godot,* Hugh Kenner is on the verge of raising a similar point about plot reversal when he tells us that Gogo and Didi appear to be supernumeraries filling in time while we laugh and wait, expecting the main action to begin at any moment:

> The tree is plainly a sham, and the two tramps are simply filling up time until a proper dramatic entertainment can get under way. They are helping the management fulfill, in a minimal way, its contract with the ticket holders. The resources of vaudeville are at their somewhat incompetent disposal: bashed hats, dropped pants, tight boots, the kick, the pratfall, the improper story. It will suffice if they can stave a mass exodus until Godot comes, in whom we all are so interested.[52]

This comic denial of our expectations goes to the heart of the structural jest: Beckett's music-hall tramps have displaced the discredited Godot and his promise of salvation, just as O'Casey's Boyle and Joxer have displaced and discredited Cathleen Ni Houlihan and her sacrificial patriots; just as Behan's Dunlavin and Neighbour lead all the prisoners in a comic displacement and exposure of the discredited system that dooms the unseen and stoical "quare fellow." Kenner's reference to "the resources of vaudeville" reminds us that O'Casey and Behan share with Beckett an affintiy for the profane delights of the music hall, the consummate theater of knockabout, with its decrepit clowns and anarchic routines, its drunken porters and randy songs, its slapstick desecration of all the respectable foundations of society. With appropriate modifications, Boyle and Joxer, Dunlavin

and Neighbour, Gogo and Didi owe as much to Gallagher and
Sheen or Laurel and Hardy as they do to Mak and Gill, Sir Toby
and Sir Andrew, Falstaff and Bardolph, Pistol and Nym. This
line of comic descent from medieval drama to Shakespeare and
the Irish clowns has been reinforced by J. L. Styan. Writing
about Empson's interpretation of the loose structure that traditionally accompanies the double plot, Styan draws some
pointed connections between structural looseness and the loose
patterns of life in the plays of Shakespeare and O'Casey, plays
that "reproduce the sensations of life with its complexities and
contradictions":

> We get the feeling that, in Empson's words, "the play deals with
> life as a whole." From the spontaneous eruption of tomfoolery
> within the sacred framework of the medieval mystery plays to the
> contrivances of O'Casey to show his subject from opposed points
> of view in, say, *The Plough and the Stars,* we are reminded again
> that the point of reference is life; but if this is true, the looseness is
> merely apparent not real.
> After the magnificent Shakespearean rhetoric of Henry's
> "Once more unto the breach . . . ," which ends, we remember with
> an injunction to "follow your spirit," what better way of having us
> keep our wits and hear a ring of truth than by dragging on Nym,
> Bardolph and Pistol immediately?
> *Bardolph.* On, on, on, on, on, to the breach, to the breach.
> *Nym.* Pray thee Corporal stay, the knocks are too hot.[53]

The dangerous knocks of war and possible death are indeed
too hot for antiheroes, and we are promptly reminded of the
complexities and contradictions of life as a whole when the
heroic king is deflated by the comic people. In O'Casey's play,
after we have heard the patriotic rhetoric of Patrick Pearse—
"The old heart of the earth needed to be warmed with the red
wine of the battlefields"—it is not necessary to drag on the
clowns for a ring of truth because they have always been there in
the center of the action, Fluther and the Covey and Uncle Peter,
Bessie and Ginnie and Rosie, all of them mocking the heroics,
helping us keep our wits. They knock Pearse and they knock
each other in a spontaneous eruption of tomfoolery that celebrates their comic survival in a rich display of what Yeats once
called "the emotion of multitude." Yeats was seldom able to cap-
ture that wild overflow of comic emotion in his own plays, but he

always knew what it was and quickly defended it in the plays of Lady Gregory, Synge, and O'Casey. It was their appeal to the comic emotion of multitude, not Yeats's heroic emotion of solitude, that gave the Abbey Theatre its greatest triumphs.

As early as 1903 Yeats had written a short essay called "Emotion of Multitude," in which he had anticipated what Empson was to say many years later about the function of the double plot. Reacting against the rigidity and rationalistic form of the too well-made French play, the *pièce bien fait*, Yeats called attention to the alternative release of a common and powerful emotion that he found in the Greek chorus and the Elizabethan subplot:

> I have been thinking a good deal about plays lately, and I have been wondering why I dislike the clear and logical construction which seems necessary if one is to succeed on the Modern Stage. It came into my head the other day that this construction, which all the world has learnt from France, has everything of high literature except the emotion of multitude. The Greek drama has got the emotion of multitude from its chorus, which called up famous sorrows, long-leaguered Troy, much-enduring Odysseus, and all the gods and heroes to witness, as it were, some well-ordered fable, some action separated but for this from all but itself.... The Shakespearean Drama gets the emotion of multitude out of the sub-plot which copies the main plot, much as a shadow upon the wall copies one's body in the firelight. We think of King Lear less as the history of one man and his sorrows than as the history of a whole evil time.... It is so in all the plays, or in all but all, and very commonly the sub-plot is the main plot working itself out in more ordinary men and women, and so doubly calling before us the image of multitude.[54]

The emotion of multitude in the Greek chorus grew out of a tragic chant or narration presented as an epic catalogue of heroic sorrows, whereas the emotion of multitude in a Shakespearean subplot grew out of a tragicomic parallel in ordinary or antiheroic characters who presented an ironic foreshadowing, a distortion on the wall, as it were, of the main plot. Yeats could not have been expected to anticipate that many years later O'Casey, and after him Behan and Beckett and many other modern dramatists, would intensify the emotion of multitude by placing the heroic figures on the wall or in the wings, and then moving their shadowy and comic counterparts from the wall to the center of the stage. Nevertheless, Yeats did experiment with the emotion of multitude in some of his own plays. He used the traditional "tragic king—comic people" double plot of Elizabethan drama for *On Baile's Strand* in 1903 by creating the Fool and Blind Man subplot as an ironic foreshadowing of the Cuchulain and Conchubar main plot. Some of the best scenes in the play illustrate the tragicomic emotion of multitude whenever the two grotesque jesters assume the mock roles of the two tragic kings and act out the legend in lowlife parodies that intensify the tragedy.

Yeats was able to exploit the emotion of multitude again with comic-ironic perceptions in an earthy character like Crazy Jane in his poems; in a drunken outcast of an antiheroic poet like Septimus in *The Player Queen* (1922); in the Blind Beggar and Lame Beggar in *The Cat and the Moon* (1926)—this latter work a remarkable prefiguring of a comically contentious Beckett-like tramp duet. In spite of these impressive achievements, however, Yeats was not at his artistic ease with comedy in his plays, and he confessed that he had difficulty writing about the comic lower orders and capturing their common folk idiom. He openly admitted that he needed Lady Gregory's help in many of his plays, particularly with the comic folk dialogue in the farcical *Pot of Broth* (1902): "I hardly know how much of the play is my work, for Lady Gregory helped me in every play of mine where there is dialect, and sometimes where there is not. In those first years of the Theatre we all helped one another with plots, ideas, and dialogue, but certainly I was the most indebted as I had no mastery of speech that purported to be of real life."[55] On another occasion, in his open letter to Lady Gregory, "A People's Theatre," Yeats began by saying he had intended to create a popular theater for the Irish people but now realized that he really needed a private theater of the right people for his own esoteric plays: "I want to create for myself an unpopular theatre and an audience like a secret society where admission is by favour and never to many. . . . I desire a mysterious art, always reminding those who understand it of dearly loved things, doing its work by suggestion, not by direct statement, a complexity of rhythm, colour, gesture, not space-pervading like the intellect, but a memory and a prophecy."[56]

This is an eloquent defense of Yeats's hieratic form of verse drama that was to be, as he had planned from the start of his career, "remote, spiritual and ideal." He wrote some of his finest plays for this concept of an unpopular theater, a poet's theater, early and late tragedies such as *Deirdre* (1907) and *Purgatory* (1939), and those ritualistic epiphany plays for dancers, *At the Hawk's Well* (1917), *The Only Jealousy of Emer* (1919), and *A Full Moon in March* (1935). These highly stylized plays present an austere denial of expectations, a denial of all conventional responses to theatrical experience, as well as a denial of comedy. The result is a rare purification of art, an accomplishment of lyrical drama that exalts the heroic emotion of solitude, in sharp contrast to the popular theater of Lady Gregory, Synge, and O'Casey, which releases the comic emotion of multitude.

Unlike Yeats, they used the common idiom of the Irish people to create a verbal denial of expectations that might be called the comic language of multitude. They created antiheroic dialogue of such exaggerated and contentious modes of expression, particularly Synge and O'Casey, that the popular audiences at the Abbey were often moved to provocation as well as pleasure and set off riots of protest in the theater. Contentious life imitated contentious art. The barbarous or irreverent language of Irish comedy was calculated to alienate audiences from their expectations of edifying behavior and national idealism. Perhaps it was the gritty Lady Gregory who set the necessary tone of comic contentiousness that was to dominate Irish drama when she made her symbolic comment about her two quarrelsome clowns, McInerney and Miskell, the archetypal comic duet, in *The Workhouse Ward:* "I sometimes think the two scolding paupers are a symbol of ourselves in Ireland—*is fearr imreas na uaigneas*—'it is better to be quarreling than to be lonesome.'"[57] If this is the symbolic experience of life in Ireland, that the heat of comic battle maintains the energy of life and is therefore preferable to the cold solitude of private peace, it may then be necessary to modify one of Yeats's well-known adages: We make out of the quarrel with others, drama, but out of the quarrel with ourselves, poetry.[58] Although Yeats would not have intended it to take this meaning, the presence or absence of contentiousness—a comic dialectic—may point to at least one fundamental distinction between the lyric and comic modes of literature.

This comic dialectic as a dramatic form of entertainment probably had its origins in the archetypal flyting, the verbal contest of farcical insult and ridicule that can be found in Greek and Roman comedy, in *Beowulf,* in Chaucer and Shakespeare, in the early Gaelic poetry of Ireland and Scotland, in the medieval "Dialogue between Oisín and Patrick" and the sixteenth-century "Flyting of Dunbar and Kennedie,"[59] and flourished in the native folk literature of practically every country. In our own time the comic strategy of the flyting appears in the verbal game of the "dozens," played with poetic virtuosity by American blacks in their ghettos and in their literature, for example, in the plays of Langston Hughes, Leroi Jones, and Ed Bullins.[60] In life as well as art, the comic flyting is a form of emotional liberation as well as aggression because it gives all the players an opportunity to transform their worldly frustrations into verbal victories.

The Scots and the Irish, who were often considered to be too barbarous and emotional by their phlegmatic British rulers, had compelling reasons to resort to the flyting in their life and literature. Hugh MacDiarmid, the forthright Scottish poet who was singularly adept at the flyting, had occasion to defend O'Casey as an eloquent Irish flyter because he believed that his kindred Celt's powerful gift of comic contentiousness grew out of the fact that his tough Gaelic spirit was fortunately unaffected by the constraint of English gentility. He wrote: "Two features of O'Casey's writing that have been severely criticised—namely, his immoderate expressions of rage and of *argumentum ad hominis*—so distasteful to English gentility—manifest his Gaelic background and have their virtues, no matter how they may go against the grain of the English tradition (and, indeed, the "flytings" are one of the great features of Scottish poetry and the English dislike them)."[61]

Another modern poet, W. H. Auden, an Americanized Englishman, admired the flyting but felt it was a lost art. Unfortunately, he didn't look to modern Irish comedy when he lamented the loss of the flyting as a literary form. He believed that this comic dialectic was practiced now only by agitated truck and cab drivers, yet in discussing the tactics of the form he recognized the dual function of the game when he wrote:

> Flyting seems to have vanished as a studied literary art and only to survive in the impromptu exchanges of truckdrivers and cabdrivers. The comic effect arises from the contradiction between the insulting nature of what is said which appears to indicate a passionate relation of hostility and aggression, and the calculated skill of verbal invention which indicates that the protagonists are not thinking about each other but about language and their pleasure in employing it inventively. A man who is really passionately angry is speechless and can only express his anger by physical violence. Playful anger is intrinsically comic because of all emotions, anger is the least compatible with play.[62]

The initial provocation to eloquent rage can grow out of the most simple as well as the most intense conflict in a play, and once the protagonists in the game get caught up in the virtuosity of their counterattacks, as Auden rightly points out, indignation is displaced by comic imagination. And the audience, as well as the characters, takes pleasure in the playful control of abusive language. The battle of words has become a dual experience of defense and delight. When Miskell hurls the curse of twenty-four men at McInerney in Lady Gregory's *Workhouse Ward*, McInerney replies with a counterinsult that has the gratifying shape and sound of a well-wrought flyting: "That the worm may chew you from skin to marrow bone."[63] When Martin Doul in Synge's *Well of the Saints* temporarily regains his sight and is mocked by the cruel villagers, and more, by the grotesque reality of his unbeautiful old wife, he resorts to counterabuse in a poetic flyting that offers some verbal pleasure as a compensation for his disillusionment: "I'm telling you there isn't a wisp on any grey mare on the ridge of the world isn't finer than the dirty twist on your head. There isn't two eyes in any starving sow, isn't finer than the eyes you were calling blue like the sea."[64] When a harmless clown such as Uncle Peter in O'Casey's *Plough and the Stars* turns on the tormentors who have been "twarting" him throughout the play, he can release a tirade of counterinsults that invests his comic rage with the mock eloquence and pleasure of a cumulative flyting: "As long as I'm a livin' man, responsible for me thoughts, words, an' deeds to th' Man above, I'll feel

meself instituted to fight again' th' sliddherin' ways of a pair o'
picaroons, whisperin', concurrin', concoctin', an' conspirin' together to rendher me unconscious of th' life I'm thryin' to
live."[65]

McInerney, Doul, and Uncle Peter are such inept and antiheroic figures that we are not quite prepared for their aggressive retaliations. Therefore it comes as something of a pleasurable surprise that such clowns who are losing the war of
tragicomic attrition should be winning some battles of farcical
insult. Imaginative and abusive words are the only weapons
available to these otherwise disarmed mock warriors trapped in
a disjointed world where the trading of comic attacks is part of
the game of survival. We do not expect such vulnerable characters to make it, yet thanks to their comic emotion and language
of multitude, they endure. Contrary to what we find in traditional comedy, where, in an affirmation of expectations, the
comic rebels are finally corrected and reintegrated into normal
society, the comic rebels of barbarous Irish comedy deny all
expectations and remain contentious outsiders, uncorrected and
unrepentant flyters.

The Comic Principle of Disintegration

"Do you know what Ireland is? asked Stephen with cold violence.
Ireland is the old sow that eats her farrow."[66]

Fortunately Stephen Dedalus was wrong. Cathleen Ni Houlihan has not been able to devour her creative children. But it is
not because the old sow has not tried to feed on her farrow in a
gruesome spectacle that might have inspired tragic legends of an
internecine curse in the grand style of the Greeks. Historically,
nevertheless, there is little if any Greek tragedy in the skirmishes
of literary Ireland because the clever farrow usually manage to
bite back and elude the bitch mother Cathleen. They bite and
run away, usually to self-exile, to live and write another day; they
write savagely comic variations on the mock-heroic spectacle of a
frustrated and outraged old sow; they create their own legends,
which tragicomically profane the excessive pieties of Irish
idealism. It is therefore necessary to reconstruct Joyce's wonderfully melodramatic myth of the devoured and martyred Irish

artist, since Cathleen is so often caught in her own religious and nationalistic nets, and in this hilarious reversal of misfortune, a comic Oedipal allegory, the ingenious farrow symbolically devour the poor old sow.

On some of those ironic occasions when the savage old sow wins, as when she voraciously devours a noble Parnell, the fault lies not so much with her as with the uncompromising death wish of the martyred victim. Parnell would never have been destroyed if he had had any bite of humor in him, expecially that dark streak of barbarous and malicious laughter which is so indispensable for survival in Ireland. If Parnell had been wiser in his domestic folly he would not have converted a bedroom farce into a political tragedy. It is precisely that instinctive and creative ability to transform the raw material of high tragedy into low comedy which characterizes a dominant aspect of the Irish imagination, particularly in the work of a Joyce, a Synge, an O'Casey, a Beckett—and also in the art and life of that minority of courageous Irish men and women who dare to ignore or question the national mystique that enshrouds Cathleen Ni Houlihan.

Joyce, Synge, O'Casey, and Beckett survived because, among other profound mysteries, they were the comic mythmakers of their own liberation. Like Blake and Yeats, they realized that they had to create their own system or become enslaved by the system of others. They survived, therefore, because they were cunning enough to construct their own mythology of self-exile—Synge survived by dying before he was forced to choose exile—for they knew that by the unwritten cannibalistic law of Irish literary life, their jealous rivals among the lesser farrow would have devoured them even more cheerfully than the atrabilious Cathleen if they had chosen to remain in Ireland. They survived because they were masters of the mythology of comic anarchy, that uniquely though not exclusively Irish form of knockabout comedy, the superbly vulgar tradition of music-hall clowning which deflates or desecrates, according to the provocation, those questionable standards of success and esteem that the political and clerical princes of society are determined to sanctify.

Knockabout comedy is an ancient and enduring art form that

always lies waiting to liberate men and women from the seemingly immutable structures of society that threaten to take away their private identity and personal freedom. By invoking a wide range of uninhibited horseplay and self-deprecation, the artist of knockabout comedy can transform grave ceremony into slapstick ritual and temporarily free us from the tyranny of the sublime. In one of his wisest and most paradoxical books, *Civilization and Its Discontents,* Freud reached the conclusion that it is in the very nature of any society—holy Ireland is not alone here— to restrict the freedom of the individual because civilization demands rigid control over people's natural desires; civilization is threatened by the unpredictable exuberance of human instincts and must therefore protect itself by imposing a system of automatic order:

> Order is a kind of repetition-compulsion by which it is ordained once for all when, where and how a thing shall be done so that on every similar occasion doubt and hesitation shall be avoided.... One would be justified in expecting that it would have ingrained itself from the start and without opposition into all human activities; and one may well wonder that this has not happened, and that, on the contrary, human beings manifest an inborn tendency to negligence, irregularity and untrustworthiness in their work, and have to be laboriously trained to imitate the example of their celestial models.[67]

When men and women begin to hesitate and to experience doubts about the repetition-compulsion system of order; when they revert to their instinctive and inborn tendency to negligence, irregularity, and untrustworthiness in their work; when they begin to question the sacred example of their celestial models; and when some or all of these life-saving signs of incipient rebellion are accompanied by the anarchic spirit of knockabout comedy, the tentative liberation of the unintimated individual may be close at hand.

This is at best a temporary and vicarious process of comic insurrection because it is of necessity more a state of mind than an overt act of violence, specifically a psychic victory of the imagination through which the artist of knockabout comedy and those who share his creative vision find the courage to endure yet another day of repressive order. Low comedy is the natural enemy of order. Indeed, wherever the instruments of order are most rigorously imposed, there knockabout comedy finds its most tempting targets for profanation. One of the chief rituals of knockabout involves a total parody of authority so that the frustration of human wishes is broken by the chaos of comic disorder. In Freudian terms, perhaps, this is the compensatory process by which the comic id force undermines the solemn superego. There is no room for guilt in a belly laugh; in fact, there is a catharsis of repressed desire in it, in the explosive release of laughter that metaphorically shakes the rigid structures of society. One can enjoy this comic catharsis in varying experiences of glorious knockabout, in the inspired antics of the Falstaffians or Chaplin and Keaton, the Pickwickians or Laurel and Hardy; the Marx Brothers or Tom and Jerry; and in Irish literature, in the mock-heroic posture of the pagan Oisín, in the barbarously comic tramps of Boucicault and Synge, as a prelude to the irreverent clowns of Joyce, O'Casey, Behan, and Beckett.

Samuel Beckett accurately described what might be the basis of this comic explosion and catharsis as "the principle of disintegration," in his review of O'Casey's *Windfalls* in 1934:

> Mr. O'Casey is a master of knockabout in this very serious and honourable sense—that he discerns the principle of disintegration in even the most complacent solidities, and activates it to their explosion. This is the energy of his theatre, the trimph of the principle of knockabout in situation, in all its elements and on all its planes, from the furniture to the higher centres. If "Juno and the Paycock," as seems likely, is his best work so far, it is because it communicates most fully this dramatic dehiscence, mind and world come asunder in irreparable dissociation—"chassis" (the credit of having readapted Aguecheek and Belch in Joxer and the Captain being incidental to the larger credit of having dramatised the slump in the human solid). This impulse of material to escape and be consummate in its own knockabout is admirably expressed in the two "sketches" that conclude this volume, and especially in "The End of the Beginning," where the entire set comes to pieces and the chief character, in a final spasm of dislocation, leaves the scene by the chimney.[68]

This brilliant insight into the knockabout artistry of O'Casey can also be applied to the comic genius of Beckett himself, as well as Synge and Joyce, for it would be accurate to say that in their various ways they all dramatized the low comic "slump in the human solid." And it is of special interest to note in this prophetic passage all the touchstone phrases on knockabout comedy that anticipate and define the kind of drama Beckett himself was still twenty years away from writing:

- the principle of disintegration in even the most complacent solidities
- activates it to their explosion
- from the furniture to the higher centres
- this dramatic dehiscence
- mind and world come asunder in irreparable dissociation—"chassis"
- the slump in the human solid
- this impulse of material to escape and be consummate in its own knockabout
- in a final spasm of dislocation

Here, from the initial disintegration and explosion to the final spasm of dislocation, is the knockabout world of comic nightmare for Gogo and Didi, Hamm and Clov, Krapp and Krapp, Winnie and Willie. It is also the knockabout dream world of Bloom in Dublin, Earwicker in the Universe; and, one must add, the knockabout folk world of Christy Mahon in Mayo, the tinkers in Wicklow, as well as the knockabout tenement and fantasy world of O'Casey's clowns in urban and rural Ireland, for all of whom mind and world come tragicomically asunder. At the conclusion of *Juno* and *Godot,* for example, no solidities remain, not a scrap of furniture on the bare stage, only the slumping couples in their final spasm of comic disintegration and dissociation. If the spectacle of this "chassis" were not accompanied by the humanizing energy of barbarous laughter, we, as well as the characters, might all go mad.

This side of madness, then, we must not overlook that brilliantly paradoxical phrase almost hidden in Beckett's profound paragraph: "this dramatic dehiscence." In its double meaning of gaping and bursting, the dramatized condition of "dehiscence" sums up the dualistic nature of low comedy, the submerged ache and the exploding energy—the dramatic enactment of the source of life in the metaphorical rituals of sex and laughter, two in one and one in two: the smiling lips agape like a surgical

wound; the bursting open or explosion of seed vessels to discharge their pollen. This hidden pain and profligate laughter
reflect the dark and bright prisms of Irish knockabout, the dual
impulse of horror and horseplay, the gallows humor that makes
it all bearable for the playboys and tramps of Synge and Beckett,
the cuckolds and paycocks of Joyce and O'Casey. And with their
related degrees of brightness and darkness, one must allow
room for the rogues of Carleton, the shaughrauns of Boucicault,
the fools of Lady Gregory, the pipe dreamers of Fitzmaurice, the
chancers of Behan, the hallucinators of Flann O'Brien. And
perhaps the beguiling dustmen and spoiled priests of Shaw.
There are many others, but finally, room must be made at the
top for that mock-heroic warrior and poet of Celtic folk myth,
Oisín, the tragicomic archetype of all Irish knockabouts—
Usheen who comically and oedipally desecrated his Da, the
noble Finn MacCool, in a ninth-century Gaelic poem, and who
later in the medieval dramatic dialogues hilariously profaned his
spiritual father, St. Patrick, the patron saint of Cathleen Ni
Houlihan.

The mock heroes of knockabout comedy may be less noble but
they are more attractive and more enduring, more human and
more accessible, than the heroic figures in Irish literature and
history. Even before he was martyred, the princely Parnell was
too noble and remote for mundane laughter. The dour De Valera was suspicious of the arts and of laughing men. Moving to
mythology, the courageous Cuchulain was a great fighter with
the terrifying instinct of a killer, and he is known to have
laughed briefly only on the occasion of his betrayal and death.
Yeats's private version of Cuchulain, in contrast to his garrulous
and tragicomic Oisín, is an aloof and tragic persona. These comparisons must bring us round directly to Yeats, who could sometimes strike a low comic note, but who was above all the incom-
parable modern master of the heroic and lyric modes. It is true
that Yeats was capable of resorting to sly and arrogant wit, and if
the public occasion demanded it he could display a devastating
tone of Olympian irony when confronted by the folly of his
countrymen. Nevertheless, and perhaps fortunately so, when
one considers the destiny of his art, he lacked the coarse-grained
and uninhibited sense of comic anarchy that was better left to

the Synges and Joyces, the O'Caseys and Becketts. Although Yeats was capable of randy comedy and malicious laughter in some of his poems and plays, particularly in his later poems, and in such an atypically mock-heroic play as *The Player Queen,* or in such a rare tramp farce as *The Cat and the Moon,* his daimonic vision was too lofty, and understandably he had little of the music-hall vulgarity so necessary for sheer knockabout.

Still, one cannot think of such plays as *The Cat and the Moon* and *Purgatory* without drawing some tentative connections between the ritualistic drama of Yeats and Beckett. Some sensitive critics, such as John Rees Moore, have suggested a link between the two beggars in *The Cat and the Moon* and the two tramps in *Waiting for Godot:*

> In a dim way, these two beggars foreshadow Beckett's "tramps" both in attitude and tone of voice. After their interesting discussion of saint and sinner, the Lame Beggar says, "We have great wisdom between us, that's certain." This is like those brief resting places of satisfaction that punctuate the storm and stress of Gogo and Didi's companionship. But Yeats's beggars *have* their Godot. The saint, indeed, requests the pleasure of their company.[69]

It is, in fact, in the resolution of the play, when the beggars *have* their Godot, when the saint offers the Blind Beggar a cure and the Lame Beggar a blessing, that Yeats achieves his epiphany and goes a different path from Beckett, a noncomic path toward the fulfillment of a miracle. Yeats's miracle play also goes a different path from Synge's *Well of the Saints,* to which work it also has dim and tentative links, for Synge's tragicomic tramps, Martin and Mary Doul, must reject the dubious miracle of sight in order to remain blind but free on their own uncertain and even dangerous terms. Synge and Beckett, therefore, retain their mock-heroic and comically skeptical view of salvation. Yeats, on the other hand, after allowing his contentious beggars their uneasy friendship and their comic flytings, finally elevates them, particularly the blessed and victorious Lame Beggar, to a condition of heroic wisdom and salvation that is celebrated through the epiphany of a liberating dance. In their miraculous quest for communion, Yeats's transmuted beggars move beyond, above comedy. In *Purgatory* Yeats creates a stark and symbolic impass that has some slight affinities to *Endgame* as well as *Godot;* however, this play is a noncomic parable with fated figures who are struck down by a family curse of tainted blood, tainted Irish history, that recalls Greek tragedy, and since there can be no miracles this time because the characters cannot be purged of their dark transgressions, the whole work moves powerfully and again far beyond and above the antic world of comedy.

Beckett may have picked up some haunting and poetic echoes of a vagrant and static world from Yeats's ritualistic theater, but ultimately he followed Synge and O'Casey along the profane and downward path of tragicomedy, which does not lead to miracles, epiphanies, or parables of tainted blood. In an attempt to make a distinction between the so-called higher and lower visions of art, the heroic and the mock-heroic paths that Yeats and Joyce followed, Richard Ellmann has added a pertinent comment to this issue of the downward thrust of comedy: "Notwithstanding numerous melancholy qualifications, Yeats and Joyce had in common an intense desire to affirm human life. Blake, whose god was Divine Humanity, was understandably a predecessor of both. For Yeats the method of literature was to raise the ordinary to the heroic, for Joyce a movement down was as required as a movement up, and he mingled ordinary, heroic, and mock-heroic without wishing to compound them."[70]

All artists can be said to affirm human life, even if they do not create their work directly under the banner of Blake, and it is not their general aim but their specific mode of expression that is relevant here. The point to be made, as Ellmann indicates, is that the downward or mock-heroic method can affirm life as intensely as the upward or heroic method. Divine Humanity is also the godhead of knockabout comedians, whose outrageous and profane pranks should not blind us to the fact that their creators choose barbarous laughter in order to champion the freedom of ordinary and repressed human beings. On the whole, Yeats followed the upward movement of the heroic mode because, among other private loyalties, his imagination was too fine to be violated by knockabout. He took a tragic rather than a comic view of the tensions in life that often lead to disintegration. And although Joyce, with his unparalleled commitment to aesthetic vision and comic disintegration, was able to mingle the heroic and the mock heroic, it is an open question whether, in perhaps the most striking comparison, his upward treatment of the artistic prig Stephen Dedalus was quite as successful as his downward treatment of the bourgeois scapegoat Leopold Bloom. In two of the outstanding chapters of *Ulysses*, "Cyclops" and "Circe," where Bloom is the central figure in the mock-heroic revels and profanations, Joyce is the consummate master of knockabout. There is of course more than knockabout comedy in those two chapters, but the movement is invariably toward a downward affirmation, as it is throughout *Finnegans Wake*, where even the glorious celebration of Anna Livia Plurabelle—like the downward celebration of Molly Bloom—would not be fulfilled without the dehiscent rituals of verbal and visualized knockabout.

Only of Synge, perhaps, can it be maintained that his upward and downward methods produced dramatic works of comparable brilliance, though unlike Joyce he never mingled the two methods. His heroic Maurya and Deirdre, in *Riders to the Sea* and *Deirdre of the Sorrows*, are figures of towering tragedy, while his Christy Mahon and Mary Byrne, in *The Playboy* and *The Tinker's Wedding*, are superbly mundane mock heroes of knockabout comedy. Like O'Casey and Beckett, Synge was a genius at comic disintegration, that dual process of dramatic dehiscence which reveals the gaping ache under the bursting laughter. Frank O'Connor, so tragically and comically adept in his fine short stories, was strangely insensitive to the nature of Synge's undeniable genius for dark comedy when, in *The Backward Look*, that sometimes perverse book of his last years, he wrote: "*In the Shadow of the Glen* fails because the story on which it is based is farcical, while the play itself is serious. . . . *The Tinker's Wedding* fails as a play because it has no Synge in it; *The Well of the Saints* because it has too much."[71] The failure here lies in the critical judgment of the aging O'Connor, who with a reckless broadside has arbitrarily wiped out three-quarters of Synge's comic work. In all these plays, as in *The Playboy*—which, by the way, O'Connor quite eccentrically called a masterpiece with a flawed first act—it is precisely that ironic interplay between the farcical and the serious, the dark wrench of alienation and the low comedy of freedom, which identifies that special quality of Synge's genius and defines what is the comic mainsteam of the Irish dramatic imagination. Farce often casts long and grotesque shadows into the territory of tragedy without moving over the line that separates the two genres, and any attempt to eliminate the shadows or soften the farce, as Frank and Willy Fay tried unsuccessfully to do, would destroy the dehiscent paradox of Synge's comic art.[72]

Similar shadows appear in the knockabout comedy of O'Casey and Beckett, similar overtones of anguish under the wild farce, or what Beckett alluded to as the "serious and honourable sense" of knockabout. In *Juno and the Paycock* and *Cock-a-Doodle Dandy*, in *Waiting for Godot* and *Happy Days,* where all the comic characters are suspended in seemingly hopeless situations, there is a farcical response to the "slump in the human solid" as the frustrated clowns retaliate with their own survival games, their fantasies of victory in defeat. Perhaps it is an ingenious method of fighting confusion with confusion: the threat of tragic chaos is exploded by comic chaos. Profane laughter may be the only answer to the dissociation and disintegration of life in the plays of O'Casey and Beckett. There is more of a gaping ache in the laughter of Beckett, more of a bursting joy in the laughter of O'Casey, especially in his later pastoral comedies; however, as masters of knockabout they both concentrate on the anarchic and liberating spirit of low comedy. The laughter in their tragicomic plays has a cathartic function: the serious disorder of society creates its own hilarious antidote in comic disorder, and the resulting laughter shakes the sacred foundations, "from the furniture to the higher centres," until Cathleen Ni Houlihan becomes as illusory and deflated as Mister Godot.

Perhaps this method of achieving a catharsis through profanation, or what amounts to a psychic release from repression, may be indigenous to low comedy, for as Wylie Sypher has observed, "The comic rites are necessarily impious, for comedy is sacrilege as well as release."[73] Commenting on the specific nature of this comic release or catharsis in relation to comic irreverence, Sypher adds further evidence in support of Beckett's "principle of disintegration" in these illuminating remarks on tragedy and comedy:

> Tragedy has been called "mithridatic" because the tragic action, inoculating us with large doses of pity and fear, inures the self to the perils we all face. Comedy is no less mithridatic in its effects on

the self, and has its own catharsis. Freud said that nonsense is a toxic agent acting like some "poison" now and again required by the economy of the soul. Under the spell of this intoxication we reclaim for an instant our "old liberties," and after discharging our inhibited impulses in folly we regain the sanity that is worn away by the everyday gestures. We have a compulsion to be moral and decent, but we also resent the obligation we have accepted. The irreverence of the carnival disburdens us of our resentment and purges our ambivalence so that we can return to our duties as honest men. Like tragedy, comedy is homeopathic. It cures folly with folly.[74]

The mithridatic cure may be more psychic than actual, the return to duty and honesty may be difficult and even undesirable, after the liberating laughter has subsided, but in their varieties of comic subversion O'Casey and Beckett dramatize the irreverent carnival of disorder and catharsis that the economy of our souls periodically require. It must also be pointed out, however, that the reverberations set off by their farcical explosions operate on different wavelengths and produce somewhat different tones of laughter. O'Casey's comedy is more inflammatory and therefore more aggressive in its sweeping disorder; Beckett's comedy is more nihilistic and therefore more portentious in its teasing irresolution. O'Casey's comic syntax is loose and voluble, more self-indulgent and playful in its rhetoric; Beckett's comic syntax is taut and hard, more stoical and astringent in its rhetoric. If O'Casey's flytings are more copious and rhythmic, Beckett's flytings are more economical and poetic. Words are more often weapons of defense for O'Casey's characters, whose comic aggression eases the burden of existence by animating a condition of merry chaos in the game of survival; words are more often scrupulously measured cries of restraint for Beckett's characters, whose comic incantations ease the burden of existence by animating a condition of merry paralysis in the game of survival. After the dark comedy of the Dublin trilogy, O'Casey's pastoral plays become progressively more urgent and joyful in their freewheeling attacks on the hardening orthodoxies of Ireland; and some of the later works, such as *Purple Dust* and *Cock-a-Doodle Dandy*, *The Bishop's Bonfire* and *The Drums of Father Ned*, call for nothing short of a comic apocalypse to redeem everyman and everywoman in Ireland, in the world. Beckett's plays become progressively more fatalistic as their ever-shrinking orbits of graveyard knockabout undermine the metaphysical structures of the universe itself; and if they call for anthing at all, it might be only an oblique form of comic subversion that may ultimately dissolve the whole system along with its farcical scapegoats, which is implicit in the dark tone of *Waiting for Godot* and *Endgame,* and more explicit and ominous in *Krapp's Last Tape* and *Happy Days,* as well as in more recent works of drama and fiction.

If there is some darkness in O'Casey's comedy, there is never despair. His comic spirit itself always contains his therapy, his faith. He was in full control of his artistic power whenever he relied on his abundant resources of knockabout comedy and irony to transcend humanity's failure to mitigate the disintegration of modern life. His work in the theater is more likely to be uneven, excessively sentimental or didactic, when he departs from his comic muse, for his noncomic characters often fail to achieve a life of their own, an authentic life apart from O'Casey's own voice of protest. Philosophy and comedy can be strange bedfellows in the theater, and even Shaw sometimes had his difficulties in trying to yoke them. It is in the nature of Beckett's stoical and objective genius that he can be philosophic and comic at the same time; it is in the nature of O'Casey's effusive and subjective genius that he can be least comic when he tries to be most philosophic.

At the top of his form, nevertheless, like Synge and Beckett, and Behan, too, O'Casey created a fine gallery of comic characters who refuse to allow the disorder of their world to destroy them. At various times his clowns succumb to what might be called the Gadshill folly, for they are comically discredited for their cowardice and mendacity; and yet they are also capable of a complementary attitude that could be called the Shrewsbury wisdom, for they all know that a corpse on the battlefield, or in the war-torn slums of Dublin, is a poor excuse for honor or patriotism. They are comically and ironically damned and saved; and in their knockabout salvation they profane whatever is too rigid or too sacred in society. And holy Ireland is a country of many sacred nets, outside of which lies comic freedom.

This is not, however, a tragicomic condition limited to Ireland, for Ionesco was referring to all modern drama when he claimed that "the comic alone is capable of giving us the strength to bear the tragedy of existence."[75] Earlier Nietzsche, reacting to the equivalent of disintegration in his own time, must have understood the cathartic power of comedy when he pointed to "the *comic* spirit, which releases us, through art, from the tedium of absurdity."[76] Artaud was also commenting on the universal power of dark laughter when he made the following charge: "The contemporary theatre is decadent because it has lost the feeling on the one hand for seriousness and on the other for laughter; because it has broken away from gravity, from effects that are immediate and painful—in a word, from Danger. Because it has lost a sense of real humor, a sense of laughter's power of physical and anarchic dissociation."[77] The comic "principle of disintegration" in the plays of O'Casey and Beckett can help the characters come to terms with that danger and dissociation, can help them and their audiences affirm the human condition through the power of farcical laughter.

The theme of affirmation emerges clearly in O'Casey's apocalyptic comedies, such as *Purple Dust* and *Cock-a-Doodle Dandy* and *The Drums of Father Ned,* but even in the dislocated urban world of his earlier tragicomedies he never doubts that there is a saving grace in his grotesque Dublin clowns, in the comically contentious and enduring women perhaps even more than in the men. Only insofar as the sheer energy of low comedy is itself a stubborn form of survival is there anything that resembles an open affirmation or celebration of life in the plays of Beckett. Nevertheless, it must be pointed out that the resilient art of knockabout comedy is in its sheer creation an act of affirmation for Beckett. On this fine point it is necessary to invoke the wisdom of Eric Bentley, who rightly insists that "artistic activity is itself a transcendence of despair, and for unusually despairing artists that is no doubt what art is: a therapy, a faith"; and Beckett, he adds, "got rid of despair, if only for the time being, *by* expressing it."[78]

Although there are different degrees of affirmation in the plays of O'Casey and Beckett, there are many comic affinities and ironies that strike common echoes in their work. Their characters continually deny our expectations by the way they respond to the elements of disintegration in their lives. "That's the Irish People all over," Seumas Shields says in *The Shadow of a Gunman,* "they treat a joke as a serious thing and a serious thing as a joke."[79] Nell in *Endgame* tries to take comfort from the fact that "nothing is funnier than unhappiness, I grant you that."[80] Laughter is difficult but essential and none of the characters in O'Casey or Beckett can go it alone. The two blundering vagrants, Jerry and Sammy, in *A Pound on Demand,* the early one-act play that appeared in *Windfalls,* form one of those Laurel and Hardy vaudeville duets that impressed the younger Beckett in 1934, comic couples who cannot live with or without each other and are so often orchestrated for knockabout frustration and communion in the plays of O'Casey and Beckett. Beckett was also fascinated by the wild game of farcical disintegration in *The End of the Beginning,* another early one-act play, in which Barry and Darry, a pair of fat and thin middle-aged duffers, perform the archetypal duet of hilarious dislocation; and all of Beckett's plays might well be subtitled "The Beginning of the End" for his duffers, though the end never comes. Hamm and Clov are *playing* the game of ending, but they can't quite end it: "Let's stop playing!" Clov says; but the helpless Hamm can only reply, "Never!"[81]

At the end of *Juno and the Paycock,* an ending that ordinarily might have come earlier with Juno's great elegiac speech, the play doesn't quite end as the drunk and bewildered Boyle and Joxer stagger onto an empty stage to play the darkest reprise of their braggart-warrior and parasite-slave duet amid the desolation. The family and the furniture are gone, their world is asunder, in "a state o' chassis," and they could well be rehearsing for or anticipating another absurd beginning, the appearance of a Gogo and Didi, or even Hamm and Clov. "The blinds is down, Joxer, the blinds is down!"[82] It is the end of a slapstick survival game that never seems to end. In O'Casey and Beckett the knockabout clowns never die; they only play games; they wait or fall down; they suffer and laugh for all of us, as well as for themselves.

Disintegration is treated as a laughing game by these characters because that is the only way they can go on living with disintegration. In *Waiting for Godot* Didi pleads, "Come on Gogo, return the ball,"[83] and in his well-meaning and incompetent way

Gogo always responds to keep the game going. In *Endgame* Clov asks, "What's to keep me here?" "The dialogue," Hamm replies theatrically, returning the ball.[84] In *Juno and the Paycock* Boyle says, "I ofen looked up at the sky an' assed meself the question—what is the stars, what is the stars?"; and Joxer faithfully returns the ball: "Ah, that's the question—what is the stars?"[85] They all grin and bear it because, as Didi says, when they decide they must fill the void with talk, "We're inexhaustible."[86] In the midst of an argument Clov says, "There's one thing I'll never understand. Why I always obey you. Can you explain that to me?"; and Hamm replies, "Perhaps it's compassion. A kind of great compassion."[87] After an argument Boyle says, "Now an' agen we have our differ, but we're there together all the time"; and Joxer returns the refrain: "Me for you, an' you for me, like the two Musketeers."[88]

So it is always for the clowns of O'Casey and Beckett. As a result of their comic duels and duets, they're all there in the chaos together; they're all inexhaustible; they're all bound together by the great compassion of low comedy. They can't affirm the disintegrating world, but they can provoke laughter and affirm each other, for all of us as well as for themselves.

NOTES AND COMMENTS

Preface

1. Herbert Howarth, *The Irish Writers: Literature and Nationalism, 1880–1940* (New York: Hill & Wang, 1958), p. 18. Howarth associated the Irish pursuit of the sacred with the heroic or messianic influence of the martyred Parnell. This noble task may explain why there is little room for a consideration of comedy in the book. I do not believe that the quest of the sacred is congenial to the spirit of comedy, in Ireland or anywhere, for the comic daimon is driven by what is essentially an antiheroic and ironic vision of life that affirms by denying.

2. Vivian Mercier, *The Irish Comic Tradition* (London: Oxford University Press, 1962), p. x. Although Mercier gives slight attention to the Irish dramatists, he is a critic of the first rank and his approach to nondramatic comedy and satire is consistently illuminating. His book is far superior to a recent work that deals with Irish drama but only in a superficial way, Elizabeth Hale Winkler's *Clown in Modern Anglo-Irish Drama* (Frankfort: Peter Lang, 1977). Winkler presents a limited and often misleading survey of satirized clowns without providing a sufficiently controlled and critical point of view. Her treatment of Synge and O'Casey, for example, is disappointing for many reasons, partly because she is almost exclusively concerned with the negative aspects of the comic characters, for she explains that she concentrates on "the clown as a butt, as object of mockery, due to his socially negative characteristics" (p. 143). Therefore, her clowns are usually the comic villains or *alazons*, the minor characters who can simply be consigned to Bergsonian automatism; whereas the major clowns—the mock-heroic "playboys" and "paycocks" in Synge and O'Casey, for example—are the flexible *eirons* whose socially negative traits are actually the source of their positive revolt, their comic victory in defeat. As I will be pointing out through a

variety of comic characters, themes, and structures, the mainstream of antic Irish comedy deals with affirmative ironies and redemptive profanations; and contrary to what Winkler claims, it is not negative or moralistic, it is not Bergsonian or corrective. For extended comment on the problems in Winkler's book, see my chapter on O'Casey in *Anglo-Irish Literature: A Review of Research,* ed. Richard J. Finneran (New York: MLA, Five Year Supplement, 1982).

1. The Barbarous Sympathies of Antic Irish Comedy

1. Claude Lévi-Strauss, *The Scope of Anthropology* (London: Jonathan Cape, 1967), p. 7.

2. Edmund Leach, *Lévi-Strauss* (London: Collins/Fontana, 1970), p. 57. Leach also makes some clarifying comments on the ambiguous meaning of myth that are pertinent here:

> Myth is an ill defined category. Some people use the word as if it meant fallacious history—a story about the past which we know to be false; to say that an event is "mythical" is equivalent to saying that it didn't happen. The theological usage is rather different: myth is a formulation of religious mystery—"the expression of unobservable realities in terms of observable phenomena" (Schniewind, 1953:47). This comes close to the anthropologist's usual view that "myth is a sacred tale."
>
> If we accept this latter kind of definition the special quality of myth is not that it is false but that it is divinely true for those who believe, but fairy-tale for those who do not. The distinction that history is true and myth is false is quite arbitrary. [P. 54]

Perhaps a useful distinction would account for at least two different concepts of truth, historical and mythical, although the whole notion of what is or is not "true" is ultimately, as Berkeley warned us, a matter of one's subjective or sensory responses. For our purposes here, then, history records the "truth" about conscious experience or past events; myth records the "truth" about unconscious experience or future wishes. This distinction is based on Leach's interpretation of Freud's and Lévi-Strauss's belief that "myths express unconscious wishes which are somehow inconsistent with conscious experience." The inconsistency between conscious and unconscious experience not only involves the difference between history and poetry, between statements of observed fact and metaphors of deep reality; it also involves the difference between what is observed and what is submerged, between what has happened and what should have happened. History is factual, myth is conditional. I have therefore borrowed from Freud and Lévi-Strauss the psychological and anthropological concept that myths "evoke a suppressed past" and project an imaginative "circumvention" of all that is repressive in civilization.

Finally, something paradoxical remains to be said about the religious view that "myth is a sacred tale." Myth is a sacred tale that must disguise its sanctity in the structure of a profane mystery, since what passes for

religious ritual in society is too often a denial of the primordial or
unconscious self—the daimonic source of all myth. The mythmaker
must say no in order to say yes. In this paradoxical light, comic myth is a
profane tale with sacred roots in the unconscious that circumvent whatever is repressively sanctified in society.

3. Sigmund Freud, *The Interpretation of Dreams* (1900; New York:
Avon, 1965), p. 630.

4. Sigmund Freud, *Jokes and Their Relation to the Unconscious* (1905;
New York: Norton, 1963), p. 110.

5. Ibid.

6. Eric Bentley, "The Psychology of Farce," the Introduction to his
edition of *"Let's Get a Divorce!" and Other Plays* (New York: Mermaid,
1958), p. x. Here and throughout this work I must acknowledge an
invaluable debt to Bentley, one of the most perceptive critics of drama.
In this seminal essay on farce as a Freudian catharsis he also makes the
following important comment: "The function of 'farcical' fantasies, in
dreams or in plays, is not as provocation but as compensation. The
violent release is comparable to the sudden relieving hiss of steam
through a safety valve. Certainly, the mental energies involved are destructive, and in all comedy there remains something of a destructive
orgy, farce being the kind of comedy which disguises that fact least
thoroughly" (p. xiii).

I would only add this qualification, that farce can function as provocation as well as compensation, as an act of comic disobedience, a comic
non serviam, as well as a safety valve. There is much more than steam in
the sound of barbarous laughter. For a further discussion of the destructive or disintegrating aspects of low comedy, see "The Comic Principle of Disintegration" in Chapter 5.

7. Wylie Sypher, "The Meanings of Comedy," in *Comedy: "An Essay
on Comedy" by George Meredith; "Laughter" by Henri Bergson* (New York:
Anchor, 1956), pp. 200–201. On a related point, Nietzsche, like Freud,
suggests that the creative process of art is man's refuge from the pain
and absurdity of life, and he distinguishes between the "sublime" and
the "comic" release of art: "Then, in this supreme jeopardy of the will,
art, that sorceress expert in healing, approaches him; only she can turn
his fits of nausea into imaginations with which it is possible to live.
These are on the one hand the spirit of the *sublime,* which subjugates
terror by means of art; on the other hand the *comic* spirit, which releases
us, through art, from the tedium of absurdity" (*The Birth of Tragedy*
[1871; New York: Anchor, 1956], p. 52).

Freud presents a similar approach to the creative art of catharsis:
"Life as we find it is too hard for us; it entails too much pain, too many
disappointments, impossible tasks. We cannot do without palliative re-
medies. . . . The substitute gratifications, such as art offers, are illusions
in contrast to reality, but none the less satisfying to the mind on that
account, thanks to the place which phantasy has reserved for herself in
mental life. . . . At the head of these phantasy-pleasures stands the en-

joyment of works of art which through the agency of the artist is opened to those who cannot themselves create" (*Civilization and Its Discontents* [1930; New York: Anchor, n.d.], pp. 14, 15, 22). And as we know from Freud's views in *Jokes and Their Relation to the Unconscious,* those who cannot create can laugh through the agency of the comic artist; they can find gratification of unconscious or forbidden wishes through the circumventing process of comedy.

8. W. B. Yeats, *The Spectator,* September 29, 1928; reprinted in *The Senate Speeches of W. B. Yeats* (London: Faber & Faber, 1960), p. 176.

9. Ibid., p. 180.

10. Freud, *Civilization and Its Discontents,* p. 90.

11. Ibid., p. 43. See also J. Bronowski, *The Face of Violence,* new and enlarged ed. (Cleveland: Meridian, 1968): "This is a book about the motives which make men take pleasure in acts which deny and can destroy their own society" (p. 5). "In this fight against natural chaos, the guilt of society is that it is a society. The guilt is order, and the guilty are those whose authority imposes order" (p. 9). Comic artists, of course, use the violence of laughter to oppose order and mock the guilty.

12. Sigmund Freud, "Humour," (1928), in *Collected Papers of Sigmund Freud,* ed. Ernest Jones, 5 vols. (London: Hogarth, 1953), 5:217.

13. Freud, *Interpretation of Dreams,* p. 480.

14. Sean O'Casey, "The Power of Laughter: Weapon against Evil," in *The Green Crow* (New York: Braziller, 1956), p. 226. Yeats took a similar view of the positive force of comedy when he wrote in *Estrangement* in 1926: "Comedy is joyous because all assumption of a part, of a personal mask, whether of the individualized face of comedy or the grotesque face of farce, is a display of energy, and all energy is joyous" (*Selected Prose of W. B. Yeats,* ed. A. Norman Jeffares [London: Macmillan, 1964], p. 114).

15. J. M. Synge, *The Aran Islands,* in *The Collected Works of J. M. Synge,* vol. 2, ed. Alan Price (London: Oxford University Press, 1966), p. 140.

16. Ibid. "These strange men with receding foreheads, high cheekbones, and ungovernable eyes," Synge wrote, "seem to represent some old type found on these few acres at the extreme border of Europe, where it is only in wild jests and laughter that they can express their loneliness and desolation" (p. 140). There is surely a significant Freudian context and function in those lonely and "ungovernable eyes," those compensatory "wild jests."

17. James Joyce, *Finnegans Wake* (New York: Random House, 1939), p. 259.

18. Charles Baudelaire, "On the Essence of Laughter" (1855), in *The Mirror of Art,* ed. Jonathan Mayne (London: Phaidon, 1955), p. 137.

19. Ibid., p. 141.

20. Ibid., pp. 135-36. Perhaps Baudelaire's Sage, who looks at literature with fear and trembling, was aware of the "heretical" implications that Eric Bentley referred to in his comment on orthodox religion and

art: "The Catholic theologian Gilson has asked whether every great work of art does not involve to some degree a renunciation of God, and the Catholic dramatist might be said to be looking for trouble" (*The Life of the Drama* [New York: Atheneum, 1964], p. 63).

21. I. A. Richards, *Principles of Literary Criticism*, 3d ed. (London: Kegan Paul, Trench, Trubner, 1928), p. 246.

22. In making these relevant changes in Richards' original statement, I have taken comfort from the realization that the heretical Pelagius was probably an Irishman. In his repudiation of original sin and his insistence that each individual is responsible for his own salvation, he seemed to possess the self-sufficient spirit of the comic outcast, though he wasn't a comic figure, except in the eyes of some of his enemies. The following portrait of Pelagius, constructed from the conflicting views of his fifth-century contemporaries by John Ferguson in *Pelagius: A Historical and Theological Study* (Cambridge: W. Heffer, 1956), confirms my view that this "barbarous Irishman," this hulking, bull-necked, hound-like, porridge-eating, unhumble, heretical priest who was quick to defy authority and gave his opponents the impression that he might butt them with his horns, might appropriately serve as the mock patron of barbarous Irish comedy:

> Jerome, after likening him to a great mountain-dog, through whom the devil barks, writes an obscure sentence: "Habet progeniem Scoticae gentis, de Britannorum vicinia," which might appear to imply that he was an Irishman, but may only mean that anyone would expect him to be a barbarous Irishman rather than a civilized Briton....
> We get some idea of what he looked like in later life through the vituperative pens of Orosius and Jerome. The overwhelming impression is one of size. He is a veritable Goliath, broad-shouldered like a wrestler, bull-necked. Jerome compares him to a great hound from the Alps: we inevitably think of a St. Bernard. By about 415 he was given to corpulence, "grandem et corpulentem," and his step was slow, like a tortoise. He was weighted down with porridge, Jerome suggests, and the very jibe is enough to refute the cheap and coarse insinuations of Orosius about his luxurious living. He was full of face, and liked to have his head bare. His brow was stern; his enemies spoke of him as butting with his horns.
> ... If he had a moral fault it lay in a real or apparent lack of humility. His enemies accuse him of the sin of pride. Yet it is an accusation too easily levelled against those who are loyal to the truth as they see it in defiance of numbers or authority. [Pp. 39, 46]

23. Albert Cook, *The Dark Voyage and the Golden Mean: A Philosophy of Comedy* (Cambridge: Harvard University Press, 1949), p. 110. Cook's theory of comedy is totally corrective and Bergsonian; it stresses the relationship between Molière and the golden mean of behavior: "Transcending the boisterousness of Plautus, Italian farce, Rabelais—indeed, of nearly all previous comedy—[Molière] developed the philosophy of the [golden] mean in all its social implications; the selfish excesses of miserliness, hypochondria, marrying out of one's generation or one's

social station, prudishness as an ego-defense against one's own lack of sexual attractiveness; finally the profound search of the soul for honesty, which brings the individual to despair in passive hybris toward his social cosmos" (p. 112).

Cook's transcendent approach to comedy tends to be too solemn and righteous, and his "philosophic" view of Molière's art is so moralistic that it threatens to wring the comic fun out of the brilliant characterizations. Several years ago I saw that fine Irish actor Desmond Perry in what was a successfully boisterous and half-sympathetic interpretation of the Miser (and I would include here similarly exuberant and farcical performances of Volpone and Fagan). The comic villainy was so wild and colorful that the appreciative audience had little time to brood about the moral lesson, about the lofty aspects of the golden mean and the social cosmos. Like Ben Jonson and Charles Dickens, Molière was a theatrical showman who understood that vice is more fascinating as well as more reprehensible than virtue. In a slightly different but related context, perhaps there is something comic as well as ironic in William Blake's observation, in *The Marriage of Heaven and Hell* (1783), that "Milton wrote in fetters when he wrote of Angels & God, and at liberty when of Devils & Hell." In the comic as well as the epic mode, virtue is fettered, vice is free.

24. Northrop Frye, *The Anatomy of Criticism* (Princeton, N.J.: Princeton University Press, 1957), p. 44. Frye also comments on the pastoral therapy in Shakespeare's romantic comedies when he describes the ritualistic escape to the forest or "green world" where all comic illusions are corrected: "Thus the action of the comedy begins in a world represented as a normal world, moves into the green world, goes into a metamorphosis there in which the comic resolution is achieved, and returns to the normal world. . . . The green world charges the comedies with the symbolism of the victory of summer over winter" (p. 182).

This comment prompts me to observe that Irish comedy, by contrast, follows a mock-pastoral ritual in which the nonromantic clowns are perpetually suspended in a winter world of dark comedy. In the mock-pastoral comedies of Synge, Lady Gregory, and George Fitzmaurice, the peasants find the green world to be so oppressive that their lives are tainted with a condition of wintry impasse and bristling ironies. "Nothing to be done." In the mock-pastoral comedies of O'Casey, Beckett, and Behan, the urban peasants are similarly trapped in a comedy of winter from which there is no escape, no metamorphosis, and no resolution. "Th' whole worl's in a terrible state o' chassis."

25. Susanne Langer, *Feeling and Form* (New York: Scribner's, 1953), p. 342. When he moves on from romantic comedy to farce and considers some of the enduring archetypes of the wise buffoon, Frye, in *The Anatomy of Criticism,* makes some comments that are very pertinent to the tradition of antic comedy:

> The earliest extant European comedy, Aristophanes' *The Acharnians,* contains the *miles gloriosus* or military braggart who is still going strong in

Chaplin's *Great Dictator;* the Joxer Daly of O'Casey's *Juno and the Paycock*
has the same character and dramatic function as the parasites of twenty-
five hundred years ago, and the audiences of vaudeville, comic strips, and
television programs still laugh at the jokes that were declared to be out-
worn at the opening of *The Frogs.* [P. 163]

Another central *eiron* figure is the type entrusted with hatching the
schemes which bring about the hero's victory. This character in Roman
comedy is almost always a tricky slave (*dolosus servus*), and in Renaissance
comedy he becomes the scheming valet who is so frequent in Continental
plays, and in Spanish drama is called the *gracioso.* [P. 173]

26. Langer, *Feeling and Form,* p. 343.

27. Ibid.

28. F. N. Robinson, "Satirists and Enchanters in Early Irish Literature," in *Studies in the History of Religions* (1912; rpt. American Committee for Irish Studies, n.d.), p. 107.

29. J. M. Synge, *Collected Works: Poems,* vol. 1, ed. Robin Skelton
(London: Oxford University Press, 1962), p. 49.

30. Herbert Gorman, *James Joyce* (New York: Farrar & Rinehart,
1939), p. 144. In this context of comic malediction see also Joyce's
flyting, "Gas from a Burner," in *The Essential James Joyce,* ed. Harry
Levin (Harmondsworth: Penguin, 1963), p. 349:

> This lovely land that always sent
> Her writers and artists to banishment
> And in a spirit of Irish fun
> Betrayed her own leaders, one by one.
> 'Twas Irish humour, wet and dry,
> Flung quicklime into Parnell's eye;
> 'Tis Irish brains that save from doom
> The leaky barge of the Bishop of Rome
> For everyone knows the Pope can't belch
> Without the consent of Billy Walsh.
> O Ireland my first and only love
> Where Christ and Caesar are hand and glove!
> O lovely land where the shamrock grows!
> (Allow me, ladies, to blow my nose)

31. O'Casey to Charlotte F. Shaw, ? September 1931, in *The Letters of
Sean O'Casey,* ed. David Krause (New York: Macmillan, 1975), 1:433.

32. Robert C. Elliott, *The Power of Satire* (Princeton, N.J.: Princeton
University Press, 1960), p. 257.

33. Bertolt Brecht, *Baal* (New York: Evergreen, 1964), p. 57.

34. Sean O'Casey, *Sunset and Evening Star* (New York: Macmillan,
1954), p. 267.

35. J. M. Synge, *The Autobiography of J. M. Synge,* ed. Alan Price
(Dublin: Dolmen, 1965), p. 13. Price constructed this "autobiography"
from the Synge manuscripts; this passage was written in 1896.

36. Ibid., pp. 16–17. This passage was written in 1898. A slightly
different version appears in Synge's *Collected Works: Prose,* vol. 2, ed.
Alan Price, pp. 5–6.

37. Synge, *Collected Works: Plays*, vol. 4, bk. 2, ed. Ann Saddlemyer (London: Oxford University Press, 1968), p. 4.
38. Synge, *Collected Works: Prose*, vol. 2, p. 349.
39. George Santayana, "The Comic Mask," in *Soliloquies in England and Later Soliloquies* (New York: Scribner's, 1922), pp. 136–38. See also Wylie Sypher's relevant comment: "The comic rites are necessarily impious, for comedy is sacrilege as well as release" ("The Meanings of Comedy," p. 223). See also Susanne Langer's parallel statement: "It is in the nature of comedy to be erotic, risqué, and sensuous if not sensual, impious, and even wicked" (*Feeling and Form*, p. 349).
40. Federico García Lorca, "The Duende: Theory and Divertissement" (1935), in *The Poet in New York*, trans. Ben Belitt (New York: Grove, 1955), p. 154. Lorca's *gitanos* or gypsies are in many ways similar to Synge's tinkers and tramps; and the mythic folk power they share is reflected in these passages from Lorca's essay: "In all Andalusia, from the rock of Jaen to the shell of Cadiz, people constantly speak of the *duende* and find in it everything that springs out of energetic instinct.... This 'mysterious power that all may feel and no philosophy can explain' is, in sum, the earth-force, the same *duende* that fired the heart of Nietzsche ... the Dionysian cry" (p. 154).
41. Synge, *Collected Works: Poems*, vol. 1, p. xxxvi.
42. George Fitzmaurice, *Folk Plays* (Dublin: Dolmen, 1969), p. 56.
43. George Fitzmaurice, *Dramatic Fantasies* (Dublin: Dolmen, 1967), p. 30.
44. W. B. Yeats, *Per Amica Silentia Lunae* (1917), in *Mythologies* (London: Macmillan, 1959), p. 334.
45. Ibid., p. 366.
46. G. Wilson Knight, "King Lear and the Comedy of the Grotesque," in *The Wheel of Fire*, rev. and enl. ed. (London: Methuen, 1949), p. 160.
47. Andrew E. Malone, *The Irish Drama* (London: Constable, 1929), p. 156. Partly as a result of his reaction against the British tradition of the stage Irishman, Malone was a firm believer in Meredith's concept of high comedy and therefore looked upon low comedy as an inferior form of cheap fun for the ignorant masses. In a chapter titled "The Necessity for Comedy" he stresses "the laughter of the mind" and constantly distinguishes between the "true humour" of comedy and the "cheap humour" of farce.
48. L. J. Potts, *Comedy* (London: Hutchinson, 1949), p. 152.
49. Enid Welsford, *The Fool* (1935; New York: Anchor, 1961), p. 321.
50. George Meredith, "An Essay on Comedy" (1877), in *Comedy*, ed. Sypher, p. 50.
51. Langer, *Feeling and Form*, p. 349.
52. Freud, *Jokes and Their Relation to the Unconscious*, p. 200.
53. Francis Macdonald Cornford, *The Origins of Attic Comedy* (1914; New York: Anchor, 1961), pp. 178–79. And Eric Bentley, in *The Life of*

Drama, added another twist to the antiheroic view of man that we find in farce: "The farceur is a heretic: he does not believe that man was made in God's image. . . . The farceur does not show man as a little lower than the angels but as hardly higher than the apes" (pp. 148, 150).

54. Cornford, *Origins of Attic Comedy,* p. 120.

55. Czeslaw Milosz, *The Captive Mind* (New York: Vintage, 1953), p. 55.

56. Ibid., p. 76. In further support of those Irish and Polish affinities, I want to draw attention to Alf MacLochlainn's review of the Polish season of films at the 1960 Cork Film Festival. At one point in his editorial-review, "A Tribute to Poland," in *Scannan: Journal of the Irish Film Society,* January 1961, MacLochlainn draws a significant analogy between Polish and Irish humor in his discussion of Jerzy Kawalerowicz's *Night Train.*

In this film a murderer stops a train at dawn, tries to escape, but is captured. This grim incident begins on a farcical note as great numbers of men leap and fall from the train in wild pursuit of the murderer. MacLochlainn describes this grotesque chase and the Cork audience's reaction to it in the following passage, which underscores the degree to which Polish and Irish audiences can share the tragicomic ironies of a thoroughly antic and barbarous experience that involves comic compassion for an outlaw-murderer—with perhaps an echo of Christy Mahon in *Playboy* in the background:

> The audience is ready to laugh. The hunted man grabs a clod as he runs and hurls it back; it strikes one of the passengers whom we don't like very much, and the unkind guffaw of slapstick bursts out. The murderer is cornered in a grove of trees surrounding a graveyard, and the crowd of pursuers closes in around him, seen in high angle like the petals of an insect-eating flower. As they draw back from the prostrate victim, the passenger who was struck by the clod arrives, makes his way into the circle, and we see him close; he breaks into sobs, stammering abuse at the murderer. The audience is frozen with embarrassment. This is the man they have just been laughing at!
>
> When the film was shown in Poland, the audience reacted exactly as the director had intended and anticipated. It was shown in England, and this sequence completely failed to involve the audience in the way intended. There was no guffaw when the passenger was hit by the clod—just a freeze of embarrassment. A freeze several degrees colder greeted the man's breaking down into sobs—not because he was a person they had just been laughing at, but because it's distressing to see anyone breaking down in public. Like hitting people with clods, it's just not done.
>
> There is perhaps some profound moral to be drawn from the fact that the Cork audience showed a response which duplicated exactly that of the Polish audience for whom the film was made.

57. Leszek Kolakowski, "The Priest and the Jester," in *The Modern Polish Mind,* ed. Maria Kuncewicz (Boston: Little, Brown, 1962), p. 323. This essay also appeared in *Dissent,* Summer 1962. I must acknowledge a debt to another brilliant Polish critic, Jan Kott, who led me to

Kolakowski's essay by referring to it effectively in his important book, *Shakespeare Our Contemporary* (New York: Doubleday, 1964).

58. Kolakowski, "Priest and the Jester," p. 325.

59. Jerzy Grotowski, *Towards a Poor Theatre* (New York: Grove, 1968), p. 22.

60. Ibid.

61. Ibid., p. 25. For an enlightening treatment of the medieval Feast of Fools as a "sacral parody" of joy and liberation, see Harvey Cox's *Feast of Fools* (New York: Harper Colophon, 1970). In view of the following passages from Cox's book, it seems possible that the extinct Feast of Fools could have been one of the archetypes for the barbarous celebration of antic comedy in modern Irish drama:

> During the medieval era there flourished in parts of Europe a holiday known as the Feast of Fools. On that colorful occasion, usually celebrated about January first, even ordinary pious priests and serious townfolk donned bawdy masks, sang outrageous ditties, and generally kept the whole world awake with revelry and satire. Minor clerics painted their faces, strutted about in the robes of their superiors, and mocked the stately rituals of church and court. Sometimes a Lord of Misrule, a Mock King, or a Boy Bishop was elected to preside over the events. In some places the Boy Bishop even celebrated a parody mass. During the Feast of Fools, no custom or convention was immune to ridicule and even the highest personages of the realm could expect to be lampooned.
>
> The Feast of Fools was never popular with the higher-ups. It was constantly condemned and criticized. But despite the efforts of the fidgety ecclesiastics and an outright condemnation by the Council of Basil in 1431, the Feast of Fools survived until the sixteenth century. Then in the age of the Reformation and the Counter-Reformation it gradually died out. Its faint shade still persists in the pranks and revelry of Halloween and New Year's Eve.
>
> Why did the Feast of Fools disappear? The question is part of a much larger one that scholars have debated for years. Are the religious patterns of postmedieval Europe the cause or the effect of the new social and economic practices that culminated in capitalism and the industrial revolution? Why did the virtues of sobriety, thrift, industry, and ambition gain such prominence at the expense of other values? Why did mirth, play and festivity come in for such scathing criticism during the Protestant era? [Pp. 3-4]

While scholars try to answer these questions, I might venture a guess, in the comic context of this study, that the proxies of Christ and Caesar, the temporal guardians of organized religion and finance capitalism, could not afford to tolerate the profane joy of these antic celebrations. Perhaps irreverent revelers could not easily be controlled or persuaded to accept their unhappy lot when the festival was over and they had to conform to the new virtues of sobriety and hard work. Cox reached a somewhat similar conclusion when he stated: "The Feast of Fools thus had an implicitly radical dimension. It exposed the arbitrary quality of social rank and enabled people to see that things need not always be as they are. Maybe that is why it made the power-wielders uncomfortable and eventually had to go" (p. 5).

Even if he had to go, the impertinent fool or jester could go underground or play Ketman; or he might turn up in comedies where he could be depended on to mock the sacred absolutes of the priests and capitalists and commissars. Cox enlists the idea of Wolfgang Zucker that the clown "affirms by denying" (p. 155), and this paradox confirms my view of the Irish clown as an antic rebel who must fall in order to rise, who must deny the world in order to affirm himself.

The implications of Cox's views are discussed further in Chapter 3. For a related treatment of this theme in Irish wake games and mumming plays, see Sean O Suilleabhain's *Irish Wake Amusements* (Cork: Mercier, 1967) and Alan Gailey's *Irish Folk Drama* (Cork: Mercier, 1969). Although the mumming plays that still survive in Ireland today, especially in Wexford and Dublin, are no longer very irreverent or provocative, Gailey provides the following documentation to indicate that the original and more profane versions, perhaps similar to the Feast of Fools, were so popular in medieval Ireland that they had to be condemned regularly by the clergy: "And in Ireland, between 1383 and 1389, a Provincial Synod was held by John Colton, Archbishop of Armagh, whereat 'The Archbishop renews the statute or statutes of his predecessors Richard (Fitzralph) and David (Mageraghty) against mimes, jugglers, poets, drummers, or harpers and especially against *kernarii* and importunate and wicked seekers, or rather extorters, of gifts'" (*Irish Folk Drama*, p. 9).

2. The Hidden Oisín

1. Frank O'Connor, *Kings, Lords, & Commons* (New York: Knopf, 1959), p. ix. This book was banned in Ireland by the government Censorship of Publications Board because it contained O'Connor's irreverent but authentic translation of Brian Merriman's *Midnight Court,* which had originally been banned when it first appeared in 1946. Yeats wrote an Introduction to Arland Ussher's more genteel translation of the poem, which was not banned, and in it he stated that this eighteenth-century Gaelic work reminded him of the "old stories of Diarmuid's and Cuchullain's loves, and the old dialogues where Oisín railed at Patrick" (W. B. Yeats, Introduction to Brian Merriman, *"The Midnight Court" and "The Adventures of a Luckless Fellow,"* trans. Percy Arland Ussher [New York: Boni & Liveright, n.d.], p. 11).

Joyce, who was also attracted to the comic irreverence of Merriman's poem, which he felt reflected the medieval Irish spirit, thought that the contradictory impulses of the sacred and the profane which existed side by side in medieval Ireland were still there in modern Ireland: "And in my opinion one of the most interesting things about Ireland is that we are still fundamentally a mediaeval people, and that Dublin is still a mediaeval city. I know that when I used to frequent the pubs around Christ Church I was always reminded of those mediaeval taverns in which the sacred and the obscene jostle shoulders, and one of the reasons is that we were never subjected to the Lex Romana as other nations were" (Arthur Power, *Conversations with James Joyce* [New York: Barnes & Noble, 1974], p. 92).

2. O'Connor, *Kings, Lords, & Commons*, p. 31.

3. Kuno Meyer, *Fianaigecht*, Todd Lecture Series of the Royal Irish Academy, vol. 16 (Dublin: Hodges, Figgis, 1910), pp. 22-23.

4. James Macpherson, *Fragments of Ancient Poetry, Collected in the Highlands, and Translated from the Gaelic or Erse Language*, 1760; *Fingal*, 1762; *Temora*, 1763. Collected and published in a two-volume edition as *The Poems of Ossian*, 1765; page references to 1822 ed. (London: Oliver & Boyd).

5. Macpherson, *Poems of Ossian*, 1:31.

6. *Boswell's Journal of a Tour to the Hebrides with Samuel Johnson*, 1785, entry for September 22, 1773; page references to Literary Guild ed. (New York, 1936), p. 204.

7. Alfred Nutt, Introduction to Matthew Arnold, *The Study of Celtic Literature* (London: Macmillan, 1910), p. 90n.

8. Macpherson, *Poems of Ossian*, 2:264-65.

9. Ernest Renan, *The Poetry of the Celtic Races, and Other Studies* (London: Scott Library, 1896), pp. 7-8.

10. Matthew Arnold, *On the Study of Celtic Literature* (1867; New York: Macmillan, 1899), p. 118.

11. Ibid., p. 116. See also Frederick E. Faverty, *Matthew Arnold the Ethnologist* (Evanston: Northwestern University Press, 1951), pp. 111-61.

12. John V. Kelleher, "Arnold and the Celtic Revival," *Perspectives of Criticism*, ed. Harry Levin (Cambridge: Harvard University Press, 1950), pp. 197-221. See also Edward D. Snyder, *The Celtic Revival in English Literature: 1760-1800* (Cambridge: Harvard University Press, 1923).

13. Alfred Nutt, *Ossian and Ossianic Literature* (1899; rev. ed., London: David Nutt, 1910), pp. 25, 26-27.

14. Ibid., pp. 24-26.

15. Ibid., p. 34.

16. *Duanaire Finn: The Book of the Lays of Fionn*, pt. 1, ed. Eoin Mac-Neill (Dublin: Irish Text Society, 1904), Introduction, p. 1.

17. Meyer, *Fianaigecht*, p. 22.

18. *Duanaire Finn*, pt. 3, ed. Gerard Murphy (Dublin: Irish Text Society, 1953), Introduction, pp. xcvii-xcix. Perhaps Murphy overlooked the fact that the Ulster cycle, in which Cuchulain (Cu Chulainn) is the central hero, contains some varieties of low comedy that do not necessarily lead to a "decay" or "degradation" of the heroic ideals. See John V. Kelleher, "Humor in the Ulster Saga," in *Veins of Humor*, ed.

Harry Levin (Cambridge: Harvard University Press, 1972). Kelleher points out a number of humorous episodes associated with Cuchulain, yet even when the noble hero is the object of the laughter he is not degraded. For example, one of the Ulster heroes, Cu Roi, becomes distressed when he is not given a share of the spoils after a fight for a beautiful woman, three magical cows, three magical birds, and a magical cauldron; whereupon the outraged Cu Roi seeks his comic revenge on Cuchulain and the men of Ulster:

> He then ran in among the cows and gathered them before him, collected the birds in his girdle, thrust the woman under one of his armpits, and went from them with the cauldron on his back. And none of the men of Ulster was able to get speech with him save Cu Chulainn alone. Cu Roi turned upon the latter, thrust him into the earth to his armpits, cropped his hair with his sword, rubbed cow-dung into his head, and then went home.
> After that Cu Chulainn was a whole year avoiding the Ulstermen. [Kelleher, "Humor in the Ulster Saga," p. 41]

Of course, this example of heroic slapstick has none of the comic blasphemy one finds in the Ossianic cycle, for unlike the mock-heroic and irreverent Oisín, Cuchulain is, as Kelleher says (pp. 38-39), "the epitome of the Celtic hero" who has many resemblances to Christ.

19. *Duanaire Finn,* pt. 3, p. 56.
20. Ibid.
21. Gerard Murphy, *The Ossianic Lore and Romantic Tales of Medieval Ireland* (Dublin: At the Three Candles, 1955), p. 5. On another occasion, in his *Saga and Myth in Ancient Ireland* (Dublin: At the Three Candles, 1961), Murphy wrote about the strong attraction of the oral tradition of the Irish legends in a way that is related to Synge's "barbarous sympathies" and Freud's view that in our discontent with the restraints of civilization we find a sense of release in the mythic freedom of the folk sagas.
22. Murphy, *Ossianic Lore,* p. 59.
23. Aodh de Blacam, *A First Book of Irish Literature* (Dublin: Talbot, 1934), p. 63.
24. Robin Flower, *The Irish Tradition* (London: Oxford University Press, 1947), p. 102. See also his *Byron and Ossian* (Nottingham: University of Nottingham Press, 1928).
25. Flower, *Irish Tradition,* p. 102. Unlike Flower, James Carney does follow up some of the "implications" of the anticlericalism and comic irreverence in medieval Irish literature. In his Introduction to his *Early Irish Literature* (London: Routledge & Kegan Paul, 1966), Carney indicates that some of the monks themselves reflected in their poetry a dissatisfaction with the rigors of monastic life. He traces one source of this attitude back to the harsh Cistercian reforms of the twelfth century: "If we were to point to one fact that changed the whole development of Irish literature we would, I think, point to the monastic reform initiated

by the Cistercians in the twelfth century. Up to this point the monasteries had been a main-stay of literary production in the vernacular. After this period it is almost as if the monasteries cleaned their cupboards of secular or semi-secular manuscripts, bringing the monks back with a jolt to things more closely connected with salvation than with the deeds of Cú Chulainn" (p. 2).

Or, one might add, the deeds of Oisín. Carney goes on to discuss the psychological aspects of that "jolt" and the difficulty some monks had in rejecting the wild and free life of the pagan myths and the palpable beauty of nature. He quotes and translates some poems in which the cloistered monks envy the freedom and song of the blackbird, in contrast to the sound of the monastic bell, and one is immediately reminded of Oisín. "The monastic bell was symbolic of settled monastic society, and the abandonment of the world, the flesh and the devil" (p. 7).

26. Kathleen Hoagland, *1000 Years of Irish Poetry* (New York: Devin-Adair, 1947), p. 121.

27. Ibid.

28. Myles Dillon, *Early Irish Literature* (Chicago: University of Chicago Press, 1948), p. 40. See the *Aislinge Meic Conglinne: The Vision of Mac-Conglinne, A Middle-Irish Wonder Tale*, ed. and trans. Kuno Meyer, with an Introduction by Wilhelm Wollner (London: David Nutt, 1892). Wollner describes MacConglinne as "a minstrel genius who had a special grudge against the Church" (p. xiii), a clerical student who abandoned his studies to become a wandering poet, "a jongleur and jester." He was a comic rebel who dressed in the costume of a minstrel and incurred the wrath of the monks of Cork, who mistreated him, stripped him naked and starved him, even condemned him to a mock crucifixion. Needless to say, the monks became the target of his irreverent satire. Wollner says that "MacConglinne suffered from the discredit attaching to his hereditary profession as a gleeman or jongleur, a profession that was always regarded by the Church as one of the most sinful... in MacConglinne we have one of those vagrants (*vagantes*) which were at the same time the plague and the delight of medieval Europe" (pp. xl–xli). For a discussion of the many levels of religious parody in the poem, see Vivian Mercier, *The Irish Comic Tradition* (London: Oxford University Press, 1962), pp. 214–17.

29. Eleanor Knott, *Irish Classical Poetry* (Dublin: At the Three Candles, 1957); reprinted in *Early Irish Literature,* ed. James Carney (London: Routledge & Kegan Paul, 1966), p. 58 (page references to 1966 ed.). Knott minimizes the humor but she stresses the important fact that the original Ossianic ballads were written in the *dán díreach* style, the strict metrical form of the early court poetry, a form of rhyming couplets with a fixed number of syllables, with internal rhyme and alliteration: "Finally, it must not be forgotten that larger in bulk in our literary heritage even than the copious court poetry is the almost completely

anonymous 'Ossianic' or 'Fenian' descriptive and narrative verse, nature poems, tales of love and courtship, the chase and battle; these also belong in origin to the *dán díreach* style, as copies of many in good manuscripts from the twelfth century amply witness, although the great popularity of this verse, which has perpetuated so much of it through the corrupting medium of oral narration, has tended to obscure this fact" (pp. 54–55).

30. Myles Dillon and Nora K. Chadwick, *The Celtic Realms* (London: Weidenfeld & Nicolson, 1967), p. 253.

31. Ibid., p. 254. In Patrick C. Power's *A Literary History of Ireland* (Cork: Mercier Press, 1969), five pages are devoted to a discussion of the *Accallam na Senórach* but no mention is made of the *Agallamh Oisín agus Padraig*. In his comment on the *Accallam*, Power suggests that he is interested only in those early Gaelic works in which paganism and Christianity are treated with mutual sympathy: "In the *accallam* we have a literary expression of the confrontation between pagan and Christian Ireland and it is singularly tolerant and peaceful. The saint, as it were, swops his Christianity for the lore of ancient Ireland; a reader feels that here is the integration of the best of two ways of thought. Let us remember, of course, that the *accallam* was written when pagan Ireland was safely obliterated by generations of Christianity! It was safe, presumably, to gather together the pagan lore in the 12th century and connect the saint who christianized some of Ireland with this act" (p. 40).

This attitude should be contrasted with the view presented by Owen Dudley Edwards in "The Burden of Irish History," in *Conor Cruise O'Brien Introduces Ireland,* ed. Owen Dudley Edwards (New York: McGraw-Hill, 1969), where we are reminded that perhaps paganism was not "safely obliterated" in Ireland in light of the provocative Ossianic dialogue that Power ignores: "The conversion of Ireland to Christianity does not seem to have been along a purely one-way street from paganism. The poetic versions of dialogue between the surviving Fianna and St. Patrick are certainly far more sympathetic to paganism than would be warranted by a climate where conversion had been absolute" (p. 27).

32. Mercier, *Irish Comic Tradition*, p. 246.

33. *Irish Times*, January 13, 1945.

34. *Irish Times*, January 17, 1945. See James Carney's account of the dispute, "The *Feuch Fein* Controversy," in his *Studies in Irish Literature and History* (Dublin: Institute for Advanced Studies, 1955), pp. 243–75. See also Frank O'Connor's translation and discussion of the poem that touched off the controversy, *Feuch fein an obair-si, a Aodh,* which O'Connor translated as "To Tomas Costello at the Wars," reprinted in his *Kings, Lords, & Commons,* pp. 84–88.

35. *Irish Times*, January 6, 1945. Standish O'Grady, often called the father of the Celtic Revival, may have been something of "a scholar on

stilts" when he disaffiliated himself from the new dramatic movement by warning Yeats not to write or produce plays based on the Celtic myths: "Leave the heroic cycles alone and don't bring them down to the crowd" (*All Ireland Review*, April 12, 1902).

36. W. B. Yeats, *Per Amica Silentia Lunae*, 1917, reprinted in *Mythologies* (London: Macmillan, 1959), p. 331.

37. Ibid.

38. Ibid., p. 362.

39. Ibid., p. 336.

40. T. W. Rolleston, *Myths and Legends of the Celtic Race* (London: Harrap, 1911), p. 270. For similar information see also Douglas Hyde, *A Literary History of Ireland* (London: Unwin, 1899).

41. Michael Comyn, *Oisín in the Land of Youth*, trans. Tomás O'Flannghaile, in *An Anthology of Irish Literature*, ed. David H. Greene (New York: Modern Library, 1954), pp. 124-25.

42. W. B. Yeats, "The Wanderings of Oisín" (1889), in *The Collected Poems of W. B. Yeats* (London: Macmillan, 1952), p. 429.

43. *Laoithe Fiannuigheachta; or, Fenian Poems*, vol. 4 of *Transactions of the Ossianic Society*, ed. and trans. John O'Daly (Dublin: Ossianic Society, 1859), pp. 223-25.

44. Ibid., p. 47.

45. Ibid., pp. 217-19.

46. Ibid., pp. 59-63.

47. See Chapter 1, notes 8 and 9.

48. Nutt, *Ossian and Ossianic Literature*, p. 41.

49. Lady Gregory, *Gods and Fighting Men* (London: Murray, 1904), p. 461. Andrew E. Malone claimed that this oral tradition prevented the development of a national drama in medieval Ireland:

> In Ireland, too, there was maintained a cultural standard, but in the very maintenance of that standard there originated a system which probably more than any other single cause prevented the growth of a distinctively national drama. That system consisted of the poetry recitals given in the homes, and the oral diffusion of stories and news by the hearthstone. This system, which had its beginnings with the bards in the halls of the nobles and the shanachies in the homes of the people, had degenerated consistently until at the end of the nineteenth century it was but a public reading of the weekly newspapers. . . . In Ireland recitation took the place taken by representation in other European countries. The nobles and the aristocracy maintained the bards, and the ordinary folk maintained the shanachies, or storytellers, to provide recreation and instruction. The spoken word was of the greatest importance, and the imagination of the listener supplied all the dramatic action that was needed. [*The Irish Drama* (London: Constable, 1929), pp. 4, 6]

50. Lady Gregory, *The Kiltartan History Book* (London: T. Fisher Unwin, 1926), pp. 22-23. Vivian Mercier refers to a parallel tale in Douglas Hyde's *Religious Songs of Connacht*, vol. 1 (London: T. Fisher Unwin,

1906), called "Oscar of the Flail," from which he quotes the following
passage:

> "Patrick," says Ossian, "for what did God damn all of that people?"
> "For eating the apple of commandment," says St. Patrick.
> "If I had known that your God was so narrow-sighted that he damned
> all of that people for one apple, we should have sent three horses and a
> mule carrying apples to God's heaven to Him." [*Irish Comic Tradition*, p.
> 178]

But I believe Lady Gregory's folk version of this episode is rendered
more successfully, thanks to the voice of the shrewd narrator who adds
his own irreverent and ironic comment on St. Patrick. Nevertheless,
Mercier also adds the following relevant comment on the verbal rebellion of the Irish writers: "The Irish rebel in word rather than deed—if
not, they would be the least conservative people in Europe rather than
the most. Swift, Shaw, and Joyce are never more Irish than when they
violate the bounds of good sense, good taste, and even sanity for the
sake of a jest" (ibid., p. 178). One might add that Oisín, along with his
kindred spirits Synge and O'Casey, was guilty of similar violations and
desecrations for the sake of a meaningful jest.

51. Maurice Bourgeois, *John Millington Synge and the Irish Theatre*
(London: Constable, 1913), p. 90.
52. Ibid., pp. 217–18.
53. Daniel Corkery, *Synge and Anglo-Irish Literature* (Cork: Cork University Press, 1931), p. 167. This popular and presumably influential
book had a fourth reprinting in 1955, and was reissued by the Mercier
Press in 1961.
54. Ibid., p. 197.
55. Ibid., 181. It should be remembered that Corkery here is referring to O'Casey's first three Dublin plays, *Gunman, Juno*, and *Plough*,
not the later anticlerical plays such as *Cock, Bonfire*, and *Drums of Father
Ned*. It is therefore ironic to note that O'Casey's Irish critics, led by Sean
O'Faolain, in urging him to abandon those later pastoral comedies and
return to the methods of his early works, had consistently ignored the
fact that the first three plays had often been exposed to the kind of
harsh treatment in Ireland that one finds in Corkery. O'Casey was
damned both ways.
56. *The Pocket Oxford Dictionary of Current English*, rev. ed. (London:
Oxford University Press, 1946), p. 943.
57. J. M. Synge, *The Collected Works, Plays of J. M. Synge*, ed. Ann
Saddlemyer (London: Oxford University Press, 1968), 3:1.
58. Ibid.
59. Ibid., p. 141.
60. Ibid., p. 149.
61. Ibid., 4:65.
62. Bourgeois, *John Millington Synge*, p. 201.

63. Synge, *Collected Works: Plays*, 4:167.

64. Ibid., p. 147.

65. Ibid., p. 149.

66. Ibid., p. 19.

67. Sean O'Casey, *The Collected Plays of Sean O'Casey* (London: Macmillan, 1951), 3:68–69.

68. Ibid., p. 69.

69. Ibid., p. 106.

70. Ibid., p. 192.

71. Ibid., p. 198.

72. Ibid., p. 199.

73. Ibid., p. 203.

74. James Joyce, *Finnegans Wake* (New York: Random House, 1939), p. 139.

75. O'Casey, *Collected Plays*, 4:124, 125.

76. Sean O'Casey, *The Bishop's Bonfire* (London: Macmillan, 1955), p. 26.

77. Ibid., p. 44.

78. Ibid., pp. 105–6.

79. Sean O'Casey, *The Drums of Father Ned* (London: Macmillan, 1960), p. 33.

3. The Comic Desecration of Ireland's Household Gods

1. *Sunday Times*, June 7, 1959. This was Rodgers' review of David H. Greene and Edward M. Stephens, *J. M. Synge* (New York: Macmillan, 1959).

2. W. B. Yeats, "The Death of Synge" (1928), in *The Autobiography of W. B. Yeats* (London: Macmillan, 1953), p. 316.

3. *United Irishman*, October 17, 1903.

4. Quoted in Lennox Robinson, *Ireland's Abbey Theatre: A History, 1899–1951* (London: Sidgwick & Jackson, 1951), p. 36. Robinson had paraphrased Cousins' account of the reaction to *In the Shadow of the Glen*, and the original account appeared in the memoirs Cousins wrote with his wife: James H. and Margaret E. Cousins, *We Two Together* (Madras: Ganesh, 1950).

5. W. B. Yeats, *The King's Threshold* (1903), in *Plays in Prose and Verse* (London: Macmillan, 1922), p. 75. In a note on the play, Yeats made a relevant comment: "It was written when our Society was beginning its fight for the recognition of pure art in a community of which one half is buried in the practical affairs of life, and the other half in politics and a propagandist patriotism" (p. 423).

6. Una Ellis-Fermor, *The Irish Dramatic Movement* (London: Methuen, 1954), p. 93.

7. *The Critical Writings of James Joyce*, ed. Ellsworth Mason and Richard Ellmann (London: Faber & Faber, 1959), p. 71.

8. Ibid., pp. 71-72.

9. W. B. Yeats, "An Irish National Theatre and Three Sorts of Ignorance," *United Irishman*, October 24, 1903: "1st. There is the hatred of ideas of the more ignorant sort of Gaelic propagandist, who would have nothing said or thought that is not in country Gaelic. One knows him without trouble. He writes the worst English, and would have us give up Plato and all the sages for a grammar. 2nd. There is the obscurantism of the more ignorant sort of priest, who, forgetful of the great traditions of his Church, would deny all ideas that might perplex a parish of farmers or artisans or half-educated shop-keepers. 3rd. There is the obscurantism of the politician and not always of the more ignorant sort, who would reject every idea which is not of immediate service to his cause."

10. James Joyce, *A Portrait of the Artist as a Young Man* (1916), in *The Essential James Joyce*, ed. Harry Levin (Harmondsworth: Penguin, 1963), p. 211.

11. *United Irishman*, October 24, 1903.

12. *The Letters of W. B. Yeats,* ed. Alan Wade (London: Macmillan, 1954), pp. 421-22.

13. It is doubtful whether much of this speech was heard by the rioting audience, but Yeats took the precaution of giving the newspapers a full report of what he said: "You have disgraced yourselves again. Is this to be an ever-recurring celebration of the arrival of Irish genius? Synge first and then O'Casey. The news of the happenings of the past few minutes will go from country to country. Dublin has once more rocked the cradle of genius. Equally the fame of O'Casey is born here tonight. This is his apotheosis" (*Irish Times* and *Irish Independent*, February 12, 1926).

14. Denis Johnston, *"The Moon in the Yellow River" and "The Old Lady Says 'No!,'"* with a Foreword by C. P. Curran (London: Jonathan Cape, 1932), p. 252. To confirm the identity of the "Old Lady," Lennox Robinson has recorded the following evidence in *Curtain Up* (London: Michael Joseph, 1942), p. 117:

> This seems a fitting place to attempt to kill the story that in the title of Denis Johnston's play *The Old Lady Says "No"* the "old lady" is Lady Gregory, that Denis Johnston waits at the bottom of the office stairs at the Abbey while the Directors are finally considering the acceptance or rejection of his play, and that I come down sadly shaking my head and saying "the old lady says 'no'." There is not a word of truth in that story; I have heard Lady Gregory called "the old lady" by some members of the Company, I never spoke of her in that way and, in point of fact, Lady Gregory loved youth and experiment and was strongly for that play's production. Yeats was against the play, I was for it but was afraid that I would make a hash of the production. The "old lady" in the title is Kathleen Ni Houlihan, I have the author's word for that.

15. Ibid., p. 193.

16. Denis Johnston, "Opus One," in *Collected Plays* (London:

Jonathan Cape, 1960), 1:16. Johnston adds that *The Old Lady Says "No!"* is "my only work that might fairly be described as anti-Irish" (p. 16). He also indulges in the popular Irish game of being anti-O'Casey, and one of the characters in the play, Seamus O'Cooney, a brash proletarian playwright, is apparently meant to be a satiric portrait of O'Casey.

17. C. P. Curran, Foreword to Johnston, *"Moon in the Yellow River" and "The Old Lady Says 'No!,'"* pp. 9–10.

18. Johnston, *Moon in the Yellow River*, p. 172.

19. Ibid., pp. 102–3.

20. Ibid., p. 59.

21. Ibid., p. 122.

22. Ibid., p. 140.

23. Denis Johnston, "Up the Rebels!," Preface to *The Scythe and the Sunset*, in *Collected Plays*, 1:4.

24. Ibid., p. 10.

25. Ibid., p. 5.

26. Johnston, *Scythe and the Sunset*, p. 97.

27. Lady Gregory, *Seven Short Plays* (Dublin: Maunsel, 1909), p. 207. Perhaps it is significant that Lady Gregory should have chosen a situation of farcical desecration as the most symbolic representation of contentious Ireland, because she must have understood instinctively what Eric Bentley meant when he described farce as a desire "to desecrate the household gods," in "The Psychology of Farce," the introduction to his edition of *"Let's Get a Divorce" and Other Plays* (New York: Mermaid, 1958), p. x. Many sympathetic critics of Lady Gregory's works seem to be embarrassed by the strong element of farce in her plays and go out of their way to insist that she did not descend into "mere" farce. See Andrew E. Malone, *The Irish Drama* (London: Constable, 1929); Ellis-Fermor, *Irish Dramatic Movement;* Elizabeth Coxhead, *Lady Gregory: A Literary Portrait* (London: Macmillan, 1961); Ann Saddlemyer, *In Defence of Lady Gregory, Playwright* (Dublin: Dolmen, 1966). Bentley objected to the generally patronizing attitude of many critics who look on farce as "mere" horseplay that "degenerates into travesty and burlesque." Relating the significant function of farce to the Freudian function of dreams, he wrote: "Repressed wishes find an outlet, surely, in all drama; many repressed wishes are gross ones; and if we take the family to be the very center of culture, we should not be surprised that gross wishes are mainly, if not exclusively, desires to damage the family, to desecrate the household gods" (p. x). In the context of Irish comedy, then, the nation itself, with all its sacred paternalism, is the largest family unit, and the desire to desecrate it is a liberating outlet for wishes that are repressed by the national hagiography of Cathleen Ni Houlihan. Of course this farcical impulse is universal and it is not limited to the household gods of Ireland.

28. Gregory, *Seven Short Plays*, p. 156.

29. Ibid., p. 159.

30. Ibid., pp. 159–60.
31. Ibid., p. 161.
32. Henri Bergson, *Laughter* (1900), in *Comedy,* ed. Wylie Sypher (New York: Anchor, 1956), p. 187.
33. W. B. Yeats, *Samhain* (1905), p. 5; reprinted in *Explorations* (London: Macmillan, 1962), p. 184.
34. Sean O'Casey, *Inishfallen, Fare Thee Well* (1949), in *Autobiographies* (London: Macmillan, 1963), 2:102–3.
35. Lady Gregory, *New Irish Comedies* (New York: Putnam's, 1913), p. 20.
36. Gregory, *Seven Short Plays,* p. 205.
37. Ibid., p. 39.
38. Ibid., pp. 47–48. The parallels to Synge continue in Lady Gregory's *Gaol Gate* (1906), a one-act tragedy about a mother's stoical lament for her dead prisoner son which achieves much of the dramatic intensity and economy of *Riders to the Sea* (1904), lacking only the lyrical power of Synge's language.
39. Gregory, *Seven Short Plays,* p. 65.
40. Ibid., p. 6. Andrew E. Malone was unimpressed by what he called Bartley Fallon's "cringing imbecility," and he felt that in most of her early comedies Lady Gregory had resorted to "mere" farce and had simply created the stock version of the ridiculous stage Irishman: "It is possible to pity Bartley Fallon, but he simply must be laughed at. He is a figure of farce not of comedy.... Lady Gregory chose to confound comedy with farce, and to play to the level of the stage Irishman.... Her creatures are all extravagantly simple—there is no Haffigan guile in them—and they are exquisitely helpless. They have none of that shrewd cunning which marks the peasant in Ireland as elsewhere. They are simple to the verge of imbecility" (*The Irish Drama,* pp. 157–58).
41. Gregory, *Seven Short Plays,* p. 30.
42. Lady Gregory, "Notes to *The Bogie Men,*" in *New Irish Comedies,* p. 155.
43. Lady Gregory, *"The Image" and Other Plays* (New York: Putnam's, 1922), p. 99. In a very similar mood O'Casey, who paradoxically mocked or celebrated some dreamers in his plays, once wrote about Yeats as a dreamer and a man of action, and he concluded by stressing the importance of image making or dreaming: "To do and never dream is worse than to dream but never to do; for to dream and never to do is at least to live in a rich state, even though it be an unnatural condition to striving humanity; but to do, and never to dream, is to humiliate that humanity into insignificance, and to dishonour the colour and form in that arrangement of things by God which man calls life" ("Ireland's Silvery Shadow," in *Blasts and Benedictions,* ed. Ronald Ayling [London: Macmillan, 1966], p. 184). See also David Krause, "The Druidic Affinities of O'Casey and Yeats," in *Sean O'Casey Centenary Essays,* ed.

David Krause and Robert G. Lowery (Gerrards Cross: Colin Smythe, 1980).

44. Gregory, *"Image" and Other Plays*, p. 8.

45. Ibid., p. 93.

46. Ibid., p. 83.

47. Ibid., p. 96. For a negative report on this play, see the views expressed by Elizabeth Coxhead: "She herself called *The Image* 'my chief play,' it was the only one she insisted on having revived, and Dr. Lennox Robinson likewise 'gives it the branch.' Yeats on the other hand said it was too slow in action and had an act too many, and reluctantly I find myself in agreement with him; indeed, I would say it has two acts too many. The notion of the statue to be erected to a non-existent hero, with the problematic profits to be made from the oil of two evanescent whales, would have done nicely for a second *Jackdaw*, which was what she originally intended" (*Lady Gregory*, p. 85).

Contrarily, I believe that the ironic theme and symbolism of the play cut infinitely deeper than the facile conflict of illusions in a short piece such as *The Jackdaw;* that the myth of image making strikes a universal chord, and is expanded with rich variations in the seven contrasting characters who are presented in greater dimension and aspiration than the characters in the one-act plays; that the mammoth whales, emblematic of more than oil and profit, are stranded on the beach as an ironic reminder of what can happen to heroic creatures, and heroic statues; that the action of the play is cumulative and circular rather than slow, and the three acts are necessary for the gradual suspense and comic reversal of expectations.

48. Lady Gregory, *Aristotle's Bellows*, in *Three Wonder Plays* (New York: Putnam's, 1923), p. 53. In a note to the play she explains the moral in the following manner: "If the play has a moral it is given in the words of the Mother, 'It's best make changes little by little, the same as you'd put clothes upon a growing child.' The restlessness of the time may have found its way into Conan's mind, or as some critic wrote, 'He thinks of the Bellows as Mr. Wilson thought of the League of Nations,' and so his disappointment comes" (p. 72).

49. Peter Kavanagh, *The Story of the Abbey Theatre* (New York: Devin-Adair, 1950), p. 147.

50. Ibid.

51. Robert Hogan, *After the Irish Renaissance: A Critical History of the Irish Drama since "The Plough and the Stars"* (Minneapolis: University of Minnesota Press, 1967), p. 33.

52. Malone, *Irish Drama*, p. 237. Basing his judgments on Shiels's first seven plays, those written up to 1929, Malone felt that these early works were mostly "antiquated" farces, and he went on to make the dubious observation that a playwright confined to a wheelchair could not possibly write "true comedy," by which he meant comedy free from farce: "Perhaps in the future George Shiels may write a true comedy,

but the disability which he suffers prevents that immersion in contemporary life from which true comedy must come" (p. 240). Peter Kavanagh also made an unfortunate allusion to Shiels's disability in judging him as a playwright: "Shiels had acquired suddenly the knack of amusing a crowd without any apparent effort. Confined to his home in the north of Ireland as a cripple, he has begun to write plays to relieve boredom" (*Story of the Abbey Theatre*, p. 147).

53. George Shiels, *Bedmates* (Dublin: Gael Co-operative Society, 1922), p. 8.

54. Ibid., p. 9.

55. Ibid., p. 13.

56. George Shiels, *Three Plays: "Professor Tim," "Paul Twyning," "The New Gossoon"* (London: Macmillan, 1945), p. 116.

57. *The Letters of Sean O'Casey*, ed. David Krause (New York: Macmillan, 1975), 1:149. O'Casey was obviously annoyed by the fact that most of the characters are sheep in wolves' clothing. For example, Hugh O'Cahan, the bankrupt young sporting squire who appears to be a failed playboy, is really a good man with an unjustly bad reputation. Mrs. Scally, the domineering and hypocritical mother, is really a well-meaning tyrant who only wanted the best for her disobedient daughter. And when the disreputable Tim becomes respectable in an eleventh-hour switch, he offers some wholesome sermons on the restored reputations of Hugh and Mrs. Scally. On Hugh's fate he remarks: "Every young man at least once should stand on the brink of ruin, with no living soul to care whether he goes over the edge. That experience is an education" (p. 93). But by the logic of the play he might have sweetened that education by adding that every young man on the brink of ruin should also be rescued by a fairy godfather like Tim. And he redeems the now contrite Mrs. Scally with this bit of heartwarming absolution: "Like every Irish mother you've a sharp tongue and a large vocabulary, and it takes both to bring up a big family of boys and girls" (p. 96). Small wonder O'Casey felt panic-stricken and wanted to run for shelter.

58. George Shiels, *Two Irish Plays: "Mountain Dew" and "Cartney and Kevney"* (London: Macmillan, 1930), p. 205. The paradoxical attractiveness of a rascal such as Dick Cartney may be compared to "the allegory of indolence" that is so brilliantly reflected in such irresponsible jesters as O'Casey's "Captain" Jack Boyle and Joxer Daly. On a previous occasion, in *Sean O'Casey: The Man and His Work* (New York: Macmillan, 1960), p. 78, I tried to account for the compensatory pleasure one finds in such comic characters, and I believe my comments could well be applied to someone like Dick Cartney:

> It is also possible that many men are more than amused by the "paycock's" game and secretly envy the "Captain" and his "buttie" their merry pranks. The average man who realizes he cannot cope with his besetting problems on an heroic scale may well have an unconscious desire to get rid of his problems entirely by emulating the "Captain" in his irresponsible and

therefore irresistible dreaming and singing and drinking. A frustrated non-hero might if he dared forsake his responsible suffering and seek the uninhibited pleasures of a clowning anti-hero; however, he probably settles for the vicarious pleasure of sitting in a theatre and watching a "Captain" Boyle thumb his red nose at responsibility. Much is made of the frustrated clown who yearns to play Hamlet, but the average man is more likely a frustrated Hamlet who if he had the strength of his weakness would cheerfully assume the role of an uninhibited Falstaff or Boyle.

Or perhaps a Dick Cartney.

59. Shiels, *Two Irish Plays*, p. 186.
60. Ibid., p. 127.
61. Ibid., pp. 134–35.
62. Ibid., p. 122.
63. Ibid., pp. 160–61.
64. Ibid., p. 209.
65. Ibid., p. 216.
66. Ibid., pp. 221–22. This ironic ending raises some questions about the nature of the "far-fetched happy ending" that appeared in the rewritten version of the play when it was revived ten years later at the Abbey Theatre in 1937, with Cyril Cusack as Cartney and Fred Johnson as Kevney. In his review of the "revised version" in the *Irish Independent*, November 9, 1937, the playwright David Sears wrote:

> To rewrite a play is always a dangerous experiment, but I congratulate George Shiels on his success in this line. The "Cartney and Kevney," produced at the Abbey Theatre, is better definitely than the first version which we saw some years ago.
>
> To some extent my more favorable impression of the play is due to Cyril Cusack's playing of Dick Cartney. This is the first time I have seen him play a big comedy role, and—well, I wish George Shiels could have seen him play the part. It was not merely that he made Cartney live, that he made us love this utterly worthless and contemptible rascal and forgive the author for his far-fetched happy ending, but that he made him so real and human that far from thinking him exaggerated, we all felt we knew him.

My conversations in 1974 with the late Gabriel Fallon, who played the role of Dr. Palmer opposite Barry Fitzgerald's Cartney and F. J. McCormick's Kevney in the original 1927 production, and with the late Ernest Blythe, who was a director of the Abbey in 1937, have failed to disclose the nature of the revisions. I have not been able to locate a revised text of the published 1930 version. As a last resort I contacted Cyril Cusack, who very kindly wrote a letter to me on July 2, 1975, in which he tried to recall some of the revisions. He rejected the idea of a "far-fetched happy ending," and also added some interesting comments on Yeats's disapproval of the play:

> Now—yes, I do remember, if distantly, how the latter version of "Cartney and Kevney" went and certainly I would say that it did *not* end on a sentimental note. It ended, if I recollect correctly, in complete triumph for Cartney and rascality with the routing and at the expense

of "the rest," Kevney benefitting, of course—to the *great enjoyment* of the
audience, and remember, an *Irish* audience, that is of the time. "The rest"
probably would be described at a much later date as "the Establishment,"
and the audience reaction may have emerged from seeing that particular
little "establishment" surrounding our friend thoroughly discomforted.
But, of course, it was received entirely as comedy, even farce—nearer to
that—not by any means as a morality play. Yeats disapproved, and, I was
told, quite loathed "Cartney and Kevney," starting from the original. I
think he even objected to its production.

67. Shiels, *Two Irish Plays,* pp. 13–14.
68. Ibid., p. 31.
69. Shiels, *Three Plays,* pp. 259–60. In 1958 a film version of *The
New Gossoon* was made, called *Sally's Irish Rogue,* produced by Emmet
Dalton, directed by George Pollock, freely adapted by Jack Kirwan and
Blanaid Irvine, starring Julie Harris as Sally Hamil, Tim Seely as Luke
Cary, and Harry Brogan as Rabit Hamil. I had an opportunity to see it
revived on Telefis Eireann on St. Patrick's Day, March 17, 1975. Unfortunately, it turned out to be a sentimentalized version of the original,
full of many visual as well as verbal stage-Irish clichés, mainly intended
for export to non-Irish audiences. Practically all of Luke's rebellious
scenes were omitted, so that he emerged as little more than a petulant
and spoiled youth, played improbably by a bland British actor. The
RTE Guide for March 14, 1975, described the film as "the warmly
humorous tale of the taming of a rural rebel," but it contained more
embarrassing warmth than genuine humor, and presented a rebel who
was so timid he didn't need taming.

70. Shiels, *Three Plays,* p. 257.
71. Ibid., p. 232.
72. Padraic Colum, *Three Plays: "The Land," "Thomas Muskerry," "The
Fiddler's House"* (Dublin: Allen Figgis, 1963), p. 4.
73. Ibid., p. 47.
74. Shiels, *Three Plays,* p. 233. Spike Island was once a convict
prison in Cobh Harbor, just off the mainland of Cork.
75. Ibid., p. 177.
76. Ibid., p. 230.
77. George Shiels, *Grogan and the Ferret* (Dublin: Golden Eagle
Books, 1947), p. 8.
78. Ibid., p. 16.
79. Ibid., p. 42. And on the matter of moral reform vs. comedy, see
L. C. Potts's comment: "But for the moralist to condemn any comedy
because of its subject matter is an error in judgment. It is not the
business of comedy to inculcate moral doctrine" (*Comedy* [London:
Hutchinson, 1949], p. 56).
80. Shiels, *Grogan and His Ferret,* p. 57.
81. See Chapter 1, notes 2 and 3.
82. Sigmund Freud, *Jokes and Their Relation to the Unconscious* (1905;
New York: Norton, 1963).

83. Brendan Behan, *Brendan Behan's Island: An Irish Sketch-Book* (London: Hutchinson, 1962), pp. 16–17. Ulick O'Connor, who takes a dim view of *The Hostage* because he believes it to be a corruption and betrayal of the earlier Gaelic version of the play, *An Giall,* wrote the following comment on Behan's defense of his music-hall methods: "Yet no matter how much he blathered about the Music Hall, the transformation must have hurt him. *An Giall* has its roots in Ballyferriter, the Blaskets and the Atlantic; *The Hostage* in a commercial entertainment world Brendan had no real contact with. It was, in a sense, a betrayal not only of the I.R.A. whom he guyed in the play but of the instinct which led him to write the first version, the compassion of the artist for a human predicament he could personally identify with" (*Brendan Behan* [London: Hamish Hamilton, 1970], p. 270). This probably means that the "transformation" hurt O'Connor's sense of Irish national pride more than it hurt Behan's artistry and compassion. And since Behan from his youth regularly attended the Queens Theatre, the traditional home of music-hall drama in Dublin, which his uncle P. J. Bourke had managed for many years, he must have developed an admiration and understanding of this type of popular theater long before he met Joan Littlewood. With respect to the original version, *An Giall,* it has been described by Kevin Casey as "a short and rather sentimental play, written in Gaelic" ("The Raw and the Honest: A Critical Look," in *The World of Brendan Behan,* ed. Sean McCann [London: Four Square, 1965], p. 125). On the matter of Behan's so-called betrayal of the I.R.A., see my discussion of *The Hostage* below.

84. T. S. Eliot, "The Decay of the Music Hall" (1923), in *Selected Prose* (Harmondsworth: Penguin, 1953), p. 225.

85. Kevin Casey, "The Raw and the Honest: A Critical Look," in *World of Brendan Behan,* p. 119.

86. Robert Brustein, *Seasons of Discontent* (New York: Simon & Schuster, 1965), p. 178. Brustein normally makes good sense on modern drama, but he is something less than reliable when he tries to write about Irish drama. For example, at one point he detects what he thinks is an O'Casey influence in what he calls Behan's inadequate plot, and this speculation inspires him to create a parody of how he presumes O'Casey might have written *The Hostage:*

> Nevertheless, the plot—which is exhausted the moment you sum it up—does seem serious in its basic outline. Set in a Dublin brothel in modern times, the action revolves around the kidnapping, and ultimate death, of a young English soldier, taken by the I.R.A. because the British are going to execute a Belfast revolutionary. This promises an Irish political drama, and one can easily imagine how O'Casey might have interpreted the same situation. The brothel would become a symbolic Temple of Love, Life, and the Dance; the prostitutes would be "pagan girls," with ample bosoms and free, sensual natures; the comic characters would emerge as personifications of bigotry, indifference, and selfishness; the death of the boy would be an occasion for commentary on the victimiza-

tion of the innocent by war; and the play would probably conclude with a vision of a better life to come. [P. 178]

But the joke must be on Brustein, for he might have noticed that O'Casey did write three "Irish political dramas"—*Gunman, Juno, Plough*—the tragicomic plots of which can in no way be compared to the Brustein parody, which apparently represents his misplaced attempt to use the later O'Casey to mock the early O'Casey.

87. Dominic Behan, *My Brother Brendan* (New York: Simon & Schuster, 1965), p. 136. And coincidentally, when O'Casey's *Plough* opened at the Abbey Theatre in 1926 it was described by Andrew E. Malone as "a cheap music-hall concoction" (*Dublin Magazine*, March 1926), and the poet F. R. Higgins called it a mere catalogue of "Handy Andy burlesque incidents" (*Irish Statesman*, March 6, 1926). See also Krause, *Sean O'Casey*, p. 41. Finally, Dominic Behan, who took Joan Littlewood's influence on his brother's work as a mixed blessing, clears some of the critical confusion about *The Hostage* with this sharp comment: "And yet *The Hostage* had a strange fascination for me, it was like a huge character-making factory. People came in one door as ponces and puffs and with a wave of a pen he turned them into Junos and Fluthers. 'A whore with a heart of gold,' Pat, the brothel-keeper, talks about, and his 'blaspheming' attack on hypocrisy took on a holiness that the Salvation Army and The Legion of Mary would not be endowed with if somebody was to offer them all ringside seats for a repeat performance of the crucifixion" (p. 147).

88. Eric Bentley, *The Life of the Drama* (New York: Atheneum, 1964), pp. 244-45.

89. Brendan Behan, *"The Quare Fellow" and "The Hostage"* (New York: Evergreen, 1964), pp. 7, 9.

90. Ibid., p. 23.

91. Ibid., p. 21. Behan used a similar irreverence in *Borstal Boy* (1958; London: Corgi, 1961), p. 286, when one of his cockney friends says: "But the best book I ever saw in the nick was the Bible. When I was in Brixton on remand, I 'ad one in the flowery. Smashing thin paper for rolling dod-ends in. I must 'ave smoked my way through the book of Genesis, before I went to court."

92. Behan, *"Quare Fellow" and "The Hostage,"* p. 25.

93. Ibid., p. 29.

94. Ibid., p. 33.

95. Kevin Casey, "The Raw and the Honest: A Critical Look," in *World of Brendan Behan*, p. 122.

96. Brendan Behan, *"Quare Fellow" and "The Hostage,"* p. 58.

97. Ibid., p. 65.

98. Ibid., p. 76.

99. Freud, *Jokes and Their Relation to the Unconscious*, p. 103.

100. Behan, *"Quare Fellow" and "The Hostage,"* p. 92.

101. Ibid., p. 133.

102. Ibid., p. 97.

103. Ibid., p. 138.

104. Ibid., p. 147.

105. O'Connor, *Brendan Behan*, pp. 201–2. See also note 89. Behan, *"Quare Fellow" and "The Hostage,"* pp. 7, 9.

106. Behan, *"Quare Fellow" and "The Hostage,"* p. 182. This was a popular song in the British Army during World War I, and Behan borrowed it for his ironic purposes.

107. Martin Grotjahn, *Beyond Laughter* (New York: McGraw-Hill, 1957), p. 256.

108. Freud, *Jokes and Their Relations to the Unconscious*, p. 229.

109. Brendan Behan, *Richard's Cork Leg*, ed. Alan Simpson (London: Eyre Methuen, 1973), pp. 10, 75, 76.

4. Manners and Morals in Irish Comedy

1. Bernard Shaw, *John Bull's Other Island* (London: Constable, 1931), p. 73. The play was written in 1904 for the Abbey Theatre, which rejected it, and was first published in 1907. It was revised for the 1931 edition.

Notice also that the description of Tim Haffigan in the stage directions ironically matches the stereotyped stage Irishman that Barry Fitzgerald was destined to play in too many Hollywood films.

2. Ibid., p. 76.

3. Roger Lancelyn Green, Introduction, *Two Satyr Plays: Euripides' "Cyclops" and Sophocles' "Ichneutai"* (Harmondsworth: Penguin, 1957), p. 12: "Silenus and the Satyrs, however, exhibit all the characteristics of burlesque or farcical figures as we would understand the term; and their determination to be on the winning side and to profess their exaggerated allegiance to the person in power sets them well in the comic tradition. Though there is a big gap in the family tree, we cannot help feeling that in some way Silenus is the ancestor of Thraso and Bobadil, of Paroles and Joxer Daly."

G. C. Duggan in *The Stage Irishman* (London and New York: Longmans, Green, 1937), p. 288, also asked a pertinent question about comic ancestry: "Is [the stage Irishman] all unwittingly the lineal descendant of the Davus of the plays of Plautus and Terence, whose wit, resourcefulness and buffoonery are not far removed from the characteristics of the nineteenth century Paddy, even as racially the Roman or Greek servant often had Celtic blood?"

4. Thomas Sheridan, *Captain O'Blunder; or, The Brave Irishman* (1738), in *Ten English Farces*, ed. Leo Hughes and A. H. Scouten (Austen: University of Texas Press, 1948), p. 230.

5. J. M. Synge, *The Collected Works of J. M. Synge: Plays*, vol. 4, ed. Ann Saddlemyer (London: Oxford University Press, 1968), p. 167.

6. *Ten English Farces,* ed. Hughes and Scouten, pp. 235–36. In creating O'Blunder as the typical stage Irishman, Sheridan used the provincial buffoon in Molière's *Monsieur de Pouroeaugnac* (1669) as his main source. He also owes a debt to the Fluellin-Pistol scenes in Shakespeare's *Henry V* when he allows O'Blunder to triumph over a cringing Frenchman by forcing him to eat a potato. Nevertheless, Sheridan endows O'Blunder with the mock eloquence of the Irish clown armed with his characteristic malapropisms and bulls. The Captain introduces himself in London with a salute: "Shir, I'm your most engaging conversation" (p. 229). Here are some of his typical Irish bulls: "I'll have 'em shot stone-dead first, and [w]phipt thorrow the regiment afterwards" (p. 228). "By my shoul, if I take my shillela to you, I'll make you skip like a dead salmon" (pp. 228–29). "Fait, my dear, I snore all night; and when I awake in the morning, I find myself fast asleep" (p. 232).

7. H. B. Charlton, *Shakespearean Comedy* (London: Methuen, 1938), p. 283.

8. Stanislaus Joyce, *My Brother's Keeper* (London: Faber & Faber, 1958), p. 164. He also deferred to his brother James on this subject: "My brother has used the phrase 'the asexual intellect of the Irish.' He did not mean that Irishmen are less virile than others (families are rather larger in Ireland than elsewhere), but that sexual motives have little influence on their lives. Sexuality is in their lives a thing apart which rarely 'gets tangled with reality'" (p. 164).

9. Brian Merriman, *The Midnight Court* (c. 1780), trans. Frank O'Connor, in O'Connor, *Kings, Lords, & Commons* (New York: Knopf, 1962), p. 157.

10. Duggan, *Stage Irishman,* p. 295.

11. Maurice Bourgeois, *John Millington Synge and the Irish Theatre* (London: Constable, 1913), p. 113.

12. Oliver Goldsmith, "An Essay on the Theatre; or, A Comparison between Laughing and Sentimental Comedy," *Westminster Magazine,* December 1772; reprinted in *British Dramatists from Dryden to Sheridan,* ed. George H. Nettleton and Arthur E. Case (Boston: Houghton Mifflin, 1939), p. 763. The "gloomy Tabernacle" is a reference to the house of worship in London where George Whitfield (1714–70), the founder of the Calvinist Methodists, preached his famous hellfire sermons.

13. Synge, *Collected Works: Plays,* 4:3.

14. Sean O'Casey, *The Green Crow* (New York: Braziller, 1956), p. 226. I should also add here that Dickens, who never allowed his sentimentality to interfere with his comedy, made the same point about instruction and entertainment when Mr. Sleary of the horse riding defended the pleasure of the circus to the utilitarian Mr. Gradgrind in *Hard Times* (1854), chap. 7: "People mutht be amuthed. They can't be alwayth a learning, nor yet they can't be alwayth a working, they an't made for it."

15. Dion Boucicault, *North American Review*, January–February 1878.
16. Dion Boucicault, *London Assurance* (Samuel French, no. 27, n.d.), p. 25.
17. *Times* (London) March 5, 1841, a review of the premiere of *London Assurance*.
18. *Times* (London), February 8, 1842, a review of the premiere of *The Irish Heiress*.
19. *The Dolmen Boucicault*, ed. with an Introduction by David Krause (Dublin: Dolmen, 1964), p. 135.
20. Ibid., p. 140. Shaw's blundering Major Swindon in *The Devil's Disciple* is very likely modeled after Boucicault's Major Coffin. Both men are comic villains who seem determined to hang somebody, anybody, because of what they call their principles. Shaw paid Boucicault the compliment of copying many of the characters and incidents from *Arrah-na-Pogue* for the parallel trial scene in *The Devil's Disciple*. Dick Dudgeon takes the place of the Reverend Anderson on the gallows, then both men are saved at the eleventh hour, just as Beamish MacCoul offers to replace the condemned Shaun, but both men are released at the last moment. There is a parallel in the condescending and ironic way Shaw's gentlemanly General Burgoyne and Boucicault's gentlemanly Colonel O'Grady treat their respectively militaristic British majors. Shaw's humorously accommodating sergeant, who allows Judith to see Dudgeon in jail, has his original in Boucicault's garrulous sergeant, who lets Arrah visit the imprisoned Shaun. Both plays are melodramatic farces, and Shaw should have bowed to Boucicault and kept his tongue in his bearded cheek whenever he belittled melodrama and farce.
21. Ibid., p. 174.
22. Ibid., p. 187.
23. To reinforce the connection between Tony Lumpkin and Conn the Shaughraun, it should be pointed out that Boucicault owed a debt to Goldsmith for the letter scene. See *She Stoops to Conquer*, Act IV, where the illiterate Tony is unable to read the conspiratorial letter from Hastings and inopportunely gives it to his raging mother. The farcical relationship between Conn and his mother has much in common with Tony's prankish fights with his mother, though Mrs. Hardcastle is much more of a Wildean "gorgon" than Conn's mother. Boucicault must have been impressed by Tony's fight for liberation from his mother, which is celebrated at the end of the play when he escapes and cries out, "Tony Lumpkin is his own man again!" and effectively characterized by his protest at the end of Act II, when he rebels against her claim that her maternal tyranny was all for his own good: "I wish you'd let me and my good alone then. Snubbing this way when I'm in spirits! If I am to have any good, let it come of itself; not to keep dinging it, dinging it into one so." All of Boucicault's rogue-heroes would agree with this attack on the "snubbers" and "dingers" of the world who would take away a man's individuality and liberty.

24. *Dolmen Boucicault,* p. 228.

25. Ibid., p. 238.

26. Lennox Robinson, *Curtain Up* (London: Michael Joseph, 1942), p. 147.

27. Lennox Robinson, *The Whiteheaded Boy* (Dublin: Talbot Press, 1920), p. 64. The play was first performed at the Abbey Theatre on December 13, 1916.

28. Lennox Robinson, *The Lost Leader* (Dublin: Thomas Kiersey, 1918), p. 5.

29. Robinson, *Whiteheaded Boy,* p. 88.

30. Lennox Robinson, *The Far-Off Hills* (London: Chatto & Windus, 1931), p. 37. This play was first performed at the Abbey Theatre on October 22, 1928. In his serious and autobiographical play *Church Street* (1934), the danger of the far-off hills for a writer becomes the main theme. Hugh Riordan, an Irish playwright who has been living in London, where one of his plays about English life has just failed, returns in despair to Ireland. In this version of you-can-go-home-again, Hugh's Aunt Moll—once more that dominating maternal figure in Robinson's work—convinces him that he must forget far-off England and find the material for his plays in his native Irish village. Incidentally, Robinson and most Irish critics often tried to play the wise Aunt Moll to the self-exiled O'Casey.

31. Lennox Robinsion, *"Killycreggs in Twilight" and Other Plays* (Dublin: Browne & Nolan, 1939), p. 159. This volume contains three plays: *Killycreggs in Twilight; Is Life Worth Living? (Drama at Inish);* and *Bird's Nest. Drama at Inish* was first performed at the Abbey Theatre on February 6, 1933. The following year, for the first London production, the title was changed to *Is Life Worth Living?*
All the scenes between Annie Twohig and her son Eddie illustrate the recurring maternal complex in Robinson's plays. Even in his early tragedy, *The Clancy Name* (1908), there is a domineering mother who is so proud and protective about the family, she urges her indecisive son to cover up a murder rather than tell the truth and taint the Clancy name. This maternal ogre calls to mind an example of pertinent Shavian irony in *The Devil's Disciple* (1897), when in Act III Dick Dudgeon says of his hapless brother Christy: "He has been too well brought up by a pious mother to have any sense or manhood left in him."

32. Robinson, *Killycreggs,* pp. 198–99.

33. William Boyle, *The Eloquent Dempsy* (Dublin: Gill, n.d.), p. 14. A revenue officer with the civil service, Boyle sided with the Irish establishment when the riots broke out over Synge's *Playboy* in 1907, and he withdrew his play from the Abbey as an indignant protest against what he considered to be the "indecencies" in Synge's work.

34. Bernard Shaw, *Collected Plays with Their Prefaces* (London: Bodley Head, 1971), 2:930. And I should point out that Joyce apparently agreed with Shaw that profound truths are often hidden in jokes. "Not 'in vino veritas,'" said Joyce, "but 'in risu veritas,'—in laughter, truth"

(quoted by W. R. Rodgers in *Irish Literary Portraits* [New York: Top-linger, 1973], p. 132).

35. Shaw, *Collected Plays*, 2:1021. The saintly Keegan's mad dream of a divine humanity has significant parallels to the heretical dreams of Shaw's St. Joan. They are both holy fools whose private visions are aimed at the salvation of their people. They are both essentially comic characters in a state of grace, wise fools who are so free from sin they cannot be seen as tragic. Joan especially has been mistakenly inter-preted as a tragic heroine by most critics. On the contrary, I would go so far as to suggest that she is a comic-rogue heroine, a barbarous peasant girl who must profane all that passes for sacred belief in a corrupted world in order to reveal her divinely inspired and liberating faith in God through the individual conscience. That act of affirmation can only be a comic vision of humanity's potential power and glory. The tragedy of her martyrdom is ours, not hers.

36. In his 1906 Preface to the play, in "Irish Catholic Forecast," Shaw disclosed his misunderstanding of the Catholic faith in Ireland when he predicted: "Home rule will herald the day when the Vatican will go the way of Dublin Castle, and the island of saints assume the headship of her own Church" (ibid., p. 835). He presented a similarly forlorn hope in the play in the following exchange between Doyle and Father Demp-sey (p. 965):

> *Doyle.* Aye; and I would have Ireland compete with Rome itself for the chair of St Peter and the citadel of the Church; for Rome, in spite of all the blood of the martyrs, is pagan at heart to this day, while in Ireland the people is the Church and the Church the people.
>
> *Father Dempsey [startled, but not at all displeased]* Whisht, man! youre worse than mad Pether Keegan himself.

37. Shaw, *Collected Plays*, pp. 905–6.

38. Ibid., pp. 909–11. I sometimes think of Larry Doyle as an original for O'Neill's Larry Slade in *The Iceman Cometh*. Both Larrys know too much, see both sides of every argument, and are paralyzed by their excess of fatalistic knowledge. As a result they are both "grandstand foolosophers."

39. Ibid., p. 923.

40. Ibid., pp. 916–17.

41. Ibid., pp. 1015–16.

42. Ibid., pp. 979–80. In this hilariously barbarous reaction of the people of Rosscullen to Broadbent's wild ride and slaughtering of the pig, Shaw the farcical playwright proved to be wiser than Shaw the puritan theorist. The low comedy of that episode links him with the knockabout fun of Synge, Fitzmaurice, O'Casey, Behan, and Beckett. But Shaw the theorist, in his harsh review of Wilde's *Importance of Being Earnest,* allowed his occasionally stiff-necked view of farce to make him reject a masterpiece as beneath his intelligence: "Unless comedy touches me as well as amuses me, it leaves me with a sense of having wasted my

evening. I go to the theatre to be moved to laughter, not to be tickled or bustled into it; and that is why, though I laugh as much as anyone at a farcical comedy, I am out of spirits before the end of the second act, and out of temper before the end of the third, my miserable mechanical laughter intensifying these symptoms at every outburst. If the public ever becomes intelligent enough to know when it is really enjoying itself and when it is not, there will be an end of farcical comedy" ("An Old New Play and a New Old One," February 23, 1895, in *Our Theatres in the Nineties* [London: Constable, 1948], pp. 42-43). Fortunately, one must believe, audiences will never become so prudishly intelligent, and farcical comedy will go on and on forever, even in the plays of Shaw. I might also point out that the laughter provoked by Wilde's great play is far from mechanical tickling, since every outburst of "sudden glory" records some sparkling exposure of Victorian earnestness or smugness, prudery or hypocrisy.

43. Shaw, *Collected Plays*, p. 982. To continue in the vein of the previous note, the gallows humor of Barney Doran's story tells us as much about Barney's significant release of inhibitions as it does about Broadbent's comic misadventure. Low comedy can therefore be a source of high irony and insight. Like Shaw, Lady Gregory could be myopic about farce when she theorized about it, but, again like Shaw, not when she created it magnificently in her plays. She was a master of farce, and yet, perhaps under the high-minded influence of Yeats, she called farce "comedy with the character left out" (*Our Irish Theatre* [London: Putnam's, 1913], p. 106). It is more likely that farce is comedy with the respectability left out; the character is defined by the farcical deeds.

44. Shaw, *Collected Plays*, p. 983. The "chaney" is the chinaware on Molly Ryan's crockery stall.

45. Ibid., p. 1021.

46. Ibid., p. 1020.

47. Ibid., p. 927.

48. William Blake, *The Marriage of Heaven and Hell* (1793). It could serve as the subtitle of Shaw's play.

49. Paul Vincent Carroll, *Shadow and Substance* (London: Macmillan, 1938), p. viii. The play was first produced at the Abbey Theatre on January 25, 1937.

50. "The Substance of Paul Vincent Carroll," *New York Times*, January 30, 1938.

51. Carroll, *Shadow and Substance*, p. 2.

52. Ibid., p. 4.

53. Ibid., p. 5.

54. Ibid., p. 6.

55. Ibid., p. 34.

56. Paul Vincent Carroll, *Three Plays: "The White Steed," "Things That Are Caesar's," "The Strings, My Lord, Are False"* (London: Macmillan, 1946), p. 2. *The White Steed* was rejected by the Abbey Theatre in 1938,

and it was first produced by Eddie Dowling in New York on January 10, 1939.

57. Ibid., p. 61.

58. Ibid., p. 100.

59. Ibid., p. 22. Canon Lavelle and Canon Skerritt, in different yet related ways, are unusual Irish priests who try to wear their Roman collars lightly in a country of religious austerity, and they remind me of the dreaming Irish priest in Pirandello's tragicomic *Henry IV* (1922). The "mad" Henry is explaining how he gains comic peace from his tragic role playing as a medieval king; he talks about the dreamlike aspect of "the everlasting masquerade, of which we are the involuntary puppets, when we mask ourselves with that which we appear to be," and this thought reminds him of an Irish priest who escapes into the poetic freedom of dreams, only to wake and return to priestly rigors, just as the playful Henry is always forced to resume his masquerade and invoke the divine right of his kingly prerogatives:

> I remember a priest, certainly Irish, a nice-looking priest who was sleeping in the sun one November day, with his arm on the corner of the bench of a public garden. He was lost in the golden delight of the mild sunny air which must have seemed to him almost summery. One may be sure that in that moment he did not know any more that he was a priest, or even where he was. He was dreaming—A little boy passed with a flower in his hand. He touched the priest with it here on the neck. I saw him open his laughing eyes, while all his mouth smiled with the beauty of his dream. He was forgetful of everything—But all at once, he pulled himself together, and stretched out his priest's cassock; and there came back to his eyes the same seriousness which you have seen in mine; because Irish priests defend the seriousness of their Catholic faith with the same zeal with which I defend the secret rights of hereditary monarchy! [Luigi Pirandello, *Three Plays* (London: Dent, 1923), p. 144]

60. Carroll, *Three Plays*, p. 105.

61. Paul Vincent Carroll, *"The White Steed" and "Coggerers"* (London: Macmillan, 1939), p. 173. *Coggerers* was first produced at the Abbey Theatre on November 22, 1934.

62. Ibid., p. 184.

63. Ibid., p. 187.

64. Ibid., p. 189.

65. Ibid., p. 190. I should point out that Robert Hogan, in *After the Irish Renaissance: A Critical History of the Irish Drama since "The Plough and the Stars"* (Minneapolis: University of Minnesota Press, 1967), makes a vague but glowing comment on *Coggerers*: "Few plays in such a short space arouse such a moving and various body of emotions as this thoroughly successful little piece does" (p. 58). It is difficult to accept this glib generalization, and it is impossible to guess where Hogan finds that "moving and various body of emotions" in this piece of second-rate sentimentality.

5. *The Victory of Comic Defeat*

1. William Empson, *Some Versions of Pastoral* (1935; London: Chatto & Windus, 1950), p. 30.

2. Frank Tuohy, *Yeats* (London, Dublin: Gill and Macmillan, 1976), p. 194.

3. Synge to Lady Gregory, September 11, 1904, quoted in Ann Saddlemyer's Introduction to J. M. Synge's *Collected Works*, vol. 1 (London: Oxford University Press, 1968), p. xxii. For a more bitter and characteristic illustration of this "neo-patriotic-Catholic" attitude toward Synge's plays, see the views of Arthur Griffith in David Krause, *Sean O'Casey: The Man and His Work* (New York: Macmillan, 1960), pp. 61, 343–44.

4. Quoted in Saddlemyer's Introduction to Synge, *Collected Works*, 1:xxi.

5. Ibid., p. xxiv. After *The Well of the Saints* opened and was attacked by most of the reviewers, George Moore came to Synge's defense with a letter to the *Irish Times*, February 13, 1905, in which he stated: "Mr. Synge has discovered great literature in barbarous idiom as gold is discovered in quartz, and to do such a thing is surely a rare literary achievement."

6. For all the quotations in this paragraph, see O'Casey to Lennox Robinson, January 10, 1926, in *The Letters of Sean O'Casey*, ed. David Krause (New York: Macmillan, 1975), 1:165–66.

7. W. B. Yeats, Preface to the first edition of J. M. Synge, *The Well of the Saints* (1905); reprinted in *Essays and Introductions* (New York: Macmillan, 1961), p. 301. Yeats here was writing about Rabelais, Villon, Shakespeare and Blake, but he also had Synge in mind, and later added O'Casey to this company. He made the connection on another occasion in one of his Senate speeches when, commenting on the cause of the riots in the Abbey Theatre, he said: "Synge's 'Playboy' and O'Casey's 'Plough and the Stars' were attacked because, like 'The Cherry Tree Carol,' they contain what a belief, tamed down to a formula, shudders at, something wild and ancient" (*The Senate Speeches of W. B. Yeats*, ed. Donald R. Pearce (London: Faber & Faber, 1960), p. 180.

8. Yeats, Preface to Synge, *Well of the Saints*, p. 304.

9. Synge, *Collected Works: Plays*, ed. Ann Saddlemyer (London: Oxford University Press, 1968), 4:173.

10. Ibid., p. 173.

11. Ibid., pp. 83–85.

12. Ibid., p. 151. Note the barbarously comic images in this irreverent speech as Michael James gives his account of Kate Cassidy's wake.

13. Ibid., p. 163. The "Unions" were the workhouses for the poor and homeless.

14. Ibid., p. 169. It was during the terrible famine years in the mid-

nineteenth century that the mouths of the starving peasants of Keel, on Achill Island, were stained green from eating grass.

15. Ibid., p. 49. I am not suggesting that the tinker Michael and the playboy Christy are entirely similar characters, but that when they are forced to retreat from the orthodox and repressive world, they adopt the role of the outcast braggart who must exaggerate his vision of the good life because his future is always a precarious improvisation. Like Nora Burke and the Tramp, like the Douls, Michael and Christy are vagabonds who must always make the best of bad situations, who must survive by their mother wit and their comic imagination. And of course the same holds true for O'Casey's strutting "paycocks."

16. Sean O'Casey, *Collected Plays* (London: Macmillan, 1951), 1:157. I am thinking of Harry Brogan's brilliant performance as Shields at the Abbey Theatre during the 1950s and 1960s. By telegraphing his Joxer-like shrug before he casually delivered his curtain line, he prepared the audience for the conclusion in which a comic twist is superimposed on a tragic scene.

17. In 1956 an Angel Records recording of *Juno and the Paycock* (ANG 35275-76), made by Cyril Cusack Productions, ended with the final speech of Juno, played by Siobhan McKenna, and the Boyle-Joxer conclusion was omitted. Although O'Casey himself reads a "Preamble" to the play, recorded separately, he was not consulted about the cut and later expressed his strong objection to this corrupted version of the play. Someone apparently decided to eliminate the low comedy, one of the most brilliant conclusions in modern drama, and end on a high tragic note with the mourning Juno, thus destroying the aesthetic balance of the tragicomedy.

18. O'Casey, *Collected Plays*, 1:255.

19. Ibid., p. 255.

20. Ibid., 2:104.

21. *Letters of Sean O'Casey*, 1:268. See also Krause, *Sean O'Casey*, chap. 3.

22. O'Casey, *Collected Plays*, 1:193.

23. Tim Pat Coogan, "The Exile," in *The World of Sean O'Casey*, ed. Sean McCann (London: Four Square, 1966), p. 115. In this forthright article Coogan provides some of the most convincing arguments written by an Irishman for the justification of O'Casey's alienation and self-exile from Ireland. To this day many of O'Casey's countrymen, unlike Coogan, still resent his role as an "exile."

24. Ibid., p. 114.

25. Sean O'Casey, *Drums under the Windows* (London: Macmillan, 1945), in *Autobiographies* (London: Macmillan, 1963), 1:623-24.

26. Michael McInerney, *Peadar O'Donnell: Irish Social Rebel* (Dublin: O'Brien Press, 1974), p. 197. In some of his later "political" plays, such as *The Star Turns Red* and *Oak Leaves and Lavender*, O'Casey stressed the need for direct action in the 1913 Dublin General Strike and World

War II, but he was very explicit and too didactic in these morality plays, which probably would have nauseated such men as O'Donnell for different political reasons.

27. Francis Shaw, "The Canon of Irish History—A Challenge," *Studies*, Summer 1972, p. 123. See also F. S. L. Lyons's review of Father Shaw's article, "The Shadow of the Past," *Irish Times*, September 11, 1972; and for a further discussion of Pearse's messianic nationalism, see Lyons's *Ireland since the Famine*, rev. ed. (London: Collins/Fontana, 1973), pp. 331–39. For some relevant comments on Irish nationalist paradoxes and hypocrisies, see Conor Cruise O'Brien's "Shades of Republicans," *Irish Times*, March 27, 1975; also O'Brien's *States of Ireland* (London: Panther, 1974) and "The Embers of Easter, 1916-1966," in *1916: The Easter Rising*, ed. Owen Dudley Edwards and Fergus Pyle (London: MacGibbon & Kee, 1968).

28. Shaw, "Canon of Irish History," pp. 117–18.
29. Ibid., p. 120.
30. Sean O'Casey, *Collected Plays*, 1:193, 196, 202–3.
31. Ibid., p. 199.
32. Ibid., p. 213.
33. Shaw, "Canon of Irish History," pp. 132–33.
34. Ibid., p. 133.
35. Ibid., p. 134. This cynical attitude toward fanatical heroism can also be observed in the popular column "Inside Politics," by Backbencher (James Healy) in the *Irish Times*, August 26, 1972. Backbencher had obviously read Father Shaw's article in the current *Studies*, had already indicated that he shared the Jesuit scholar's view of Pearse, and was now replying to an irate nationalist reader who had written a letter of protest. In his reply Backbencher referred to 1916 as "a mickey-mouse Rising," and he went on to make an ironic comparison between Pearse's rabid chauvinism and its counterpart in England during World War I:

> I am taken to task by a private correspondent for having some words about the blood lust of Pearse and that his exhilarating wine of the battlefield quotation should be set against the mood of the times. I accept the point completely: he was in the best tradition of the cultural stream of the Brits: the last flourishing of the poets who glorified war as noble and death on the battlefield as a glorious thing was very much a British thing just then. The poetic literature of disillusionment came five bitter Owen and Sassoon years later when, having found out how it wasn't, they told it how it was and what a squalid thing it was.
> But British anti-war poets are not for the Irish classroom because that would be cultural shoneenism.
> The corners of our land which will remain forever English are very odd indeed, when you come to think about it.

36. Sean O'Casey, *The Drums of Father Ned* (London: Macmillan, 1960), p. 10.

37. P. O Cathasaigh, *The Story of the Irish Citizen Army* (Dublin: Maunsel, 1919), p. 52.

38. Ibid., p. 52.

39. Ibid., p. 55. O'Casey's reference to Yeats's *Cathleen Ni Houlihan* (1902) calls to mind a comment by Conor Cruise O'Brien on the audience reaction to this chauvinistic play, and it could also be applied to the Irish audiences at *The Plough and the Stars:* "It doesn't seem to have occurred to the earlier audiences of Yeats's *Cathleen Ni Houlihan* that there might be something unhealthy about a mother who shuffles round promising her sons that 'they shall be remembered for ever,' provided they get themselves killed for mother's sake" (*States of Ireland,* p. 295n).

40. R. M. Fox, *The History of the Irish Citizen Army* (Dublin: James Duffy, 1944), p. 179.

41. Leon Trotsky, *Nashe Slovo,* July 4, 1916; quoted by P. Berresford Ellis in the Introduction to *James Connolly: Selected Writings,* ed. P. Berresford Ellis (Harmondsworth: Pelican, 1973). Berresford Ellis also prints the relevant passages from the works of Marx and Lenin in support of Connolly's position. For another defense of Connolly's attempt to unite nationalism and socialism in Ireland, see C. Desmond Greaves, *The Life and Times of James Connolly* (London: Lawrence & Wishart, 1961).

42. Francis Sheehy-Skeffington, "An Open Letter to Thomas MacDonagh," *Irish Citizen,* May 1915; reprinted in *1916: The Easter Rising,* ed. Edwards and Pyle, pp. 150–51. In the same volume see also Owen Sheehy-Skeffington, "Francis Sheehy-Skeffington," pp. 135–48.

43. O Cathasaigh, *Story of the Irish Citizen Army,* pp. 63–64. It may help to tilt Sheehy-Skeffington's halo and humanize him by recording an amusing story about the ardent feminist's attempt to heckle the British prime minister, Herbert Asquith, at a meeting of the old Redmondite Irish National Party in Dublin. O'Casey would have enjoyed this episode, though in all probability he knew about it and many others like it so typical of Sheehy-Skeffington. George Dangerfield tells the story in *The Strange Death of Liberal England* (1935; London: Macgibbon & Kee, 1966), pp. 154–55:

There was the famous story of Mr. Sheehy-Skeffington, an ardent suffragist of Dublin, who determined to heckle Mr. Asquith at a Nationalist meeting in July 1912. Now the Dublin Nationalists had issued their tickets with special care; no suspect women were to be admitted; and as for Mr. Sheehy-Skeffington, he had been warned that if he attempted to get in he would be severely handled.

But Mr. Sheehy-Skeffington was not to be intimidated. He procured a ticket made out in a priest's name, and, with the help of Dudley Digges, disguised himself as a priest. His make-up was extremely effective except that he refused to shave off his red beard, of which he was inordinately proud; and beards, among Catholic clergy, are rather the exception than the rule. Arrived at the meeting somewhat late, owing to the fact that his cabby was completely intoxicated, Mr. Sheehy-Skeffington presented his ticket with some trepidation; but in Dublin, a priest is a priest; and the bearded apparition was admitted inside. And so it came about that Mr. Asquith, in the middle of one of his finest periods, was completely put off with the cry of 'Votes for Wee-men!' There was no mistaking that high, shrill voice: with a howl of 'Skeffy!' the enraged ushers started a man-hunt, discovered their priest, and—with shouts of rage and laughter—bundled him bruised and dishevelled, out into the street."

44. Seamus Deane, "Irish Politics and O'Casey's Theatre," *Threshold,* Spring 1973; reprinted in *Sean O'Casey: A Collection of Critical Essays,* ed. Thomas Kilroy (1975). Deane argues that in all the Dublin plays, *Gunman* and *Juno* and *Plough,* O'Casey errs by stressing the family situation of the Dublin poor at the expense of the political situation of the nation. Along with this political failure, he faults O'Casey for not being able to write a classical tragedy because his characters "are not in any sense heroic or in any tragic way flawed." For a reply to Deane, see my "Some Truths and Jokes about the Easter Rising," *Sean O'Casey Review,* Fall 1976.

William Irwin Thompson, in *The Imagination of an Insurrection, Dublin, 1916* (New York: Oxford University Press, 1967), complains that the mock-heroic women in *The Plough* are not tragic heroines and dismisses the play as a failed classical tragedy: "O'Casey is trying to lift Nora's lament into the realm of tragedy, but Nora is incapable of understanding her situation, and therefore is incapable, as a dramatic figure, of generalizing her situation into anything resembling a tragic predicament.... Medea, Clytemnestra, Lady Macbeth: these are tragic heroines, but poor Nora is only an object of pity" (pp. 219-20). But since poor Nora is obviously a tragic victim, not a tragic heroine, what is the point of protesting that she is not a Medea et al.? Thompson goes on to flog O'Casey with Marx as well as Aristotle when he shifts to a political stance and explains the failure of the play in different terms: "O'Casey was a voice out of the slums that spoke of the rebellion, not as a holy rising enkindled by Saint Pearse with a leaf from Irish legend, but as a class struggle lit by a page torn from the book of Marx" (p. 205). Thompson here sounds as if he had been reading Jenersky instead of O'Casey! *The Plough* is not an apology for Marxist dogma, any more than it is an apology for nationalist dogma. Nevertheless, Thompson invokes his syllogistic conclusion: O'Casey is a Marxist; tragedy is not a Marxist genre; therefore, the play is not a tragedy.

45. Bernard Shaw, *John Bull's Other Island* (1907; London: Constable, 1931), p. 101.

46. T. S. Eliot, *Poetry and Drama* (London: Faber & Faber, 1951), p. 32.

47. Enid Welsford, *The Fool* (1935; New York: Anchor, 1961), p. 322.

48. George Santayana, *Soliloquies in England and Later Soliloquies* (New York: Scribner's, 1922), p. 141.

49. James Agate, *Sunday Times*, November 16, 1925; reprinted in *Sean O'Casey*, ed. Ronald Ayling (London: Macmillan, 1969), p. 76.
50. *Aristotle's Poetics* (New York: Dramabook, 1961), p. 52.
51. Empson, *Some Versions of Pastoral*, p. 27.
52. Hugh Kenner, *Samuel Beckett: A Critical Study* (New York: Evergreen, 1961), pp. 134–35. And Jan Kott, in *Shakespeare Our Contemporary* (New York: Doubleday, 1964), makes a similar point about grotesque characters: "In Shakespeare's world prose is spoken only by grotesque and episodic characters; by those who are not a part of the drama proper" (p. 275). The contemporaneous point is that in the plays of O'Casey and Beckett the grotesque and episodic characters themselves *become* the drama proper, while their poetic and social betters are discredited or hidden in the wings.
53. J. L. Styan, *The Dark Comedy: The Development of Modern Comic Tragedy* (Cambridge: At the University Press, 1968), p. 284.
54. W. B. Yeats, "Emotion of Multitude," in *Ideas of Good and Evil* (London: A. H. Bullen, 1903), pp. 339–41.
55. W. B. Yeats, *Plays in Prose and Verse* (1922); reprinted in *The Variorum Edition of the Plays of W. B. Yeats*, ed. Russell K. Alspach (New York: Macmillan, 1969), p. 254.
56. W. B. Yeats, "A People's Theatre: A Letter to Lady Gregory," *Irish Statesman* (1919); reprinted in *Explorations* (London: Macmillan, 1962), pp. 254-55.
57. Lady Gregory, *Seven Short Plays* (1903; Dublin: Maunsel, 1909), p. 207.
58. W. B. Yeats, *Per Amica Silentia Lunae* (1917); reprinted in *Mythologies* (London: Macmillan, 1959), p. 331.
59. William Dunbar's "Flyting of Dunbar and Kennedie" (c. 1505), a poem of 522 lines, written in octosyllabic couplets in dialogue form, is a formal flyting or comic debate between two word-battling poets. John Small, in his three-volume edition of *The Poems of William Dunbar* (Edinburgh and London: Blackwood, 1893), comments in his Introduction: "The group of vituperative poems consists of the singular 'Flyting' with Kennedy, where the abuse is probably chiefly mock, a sort of poetical tournament or contest of wit, and a few where the censure was certainly real. . . . The 'Flyting' belongs to a form of poetry of which the literature of almost every nation has examples. The 'Ibis,' in which Ovid, or some like Roman poet, abused an unknown rival, was copied from the poem of the same name and purpose by Callimachus against his former pupil Apollonius Rhodius" (pp. cix–cx). Small also cites as examples of flytings "The Loki Sennar," an early Scandanavian work, and refers to a number of Italian Renaissance and sixteenth-century Scottish Gaelic poets who used the flyting in their satires. As a proper Victorian gentleman, however, Small disapproves of the flyting because it is too abusive and vulgar, and he concludes: "Modern poets have taken to lauding instead of abusing each other. Byron was perhaps the last of the 'flyters'" (p. cxii). Well, not quite the last.

60. See John Dollard, "The Dozens: Dialectic of Insult," *American Imago I* (1939). See also Robert C. Elliott, *The Power of Satire* (Princeton: Princeton University Press, 1960), pp. 73-74. The flytings or verbal games, Elliott writes, "have entertainment value (socialized ridicule seems always to provide popular entertainment), and they act, as Dollard says of the Dozens, as a safety valve for aggression."

61. Hugh MacDiarmid, "Slainte Churamach, Sean," in *Sean O'Casey*, ed. Ayling, pp. 255-56.

62. W. H. Auden, *The Dyer's Hand* (New York: Vintage, 1968), p. 383.

63. Gregory, *Seven Short Plays*, p. 160.

64. Synge, *Collected Works: Plays*, 3:97. I am tempted to put down here one of my favorite flytings from *The Playboy of the Western World*, Pegeen Mike's blast at the Widow Quin when the two women are fighting over the bewildered Christy Mahon. It is actually a double-barreled flyting: "Doesn't the world know you reared a black lamb at your own breast, so that the Lord Bishop of Connaught felt the elements of a Christian, and he eating it after in a kidney stew? Doesn't the world know you've been seen shaving the foxy skipper from France for a threepenny bit and a sop of grass tobacco would wring the liver from a mountain goat you'd meet leaping the hills?" (p. 29). And here is another Synge flyting, spoken by Sarah Casey in *The Tinker's Wedding*, when she puts Mary Byrne down and insists that even a lowly tinker woman who has been living with a man has a right to demand a proper marriage: "Let you not be destroying us with your talk when I've as good a right to a decent marriage as any speckled female does be sleeping in black hovels above, would choke a mule" (p. 200).

65. O'Casey, *Collected Plays*, 1:253. One could draw up a formidable list of flytings from O'Casey's plays, beginning with "Captain" Boyle in *Juno and the Paycock*, continually outraged, and at one point furious because Devine has been looking for him in a pub about a job: "Is a man not to be allowed to leave his house for a minute without havin' a pack o' spies, pimps an' informers cantherin' at his heels?" (p. 16). Or Fluther Good in *The Plough and the Stars*, in a slow burn when he is fighting with the Covey over the honor of the prostitute Rosie Redmond: "Sing a little less on th' high note, or, when I'm done with you, you'll put a Christianable consthruction on things, I'm tellin' you!" (p. 211). See also the enlarged edition of my *Sean O'Casey* (1975), pp. 318-20, where I have set down half a dozen flytings from O'Casey's one-act plays.

66. James Joyce, *A Portrait of the Artist as a Young Man* (1916; New York: Viking, 1964), p. 203.

67. Sigmund Freud, *Civilization and Its Discontents* (1930; New York: Anchor, n.d.), pp. 37-38.

68. Samuel Beckett, "The Essential and the Incidental," *Bookman*, December 1934. I drew attention to this little-known review in "The Principle of Comic Disintegration," *James Joyce Quarterly*, Fall 1970; and since that time it has been reprinted in *Sean O'Casey: A Collection of*

Critical Essays, ed. Thomas Kilroy (Englewood Cliffs, N.J.: Prentice-Hall, 1975).

69. John Rees Moore, *Masks of Love and Death: Yeats as Dramatist* (Ithaca: Cornell University Press, 1971), p. 246.

70. Richard Ellmann, *Eminent Domain* (New York: Oxford University Press, 1967), p. 54.

71. Frank O'Connor, *A Short History of Irish Literature* (New York: Putnam's, 1967), pp. 170, 187.

72. See my comments on the Fays' unsuccessful attempts to urge Synge to make his comic characters more "decent" and "lovable": *Sean O'Casey*, pp. 63-64, 345-46.

73. Wylie Sypher, "The Meanings of Comedy," in *Comedy: "An Essay on Comedy" by George Meredith; "Laughter" by Henri Bergson* (New York: Anchor, 1956), p. 223.

74. Ibid., p. 222.

75. Eugene Ionesco, "*La demystification par l'humour noir,*" quoted by Martin Esslin in *The Theatre of the Absurd,* rev. ed. (New York: Anchor, 1969), p. 159.

76. Friedrich Nietzsche, *The Birth of Tragedy* (1872; New York: Anchor, 1956), p. 52.

77. Antonin Artaud, *The Theatre and Its Double* (1938; New York: Grove, 1958), p. 42.

78. Eric Bentley, *The Life of Drama* (New York: Atheneum, 1964), p. 350.

79. O'Casey, *Collected Plays,* 1:100.

80. Samuel Beckett, *Endgame* (New York: Grove, 1958), p. 18.

81. Ibid., p. 77.

82. O'Casey, *Collected Plays,* 1:88.

83. Samuel Beckett, *Waiting for Godot* (New York: Grove, 1954), p. 9.

84. Beckett, *Endgame,* p. 58.

85. O'Casey, *Collected Plays,* 1:26.

86. Beckett, *Waiting for Godot,* p. 40.

87. Beckett, *Endgame,* pp. 75-76.

88. O'Casey, *Collected Plays,* 1:37.

INDEX

328

INDEX

Behan, Brendan (*cont.*)
Boy, 23, 35, 44, 154, 170, 311; *Brendan Behan's Island: An Irish Sketch-Book*, 155; *An Giall*, 168, 310; *The Hostage*, 35, 154, 155, 156, 157, 164–70, 310–11; *Quare Fellow*, 154, 157, 158, 159–64; *Richard's Cork Leg*, 154, 170
Behan, Dominic: *My Brother Brendan*, 311
Belch, Sir Toby, 32, 49, 257, 263
Ben Bulben, 81, 82
Benign comedy, 48, 135, 145, 150, 195–97, 201, 202
Bentley, Eric, 20, 159, 207, 281, 292–93; *Life of the Drama*, 288–89; "Psychology of Farce," 20, 287, 304
Bergin, Osborne, 77, 78
Bergson, Henri, 31, 49, 93, 125, 134, 173, 203, 289; *Laughter*, 123
Berkeley, George, 225, 286
Beowulf, 267
Berrigan, Fathers Daniel and Philip, 55
Bim and Bom, 224–25, 233
Blacam, Aodh de, 74, 75
Black and Tans, 248–49
Blake, William, 66, 212, 258, 270, 276, 319; *Marriage of Heaven and Hell*, 120, 290
Bloom, Leopold, 23, 52, 159, 277
Bloom, Molly, 35, 177, 178, 277
Blythe, Ernest, 308
Boru, Brian, 131, 226
Boucicault, Dion, 21, 272, 274; discussion of his work, 175–77, 181–95; influence on Shaw, 314; influence on Synge and O'Casey, 175, 177, 182–83; influence on Wilde, 186; influenced by Goldsmith, 185, 314; *Arrah-na-Pogue*, 182, 191–92, 314; *Colleen Bawn*, 182, 187–91, 192; *Irish Heiress*, 186; *Legend of the Devil's Dyke*, 184–85; *London Assurance*, 185–86; *Lover by Proxy*, 186; *The Shaughraun*, 171, 176, 182, 192–95

Bourgeois, Maurice, 91, 96, 180
Bourke, P. J., 310
Boyle, "Captain" Jack, 79, 123, 151, 159, 162, 173, 194, 203, 233, 256, 257, 262, 282
Boyle, William, protest against Synge, 315; *Eloquent Dempsy*, 202–3; *Family Failing*, 203
Brecht, Bertolt, 234, 256; *Baal*, 37; *Caucasian Chalk Circle*, 167, 262
Brehon laws, 34–35
Brigid, saint, 213, 214
Brogan, Harry, 320
Bronowski, J.: *Face of Violence*, 288
Brooke, Charlotte: *Reliques of Irish Poetry*, 69
Brustein, Robert, 157, 158; on Behan and O'Casey, 310–11
Buile Suibne (Mad Sweeney), 35
Bull, John, 165, 167, 174, 208, 261
Bullins, Ed, 267
Byron, George Gordon, 66, 297, 324

C

Cailte, 61–63, 70
Campbell, J. F.: *Leabhar na Feinne*, 69
Carleton, William, 44, 247, 274; *Traits and Stories of the Irish Peasantry*, 175; *Willy Reilly and His Dear Colleen Bawn*, 188
Carney, James, 297–99
Carroll, Lewis: *Alice in Wonderland*, 120
Carroll, Paul Vincent, 318; discussion of his work, 212–22; *Coggerers (Conspirators)*, 219–22; *Shadow and Substance*, 213–16; *White Steed*, 213, 216–19
Casey, Kevin, 157–58; on Behan's *An Giall*, 310
Cathleen Ni Houlihan, 65, 104, 126, 148, 167, 206, 208, 214, 220, 242, 245, 251, 261, 274, 303; defense of, 254, 255; disillusionment with, 204, 262; hagiography of, 239, 304; in

Swift, Carolyn, 158
Swift, Jonathan, 116, 247, 301
Synge, J. M., 17, 18, 27, 32, 43, 44, 64,
77, 100, 107–8, 112, 121, 129, 132,
148, 177, 181, 183, 187, 195, 209,
210, 223, 270, 272, 275, 277–78, 280,
285, 290, 301, 316; discussion of his
work, 91–99, 178–80, 225–35, 258–
60; defended by Moore and Yeats, 21,
88, 319; flytings in his plays, 268,
325; on Irish nationalism, 107–9;
Ossianic affinities, 88–98; "The
Curse," 36; Preface to *Poems*, 41;
Preface to *Tinker's Wedding*, 39;
Deirdre of the Sorrows, 97, 277; *In the
Shadow of the Glen*, 41, 93–94, 108,
149, 178, 179, 195, 225, 229, 234,
302; *Playboy of the Western World*, 21,
35, 36, 39, 41, 92, 95–97, 126, 128,
139, 209, 226, 230–33, 277, 293, 325;
Riders to the Sea, 97, 277; *Tinker's
Wedding*, 35, 41, 97–98, 181, 225,
229–30, 235, 277, 325; *Well of the
Saints*, 41, 94–95, 125, 225, 226–27,
228–29, 234–35, 258–59, 268, 275,
277, 319; *Aran Islands*, 27, 288; *Autobiography*, 37–40
Sypher, Wylie, 20, 278–79, 292;
"Meanings of Comedy," 20, 287

T

Táin Bo Cuailnge ("Cattle Raid of
Cooley"), 79, 246
Tasby, 44
Theatre Royal, London, 158
Thompson, William Irwin, 255, 323
Tir na nOg (Land of Youth), 64, 82,
217
Titanism, 68–69
Tolstoy, Leo, 200
Tone, Wolfe, 100, 220, 251
Tragedy, 23, 28–30
Trotsky, Leon, 252
Twain, Mark, 31, 210

U

Ulster cycle, 66, 74, 296
United Irishman, 111, 112
Ussher, Arland, 295

V

Villon, François, 319
Vision of MacConglinne, 35, 75, 247,
298

W

Wake games, 295
Welsford, Enid: *The Fool*, 48, 258
Whitfield, George, 313
Wilde, Oscar, 21, 176, 182, 186, 187,
247, 257, 314; *Importance of Being
Earnest*, 186, 316–17
Winkler, Elizabeth Hale: *Clowns in
Modern Anglo-Irish Drama*, 285–86
Winnie and Willie, 273
Wollner, Wilhelm, 298

Y

Yeats, W. B., 35, 39, 56, 57, 77, 88, 97,
116, 124, 154, 156, 182, 197, 203,
204, 225, 226, 227, 228–29, 238,
246, 247, 270, 295, 300, 306, 309;
discussion of his work, 44–47, 263–
66, 274–76; defense of Synge and
O'Casey, 22, 88, 303, 319; "Emotion
of Multitude," 264–66; on Irish
nationalism, 107–13; "An Irish
Theatre and Three Sorts of Ignorance," 111, 303; "A People's
Theatre," 265; Crazy Jane poems,
21, 44; "Lapis Lazuli," 110; "Sailing
to Byzantium," 110; "Second Coming," 46; "Wanderings of Oisín," 83;
At the Hawk's Well, 44, 266; *On Baile's
Strand*, 265; *Cat and the Moon*,

The Profane Book
of Irish Comedy

Designed by G. T. Whipple, Jr.
Composed by The Composing Room of Michigan, Inc.
in 10 point VIP Baskerville, 2 points leaded,
with display lines in Baskerville.
Printed offset by Thomson-Shore, Inc.
on Warren's Number 66 text, 50 pound basis.
Bound by John H. Dekker & Sons, Inc.
in Holliston book cloth
and stamped in Kurz-Hastings foil.

Library of Congress Cataloging in Publication Data

Krause, David, 1917–
     The profane book of Irish comedy.

     Includes bibliographical references and
index.
        1. English drama (Comedy)—Irish authors—
History and criticism.   I. Title.
PR8793.C6K7   822'.0523'099417   81-17454
ISBN 0-8014-1469-5   AACR2